AF395618

*To the memories
of my grandmothers.*

I WANT ORGASMS, NOT ROSES

Éva Szombat

KEHRER

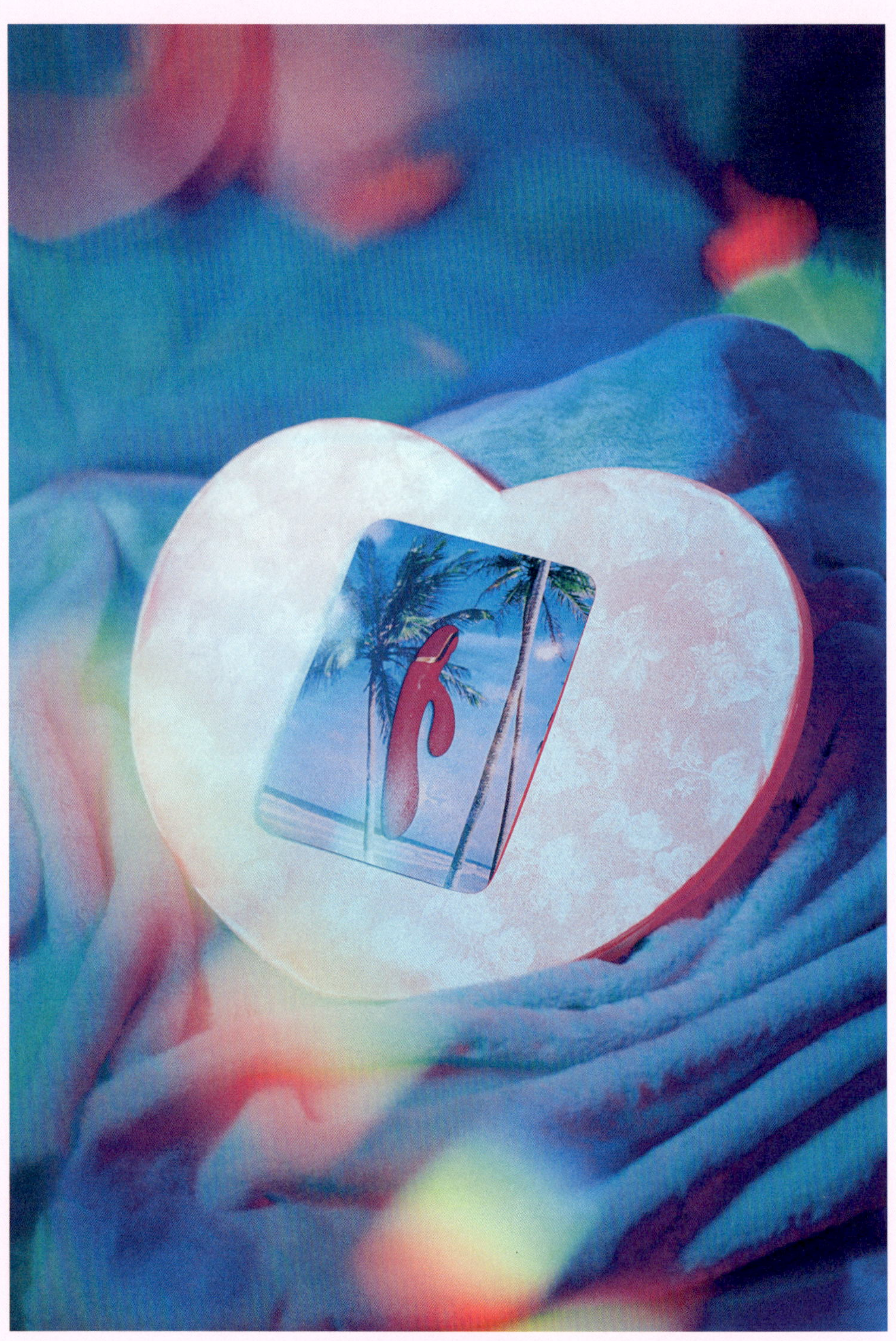

The Story

I was 29 when I bought my first ever vibrator. I have always had fantasies about such objects, but I was too shy to realize them. When I found myself in a serious relationship I overcame that obstacle. I played alone, we played together, I started to open up. I photographed, posted, and even exhibited said first vibrator. I was terrified of what other people would think but my world wasn't turned upside down after all.

My whole life I've been interested in sexuality more than I dared to admit to myself. I believed it was bad manners for girls to be interested in such a thing so openly. I believed this until I met people who would fearlessly talk about sex, masturbation, orgasms, the clitoris, porn, and fantasies. It was liberating to belong to this group.

In 2017 I posted a public advertisement. I was looking for people who would show their sex toys to the public. To my great surprise many answered my call. They also had a strong desire to talk about their sexuality without shame. The contributors came from various walks of life: students, social workers, hairdressers, translators, artists, dominatrixes, entrepreneurs, employees, unemployed people, freelancers, wives, girlfriends, single people, divorcees, mothers-to-be, mothers, and even a grandmother. In addition to taking pictures, I was conducting interviews, which let me dive deeper, dredging up serious traumas in more than one case. I learned something new in every single session.

While working on this project I found my grandmother's memory book, which she got during World War II. Memory books are a centuries-old tradition in Hungary—equal parts souvenir and scrapbook, they are given to schoolchildren during their education, full of inspirational quotes, jokes, and advice for their future life, all written by their friends, family, and teachers.

The messages in it, that were meant to prepare one for life, often corresponded with the thoughts my participants had told me about their own inhibitions. These lines from many generations before served as pointers for girls. They implied that if you were born a woman you should be modest and obedient, bear the pain and suffering. The participants, just like myself, internalized these thoughts.

My relationship with sexuality has changed a lot throughout the years and the project itself has changed along with it. The objects became less important, as I became a lot more interested in the owners and their stories. I was looking for a means to get rid of the shame connected to sexuality, overcome societal conventions, and break free from inherited behavioral patterns. The toys became the key to establishing honest communication.

I'm deeply grateful to all the contributors for their trust.

ÉVA SZOMBAT
2022
Budapest, Hungary

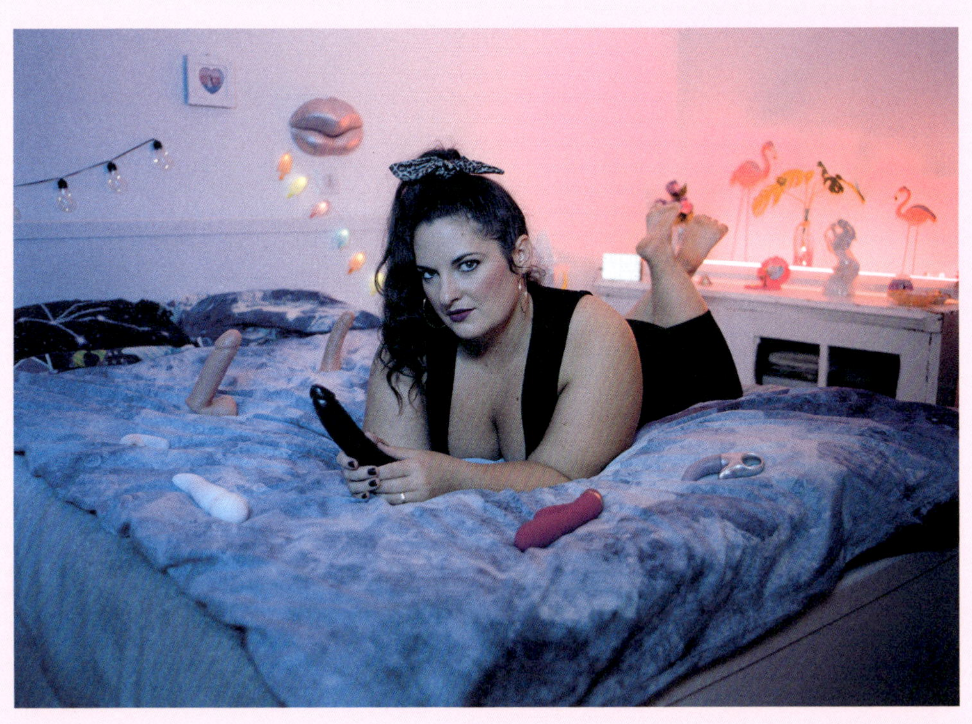

'Roses are red,
Violets are blue,
Modesty makes you
A woman of
virtue.'

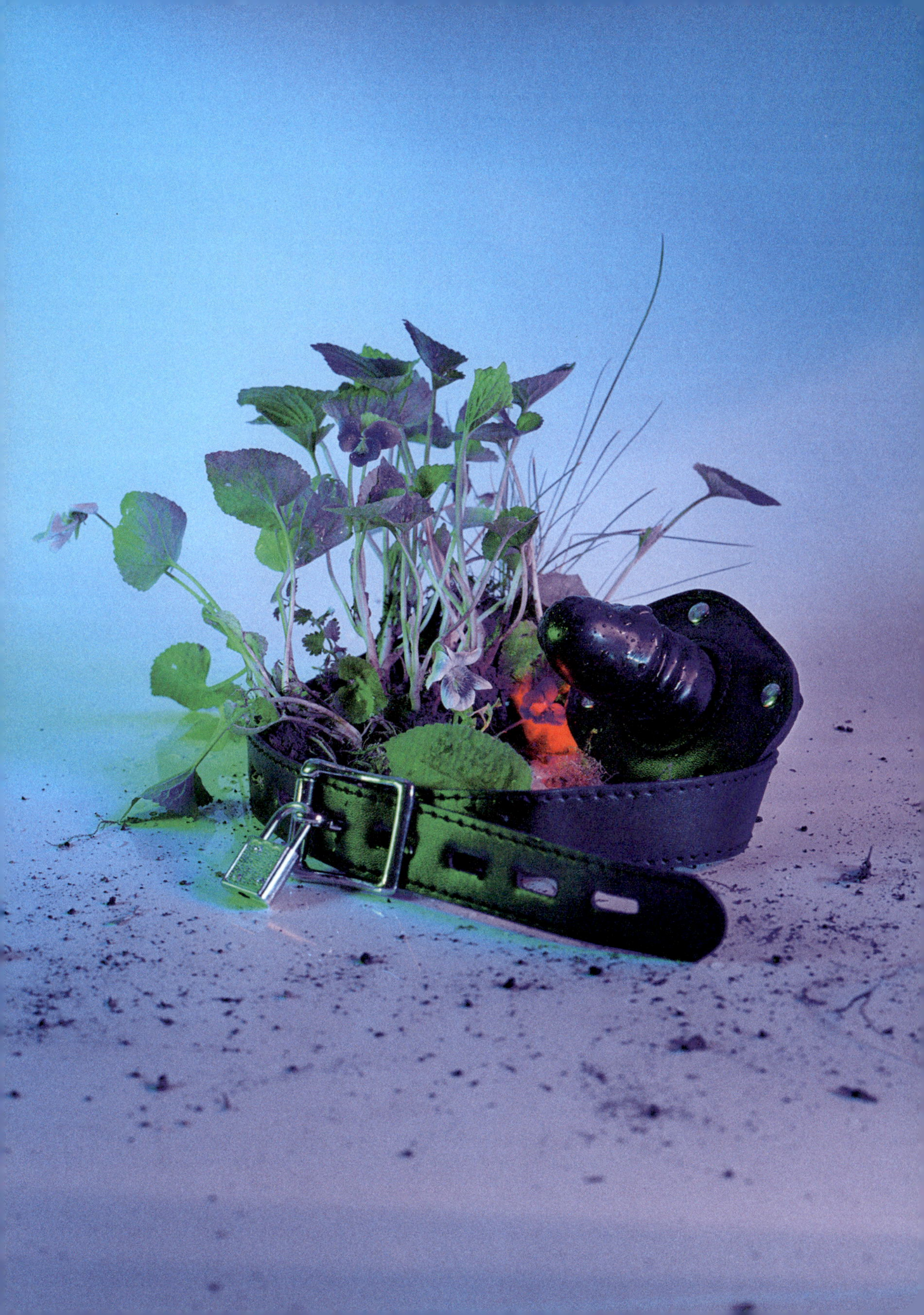

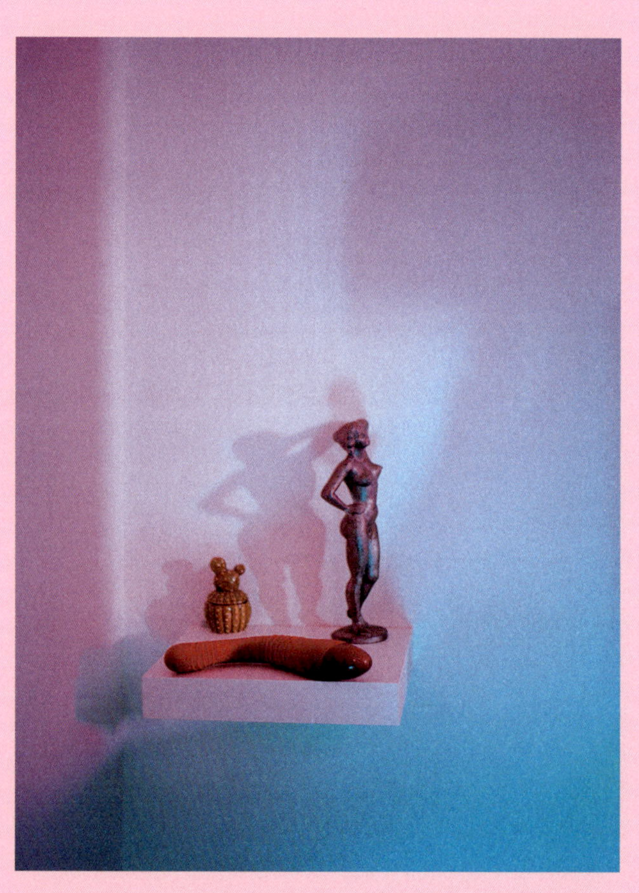

Whether you should follow patterns is always a big question. You don't want to do things like this or like that, but for some reason you will in the end. Because it's in your blood, it's in your genes. But then you might be a fixed version of that inherited pattern.

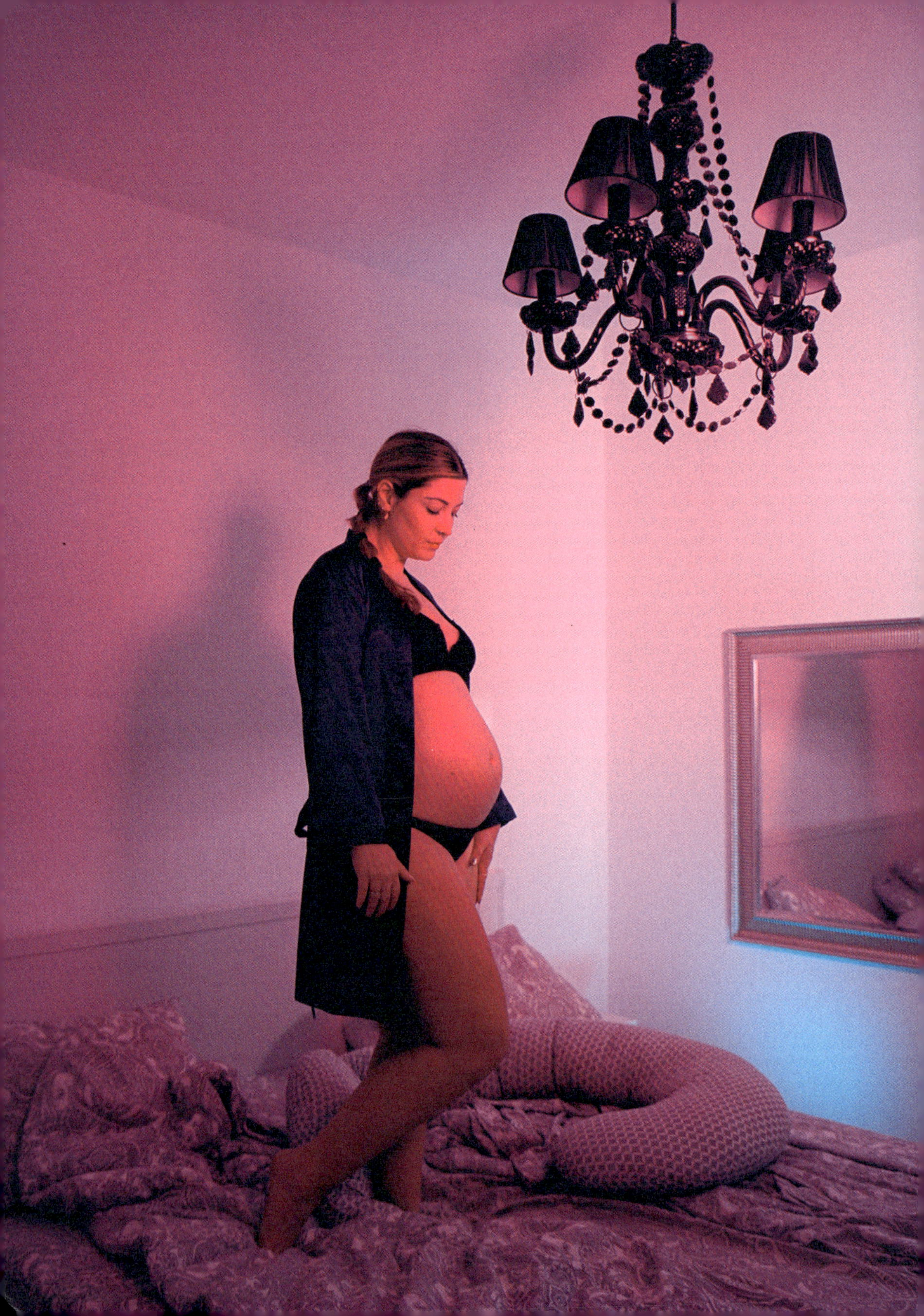

My grandparents buried my mom and, when he was just a few days old, also their little boy. A tumor grew right around my grandma's clitoris. She never was the spiritual type, yet she was not surprised that it affected her female body parts—she did not process the death of her children. She told me of the emotional burdens I carry by being related to her, and she pointed out what to do differently than she had. Back then people were happy to have a pot to piss in, they weren't the generation to decorate their walls with Buddhist quotes.

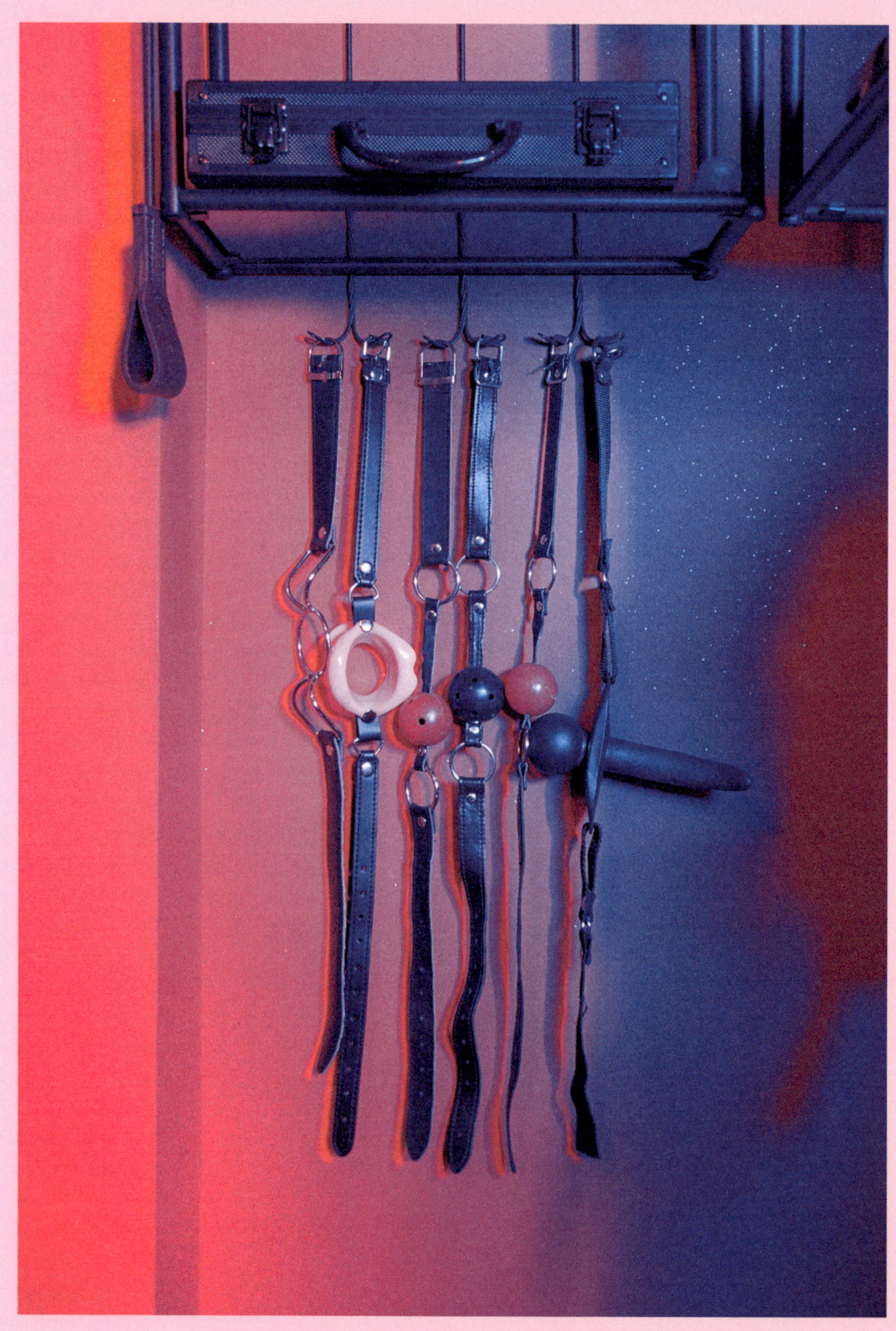

*My dad often
hurt my mom with
words. She cried
a lot, yet she stayed
with him.
I tried to accept it
as normal.*

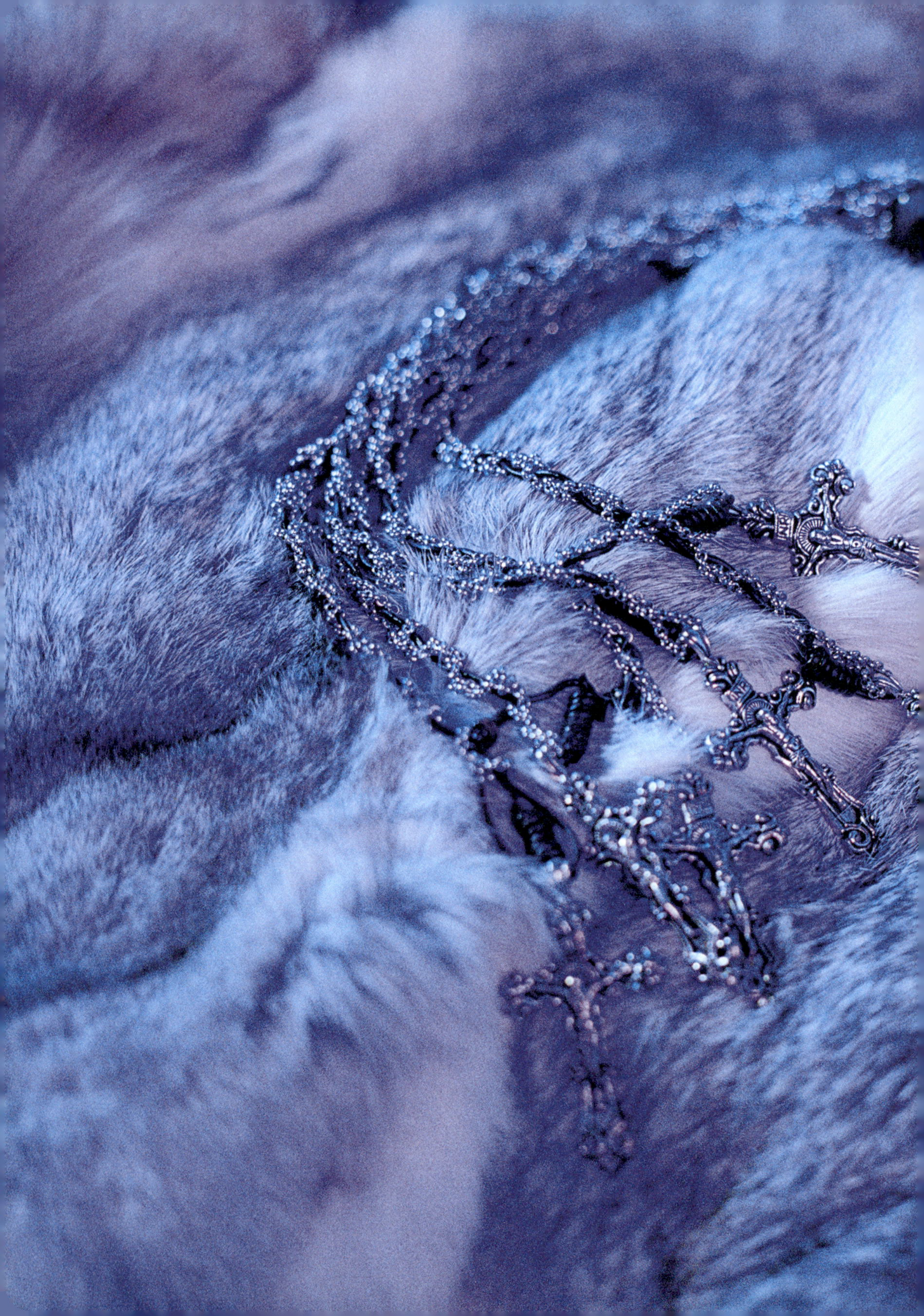

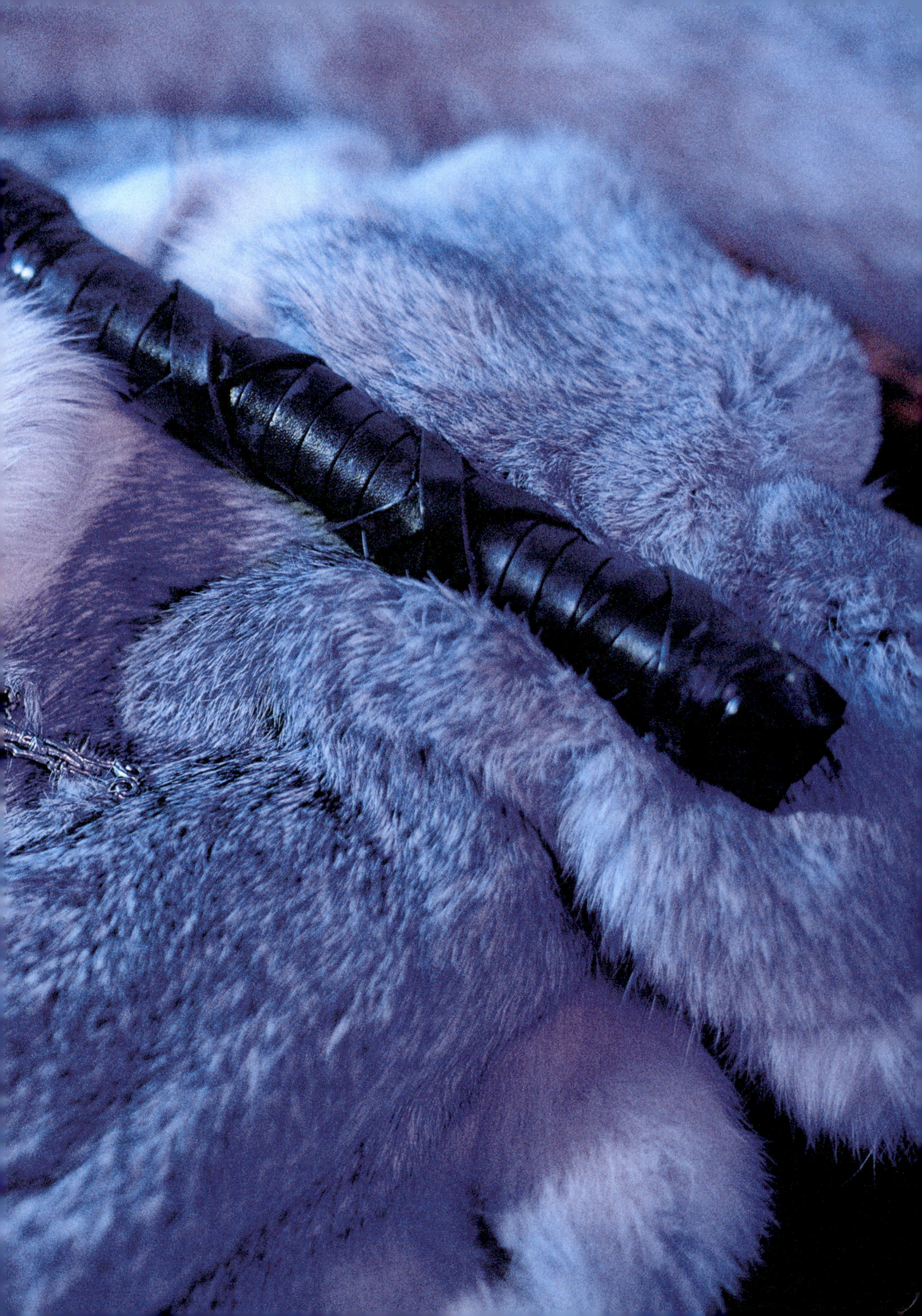

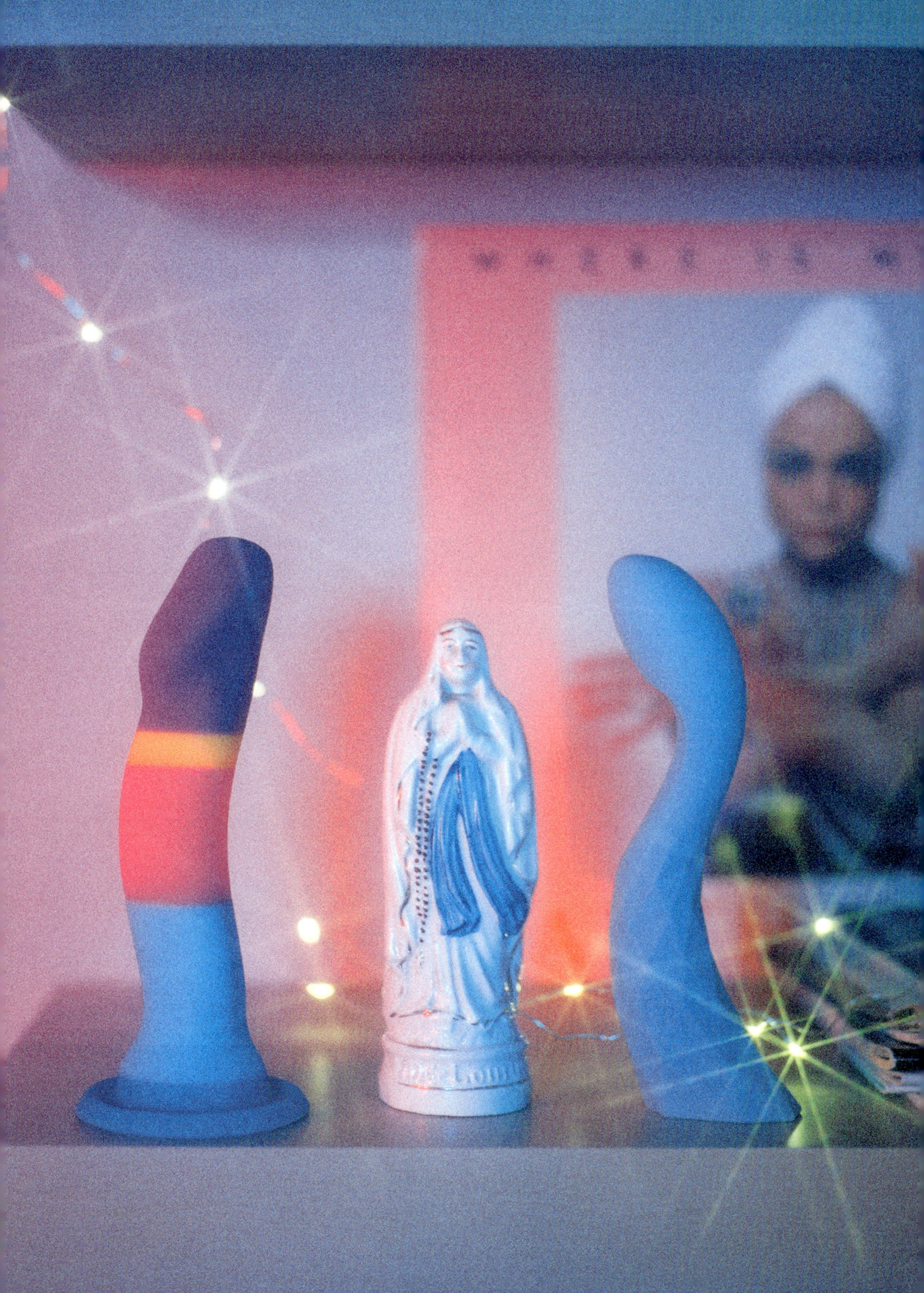

ZSÓFIA

I was born into a Christian conservative family. By the time of my First Communion, I had to confess sins of promiscuity. It was incredibly awkward to talk to a priest about these things. Within two years I abandoned the Church. I was dating boys, going to pubs, and listening to rock music. I argued a lot with my parents.

In my family, sexuality was an awfully big taboo. They didn't express anything about sexuality because they also grew up this way. They didn't have any words for it, so I didn't have any either. It's a trap to be together with someone who can't communicate. I've accepted that I always have to work on this.

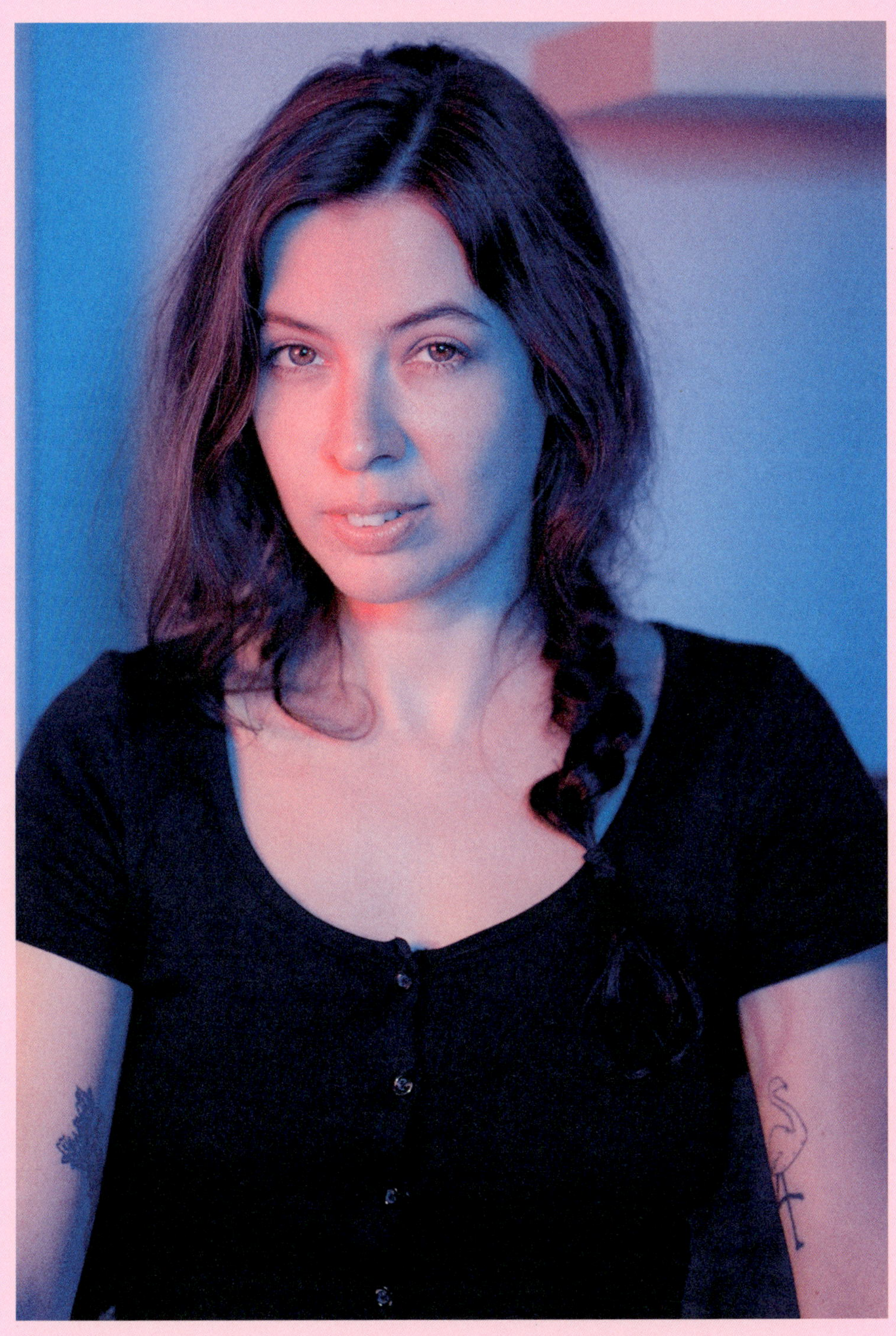

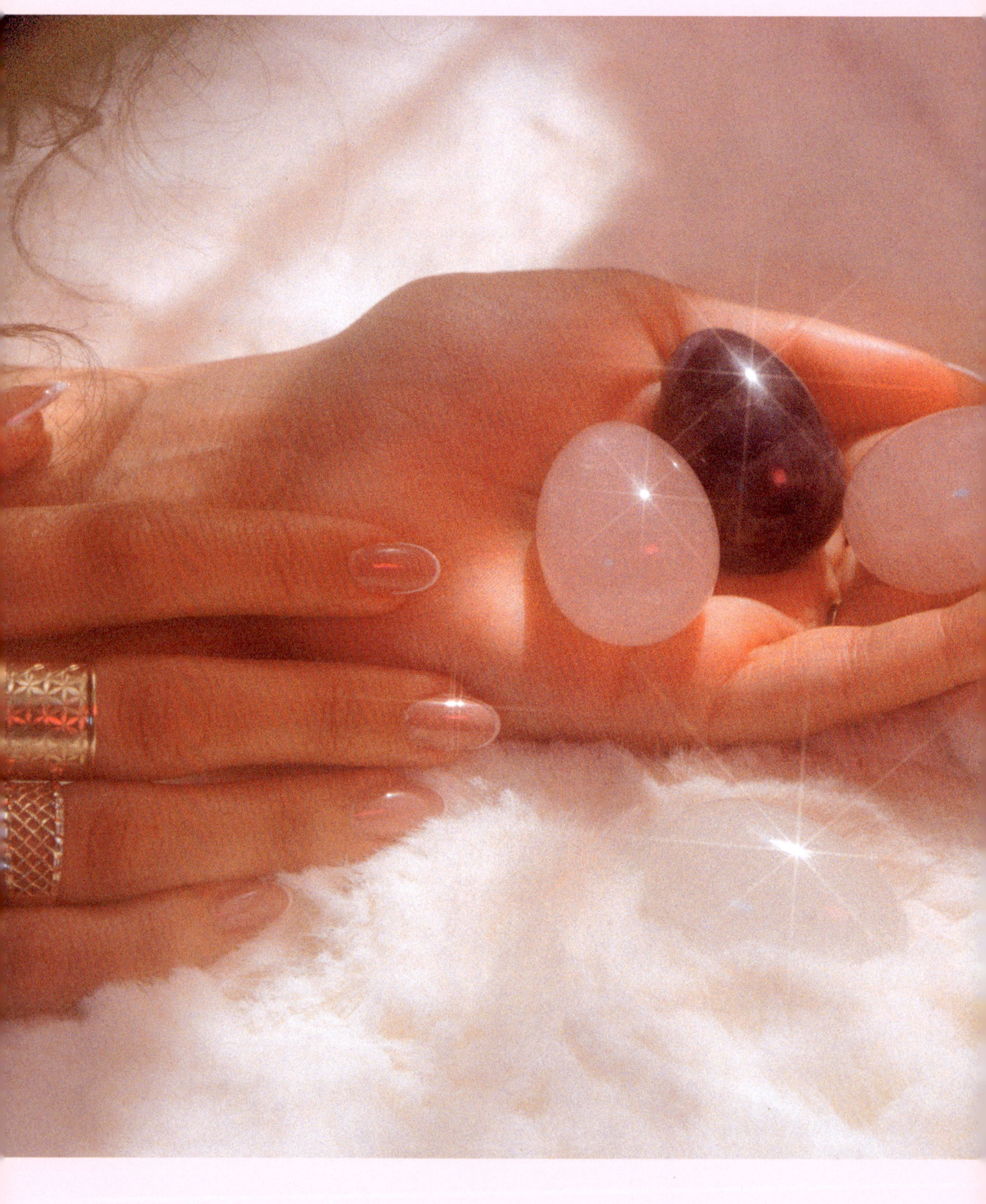

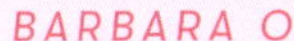

BARBARA O.

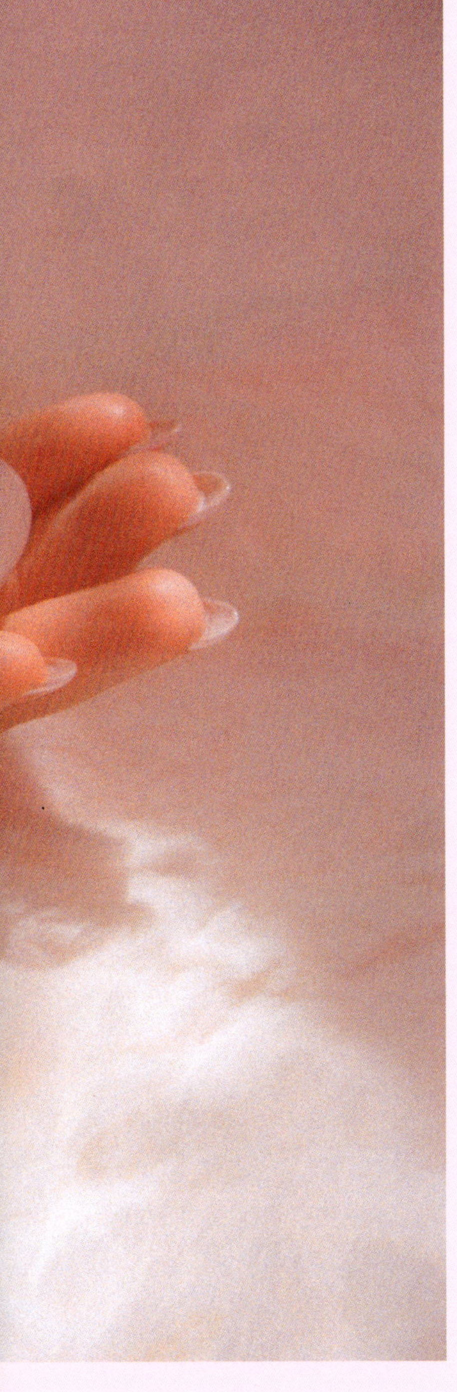

I come from a family where everyone is born as and conceived by a virgin. We are also gypsies. In gypsy culture men can let go and have a bit of freedom but it is considered taboo for women to do the same. We didn't talk about sex, but I knew I was very interested in it, even when I was little.

I grew up in a sex-positive family; still, I was clueless about a lot of things. I was on good terms with my mom but we didn't talk about everything. I was a very good girl, obedient, and a good student. My sex life started out like this too. I was even shy to touch myself. I only had one friend with whom it was okay to talk about this stuff. She talked more, I didn't dare to because I thought it was so awkward.

Life has shown me a lot of stories. I heard people saying sex is only enjoyable for men. When I was working for a women's magazine, plenty of readers sent us letters. There was one woman who only realized what an orgasm was at the age of 50, after the death of her husband.

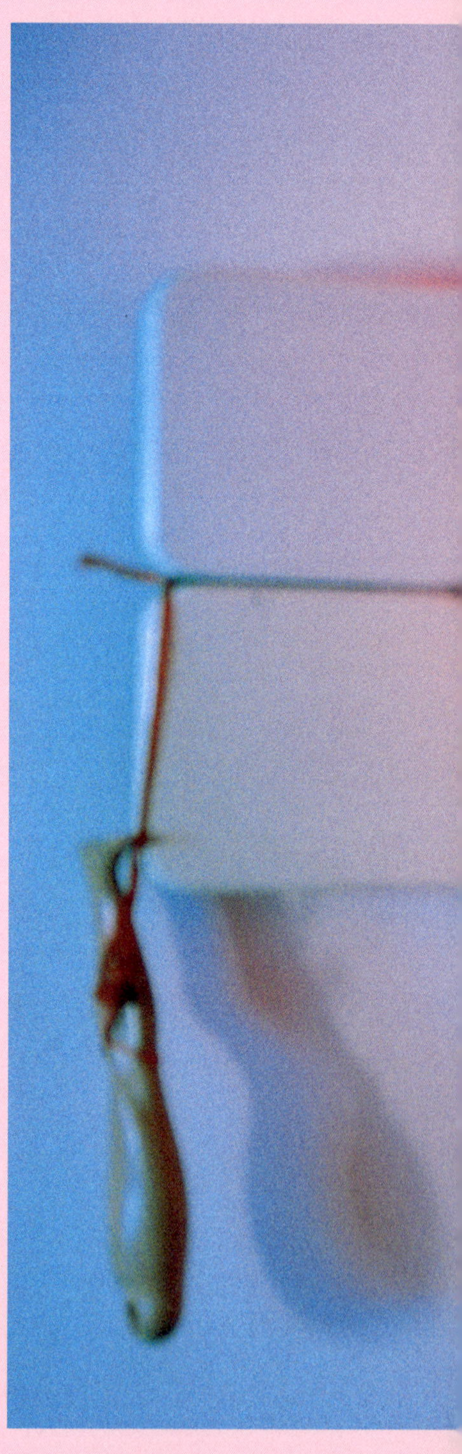

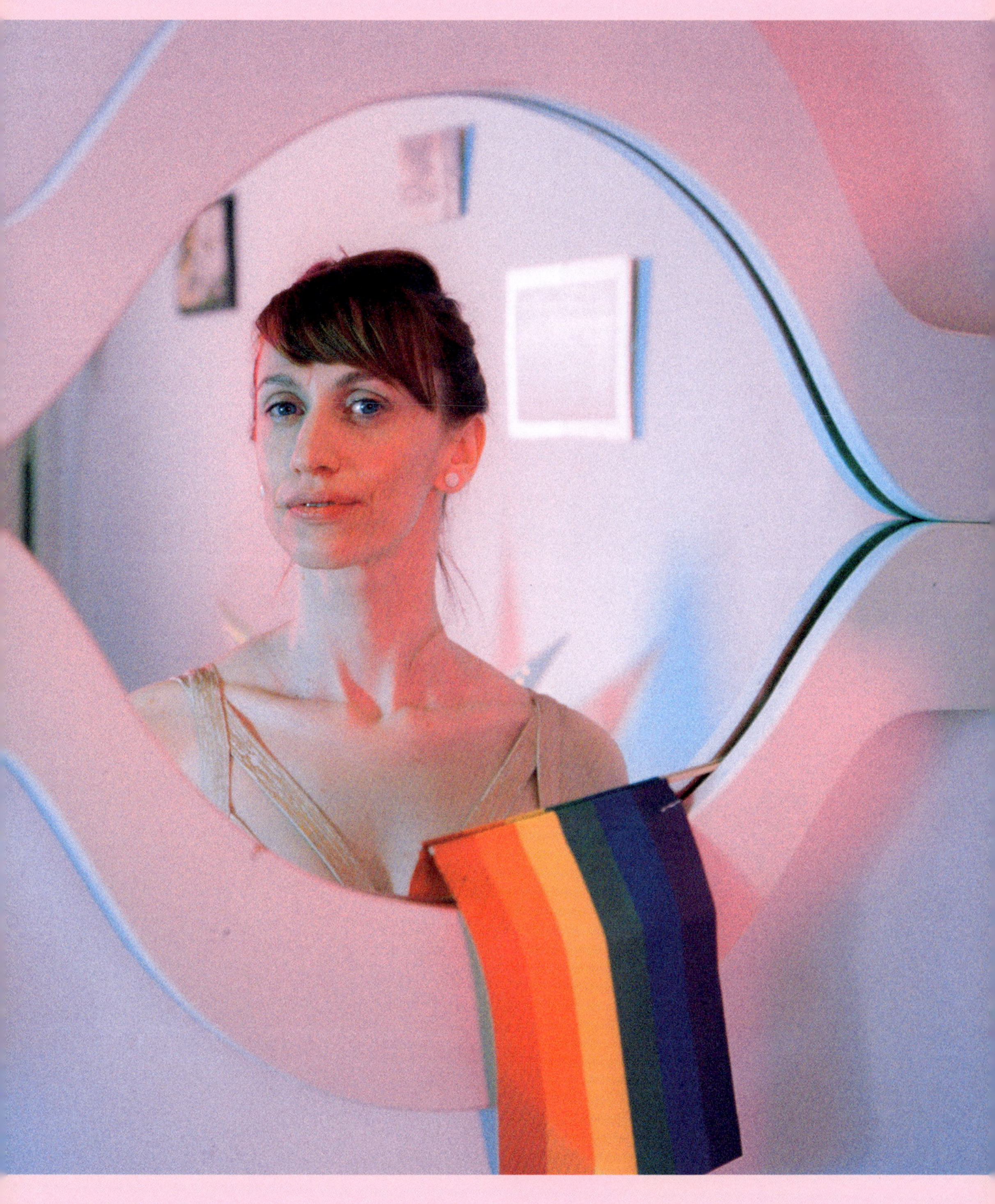

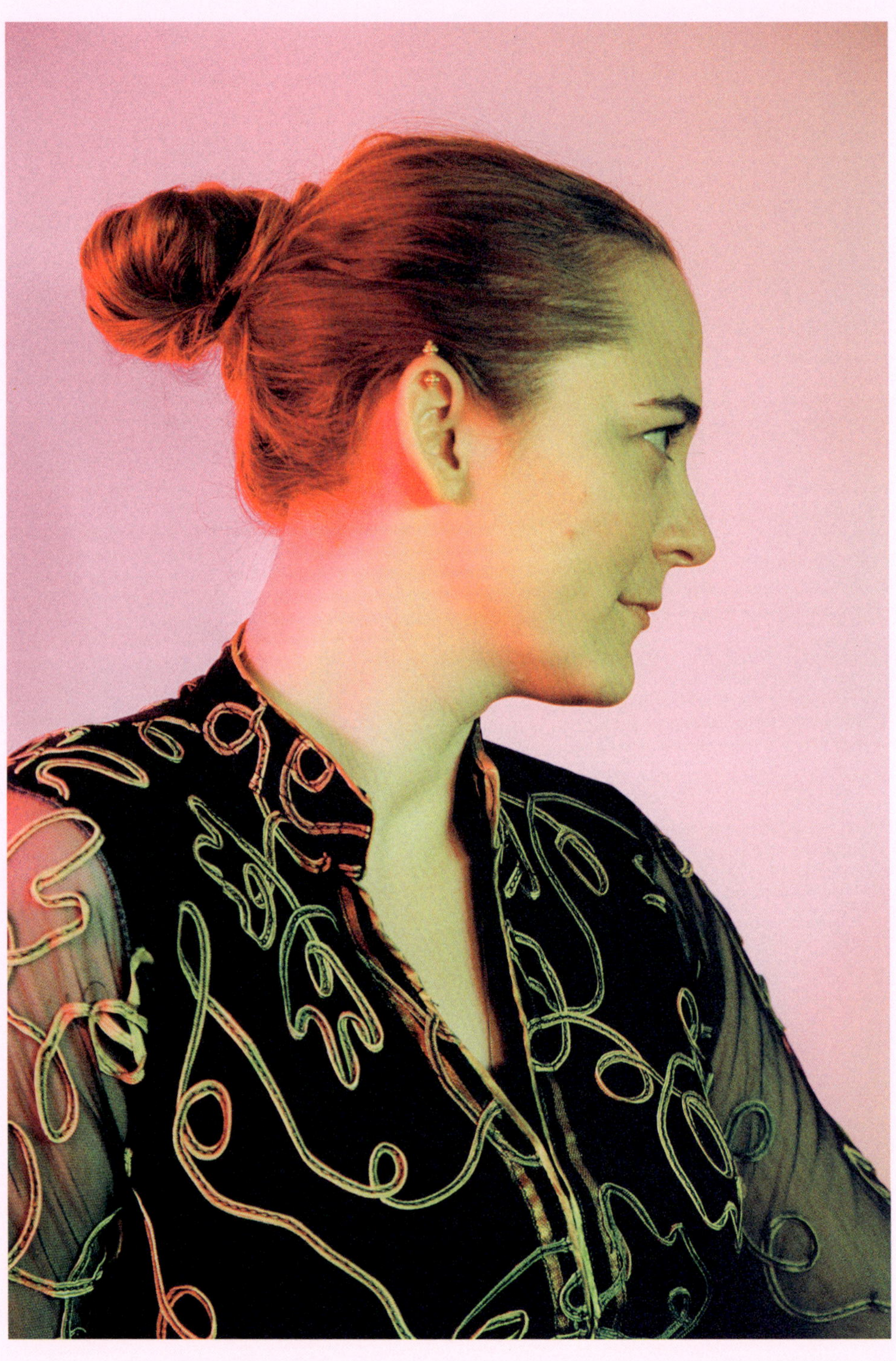

BARBARA M.

When I was a child I suffered serious abuse and the shame of it all turned into extreme curiosity. I was way more interested in sex than my peers. As soon as I could, I watched porn and bought porn magazines. I was only sixteen when I bought my first vibrator.

It wasn't with boys in real life but in my own fantasies that the whole thing was really intense. It was an important part of my life. I lost my virginity quite late, at the age of eighteen. It was a one-night stand with an older guy, a complete stranger. Perhaps I wanted to hurt myself with the act. In my fantasy anything could happen, while reality was more like this.

I must've felt like I didn't deserve good sex. Many times in my life I was in a state that could be called "emotional vaginismus." I either fell in love with people who I couldn't have a sexual relationship with whatsoever, or they were extremely rejective. I feel that I've worked a lot to change for the better.

For me this boyfriend stuff is strange. I have trust issues. I've never been in a relationship but I have my libido just the same. I feel the need for it to happen but I have no patience to get there. I'm sure my childhood affects my sexuality. My mother is overly sensitive, my father is a stronger character. Many conflicts stemmed from this. When I was a kid, my parents used me as their punching bag to release the tension. I think they noticed this in school but they didn't care because my family was well off. For us this was normal, I grew up like this. Once, when I was thirteen, I didn't want to go to the beach. My father hit me and my mom just stood there watching. I had a black eye and my head was so beaten up that I stayed in my room. I was a really anxious kid. My mental health took a huge hit and all of a sudden I put on weight too. When I got better, I could see how depressed I was as a kid. If I had been in this position as an adult, I may have just lost my mind.

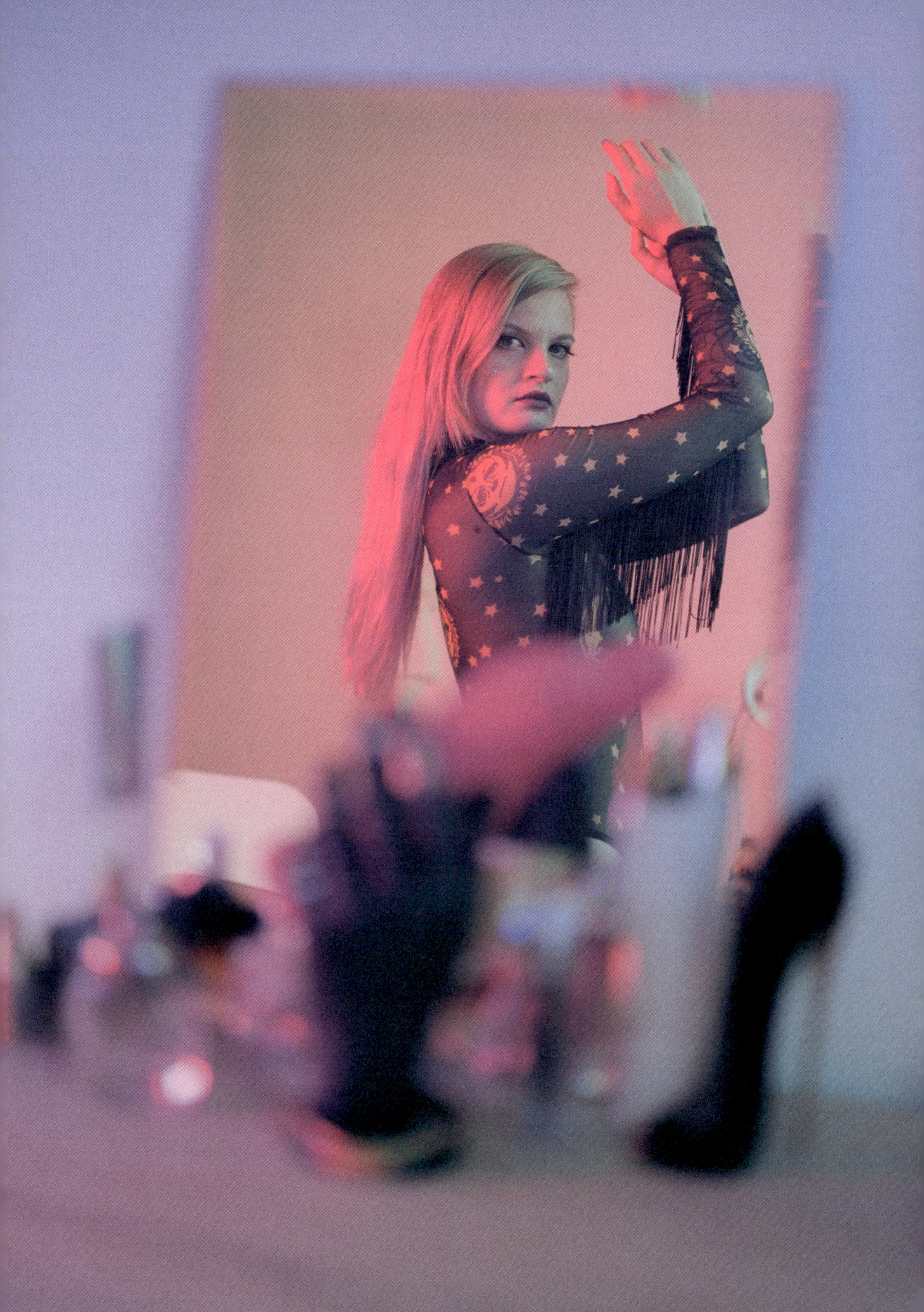

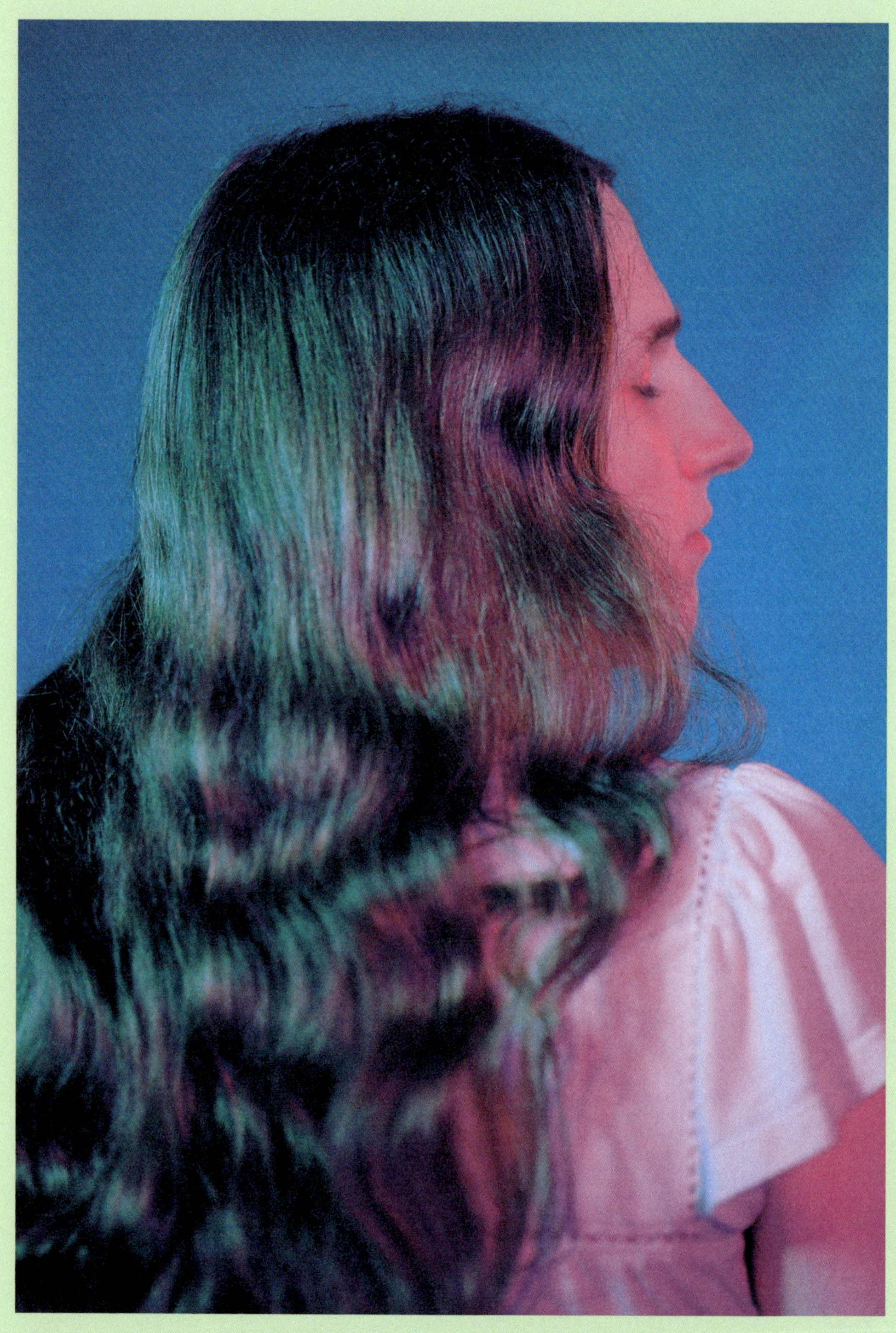

DANIELA

My dad had four children before I was born. I was about six months old when my parents separated and six years old when my father died. I hardly saw my siblings during my childhood but I yearned for their company still. My mom has a very complicated personality; she has many emotional wounds from childhood. It's difficult to deal with her. If I opened up to her as a child, she would often hurt me, generating fear and doubt. She means well but she never knew any better. When I was nineteen my mom was diagnosed with cancer and we thought she would die. In the hospital she was a different person. She was carefree and we laughed a lot together. Then she got better and everything went back to "normal." In primary school I was badly bullied, physically too. I shut down, not opening up to anyone. I got used to keeping my biggest secret to myself.

JUDIT

My parents died when I was just a child. I didn't have a father figure, so I was attracted and attached to men very early on. I expressed a lot—if not with sex itself, with sexual communication and with the need to love, even as a preteen. For me sex is not just the act but the hugs, the touches and the eye contact too. These are easy to misread if someone is not aware of the power of their own sexuality. They will flirt with everyone, intended or not. I was mature for my age, older men found their way to me. I trusted them, then I realized that their approach was not friendly or fatherly and they wanted more. My teachers paid special attention to me. I was aware that it was not ideal to be an orphan at age thirteen with my older sister as my legal guardian at age eighteen. I started to process this and by the time my first love found me, everything was in its right place.

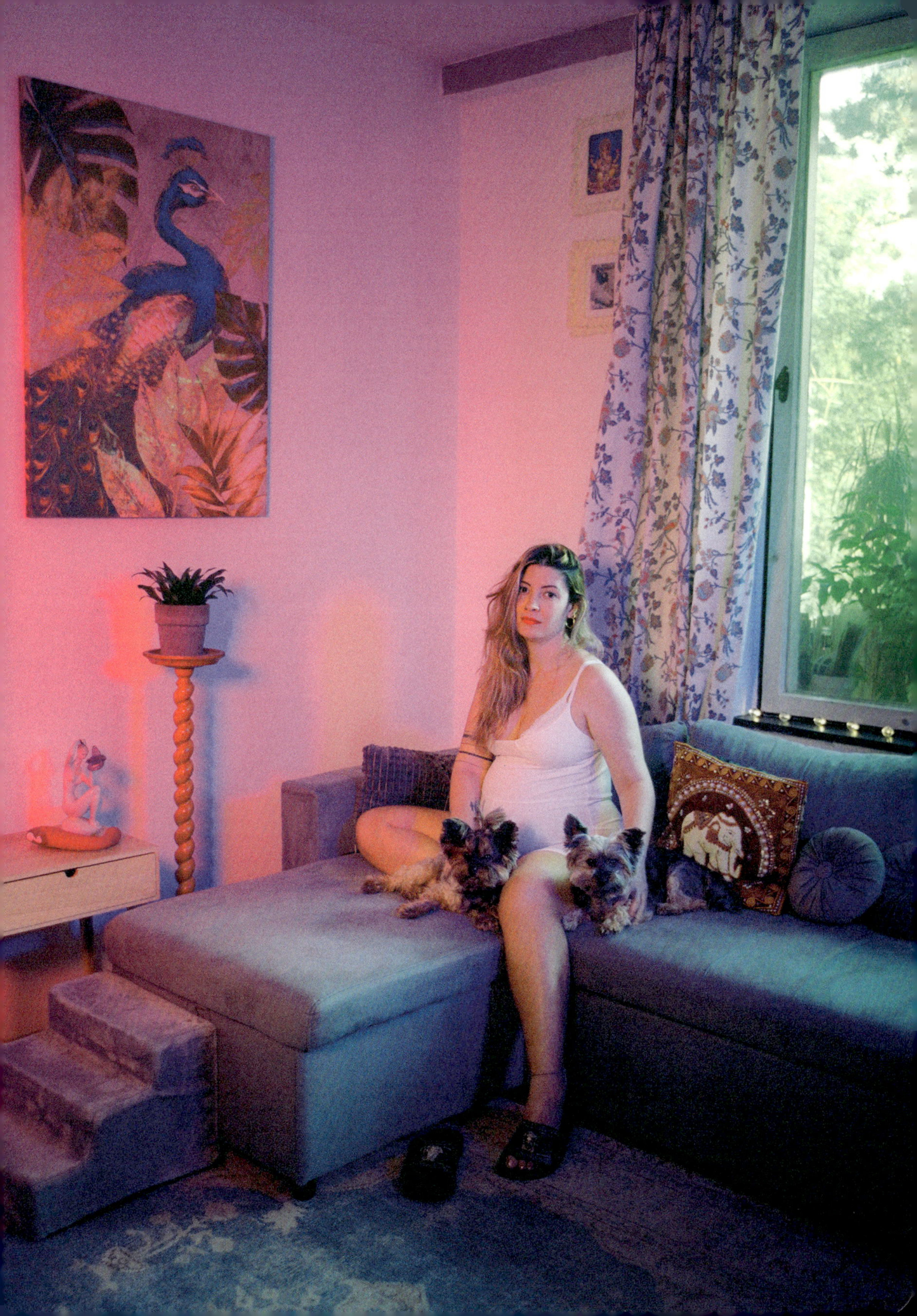

From a very early age, as sexuality appeared in my life with masturbation, I had extremely brutal dominant and submissive fantasies. I felt what I wanted was not acceptable. I've been told several times that I should be more modest and cute. In school we got a sex education booklet, I remember so clearly it said you can fantasize about anything, as long as it's not violent. I always thought something was wrong with me, until I found the BDSM community. I've learned to accept myself just as I am. It should be emphasized during sex education that what two people do with mutual consent is fine. Except if it causes permanent disfigurement.

BDSM:
B/D (Bondage and Discipline),
D/s (Dominance and submission),
S/M (Sadism and Masochism)

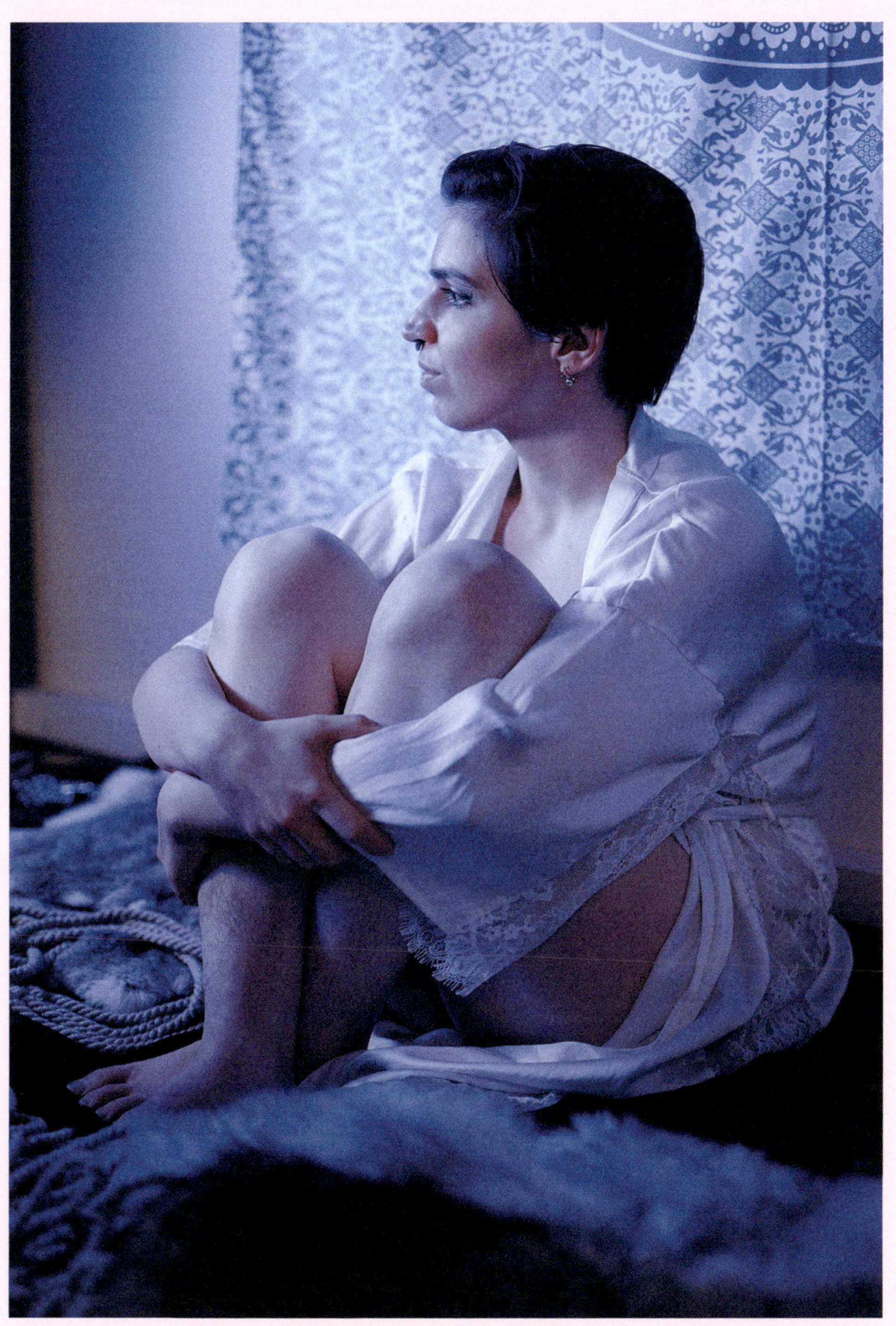

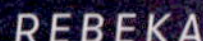

My earliest sexual memory is when I put my feeding bottle in my tights, between my legs to pleasure my pussy. I was about seven when I found porn on the home computer. I had a female friend in first grade and we, as a playtime activity, laid on top of each other, mutually fingering one another. We knew what we were doing, too. We grew up extremely interested in sex. We also found a lot of porn at her place, her parents didn't really try to hide it. This friend and I still talk about sex very openly but since then I've moved to Budapest and she stayed in the area where we grew up.

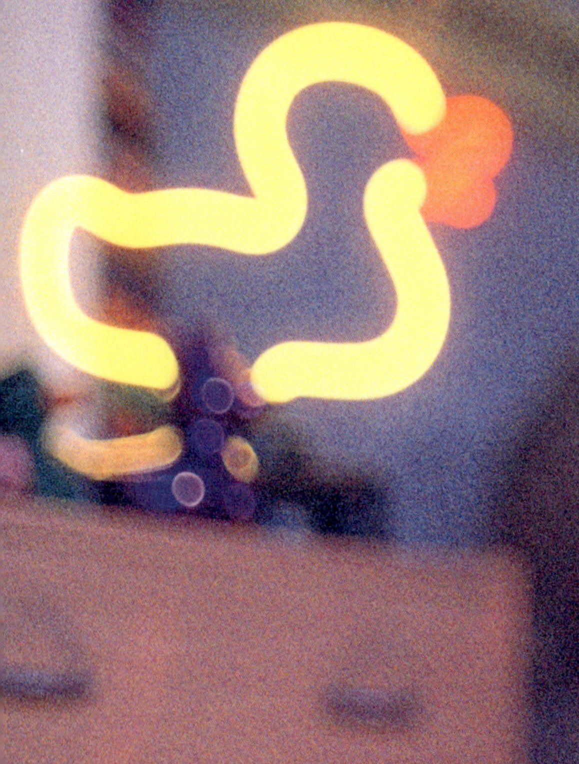

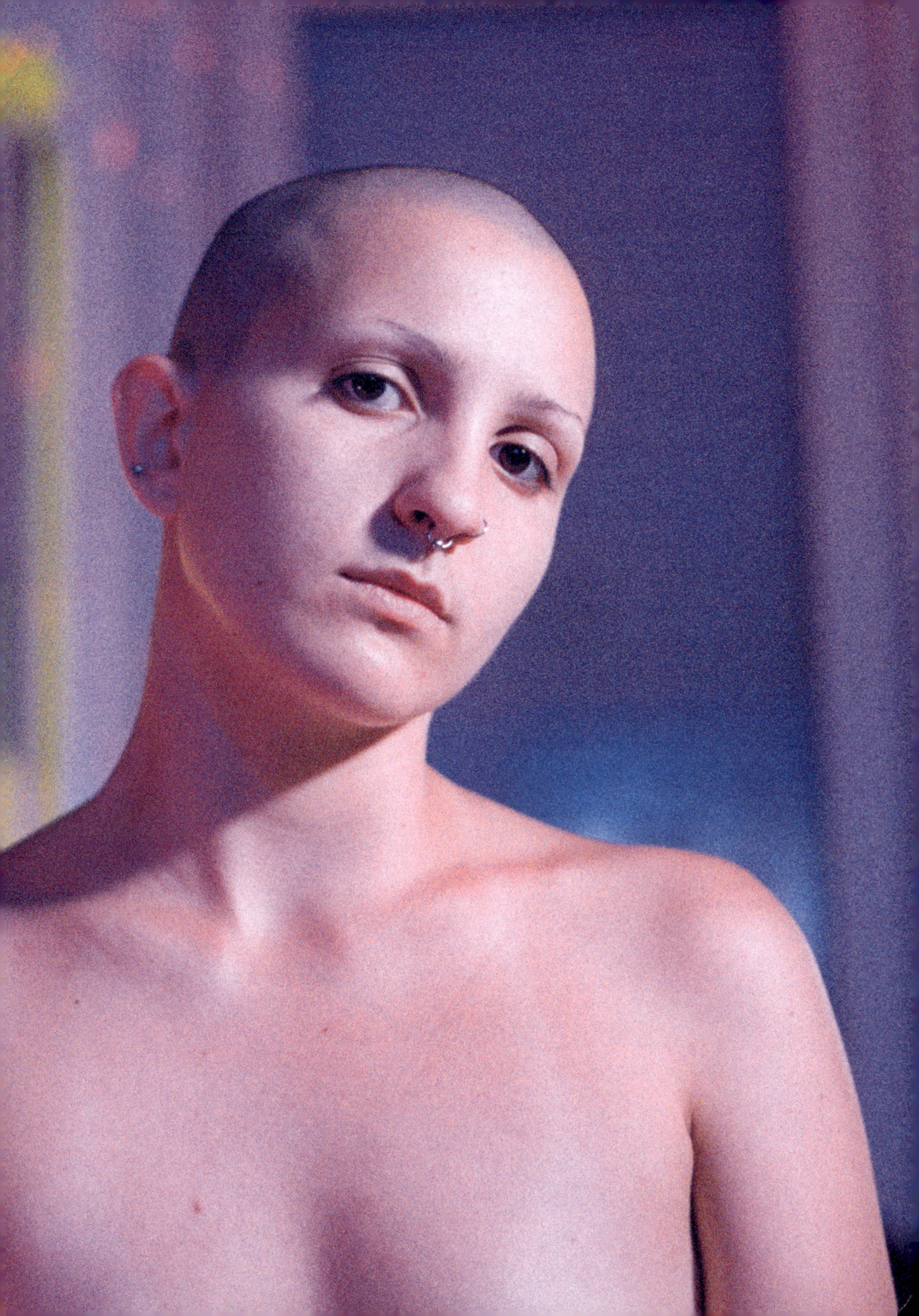

*In our teens,
sexual pop culture
is traumatizing.
We have to process
the violent porn
flicks in which they
don't care for
the women.*

*It takes a long
time until
those stereotypes
wash away.
We have to
take shame out
of sexuality.*

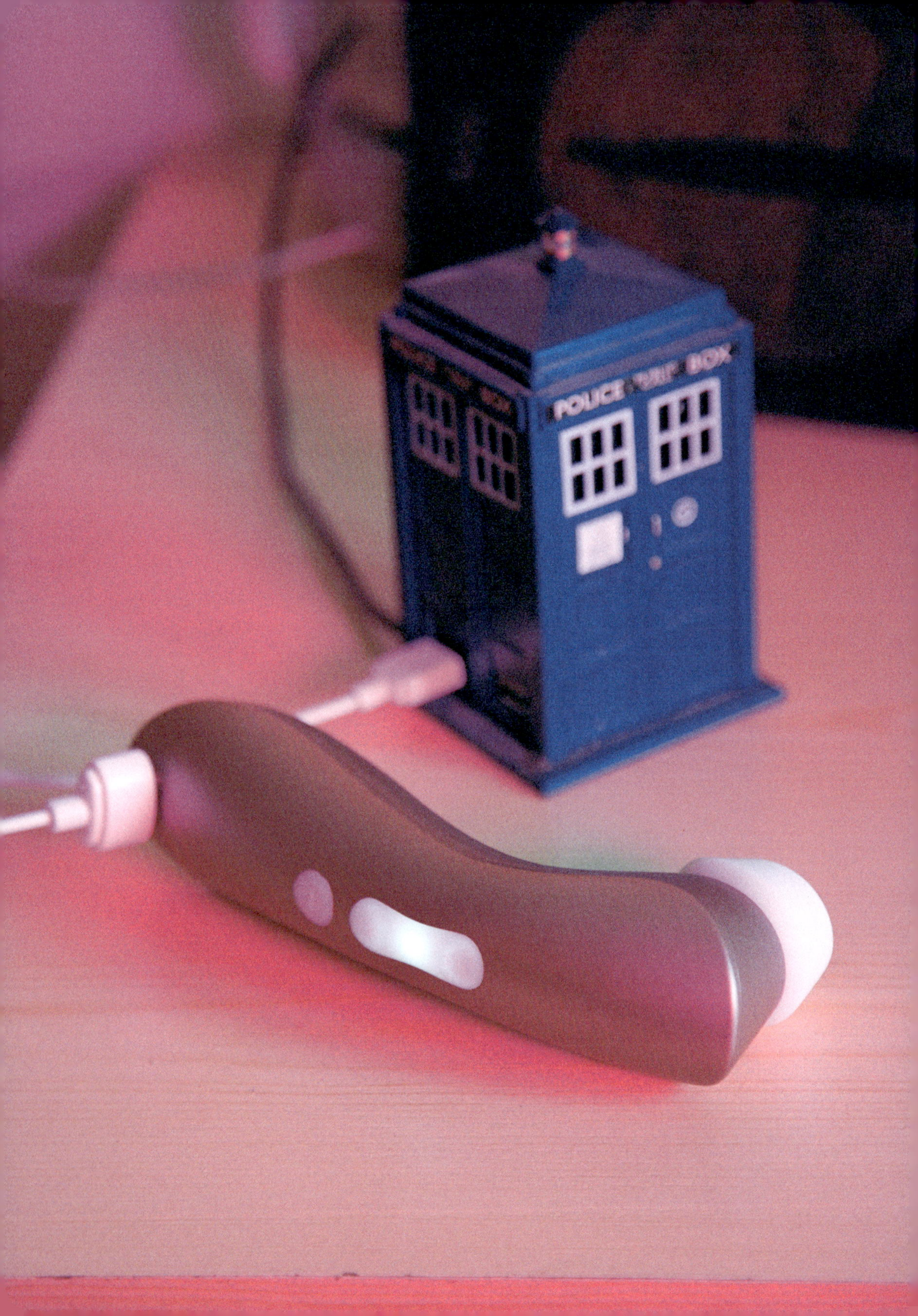

POLICE PUBLIC BOX

NÓRA

We played a game where we either had to confess that we masturbate or say that it is a "private matter," effectively still confessing. It was my turn and I said it was a private matter. Then everyone started laughing at me and gossiping about me masturbating too. Everyone was doing it. We were fourteen, why would I have been the odd one out?

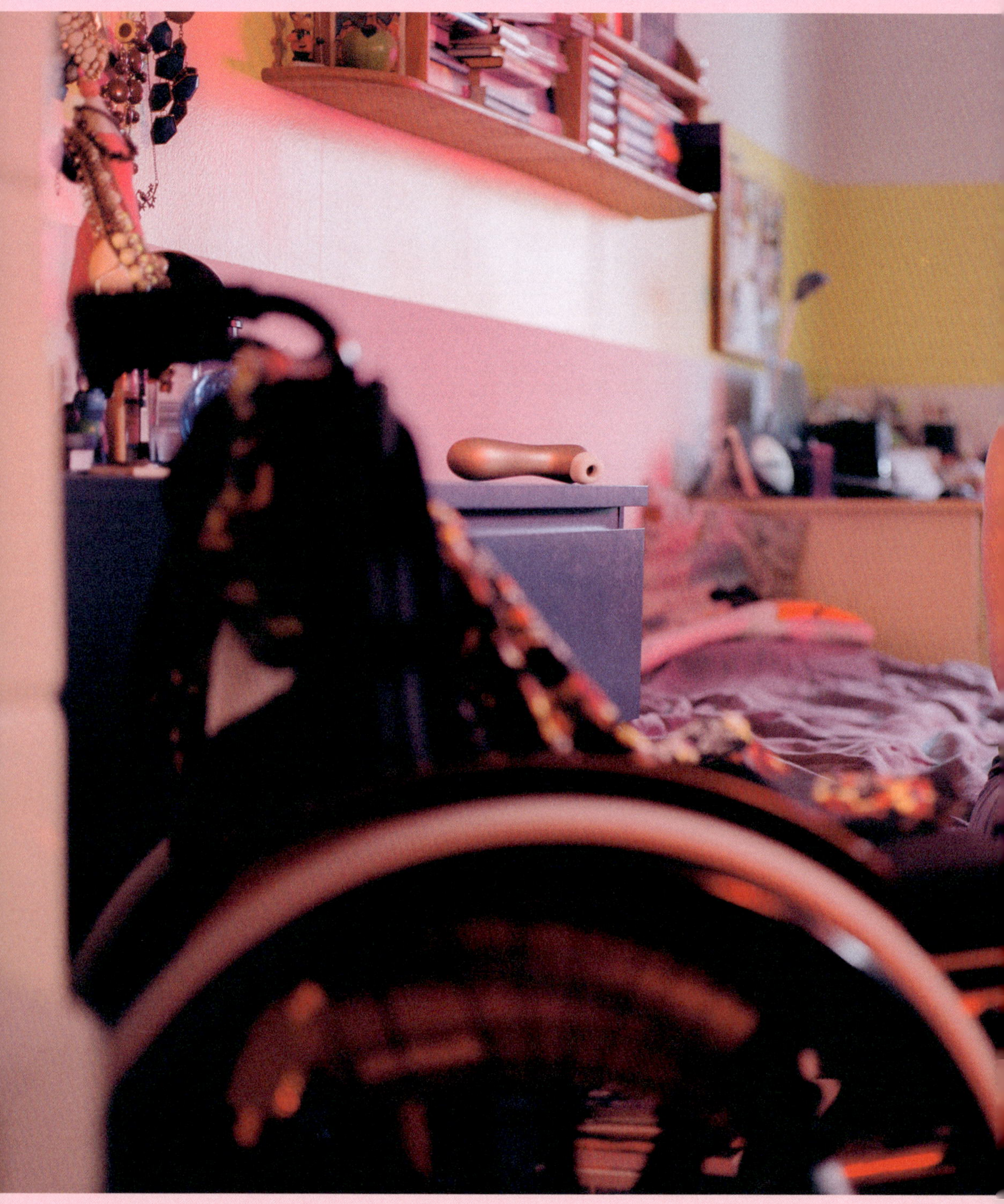

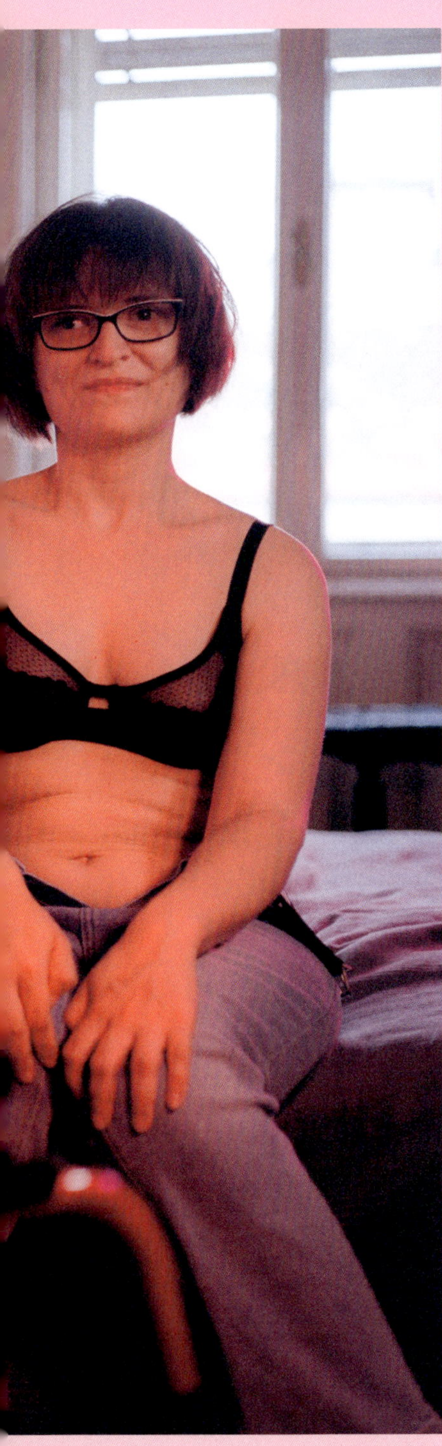

In my teen years I couldn't find anything regarding my sexuality. I had to google "wheelchair Kama Sutra" for example. Yet, it didn't work for me. Everyone is different.

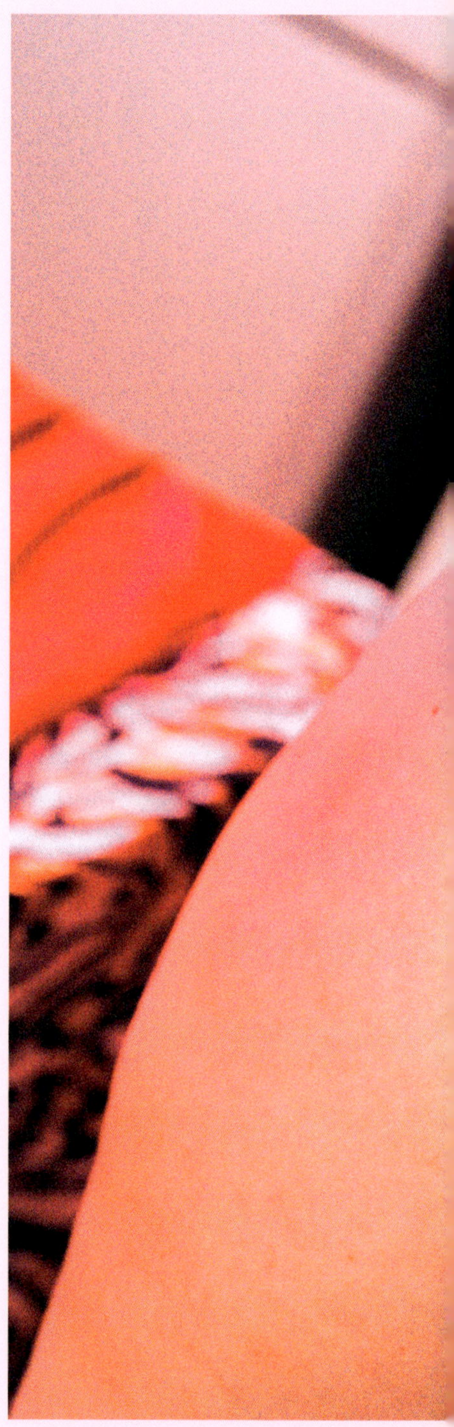

I had my first sexual relationship when I was fourteen years old. I thought it was normal that he should tell me what to do. I went to the bus stop to masturbate because he wanted me to. I went down to the pub and picked up guys because he asked. I've been sexually abused several times, but I am very positive about my sex life nowadays. I bought a vibrator because I didn't orgasm. I have been able to for about four years now. Occasionally 20-30 times during a sex act, that's why I'm grinning like a Cheshire cat.

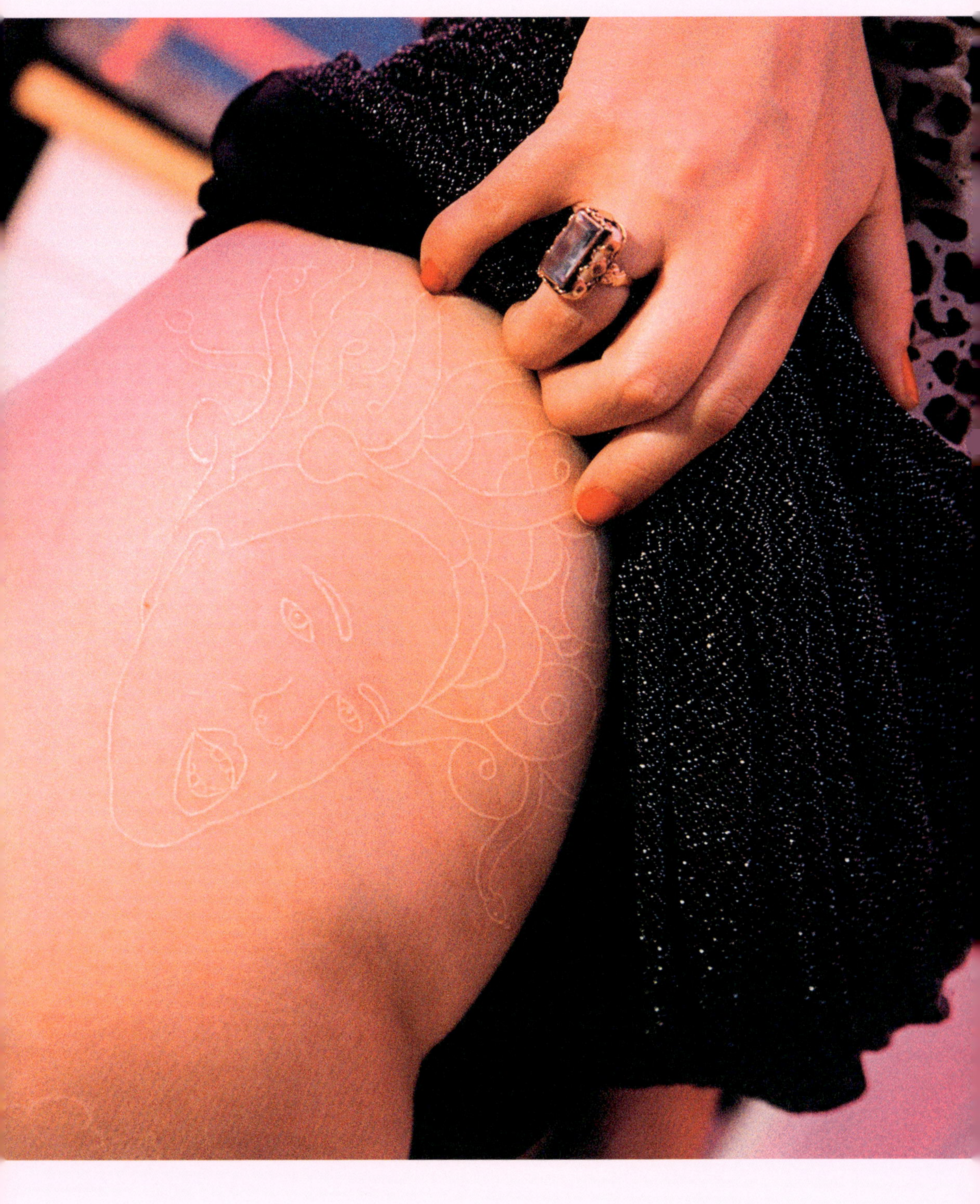

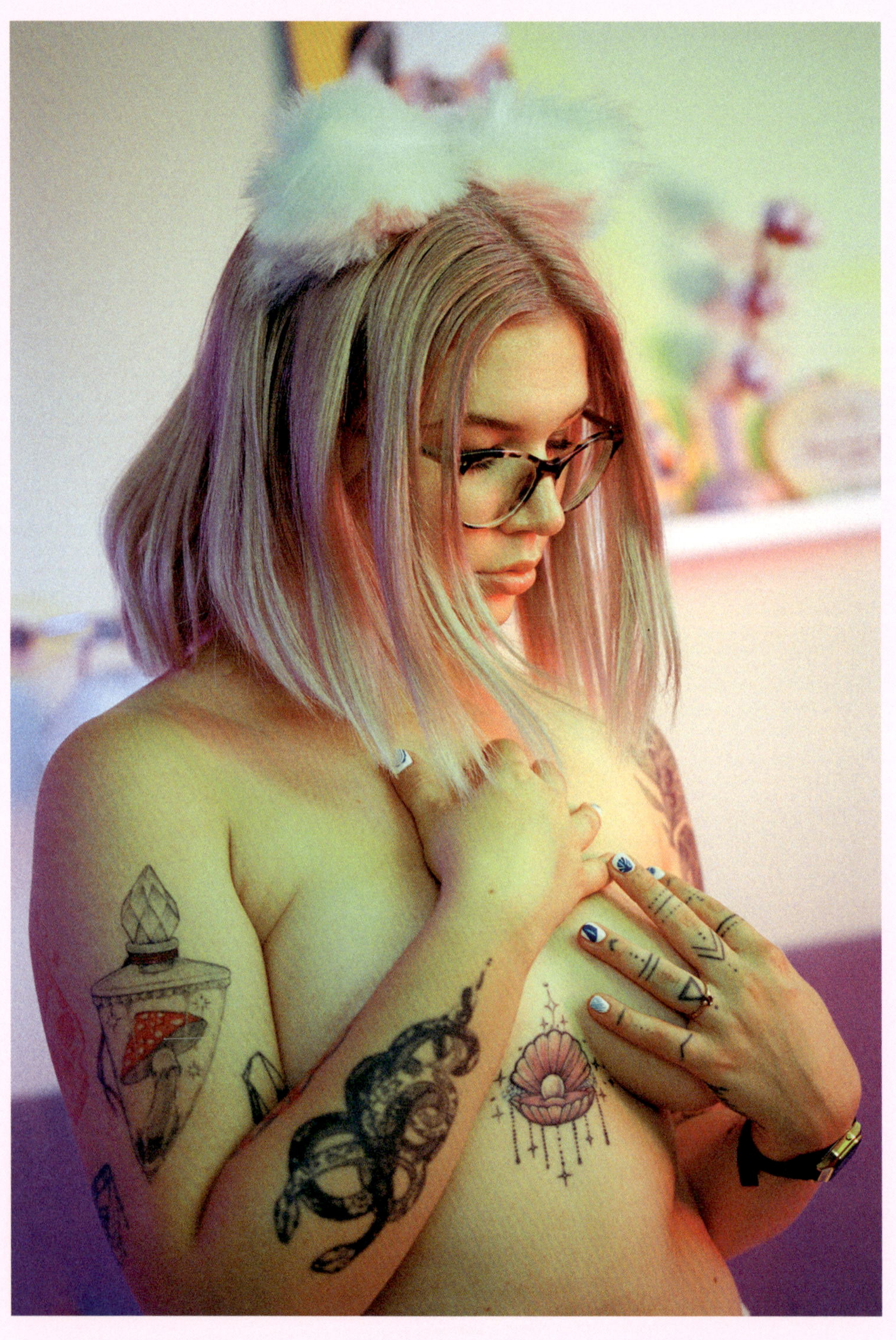

FRUZSINA

When I was twenty, I was in an abusive relationship. He damaged me deeply with his words, and almost physically too. He demolished my self-esteem, I wasn't myself. I went numb. I had a relationship after that one and I became pregnant right at the beginning. We had been going out for two months, I didn't want to keep the baby. The abortion was a serious trauma for me, and I think for him as well. After that he didn't touch me for a year. I cheated on him, too. I had never cheated on anyone before but I just couldn't take it anymore. Tamás, my fiancé, and the last three years brought me back.

Four years ago, I suddenly put on 30 extra kilos due to emotional reasons. I shouldn't have dated anyone at that time. I met a guy and he seemed to fancy me. After meeting a few times he suggested we go to his place. As we were having sex, he stopped and said he couldn't do it. He was embarrassed and said that I was fat and I disgusted him. It felt awful, especially considering my emotional state.

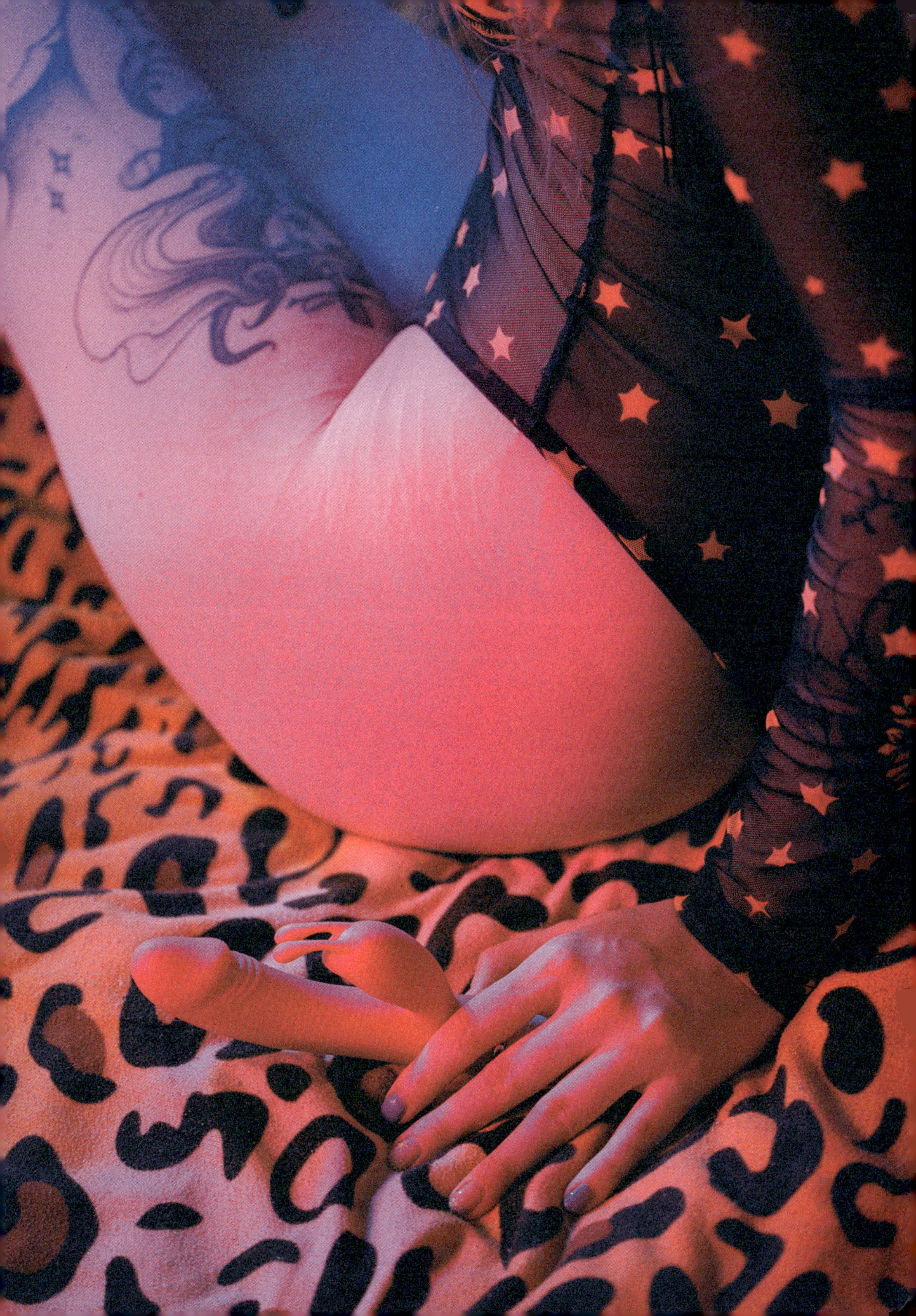

LILLA T.

My sex life didn't have the best start. I was always in pain. In my first relationship I was traumatized by the pain that had no specific reason, probably causing my vaginismus. For some time I was unable to have sex in the traditional sense. It's possible that my body reacted to intimacy and pleasure in a way that I couldn't accept easily. The acceptance was more difficult because I didn't see any healthy examples before me. My parents' relationship lacked stability, open and calm communication, and loving touches. This made similar dynamics strange and scary to me.

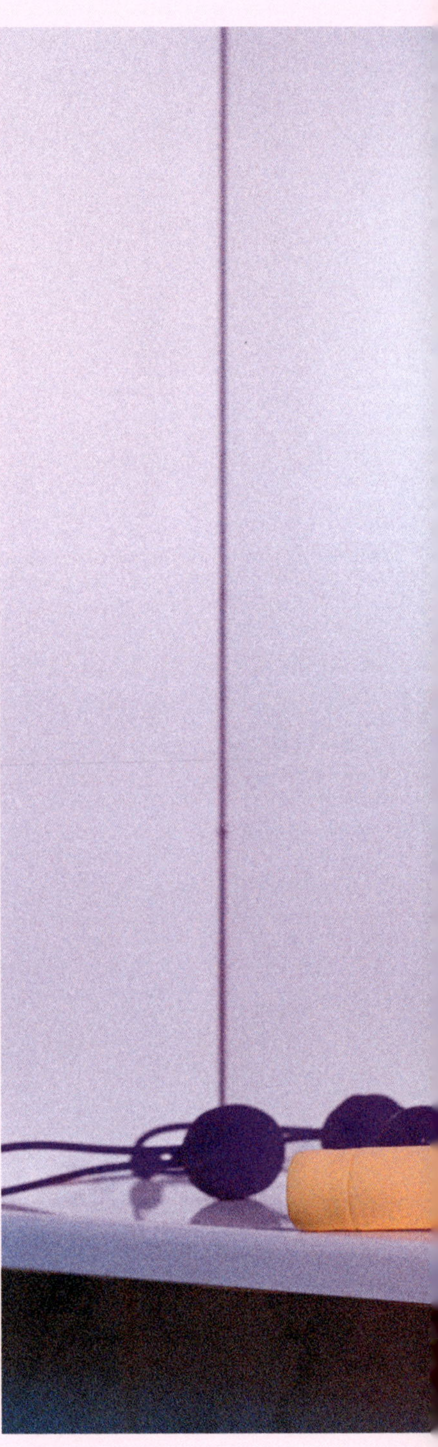

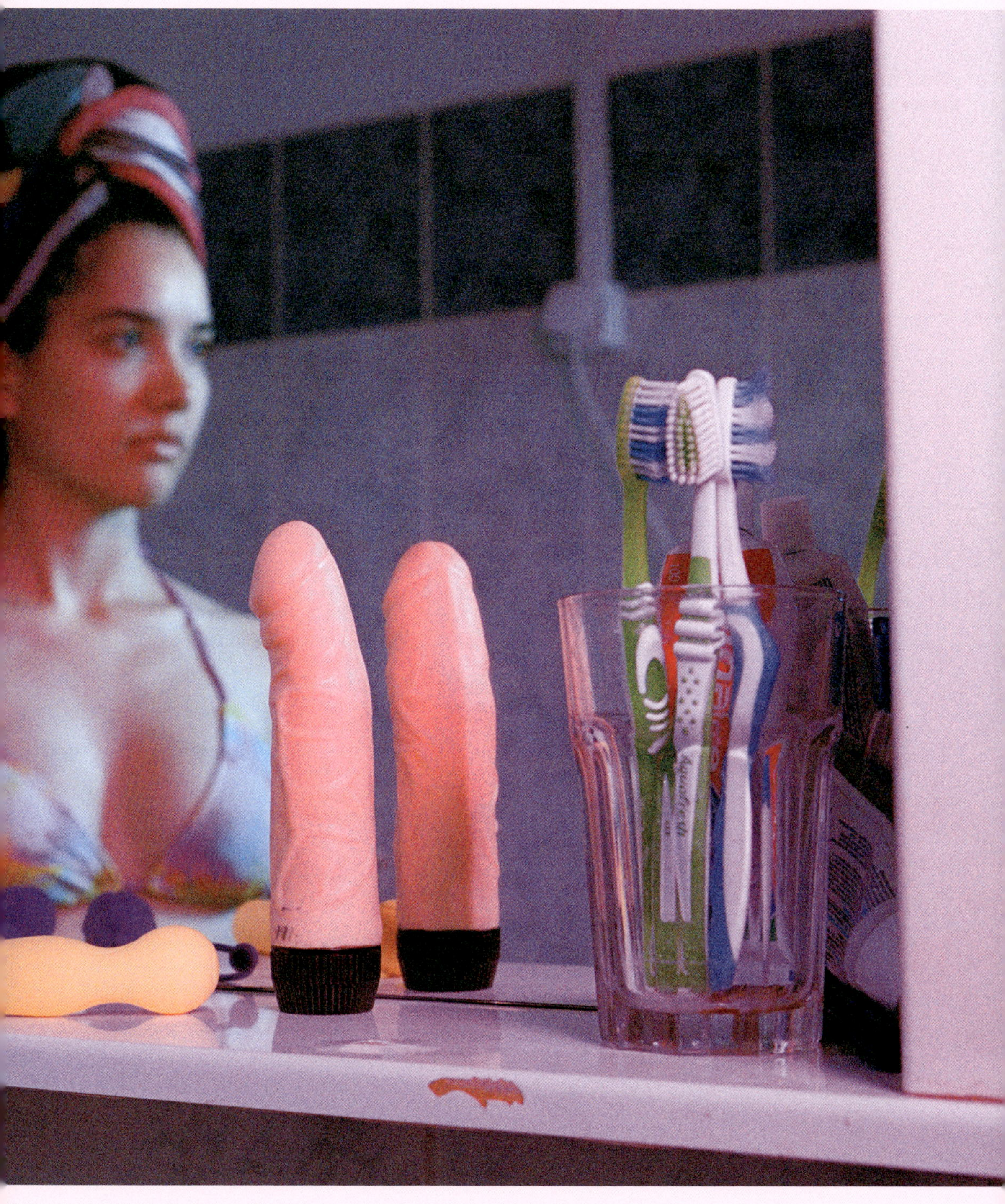

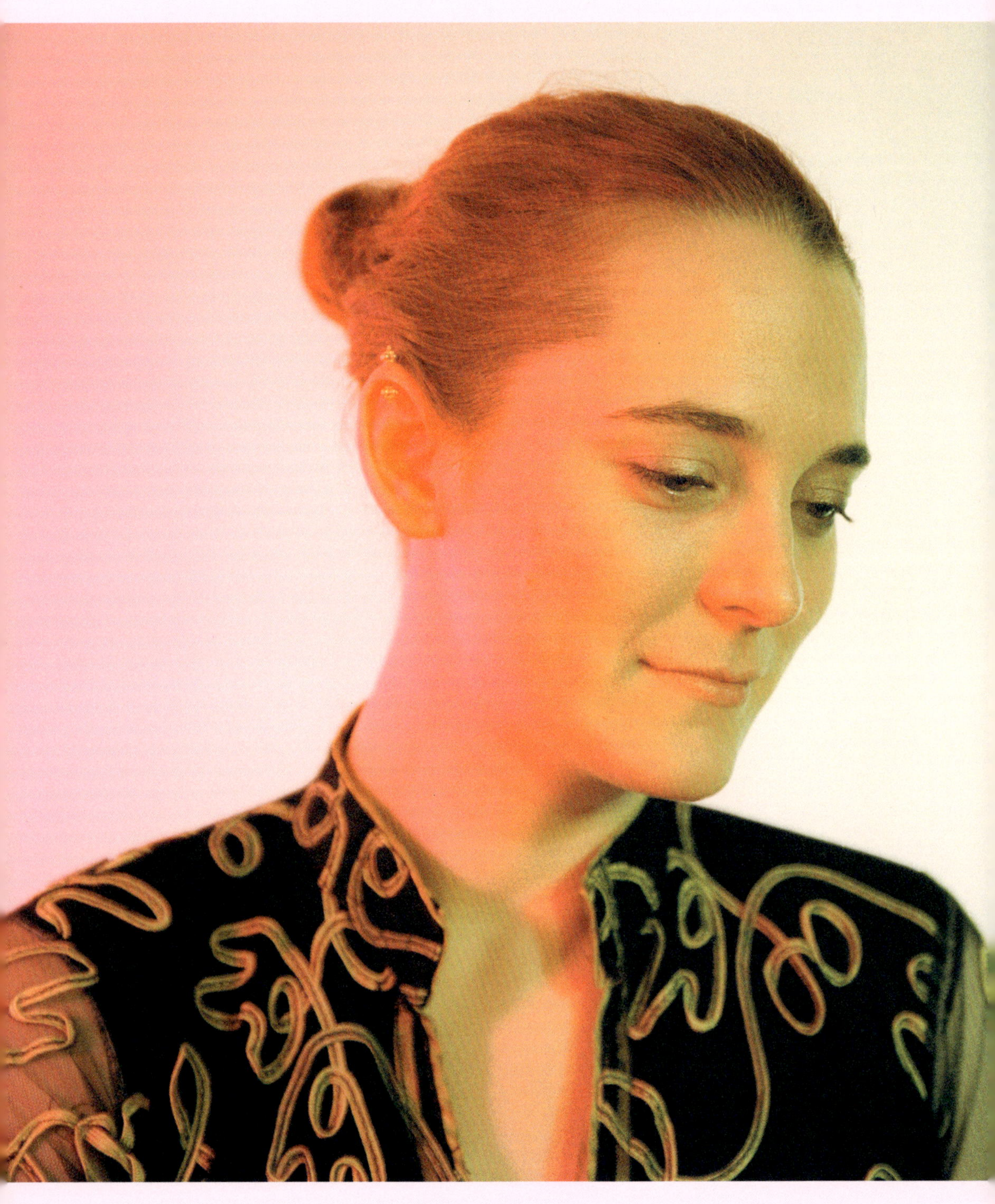

BARBARA M.

Now I can access my shame. I can revert to being that little girl who is ashamed by the sexual abuse she suffered. Somehow, I still feel that my sexuality is dangerous and puts everyone at risk.

BARBARA O.

I experienced orgasms even as a child. Yet, the first two guys I slept with didn't make me come, so I just kept telling myself that I did. I even messaged my friends about my great orgasm. Meanwhile I knew well what an orgasm really was. I thought there was a limit to the time I deserved and if I couldn't come until it was up, I just faked it. The sex was phenomenal, I just didn't even give myself a chance. I don't know where this came from. Later when I orgasmed for the first time with a man, he just pushed all the right buttons, so I realized that was it and I was able to experience orgasms from then on.

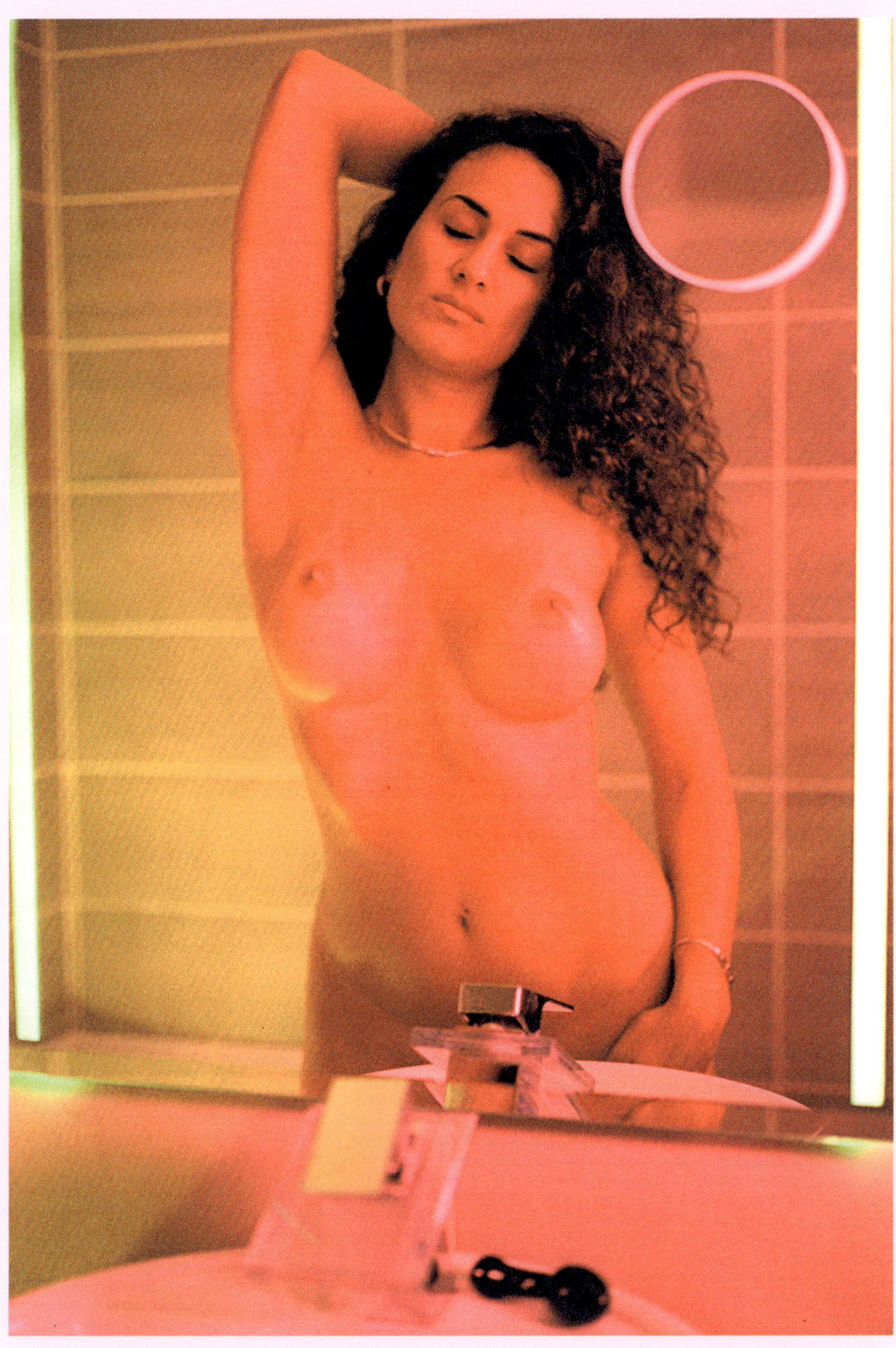

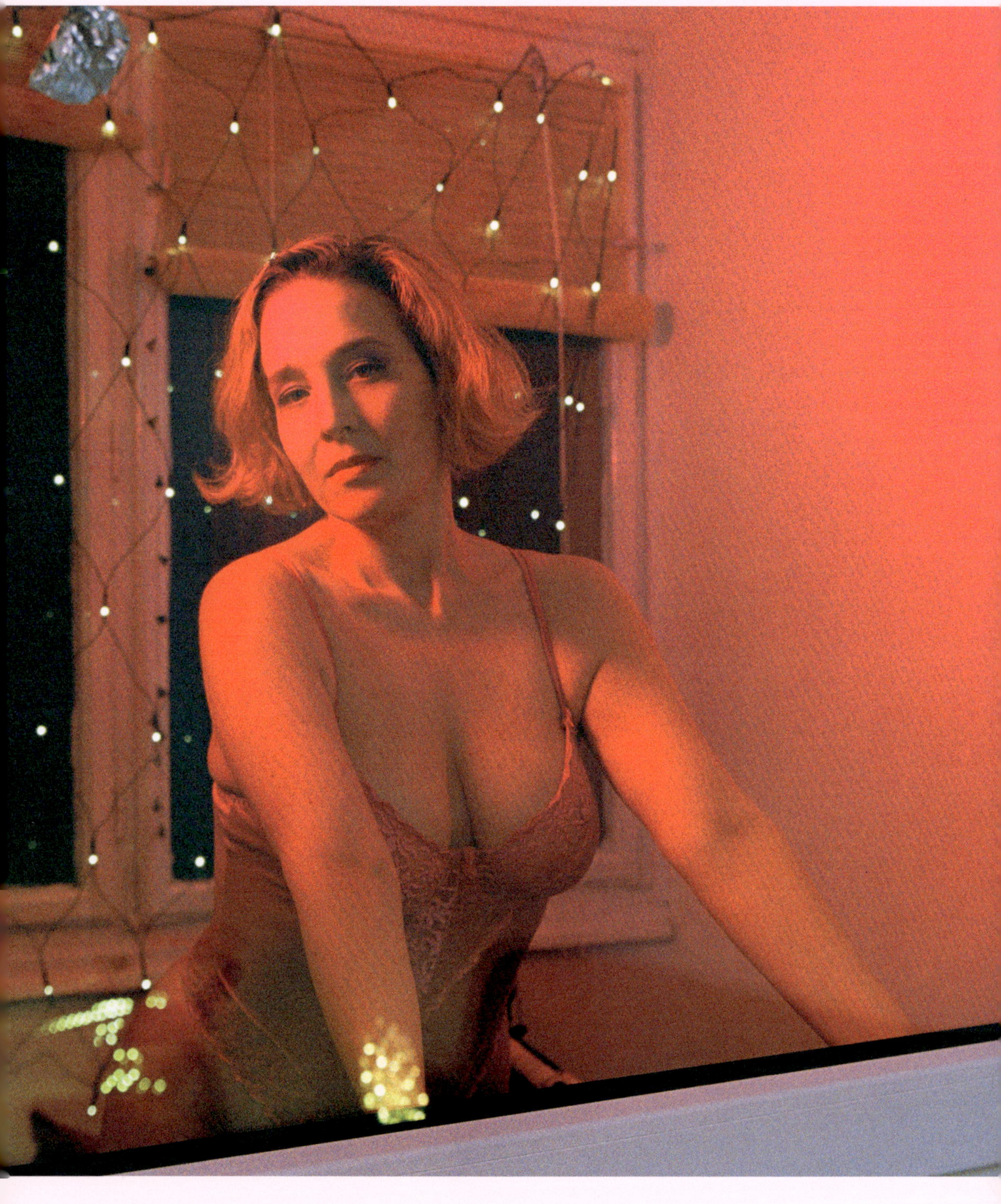

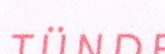

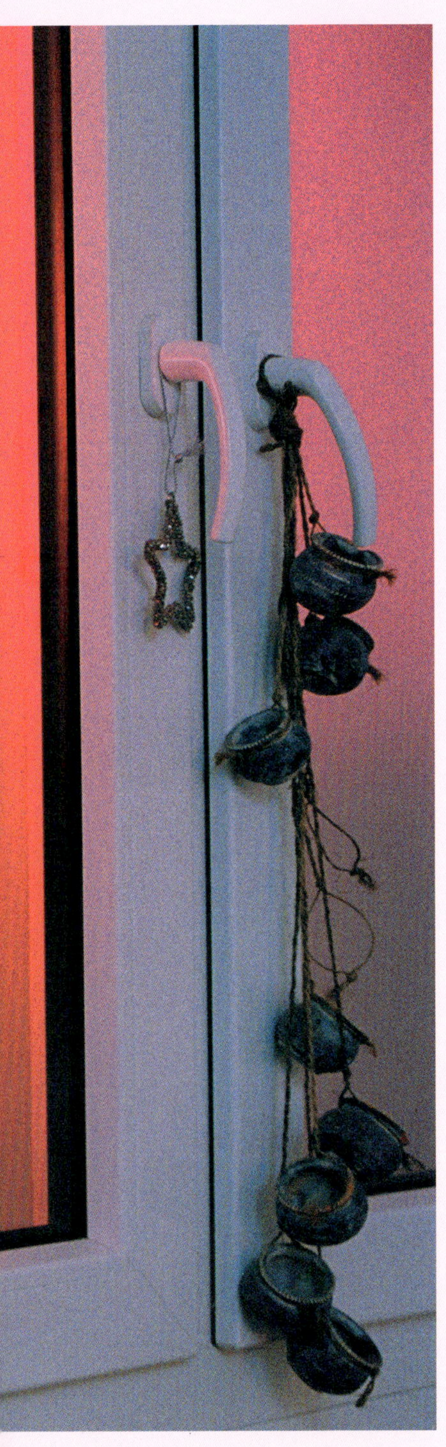

I've fallen in love with men who were very different. I've always wanted the guy to be smarter than me but it didn't always work out that way. When he was smarter than me for real, I tried to subordinate myself to his life. This affected sexual matters as well.

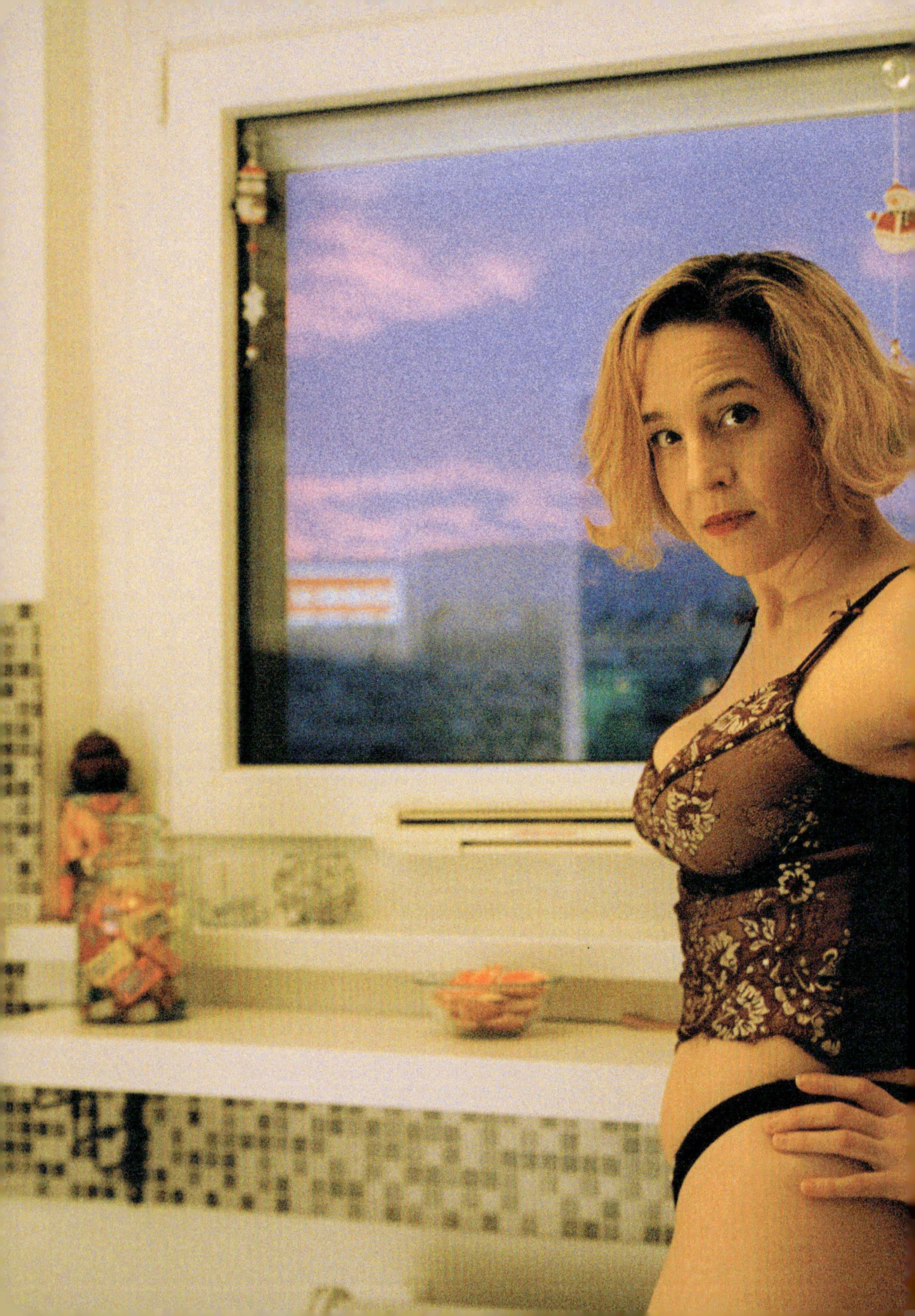

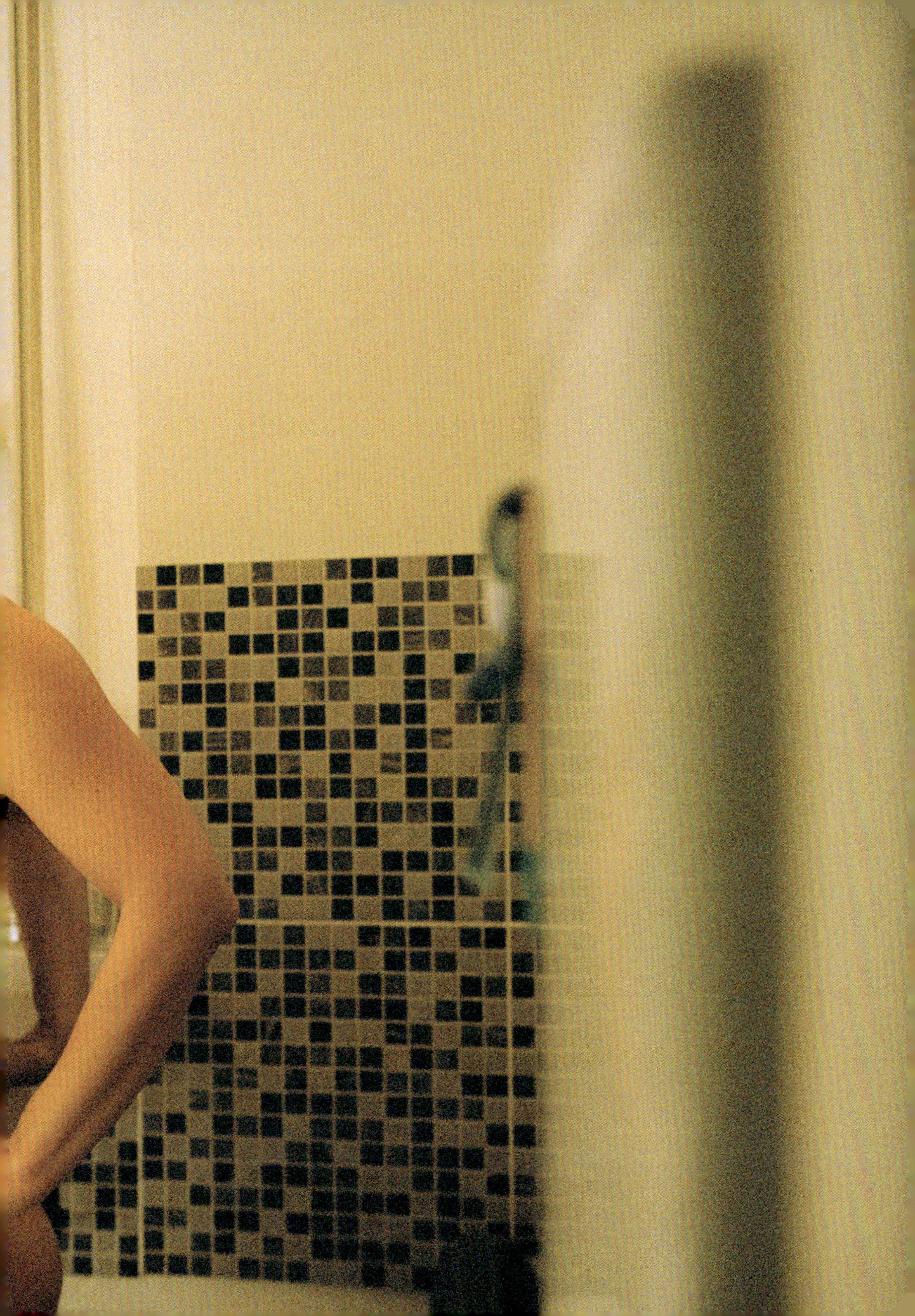

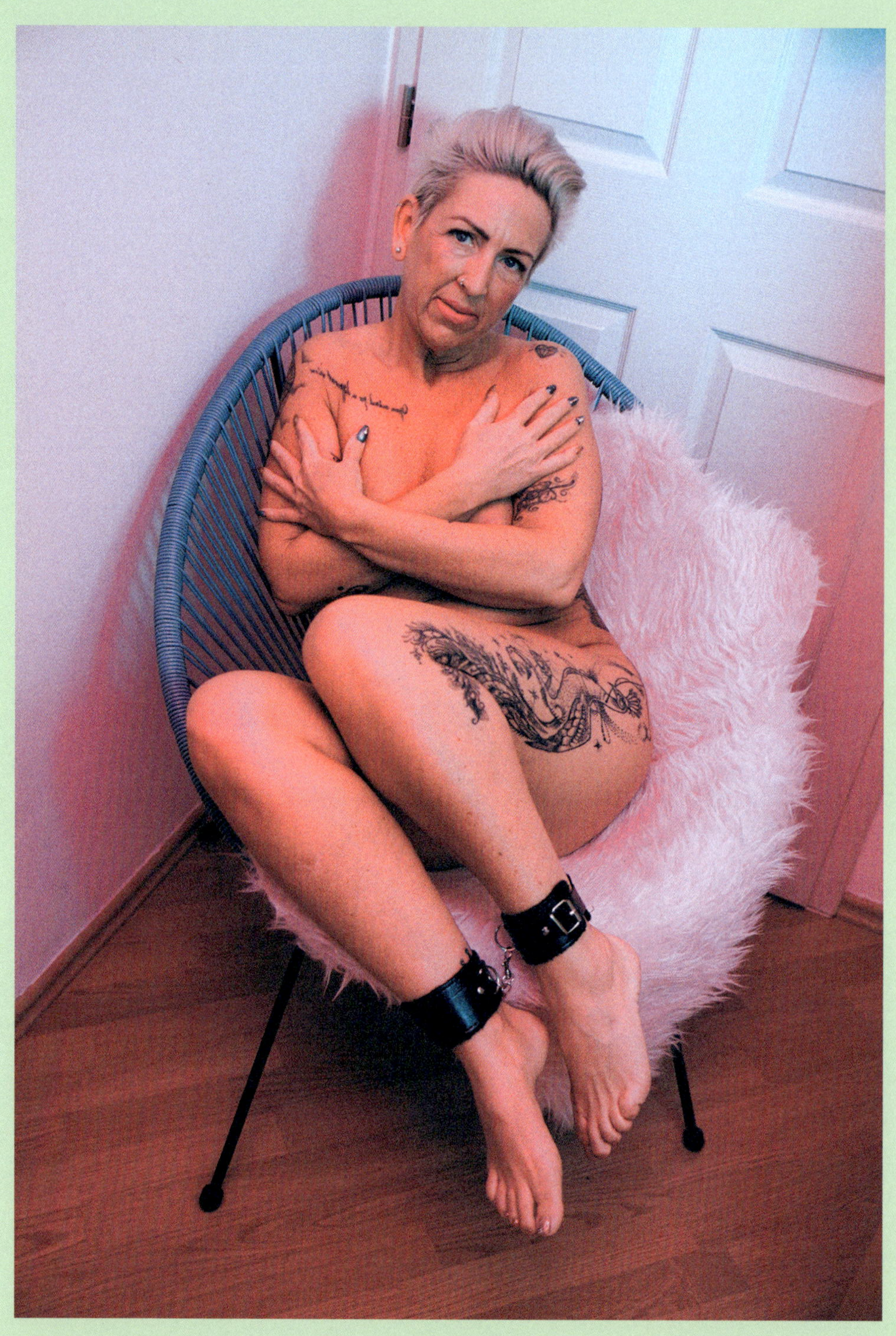

I've always wanted to be an "it girl," but I wasn't going out with anyone. Before my husband, I didn't have a normal relationship. I was 32 when I gave birth to my child. After my divorce, I had zero sexual self-awareness. I met a rock musician who was pretty reckless, he wanted to try everything with me. At first, I only agreed to do it for him but then I realized it is a pretty cool thing. But he was really violent, I can't even comprehend how I could go out with him.

When he left me, I didn't give a shit. There was just this one thing: I'm never gonna have such great sex as I did with him. Then I met another one of these reckless men. Beware, because you might have amazing sex with dudes like them but they are very dangerous. One abused me physically and the other abused me verbally. It wasn't worth it to be honest. My soul was damaged, then I went to a psychologist and we figured out why these things had happened to me. I know now how to distance myself from this type of guy. I discovered I'm a sexual being, I got to know good sex and I'd missed it too. I thought I'd buy myself a vibrator; at least it can't slap me in the face.

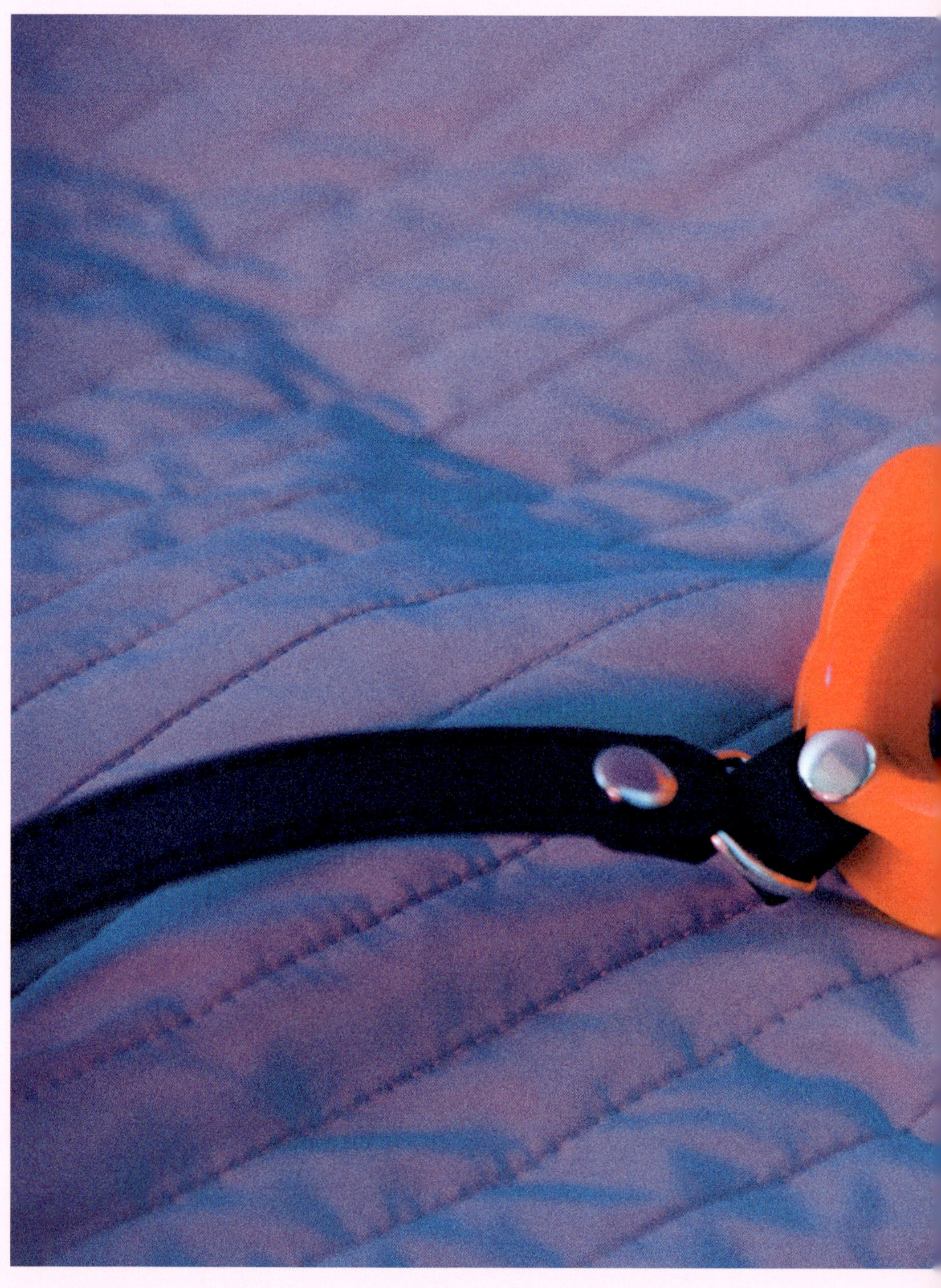

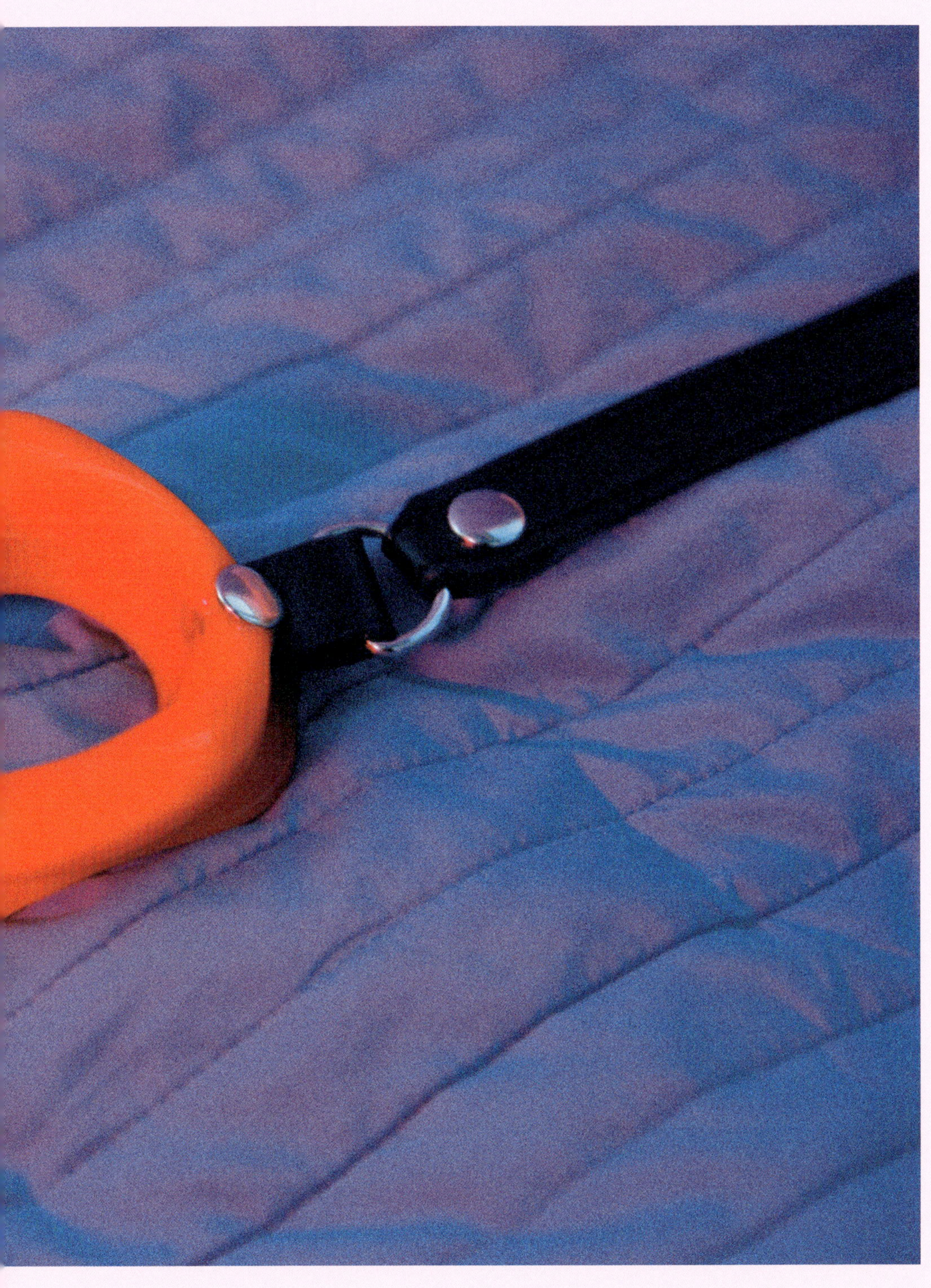

Vanilla relationship. Chaos. The End. The guy wanted to oppress me but when he had an itch, he wanted me to be his goddess in bed, or his mom. Whichever he was in the mood for. I couldn't be myself. I got sick. He wanted to tie me down with fear. And I hate to be scared; I'm brave. I had had enough, I wasn't happy. I could see how humiliating my circumstances were, just because I thought it was normal. After six years I got out of that relationship.

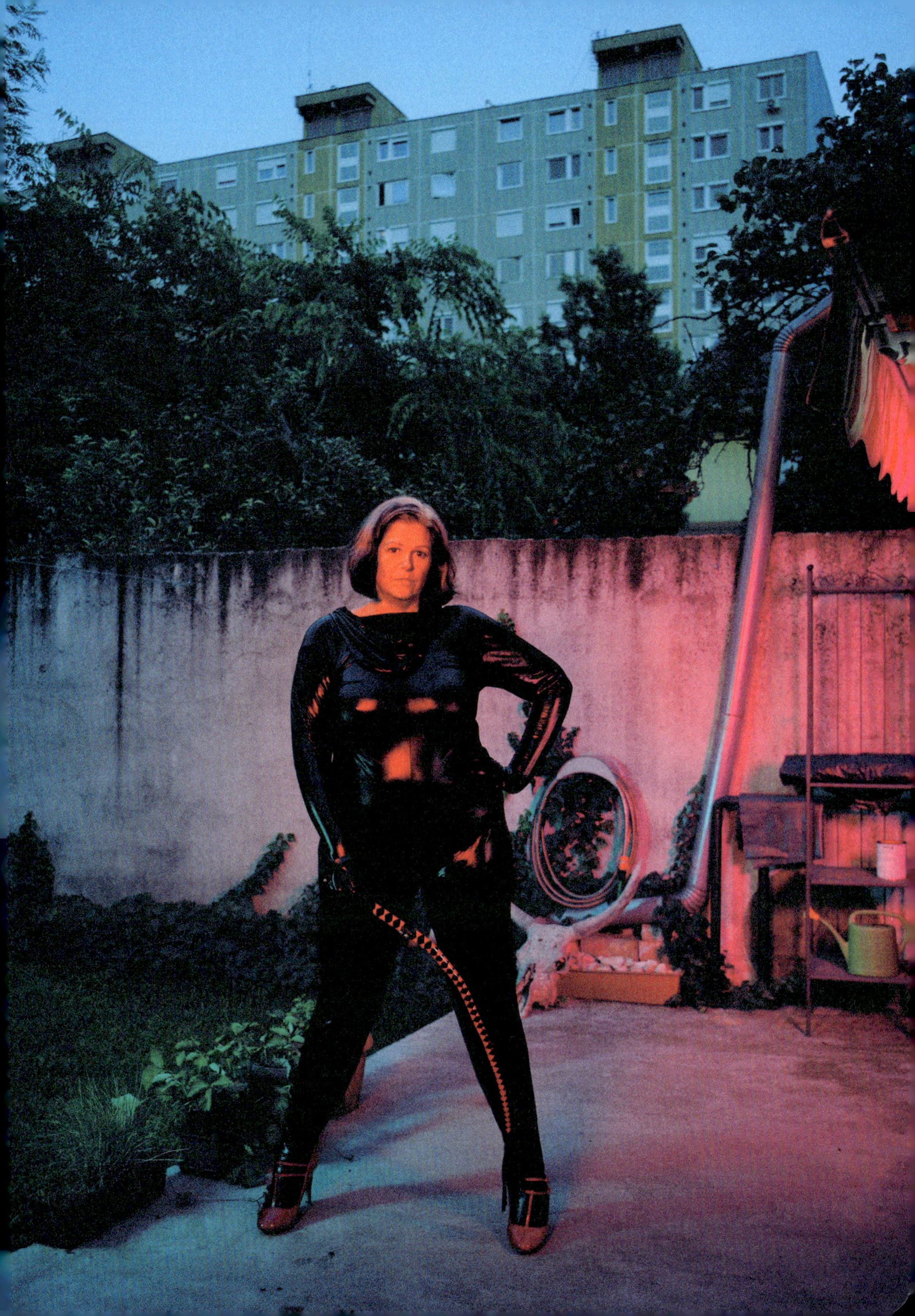

ÉVA B.

I've never had a relationship that was good for me. I was hung up on people I shouldn't have been. They destroyed me so much that I didn't even feel like a woman most of the time. During sex I thought "Let's get it over with." Even if the sex was shitty, I couldn't let go of the relationship. I don't know why.

I've only ever really been in love once, with a younger guy. He was the typical golden boy of an educated family. I already had my three children, I was about 36. That's when I experienced orgasm for the first time. I didn't get why he wanted me. I was heavier back then, with two legs and three kids. He explained that for a long time he was just one of the boys who ranked women by their appearance. Then he saw the movie *Shallow Hal* which changed his mind. He realized women have much more inner value than he had previously thought and aren't just objects to be judged by what they got from mother nature. He always called me "princess." I was awfully sick after we broke up.

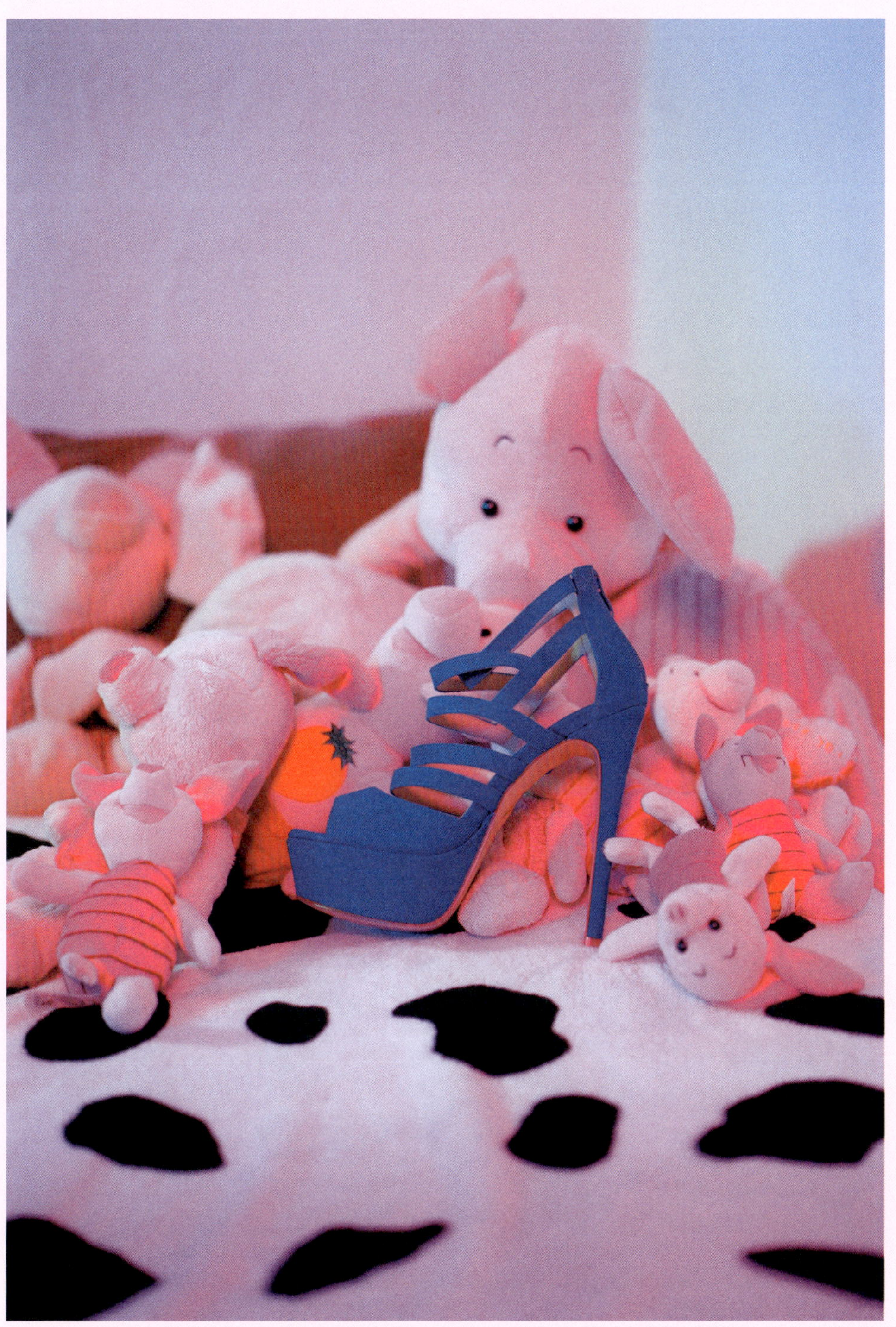

The world is so colorfully diverse, see how colorfully diverse it is.

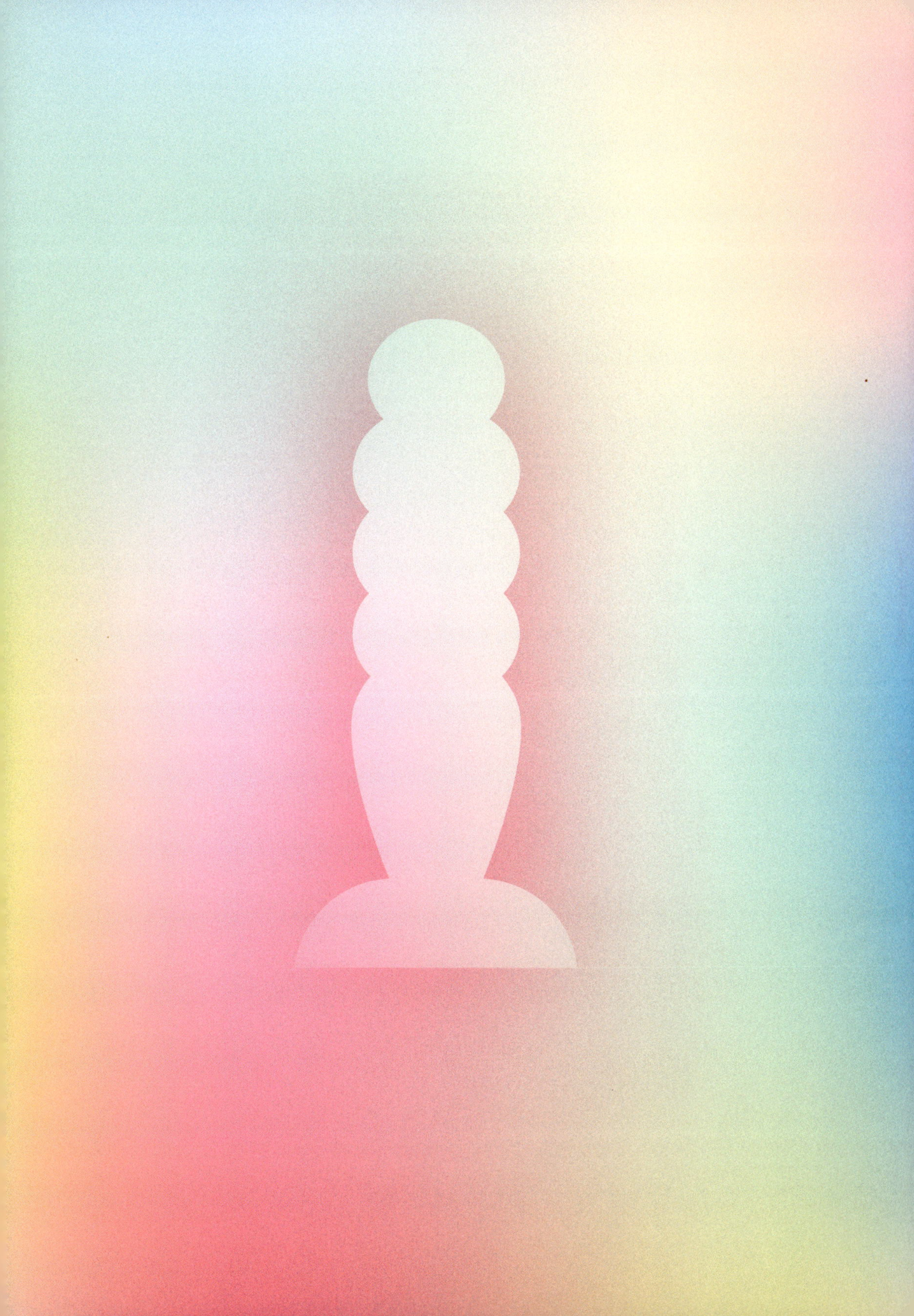

*I remember
how shitty it was
to live without
information.*

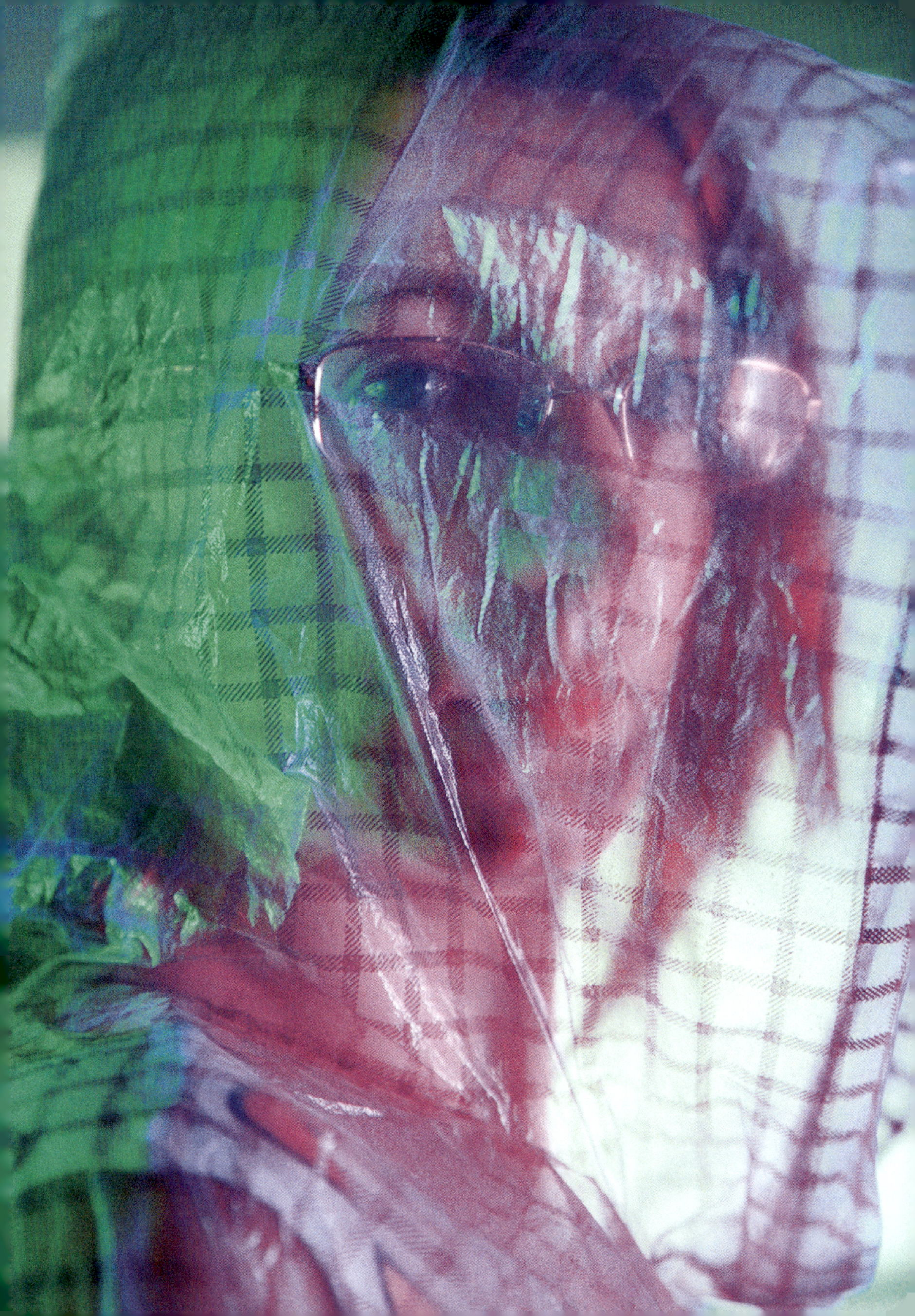

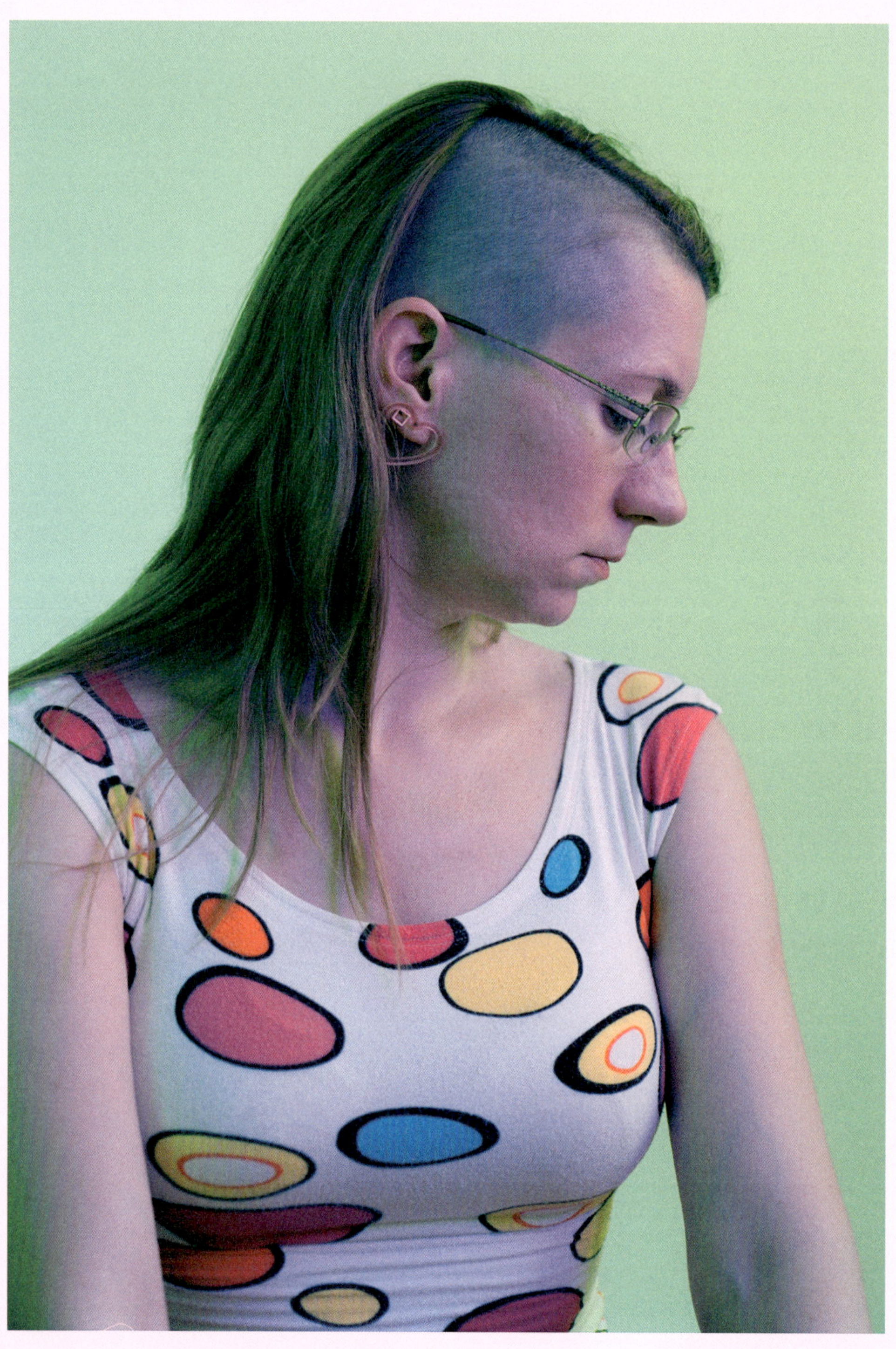

VIKTÓRIA

I noticed that I'm not interested in men at all. I'm not a lesbian, I don't have those feelings lesbians have. I had boyfriends and girlfriends too, so I figured I was just a picky bisexual. Ten years passed without having sex with another person. I thought this was really weird, everyone was having sex around me. In 2016, I read an article on asexuality and I realized you can separate libido from attraction. I desire orgasms but the act of getting there with someone else leaves me dry. I'm not only asexual, I'm also aromantic, so I don't feel romatic love.

I'm not attracted to anyone. It's not about them, it's about me.

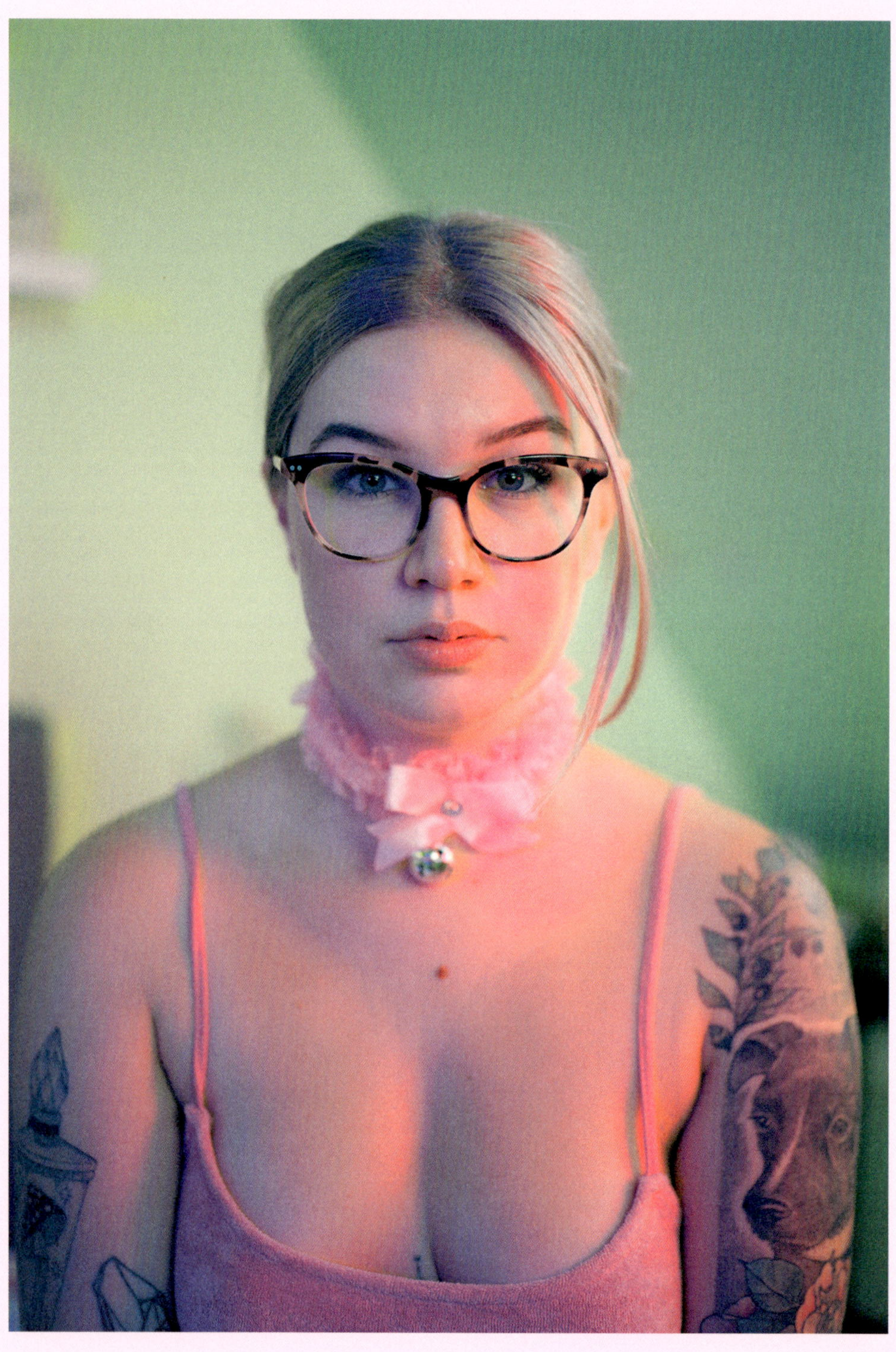

I've told my family several times that I'm bisexual but they never believe me. I was already dreaming about girls back in kindergarten.

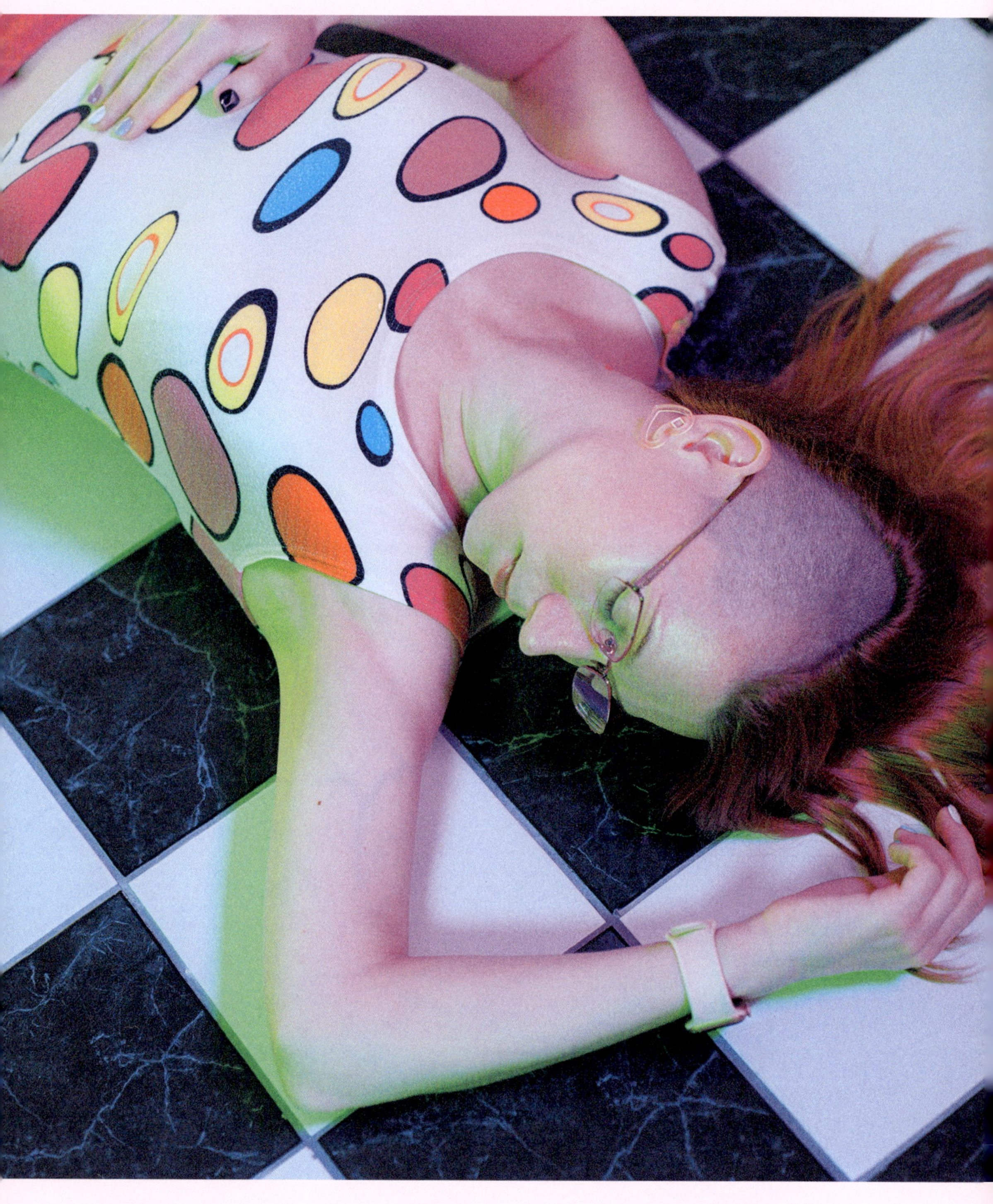

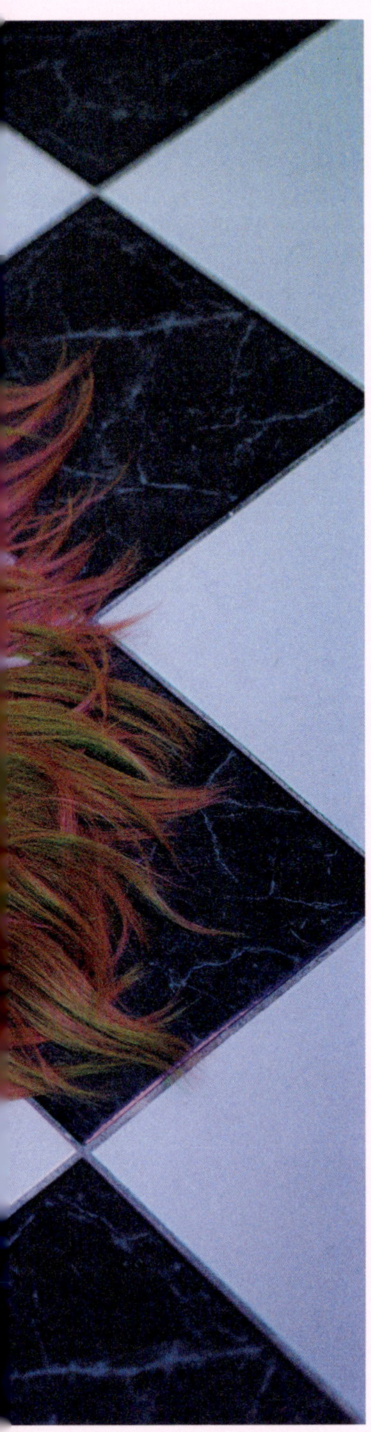

I'm not sure my family fully understands but it's no problem. They just have to accept me as I am.

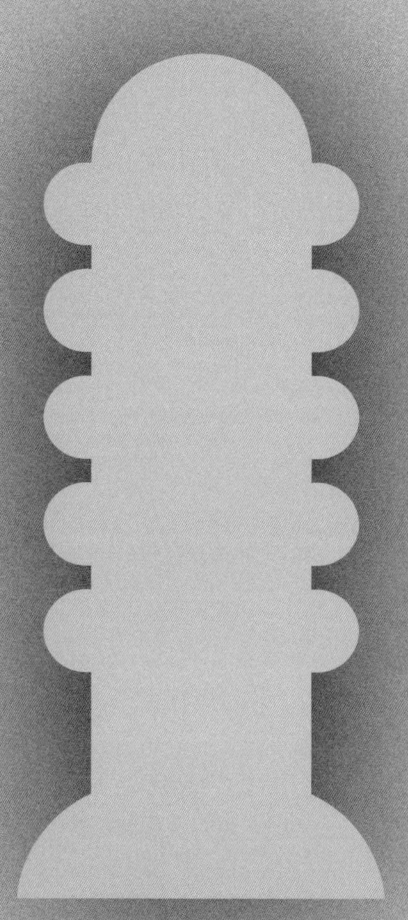

*It would be so cool
if they taught us that
"your body is yours."
You have the
right to decide what
to do with it.*

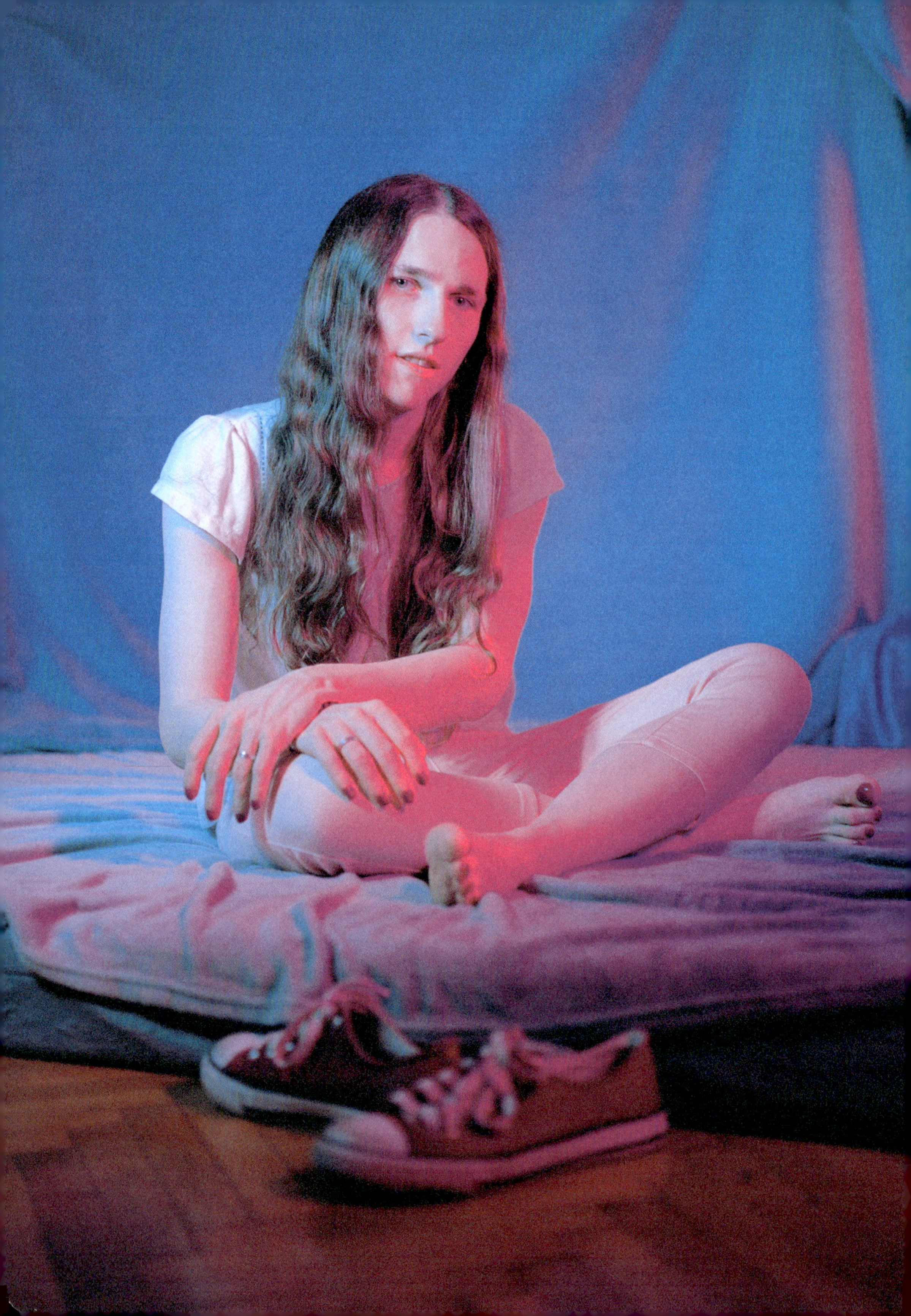

DANIELA

Even when I was eleven years old, I could form the thoughts that I was born in the wrong body and I was never ever supposed to talk about this to anyone. My homeroom teacher once asked the class if anyone felt like they were born in the wrong body. It crossed my mind that I could talk to her about this. When no one put their hand up, she said: "Well, it's not that normal, is it?" So, I quickly pushed that thought away. I had struggled with my transgenderedness my whole life; I felt it wasn't an option for me, not in my family. My mom often said: "I love you so much but if you end up being a faggot, you can go live on the streets."

I struggled with my sexuality a lot too. I never dated anyone, masturbation also made me feel sick. The message was that it was a bad thing and I felt guilty.

I was conflicted about transitioning because I knew it was forbidden but I also needed it. I had suicidal thoughts. I felt it was never going to get better. The idea that this could end was wonderful. I have siblings, but we grew up separately. I remembered a photo of them, I imagined them meeting again without me, like nothing had happened, and it hurt a lot. It just dawned on me that I could change this. I could be in that photo too. I also figured if I was going to die anyway, why shouldn't I live the way I want to first? And I'm here now. That was when I realized I did have something in life that I wanted. All the bad feelings were gone, and a sense of calm came over me. I found a novel about a trans girl. I could see through the eyes of a girl who had already transitioned. That was the last step towards making the decision that I wanted to transition. I started seeing a psychologist, I took a course, everything was getting better.

I was 24 when I came out to my sister, the first time ever in my life. I started opening up to others. I got a job. They supported me in using my chosen name, so I know what it's like to use my own. That's when I realized what the government took away from me.[1] After two years of therapy, I started my transition.

[1] *Hungary's parliament passed a law in 2020 that requires the use of birth gender only for transgendered and intersex people. They are legally unable to use any other gender marker.*

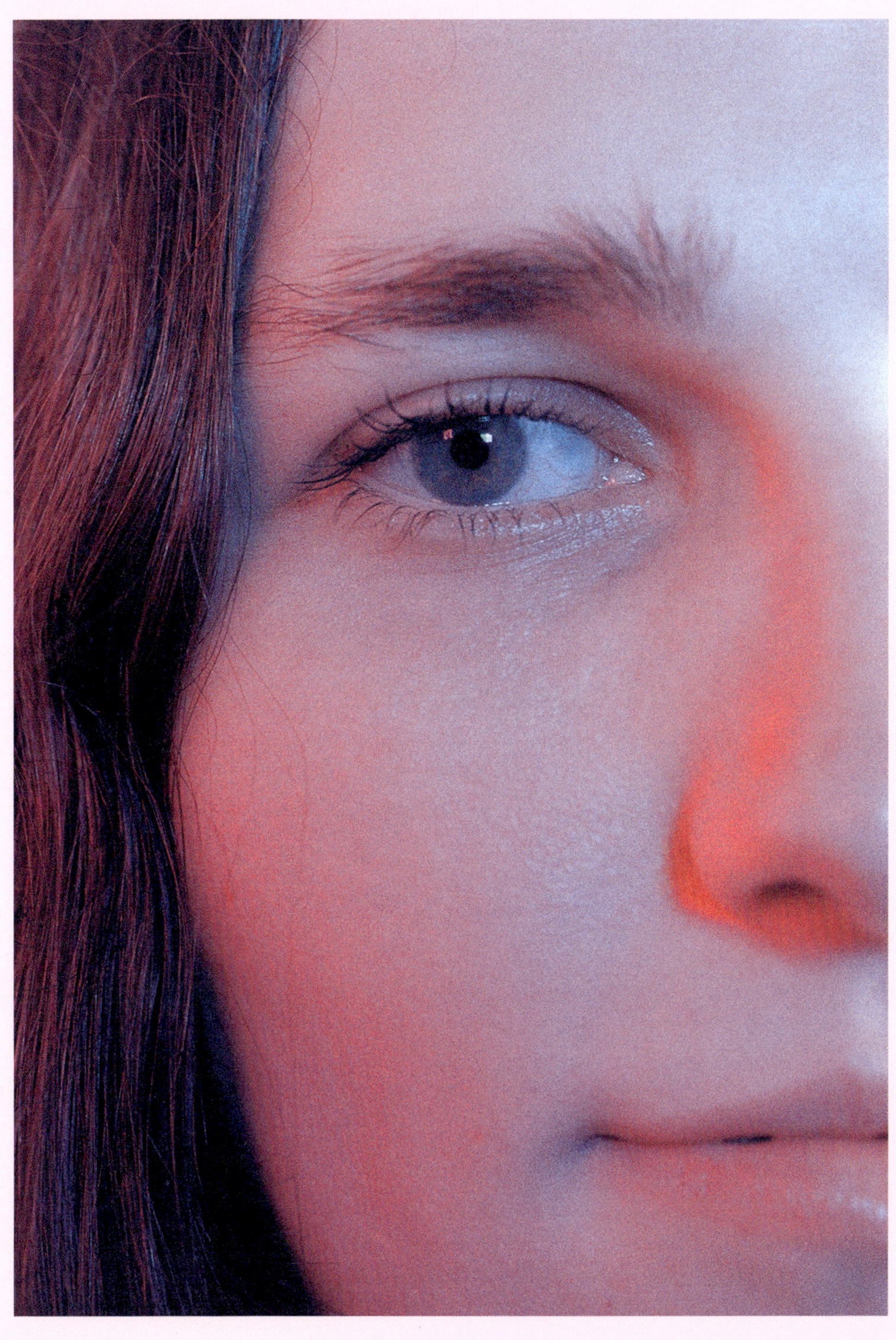

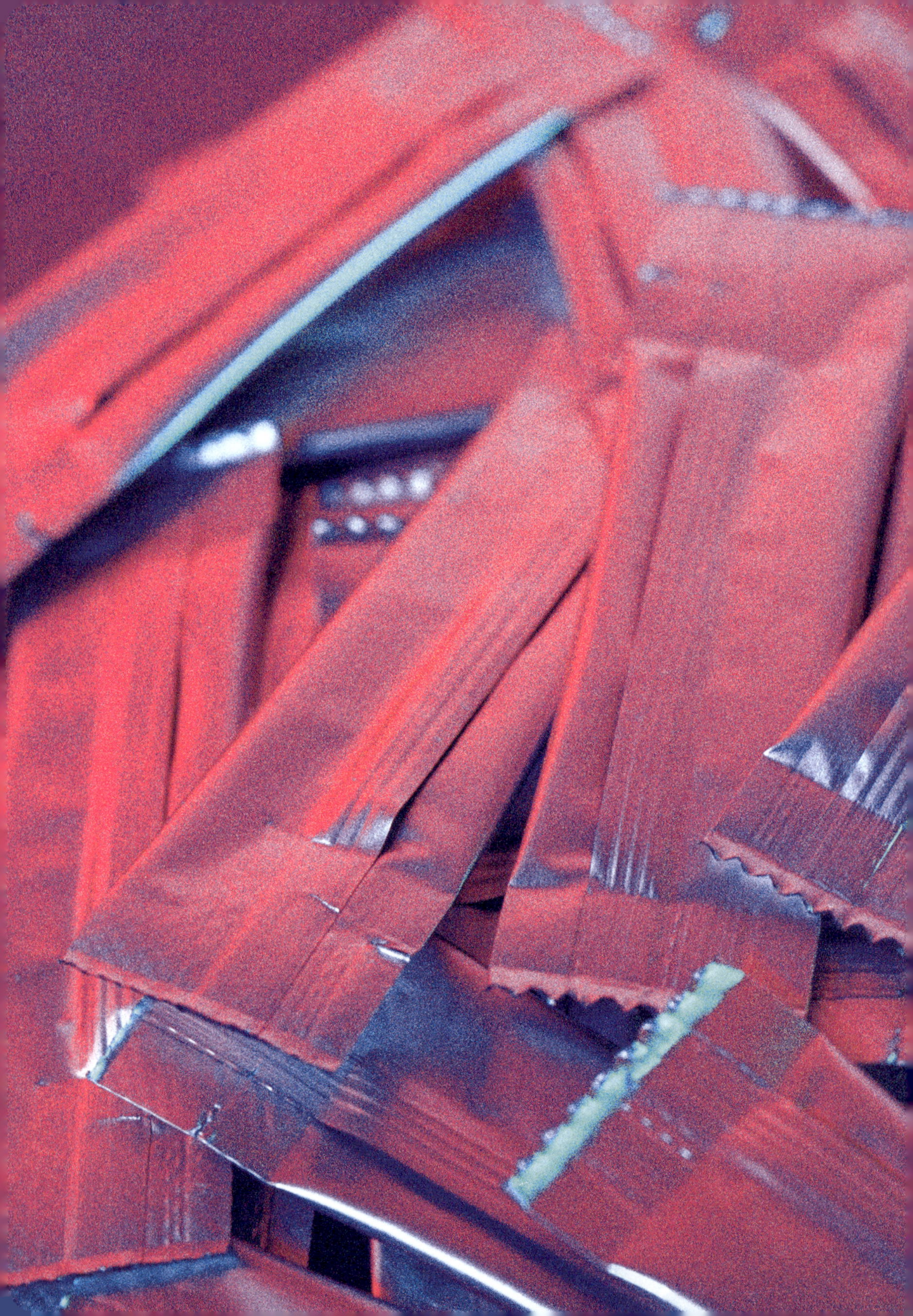

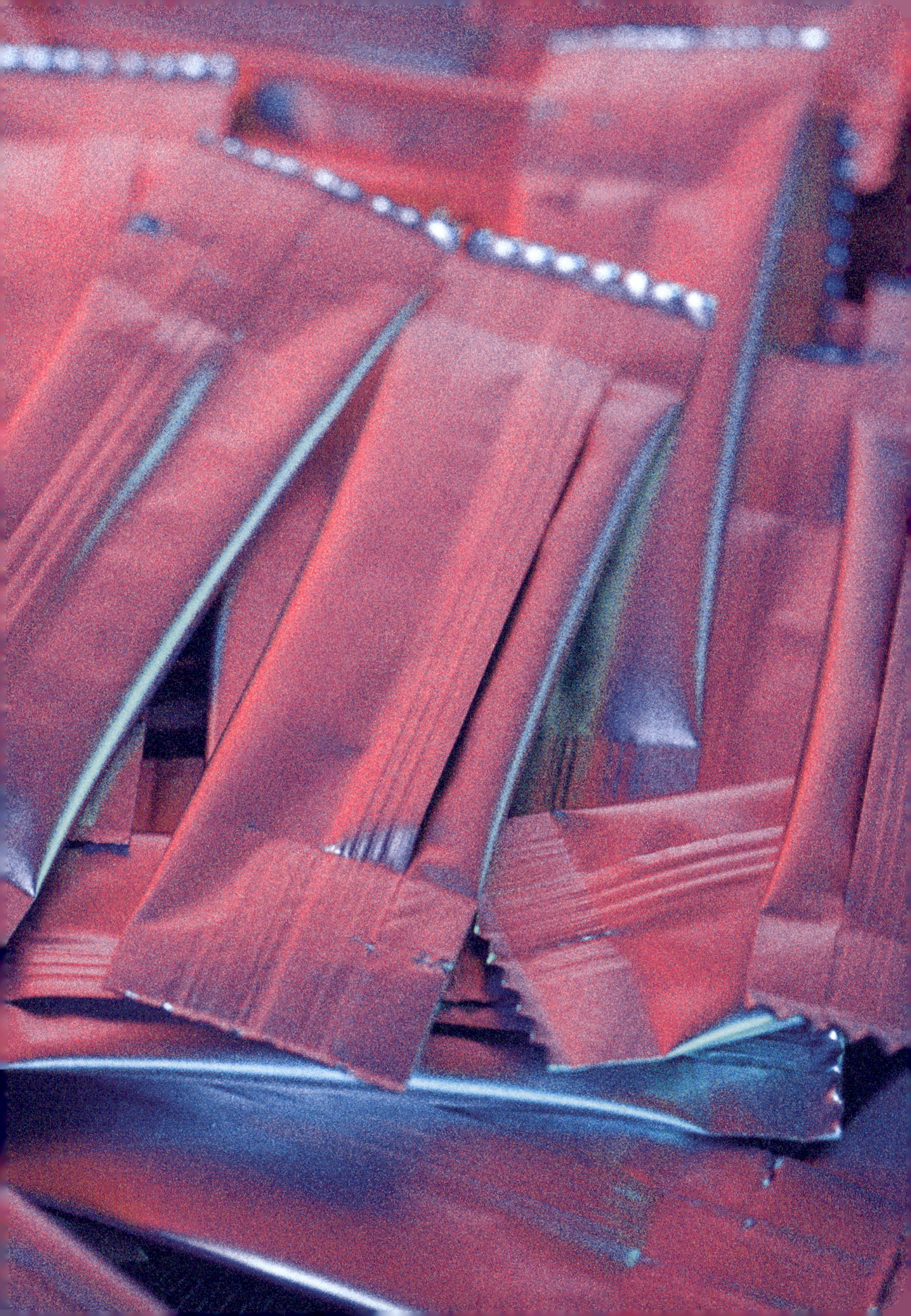

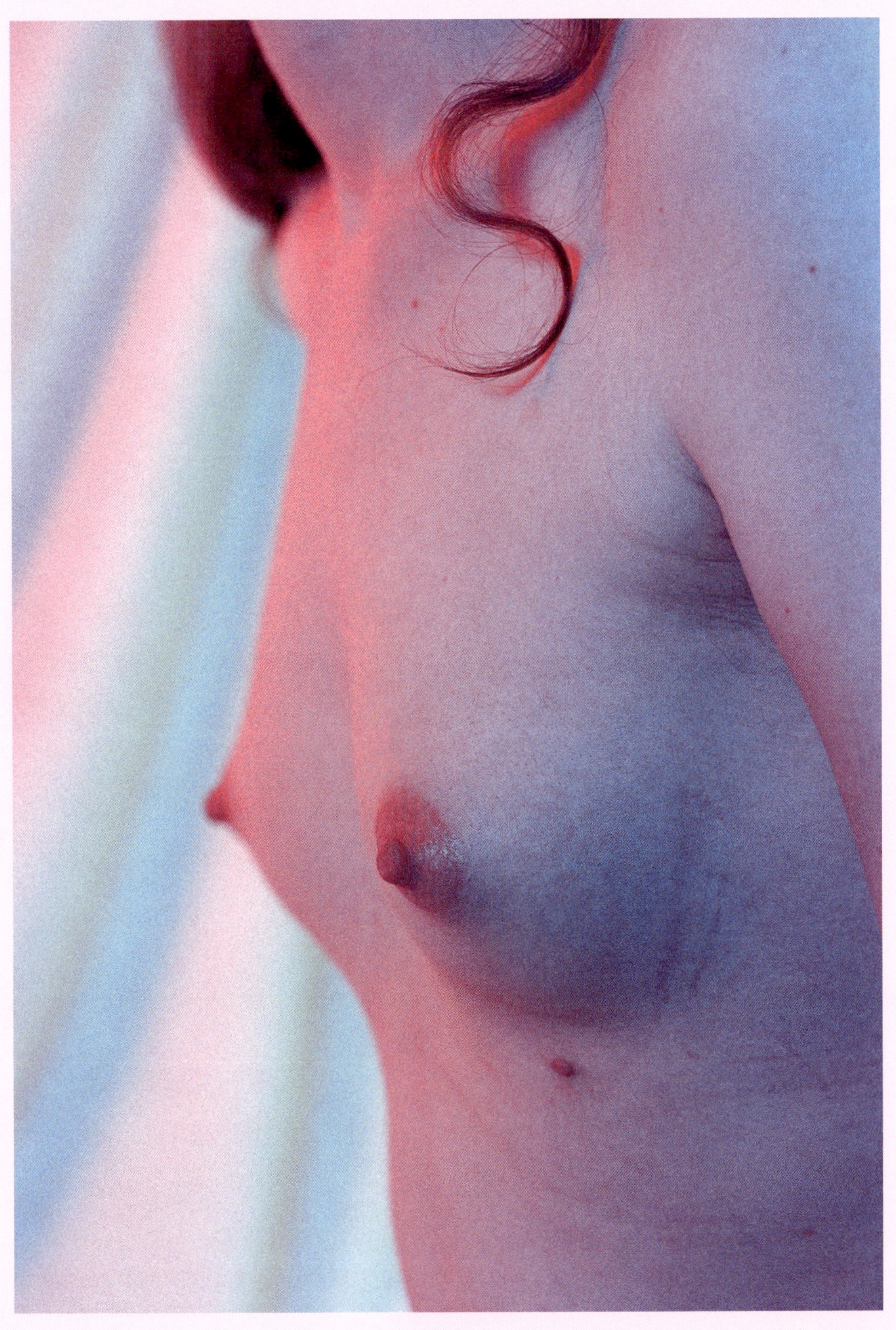

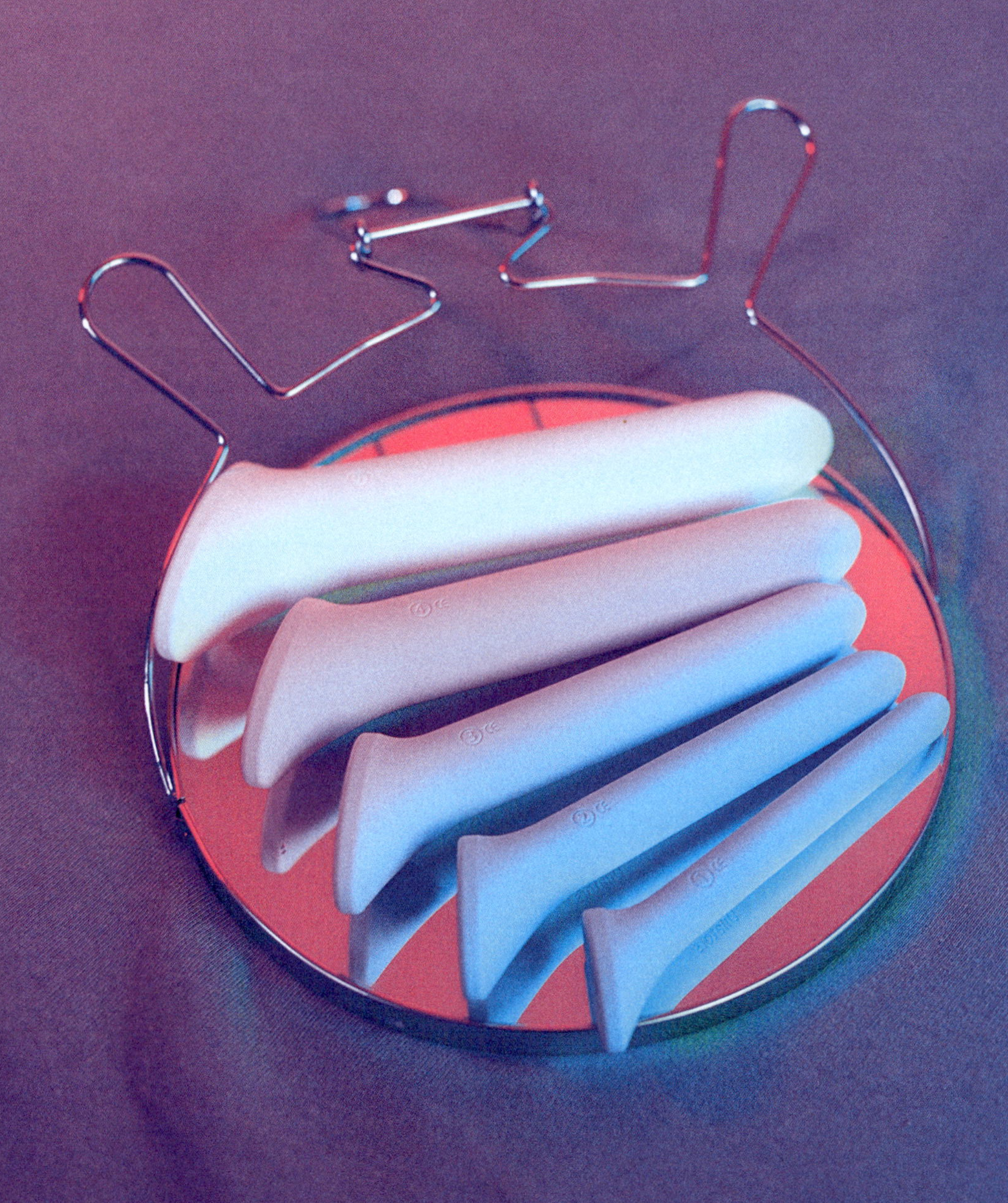

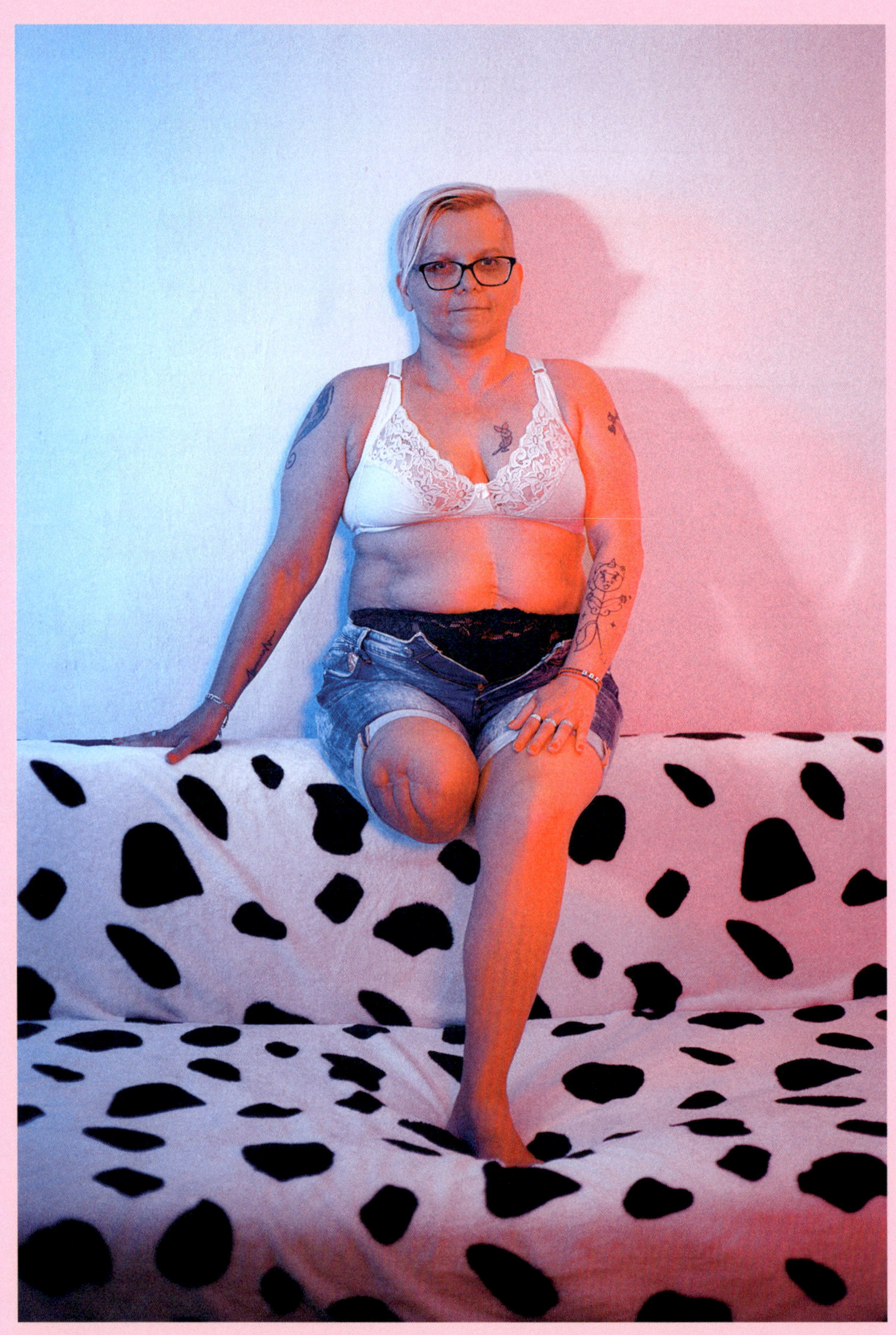

For most men I'm a monster, a disfigured being. But then there are some who treat me like I'm their everything. I first heard the expression "devotee" on message boards. Most of them are married, secretive and ashamed about this attraction. The ones I talked to realized this attraction to amputees during their teen years. These men taught me not to be ashamed of my body and that I'm perfect the way I am. Without them the past couple of years would've been terribly shitty. For me, it's just like when someone is into big boobs or big asses. Some like amputated bodies. They encourage me mentally to be myself and fend for myself. They need this too, to dare to be themselves. One of them tried to take me for an object. But I'm not an object, I'm a person. So we cut it short very quickly.

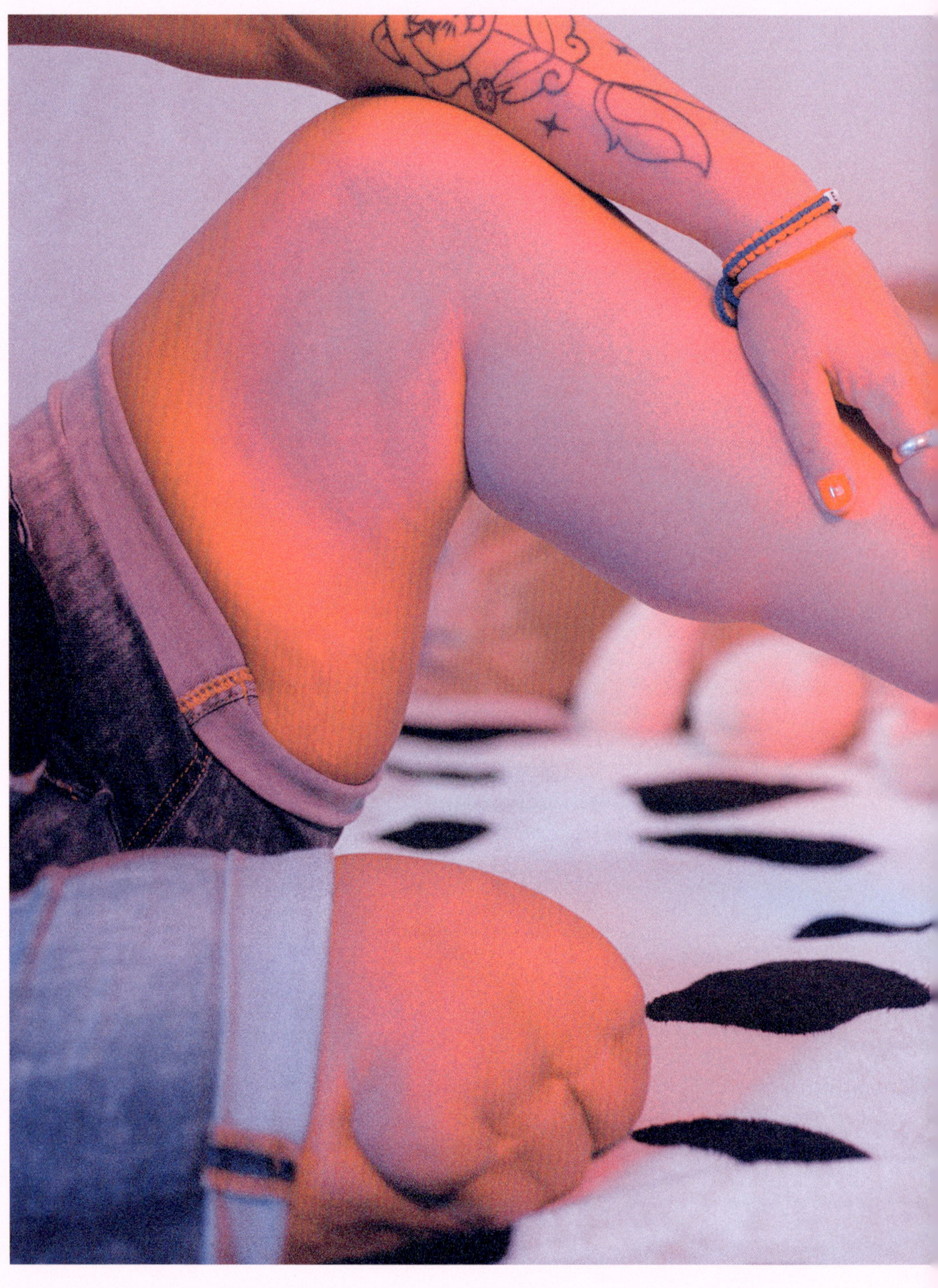

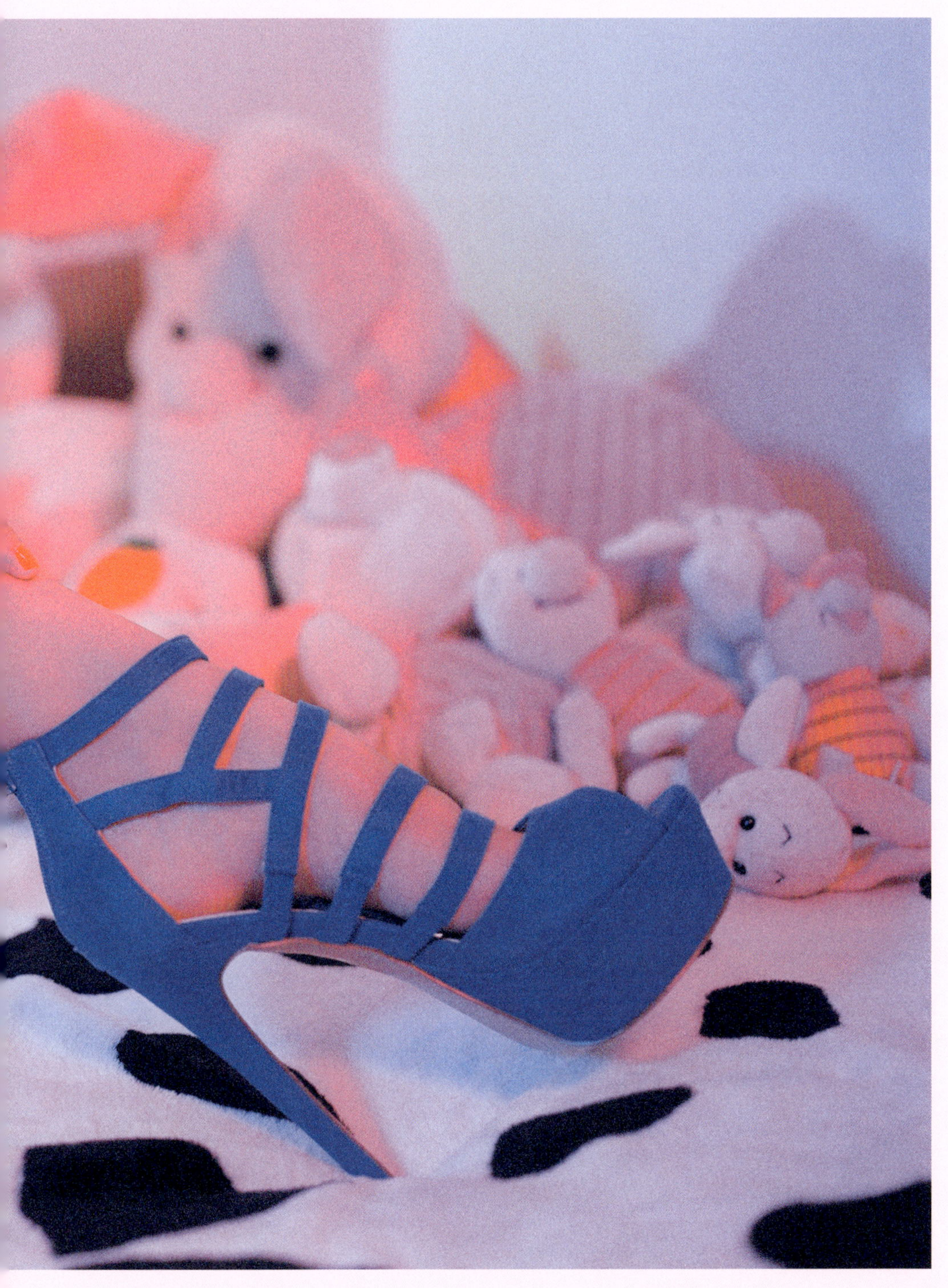

Two years after my amputation I had my first sexual encounter with a devotee. It was hard to imagine the stump could be an erogenous zone. I need sex very much. They didn't cut my libido off. People always ask me how I have sex. I just say that apart from getting on my knees to give them some lovin', I can do anything! And that I'm just a bit wobbly. A woman nearing 50 must be proud of her body because it's full of memories: childbirth, losing weight, gaining weight, the amputation. I have scars that remind me that I gave life and I have scars that remind me that I've been given an extra one. I feel good in my skin.

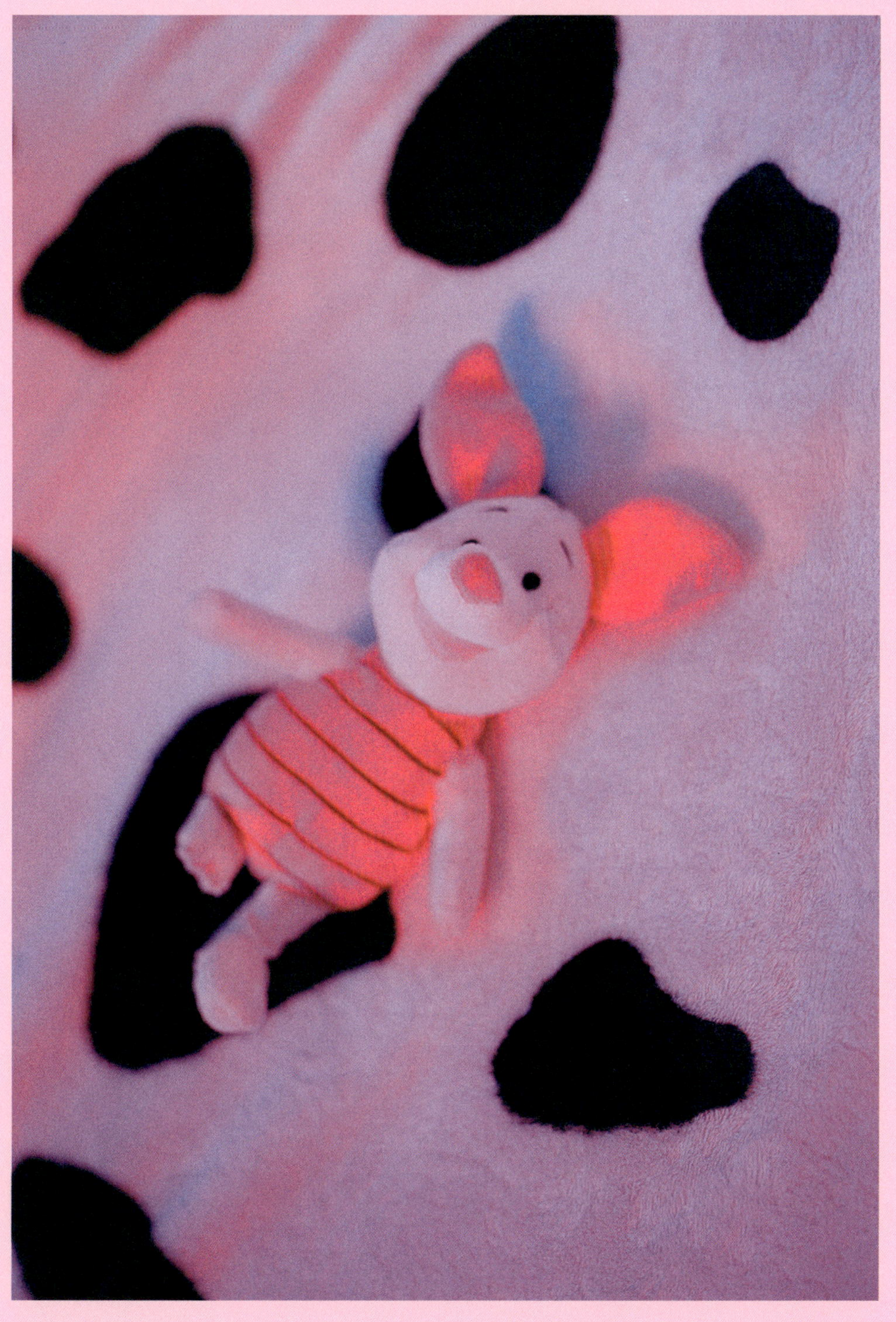

*I didn't write
myself off.
My friends in
healthcare said
that the best
is yet to come.
Finally
I don't menstru-
ate anymore.*

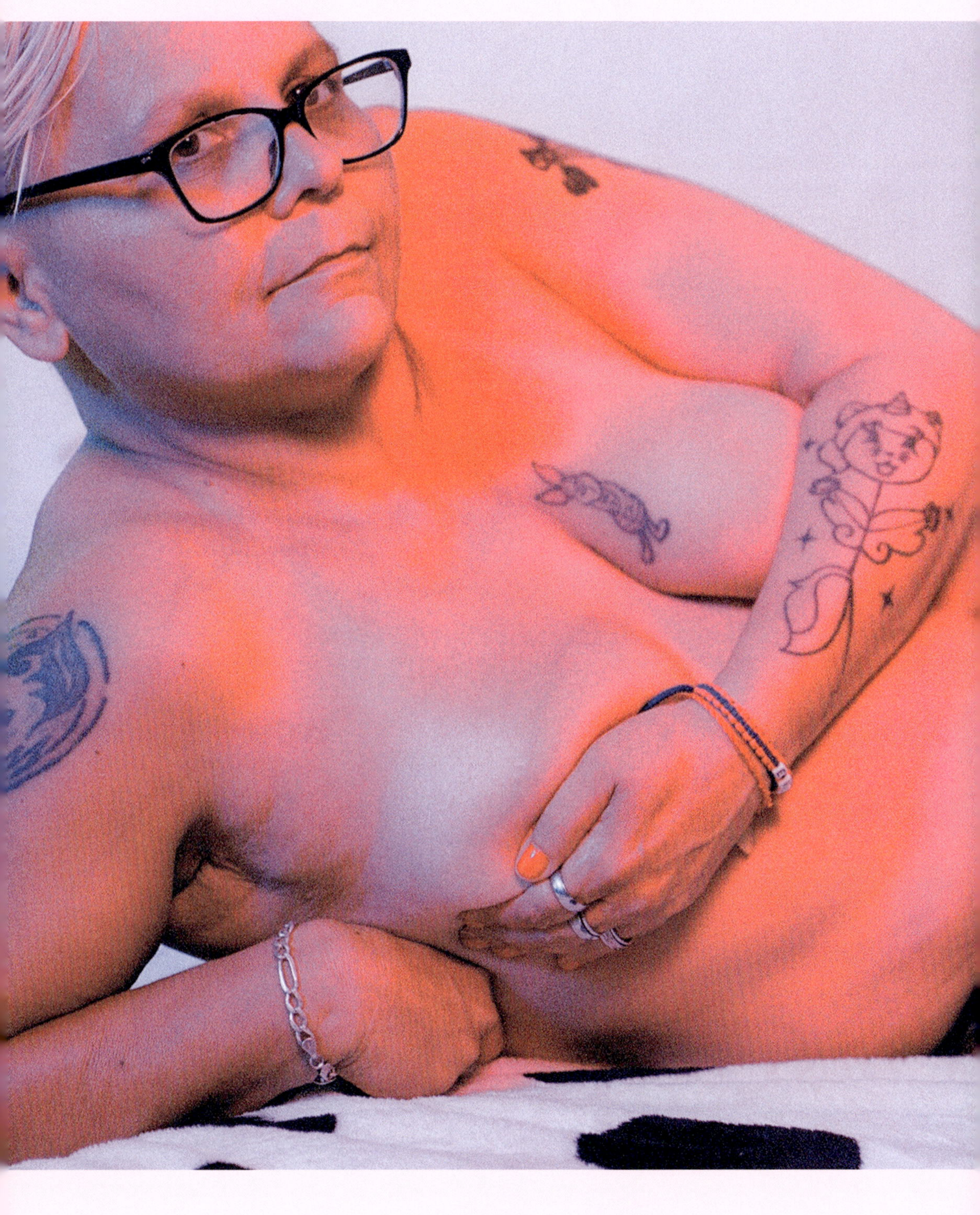

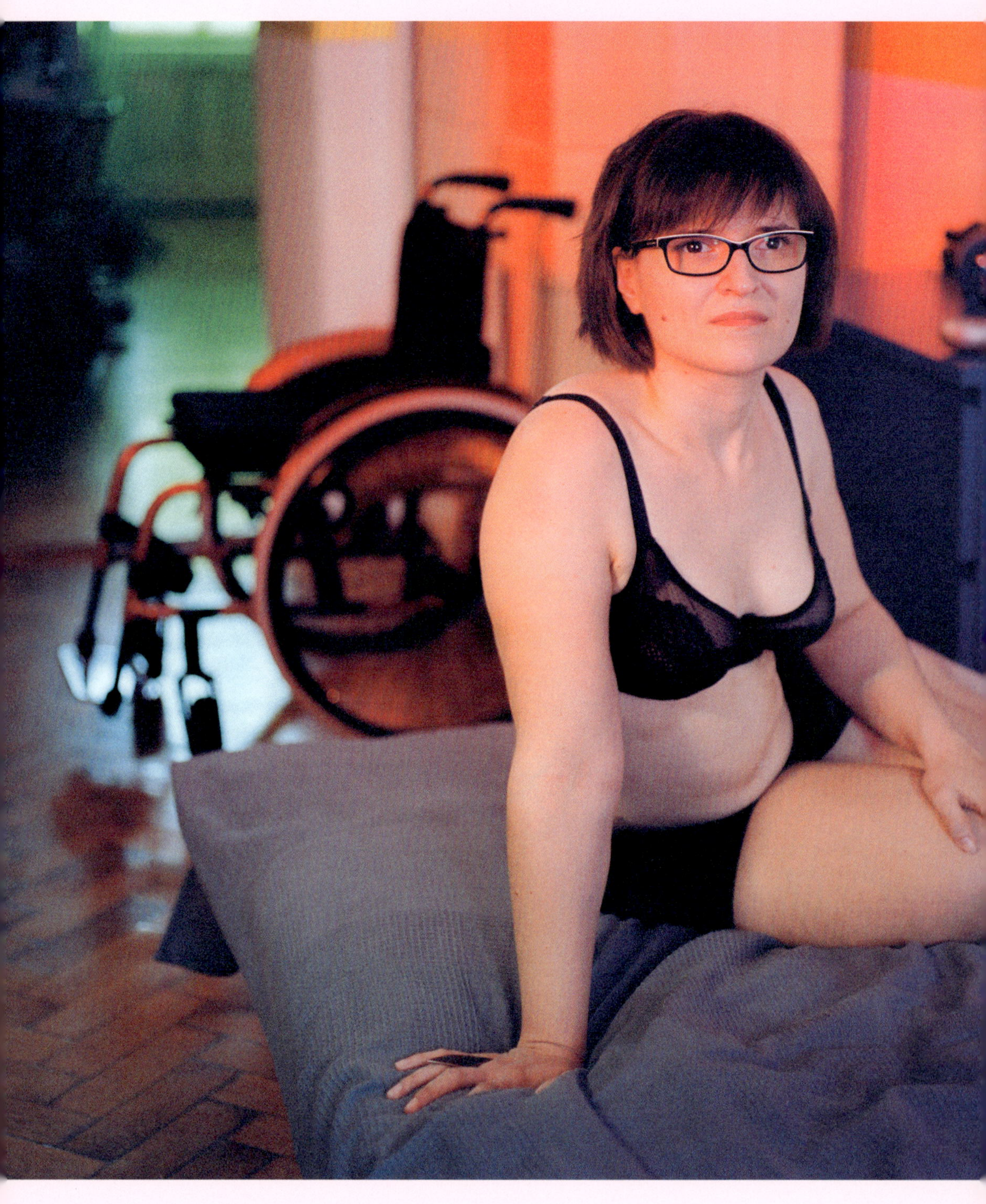

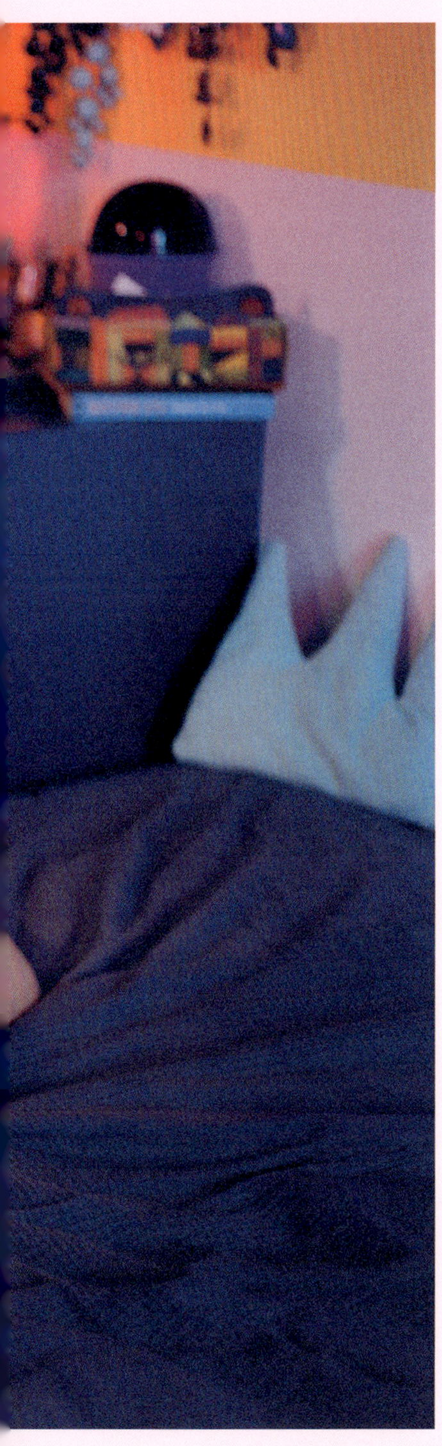

*People look
at me and all
they are
interested in
is how I have
sex.*

I moved from home fairly early on and I was involved with some internet communities. It had the advantage of a personal life and new opportunities but it was also a space for emotional abuse. There was one guy who held onto the idea that because I was disabled, I would settle for him for sure. And when I said no he was deeply hurt. Sexuality has its own set of rules too: good communication, asking first, touches only when I let them.

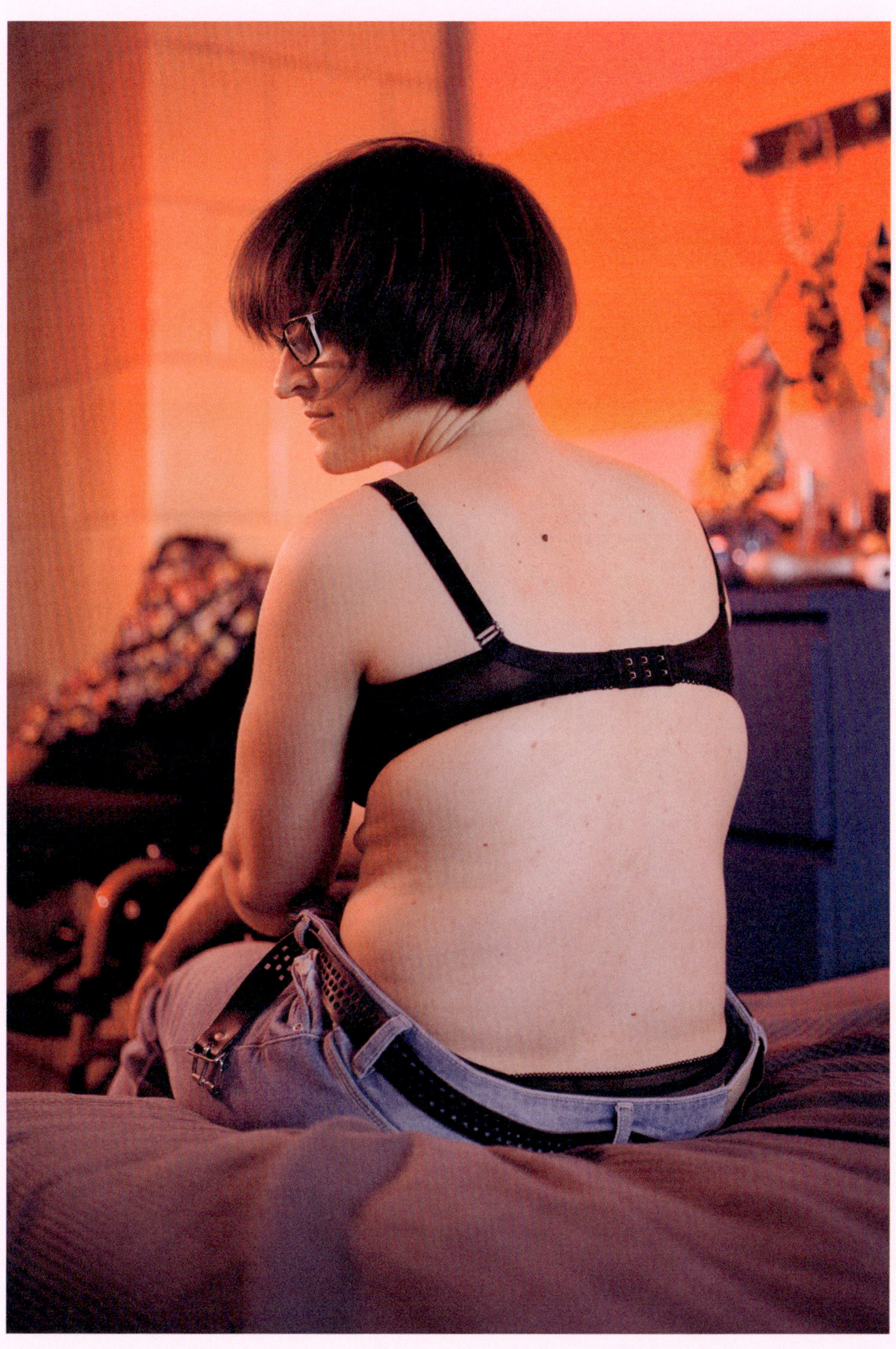

BARBARA M.

*I got bored
of the shame.*

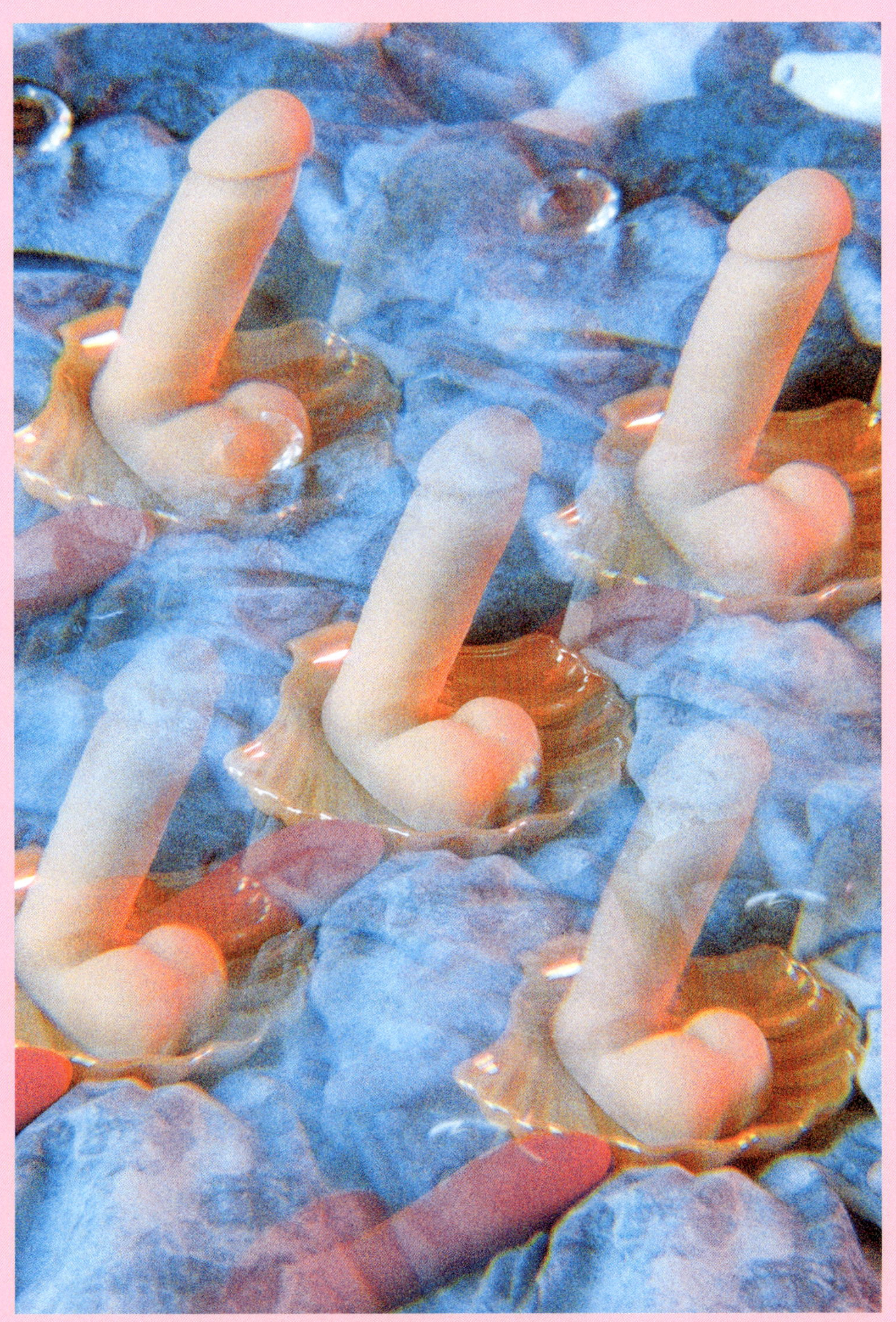

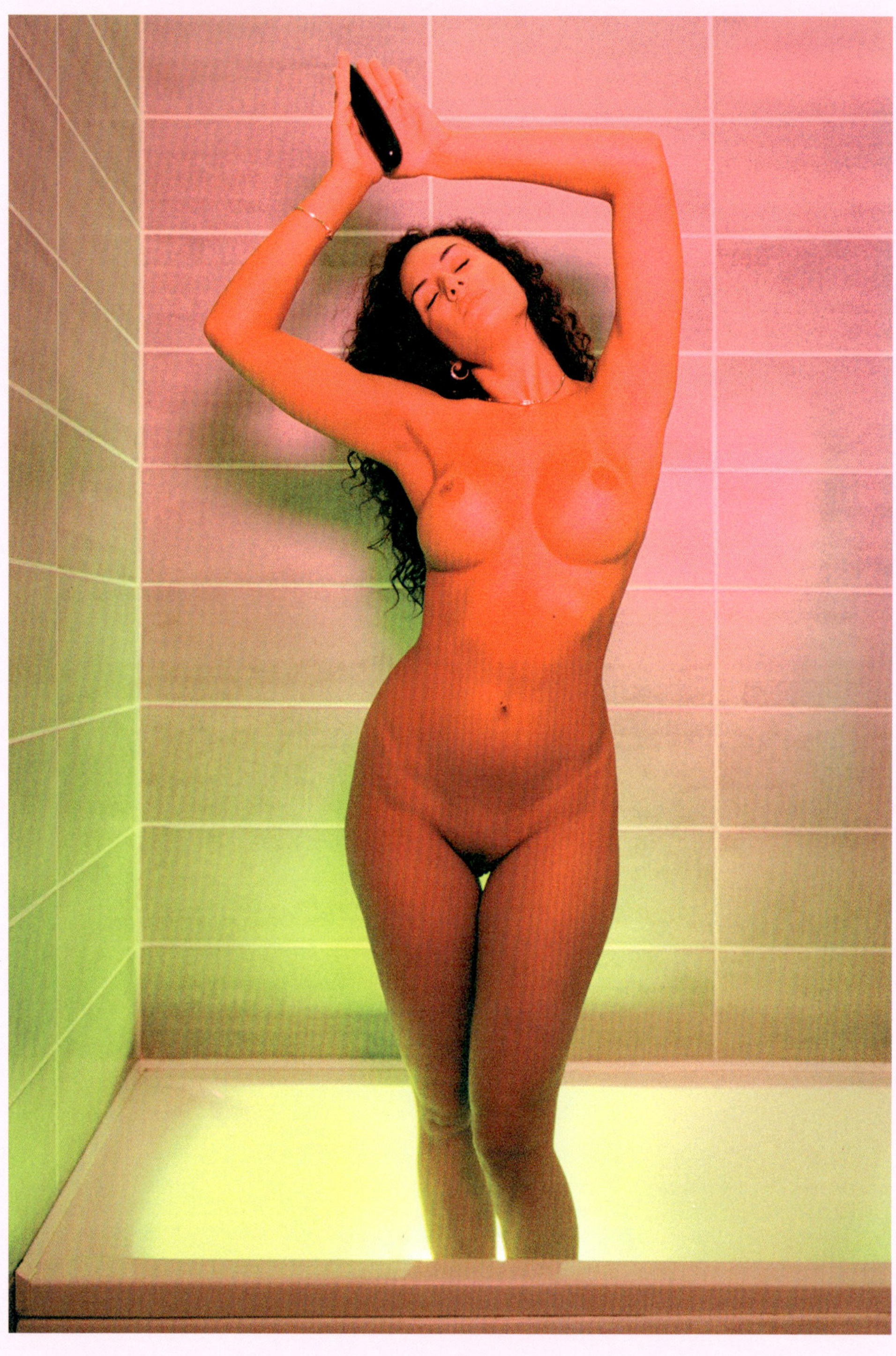

BARBARA O.

Sexuality was a truly closed off part of me. Even when I was little I had some sexual interest. I couldn't stop self-pleasuring, I was interested in boys and love. I've been in love since kindergarten. Still, I kept thinking that girls who jump from man to man are sluts. I had to be virtuous, honest, and save myself for the right man. My mom raised me like this and it took me a while to put it into perspective. I realized that not following these values is not a sin and I became liberated. I learned who my mom and her core values were and who I was. That's when I grew up for real.

LILLA K.

After my nervous breakdown and a lot of anxiety, suddenly I'd had enough. Why waste time on struggling with myself? I got this huge chip off my shoulder, just like that. I was fed up with being on edge all the time due to things that I can't change anyway.

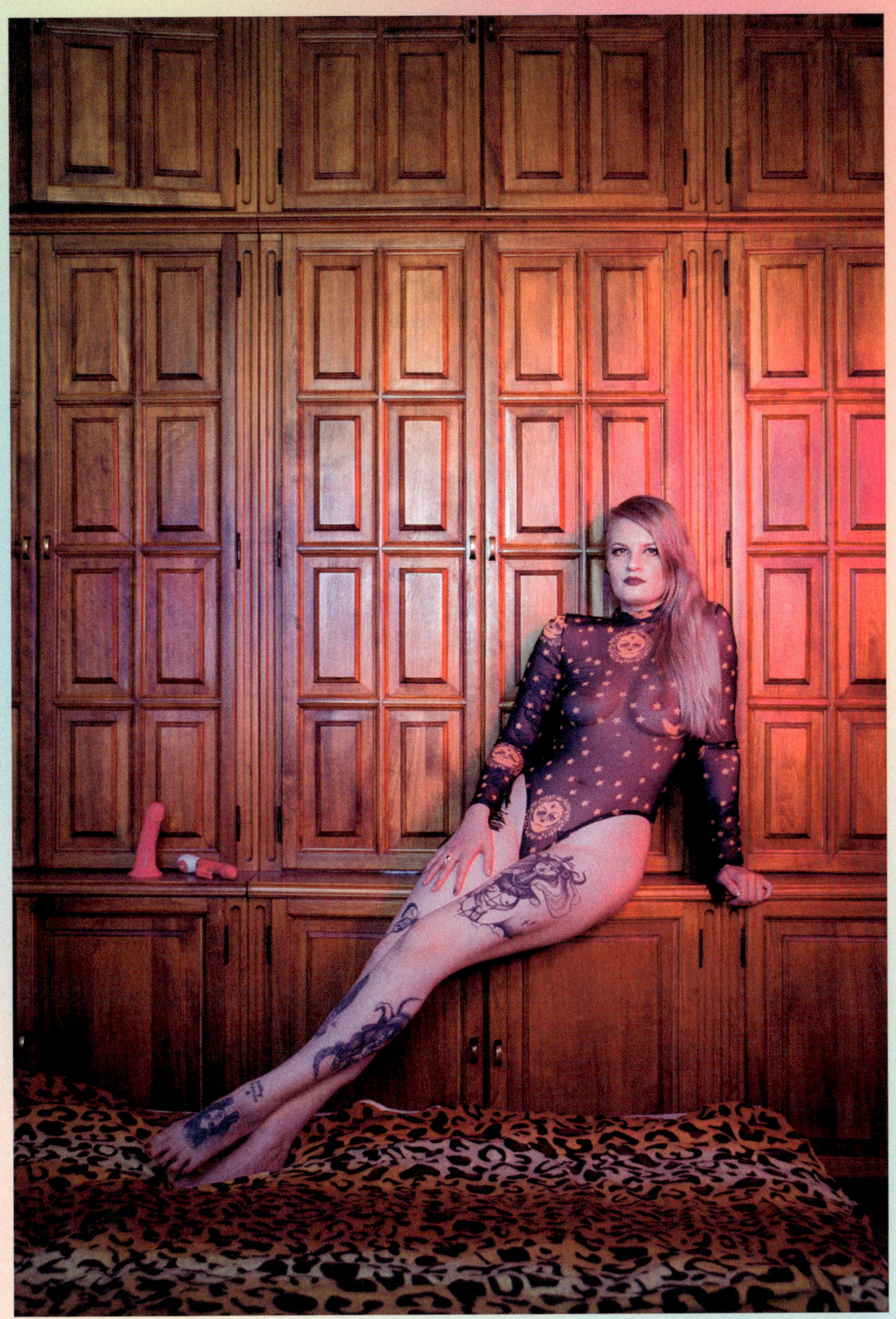

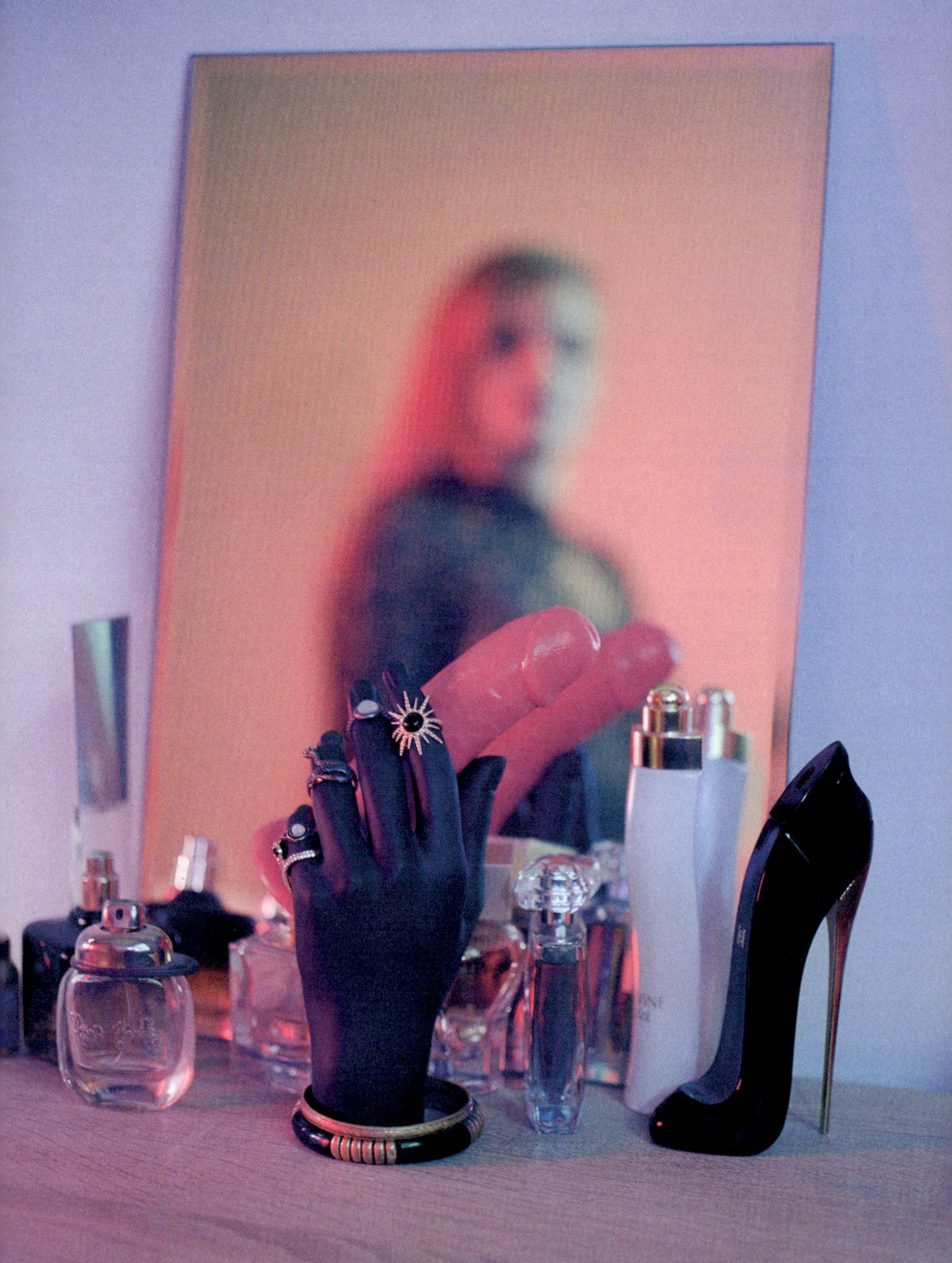

I wasn't a very
popular teen,
no one really asked
me out, so I thought
I would take care
of it for myself and
bought a dildo.

*No one told me
that my clit was
a fucking cool organ.
I had to realize
that for myself.*

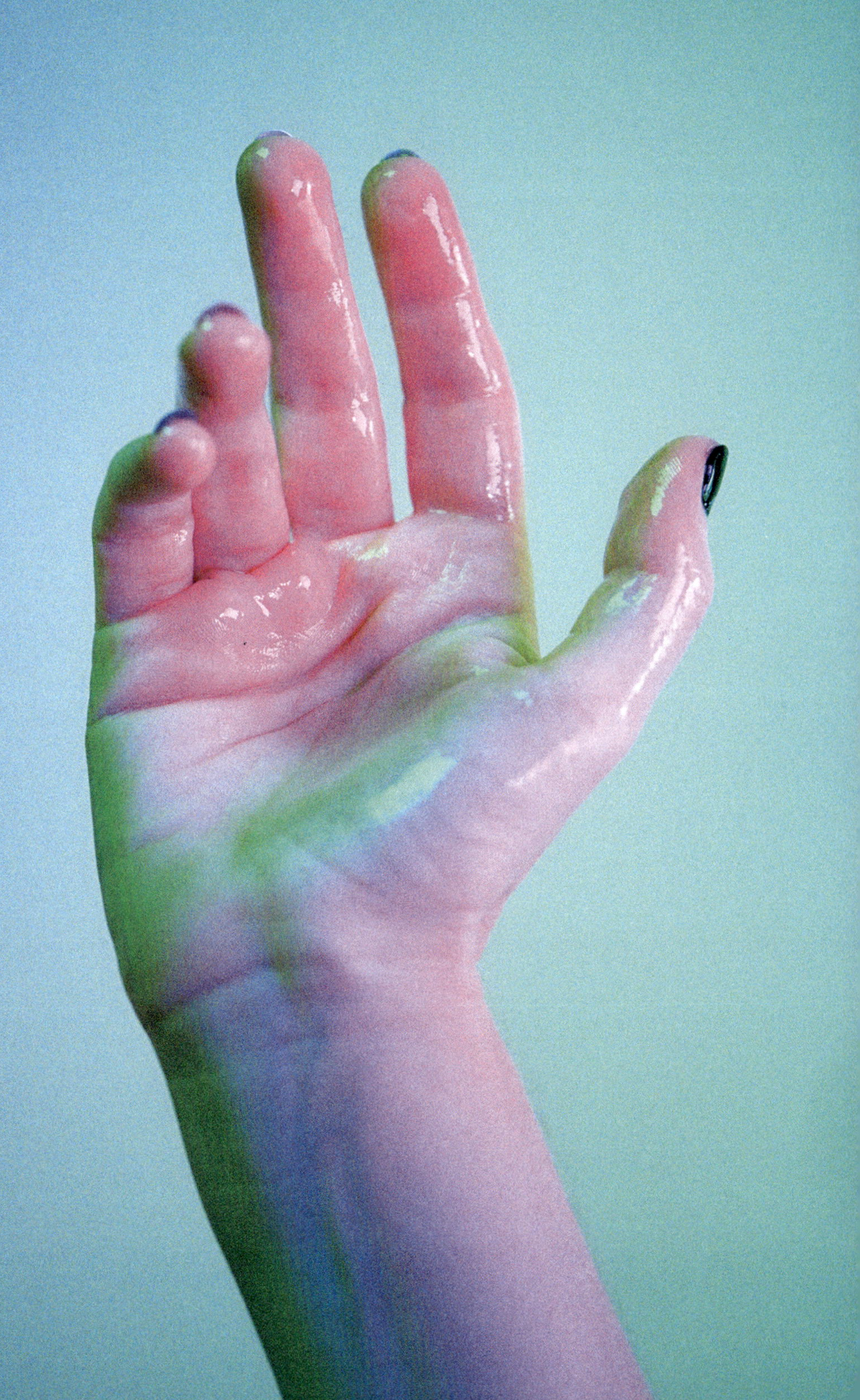

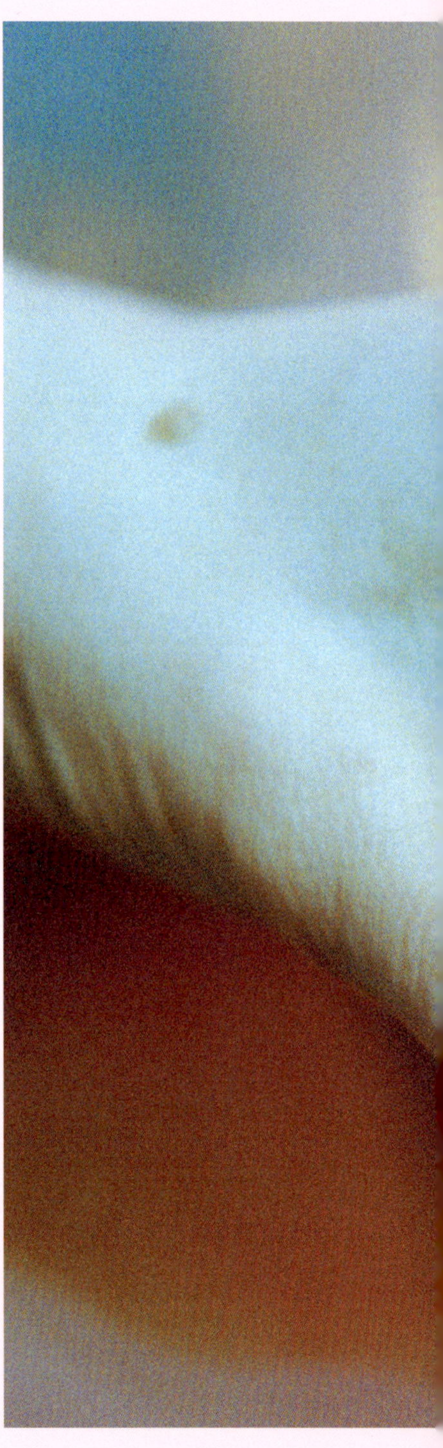

It's a common misconception that you can't touch the clit during sex.

Society was built in a way that men own sex and you are just there to cater to them. Thinking back to my sex life, it could've been so much better if I'd opened my mouth. You mustn't wait for them to ask you. You have to say what's working for you. I don't know everything about sex either, I've faked orgasms before. Here I am at 40 years old and there is still room to improve.

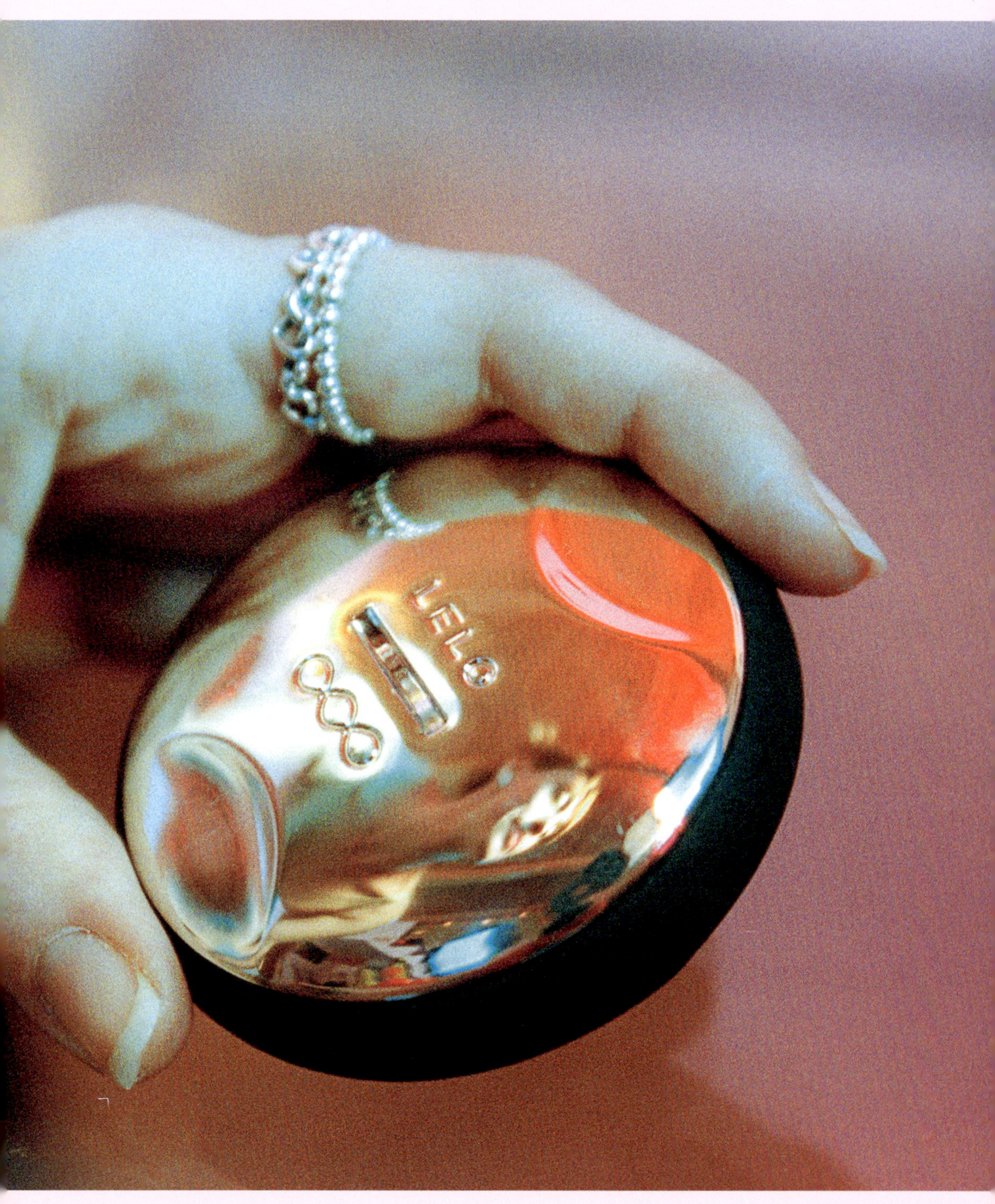

LELO

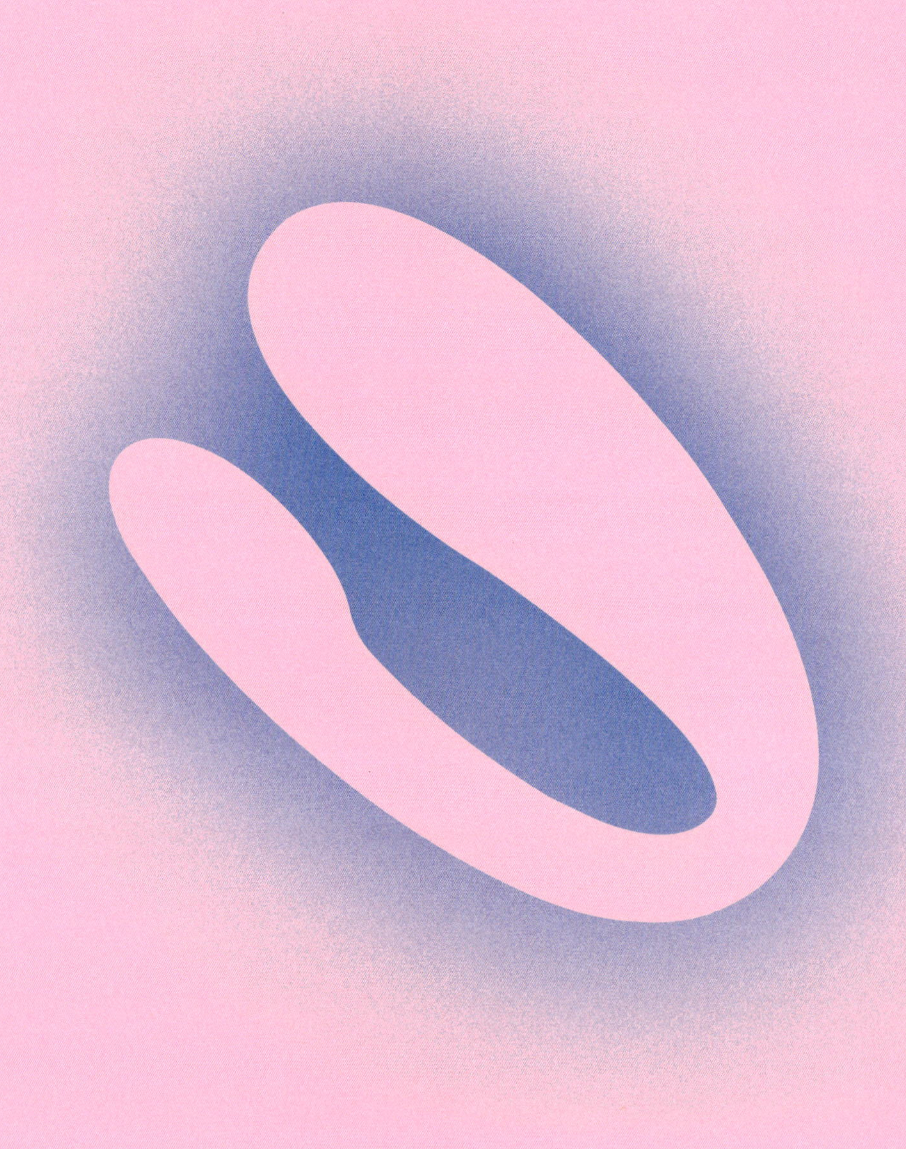

ZSÓFIA

After my 30th birthday I got fed up about the fact that I couldn't let go, that I was hurt and I wasn't enjoying sex the way I was supposed to. Freud caused massive damage with the myth of the vaginal orgasm. Most men still go white when I mention I'm not much into vaginal orgasms, because the clit is still a part of the same organ. They instantly think I'm frigid. Not touching the clit is real self-sabotage. You can swim with your hands tied back but why the fuck would you do that?

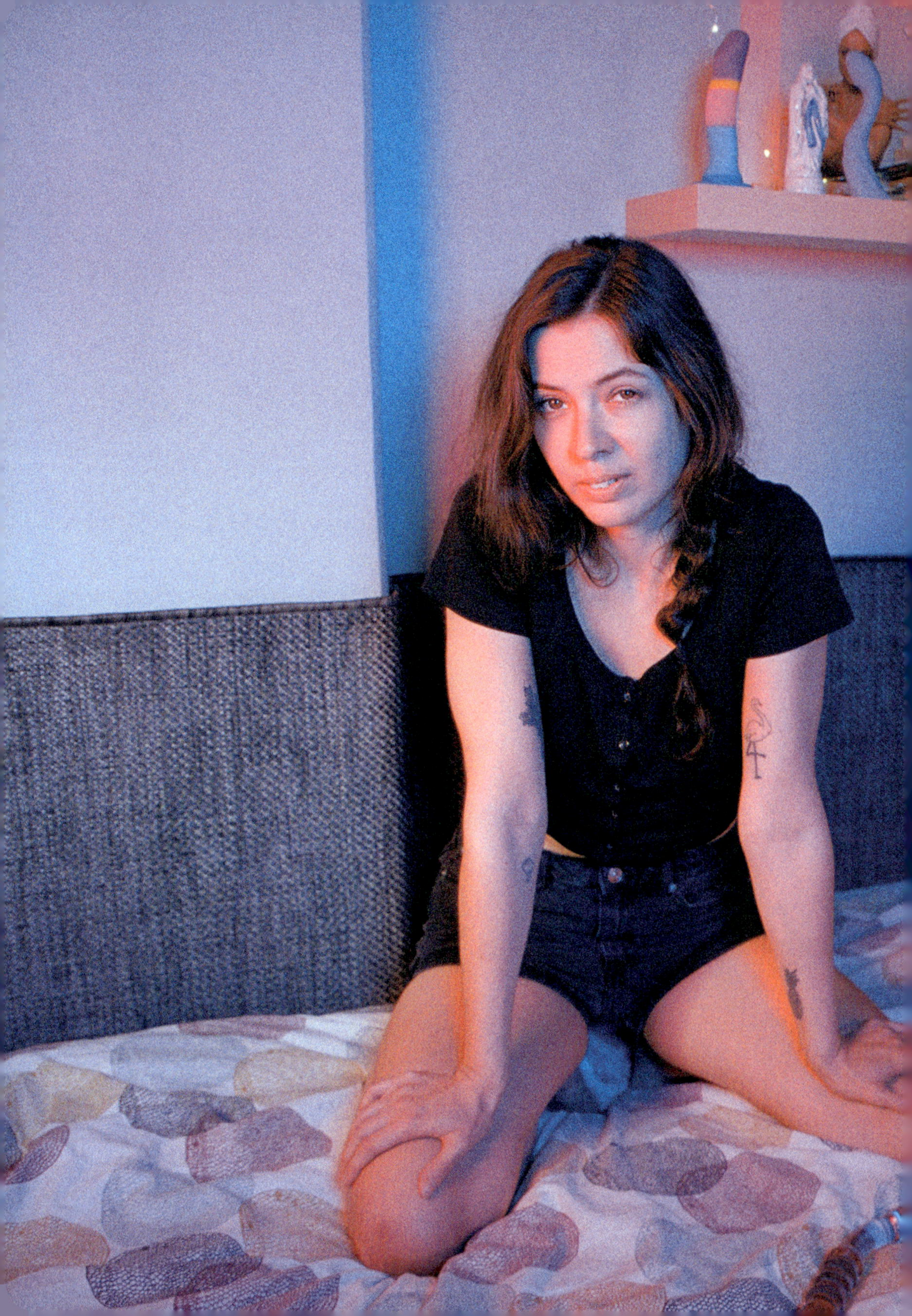

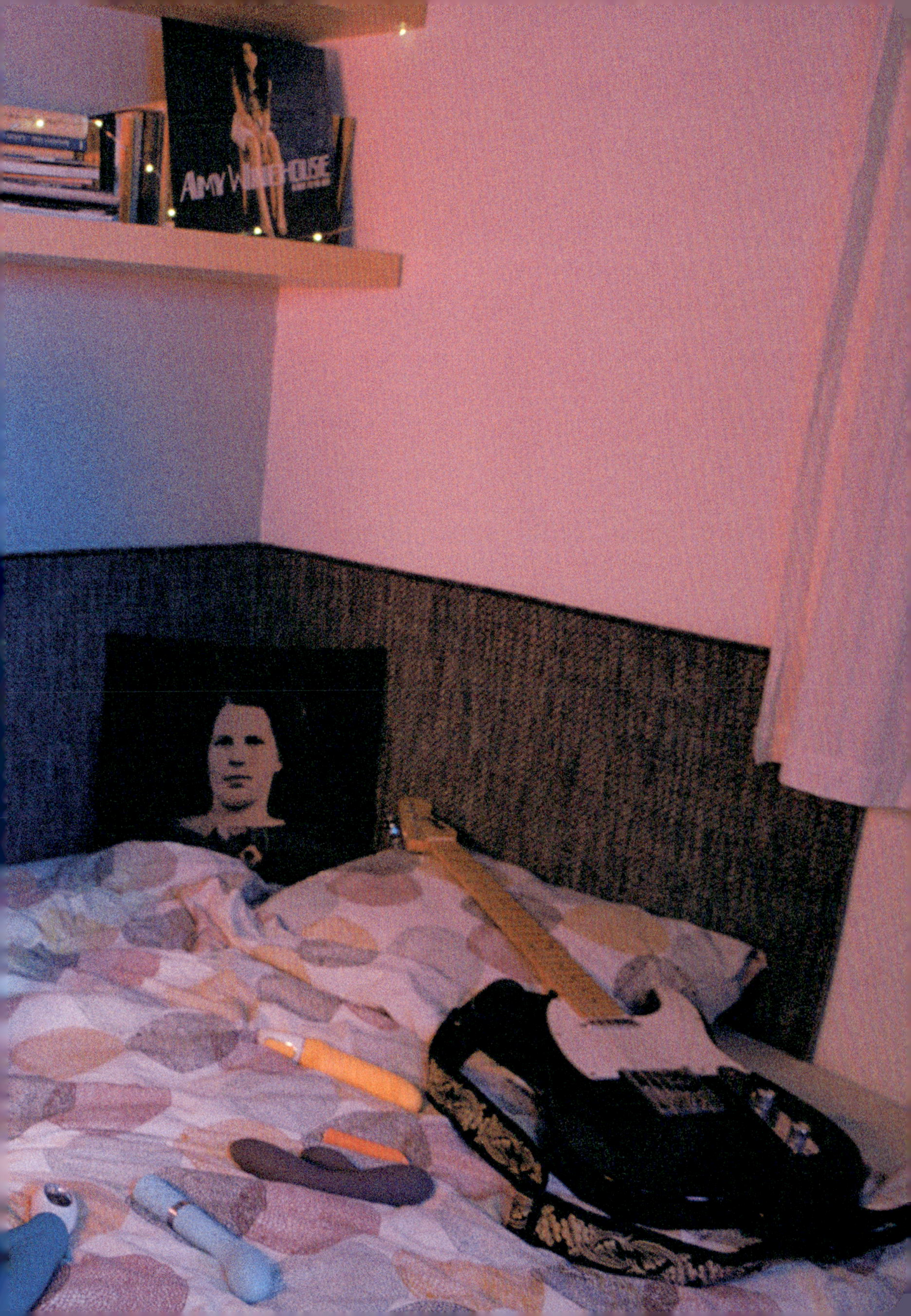

These are some sort
of educational toys too.
I often buy sex toys and
I imagine how it would
be good for me. But when
I use them it's something
totally different and
I learn something new
about myself that I didn't
see coming.

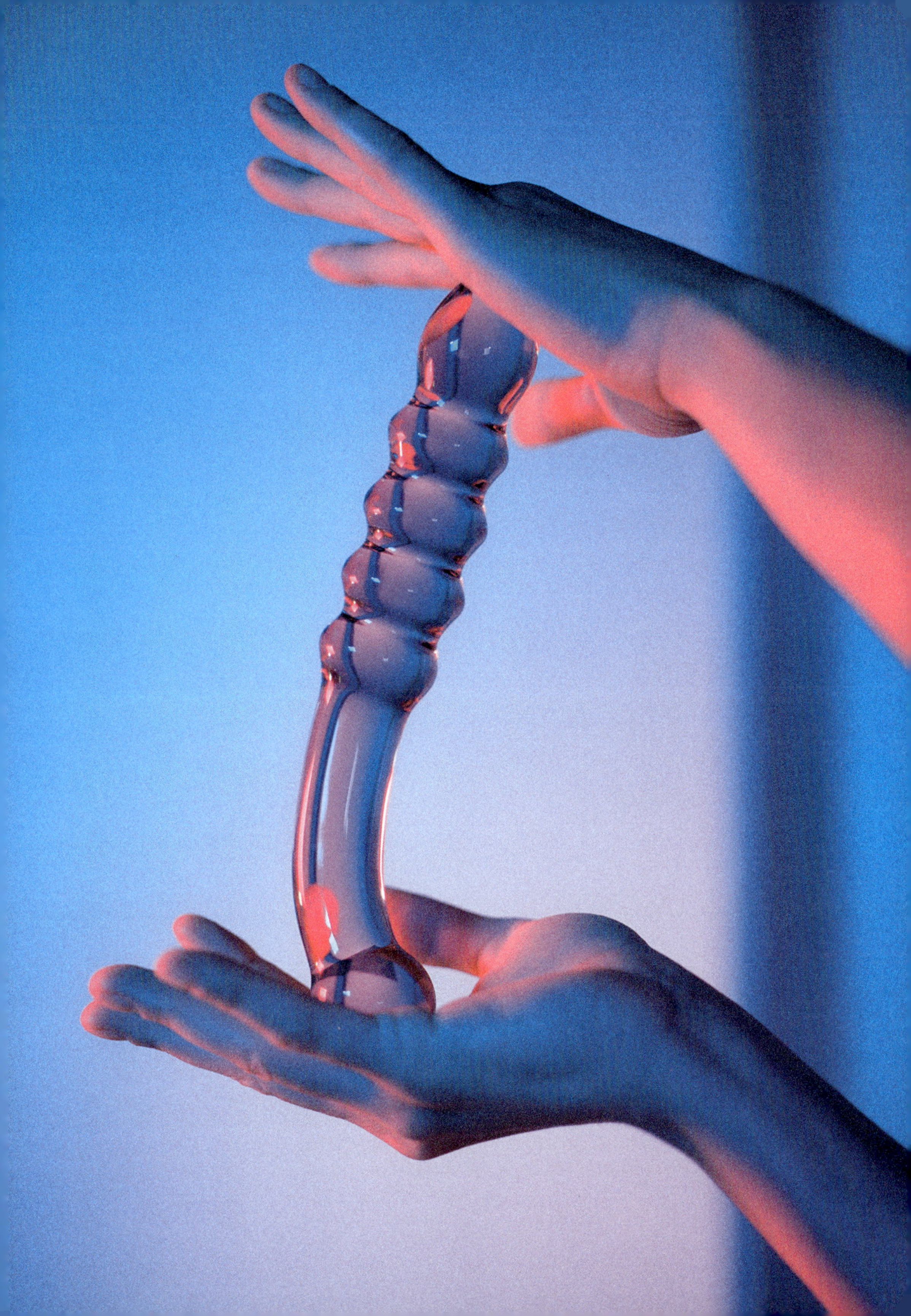

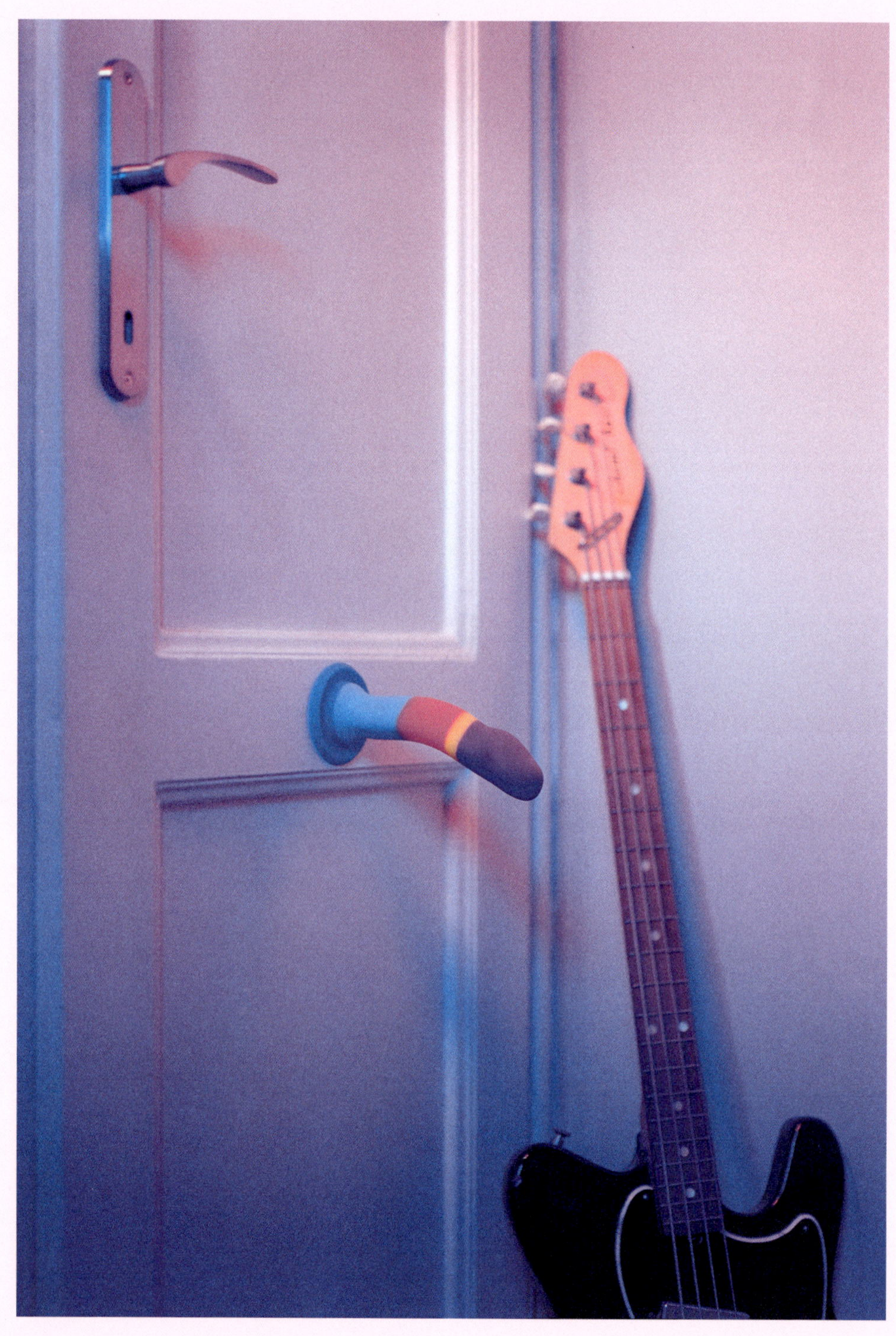

In the past few years I was more often single than not. That's why my drawer looks like this. I think it's a more mature decision than to chase one-night stands, which are not necessarily satisfying for women, although men are not always at fault. I need time to let loose and let someone into my intimate space.

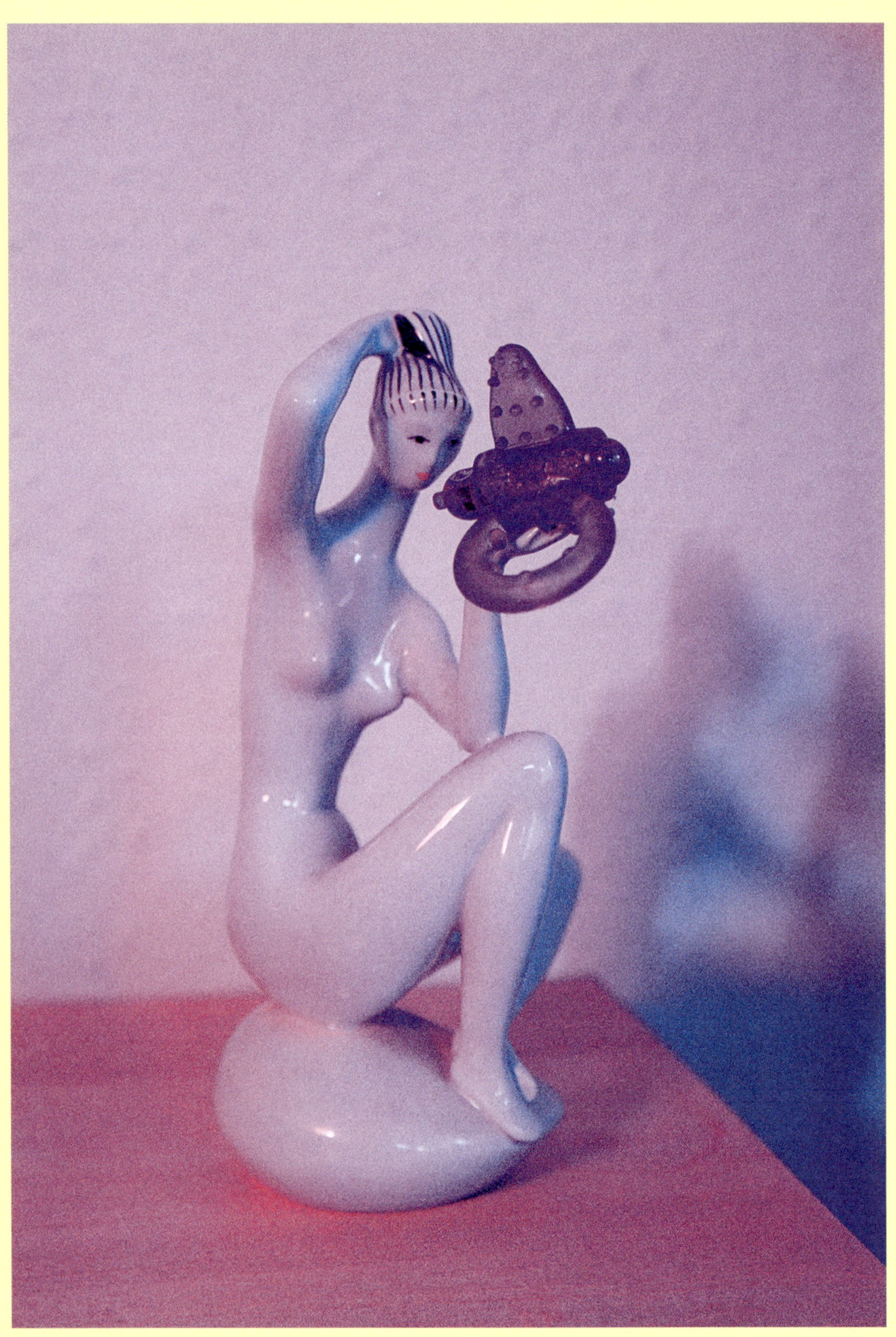

JUDIT

A couple years ago my girlfriends and I celebrated that one of us finally had an orgasm. I said it's not okay if you are together with someone and you don't have any orgasms, ever. And then she asked if it's necessary to have them if the sex is good. I think so. If you can, why not? I think there is this false belief that you should have sex, even if you don't have anyone. That's when meaningless flings happen. Have sex with someone you'd really like to and until then buy a vibrator. Orgasms and sexuality can be experienced in different ways. You can keep a plethora of sources.of pleasure at home.

Interesting that boys react to toys differently. In a former relationship it didn't work at all to use a vibrator because he didn't like it. I think he felt he had a small-er role during the activities. But my next partner asked for it specifically. He loved it because it was like having an extra hand.

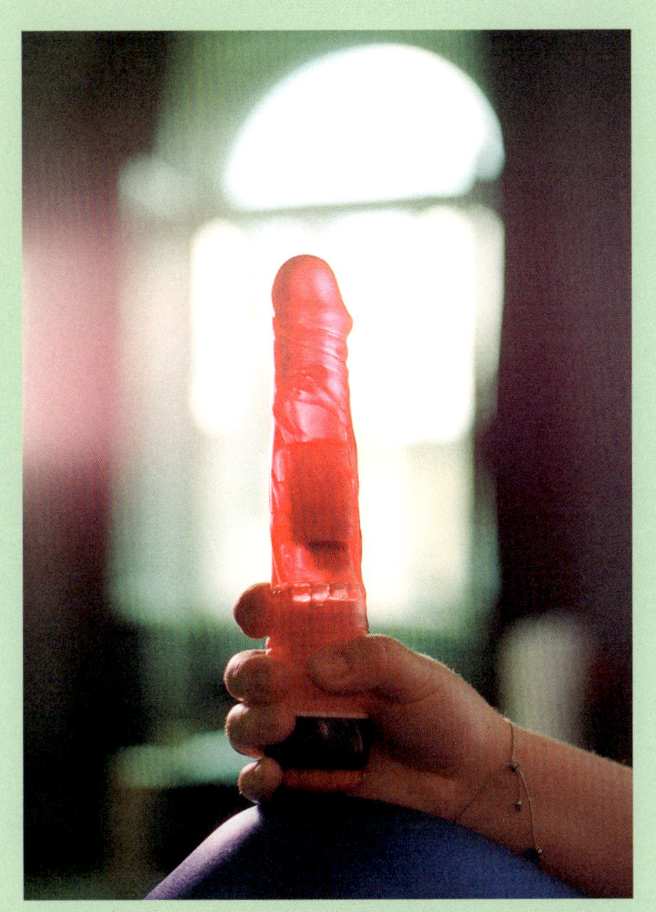

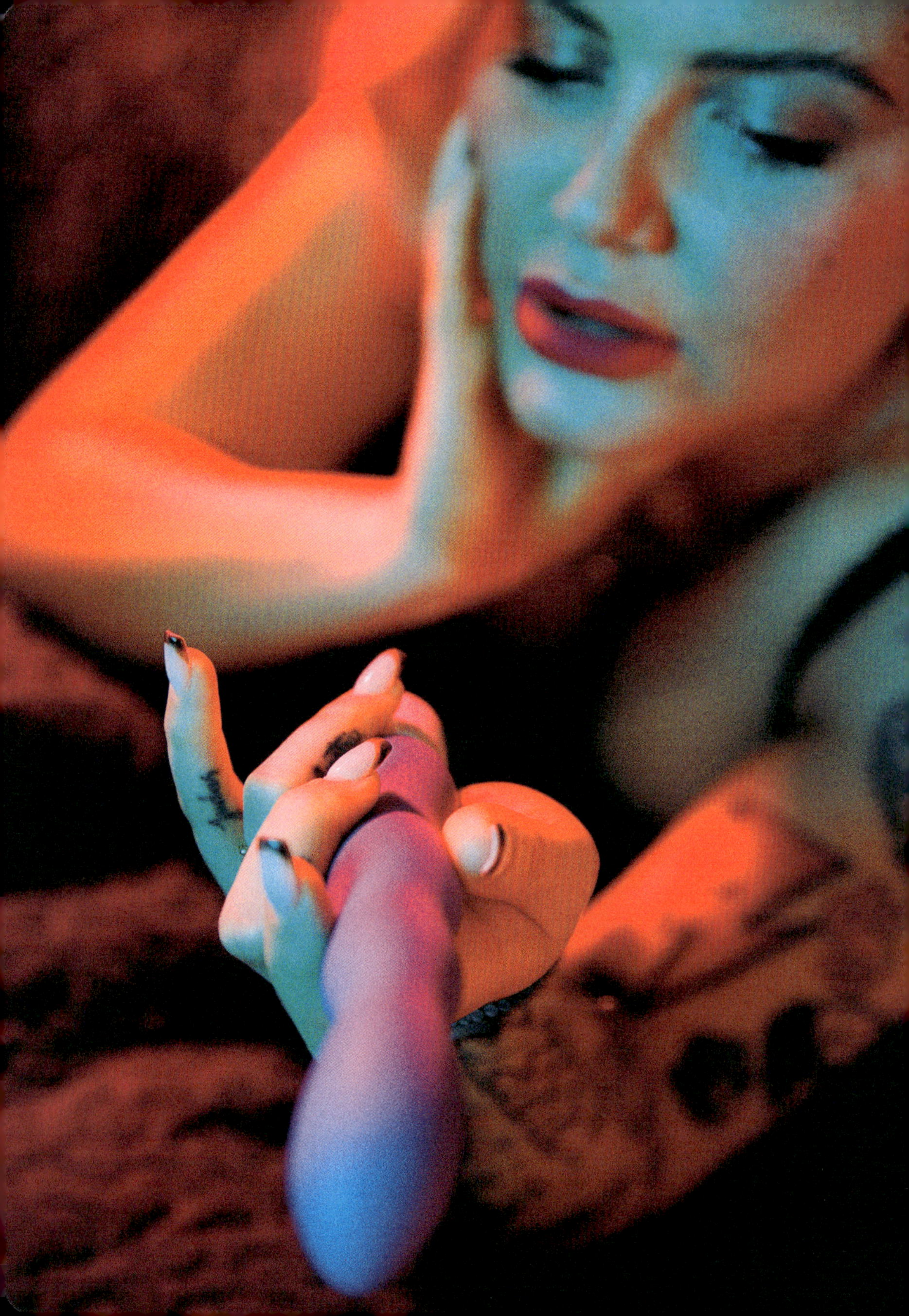

EMÍLIA

Guys reacted very differently to my toys. One was interested, one shopped for me, and one even brought over his own stuff. Once it didn't even cross my mind to show him, I wasn't ashamed, he just wasn't the type. Some were not interested at all.

*After a breakup
I throw away my
toys because they
are like pieces of the
past. It's hard to
separate them from
a relationship.*

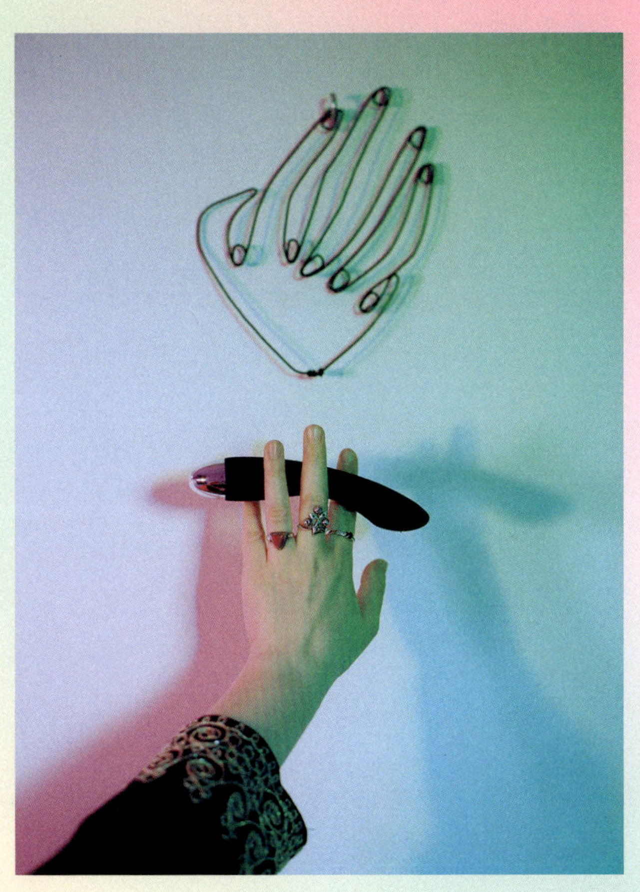

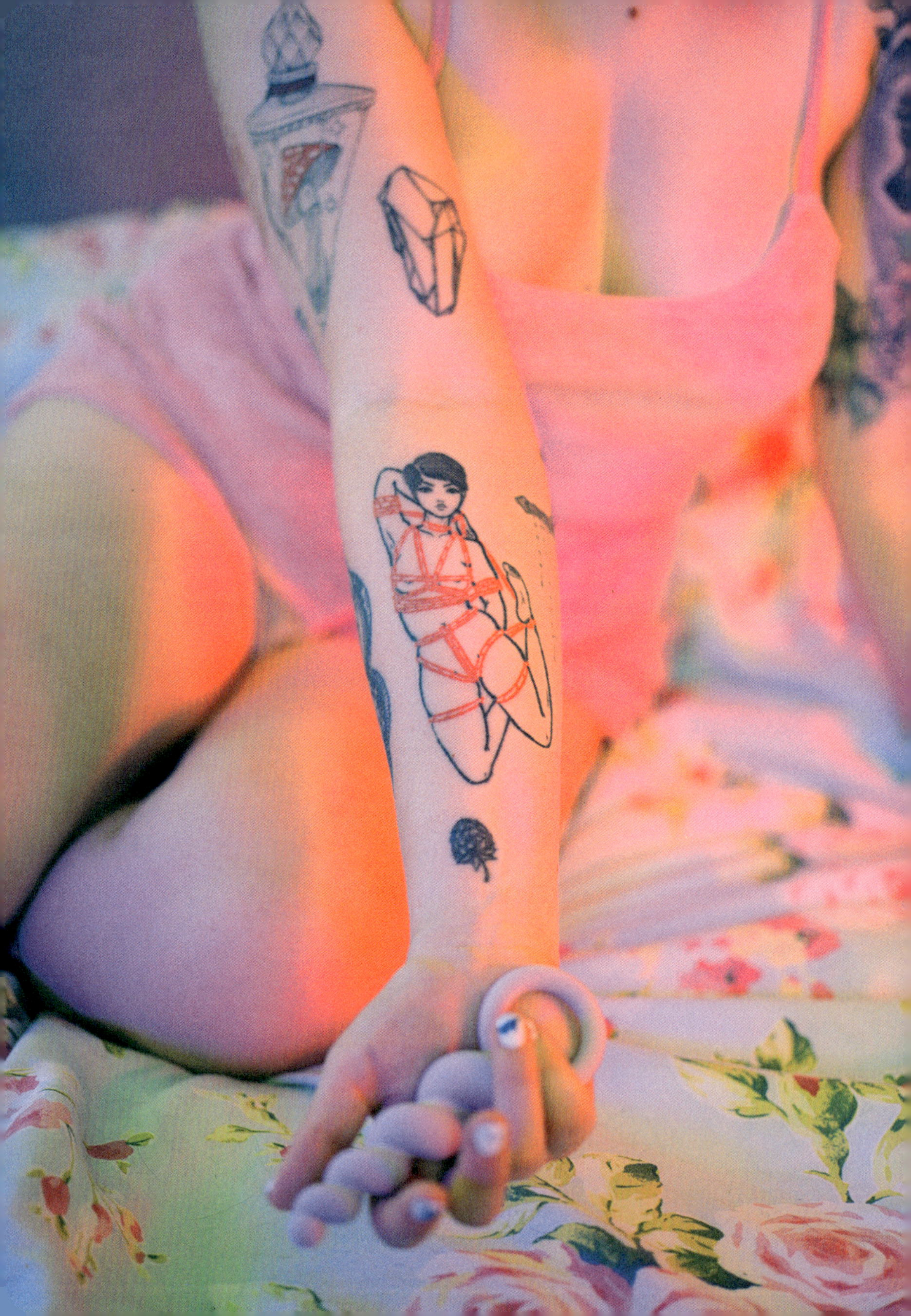

FRUZSINA

I love kinbaku. I saw it in photos by Araki first, that's how it started. I had always wanted to try it, then I met a guy on Tinder and I tried it with him. The tight rope on my skin was a great sensation. It was really sexy how he was getting into it. No words, just concentration, all I could hear was his breathing.

LUCA

My sex life with my boyfriend is fucking great. But sometimes I can't wait to be alone, get the sex toys and handle my body own my own. It releases some kind of extra energy and the whole thing makes me feel like I'm the Rihanna of the 7th District.

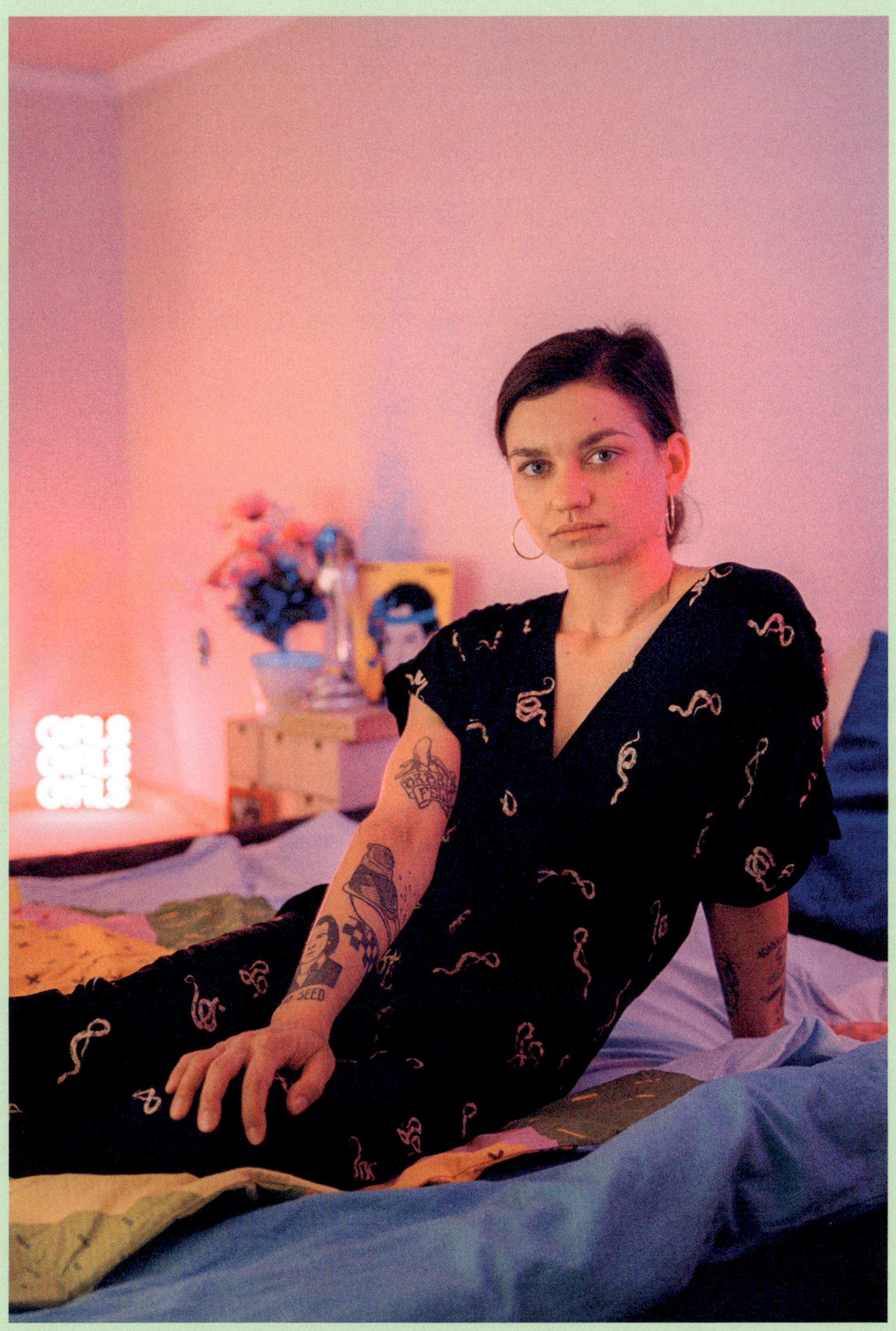

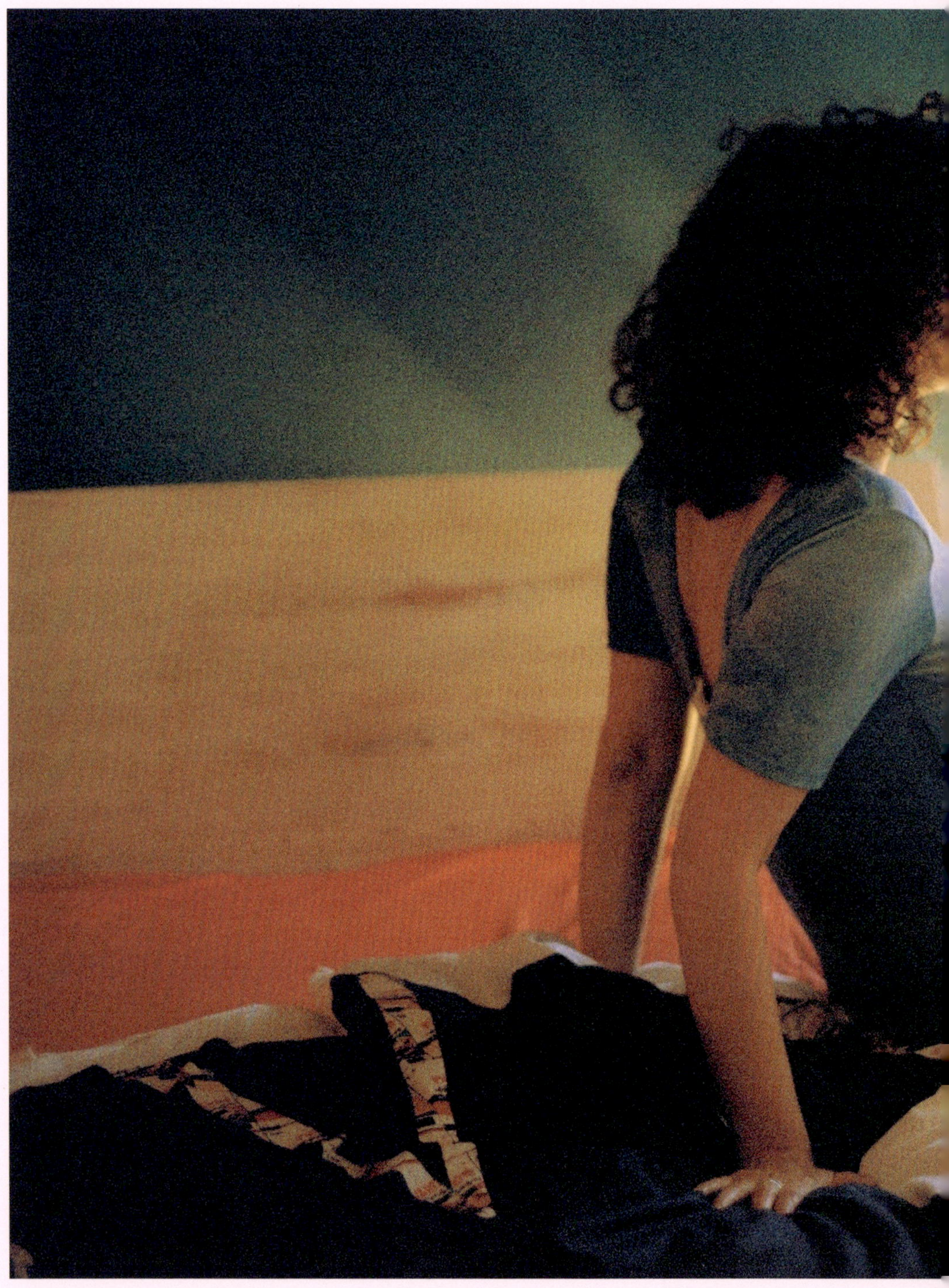

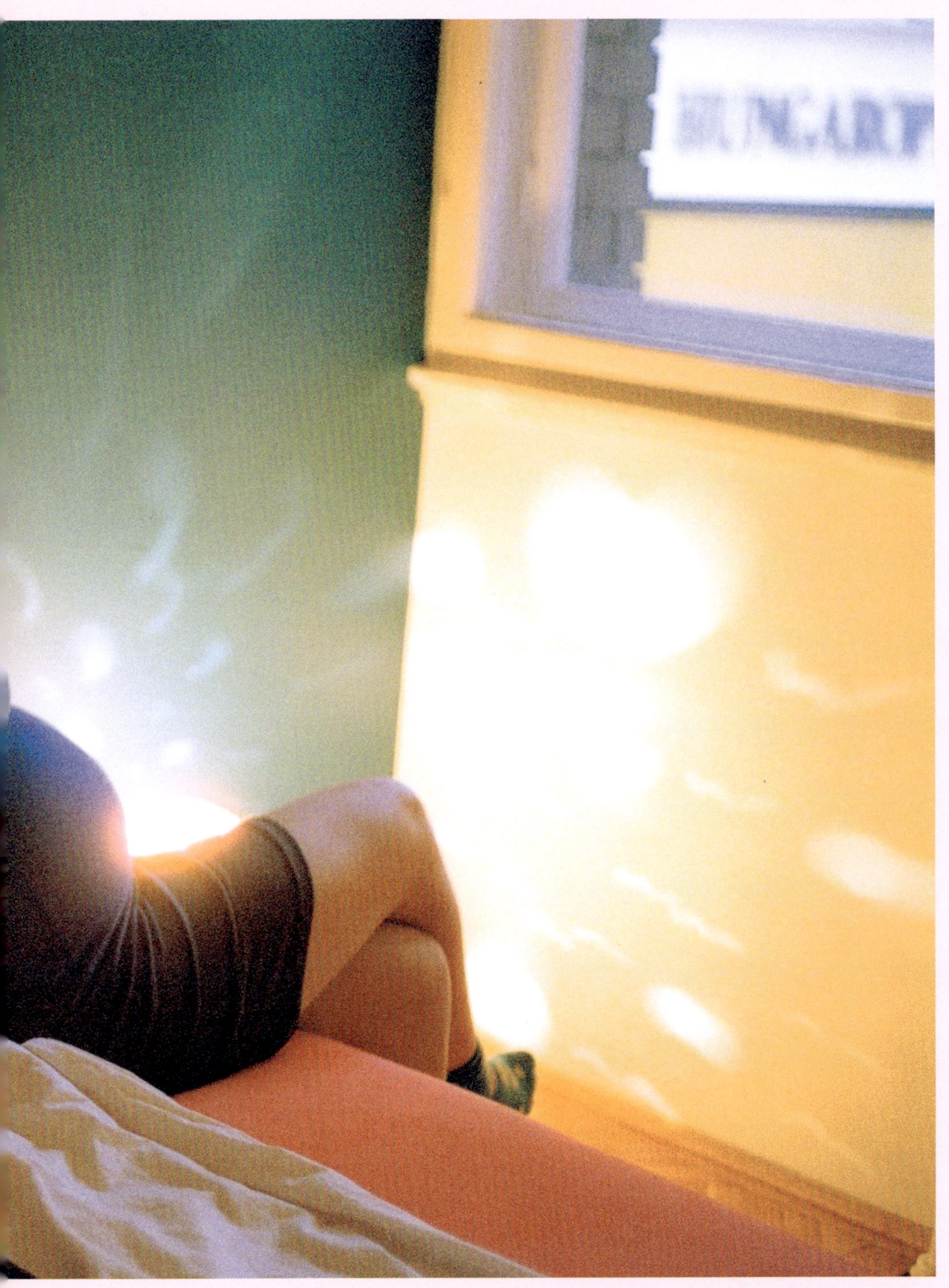

During pregnancy, sex is without any fuss, it's a more gentle experience. It's a great muscle relaxant too, I recommend it for pregnant women. When the belly gets hard, after a quickie it's not tight anymore. It's better than pumping yourself full of magnesium.

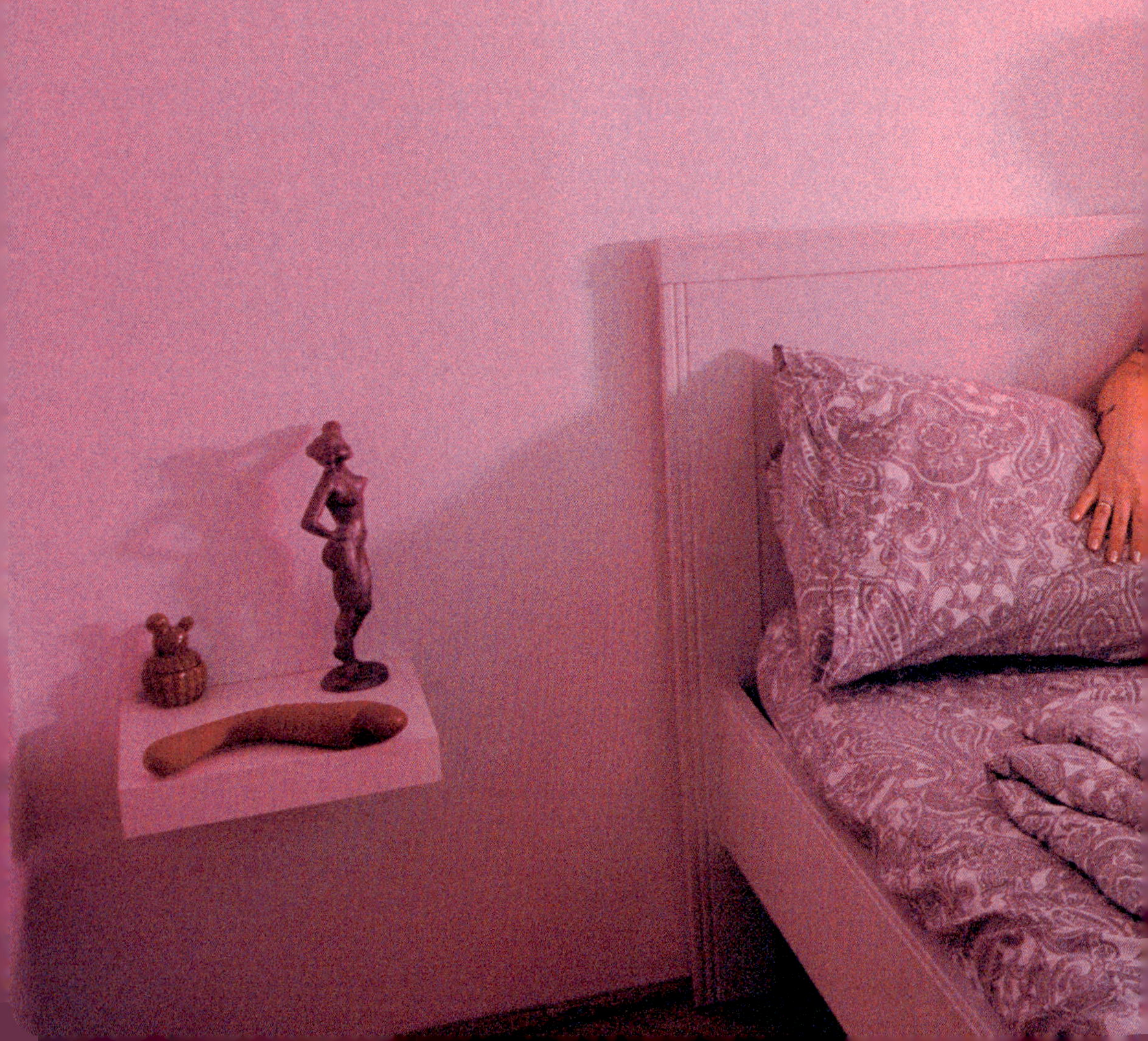

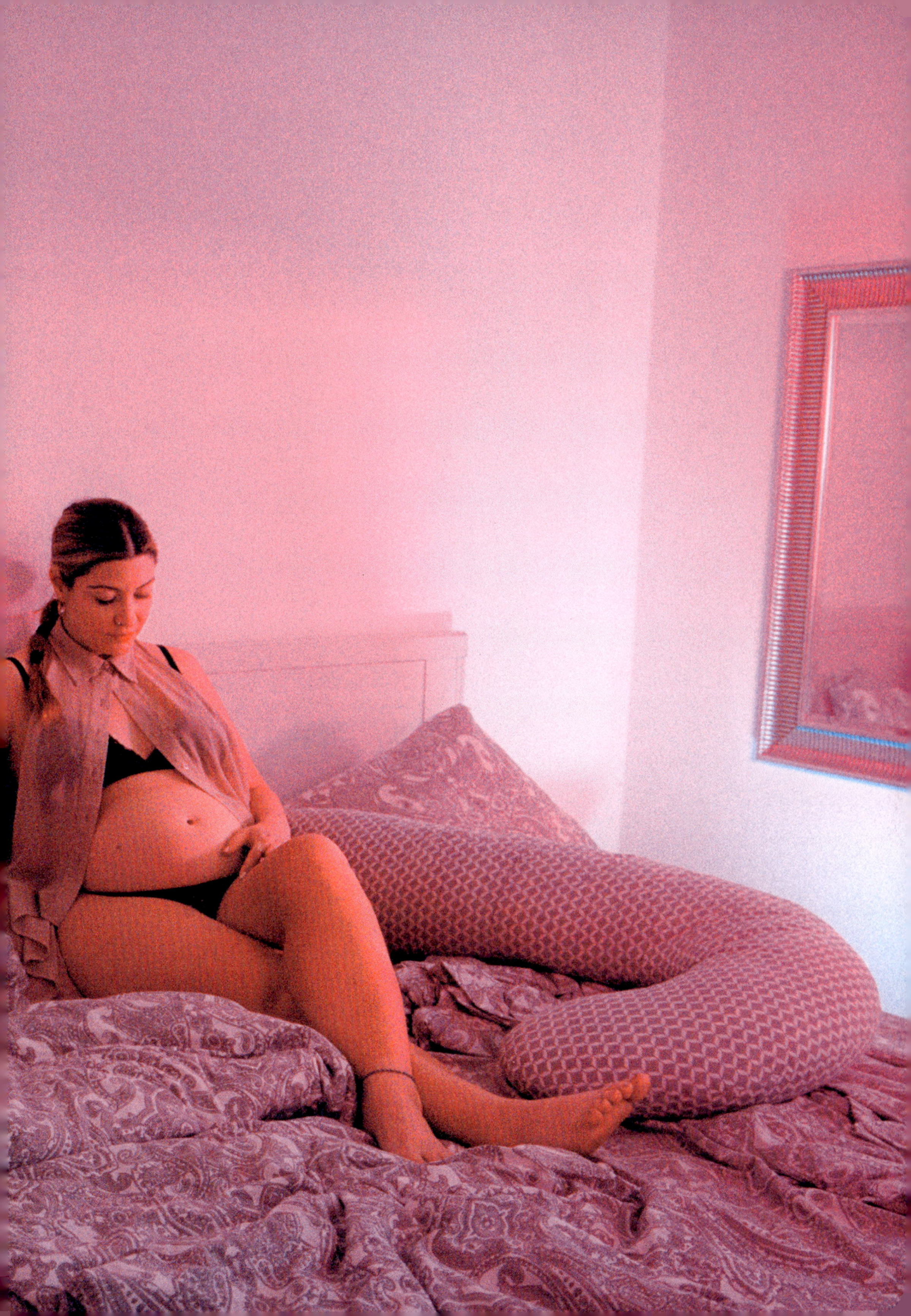

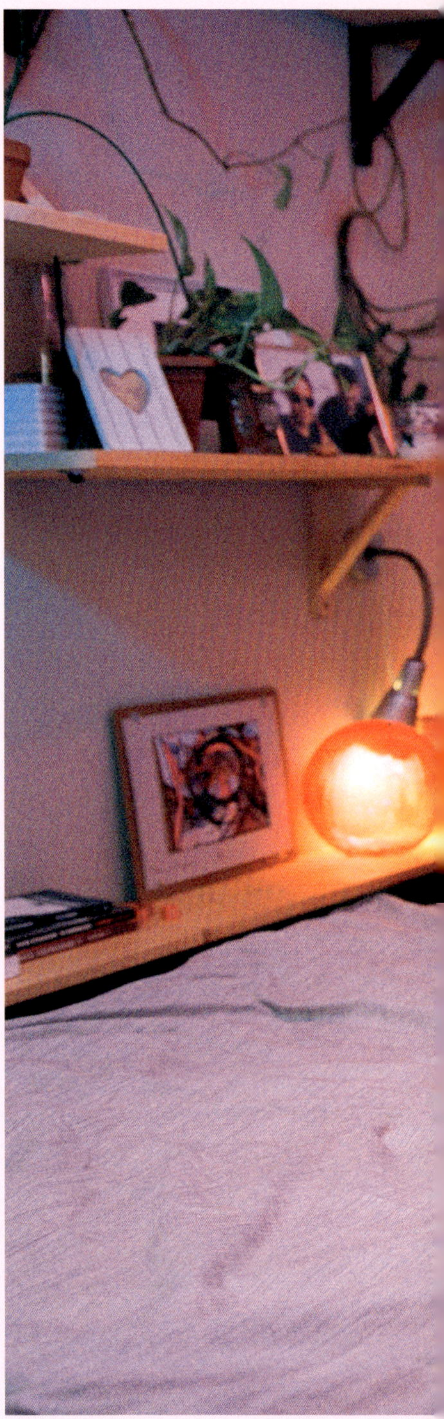

Very few guys ask me about what I like, what is good for me. They're guessing instead. Asking questions is a more frank way to the other person. I often hear it from guys in long-term relationships that their girlfriends don't want to have sex with them anymore. I think it stems from people not discussing what's good for them. Especially at the beginning. How would they notice if the other just pretends it is good for them? Everyone wishes to show their best and most charming selves and this can derail things later.

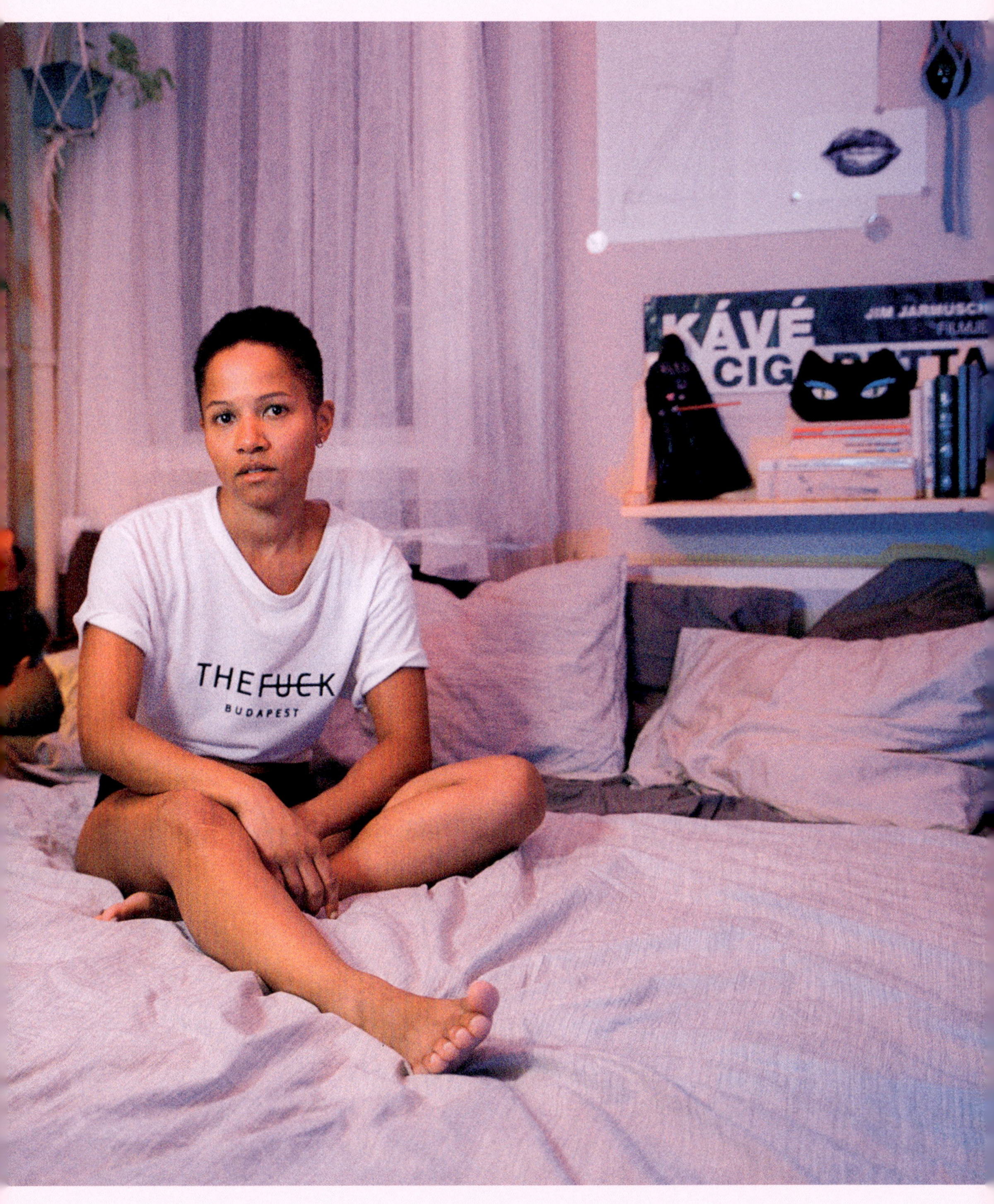
THE FUCK
BUDAPEST
KÁVÉ
CIGARETTA
JIM JARMUSCH
FILMJE

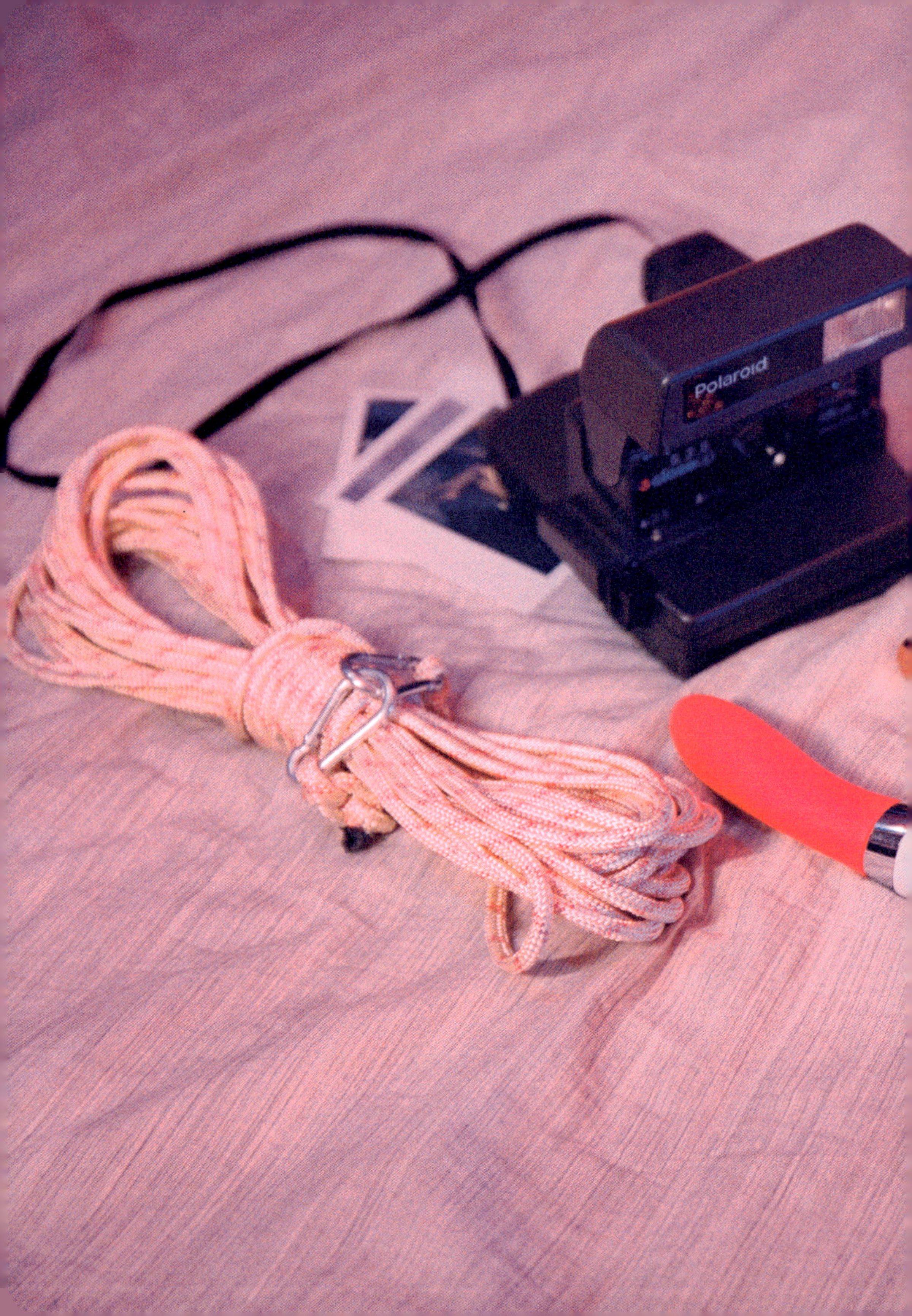

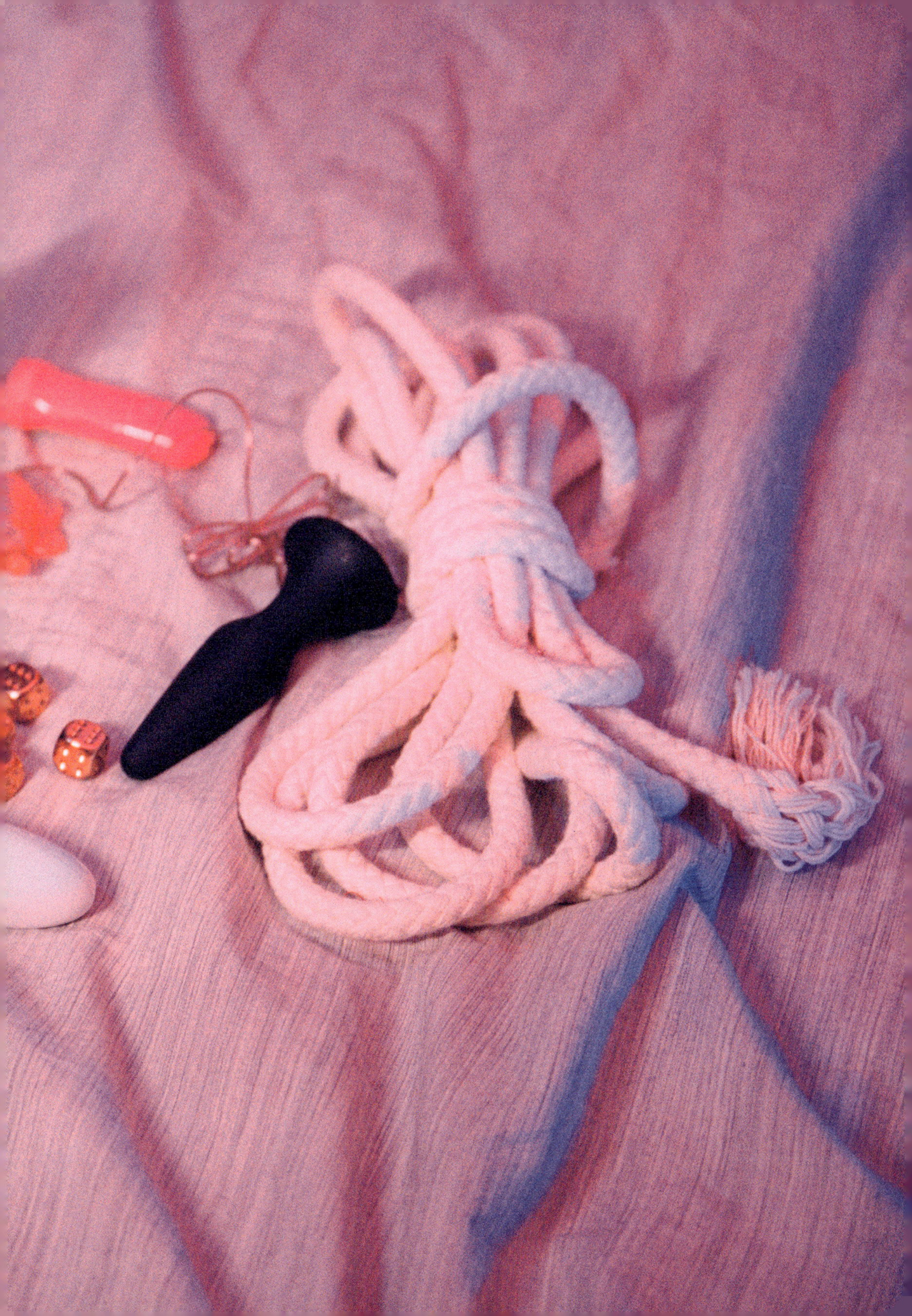

◆

LILLA T.

I used to have low self-confidence. I was afraid my performance wasn't good enough, so I was stressed. That's when I bought my first vibrator, hoping it would change things. The change didn't happen at once, but exploring my own joy improved my sexuality a lot. This improvement, I think, is a lifelong, conscious effort that's worth your energy. You have to open up to new things. The point is that it should be good for you, so it will be good for the other person as well.

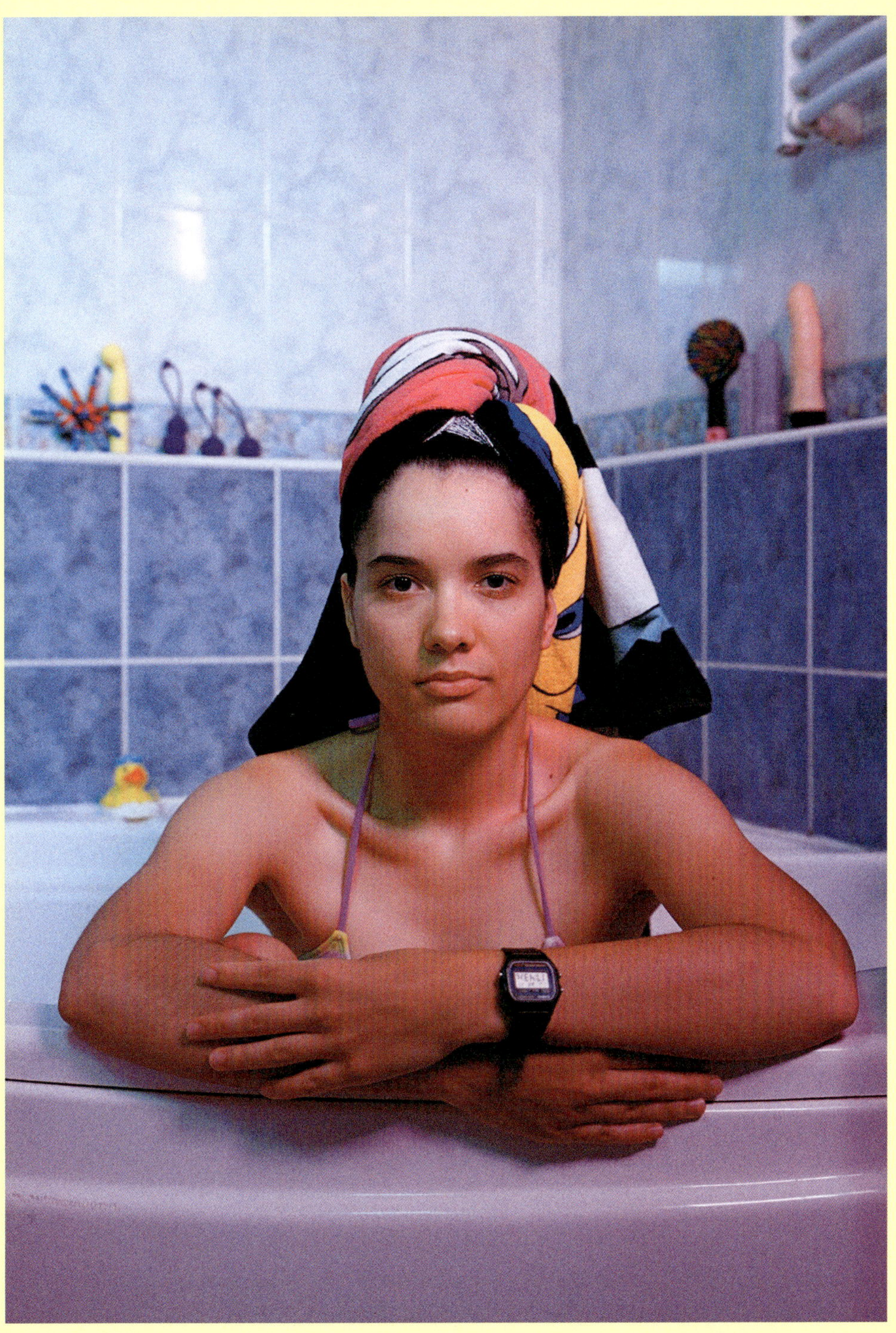

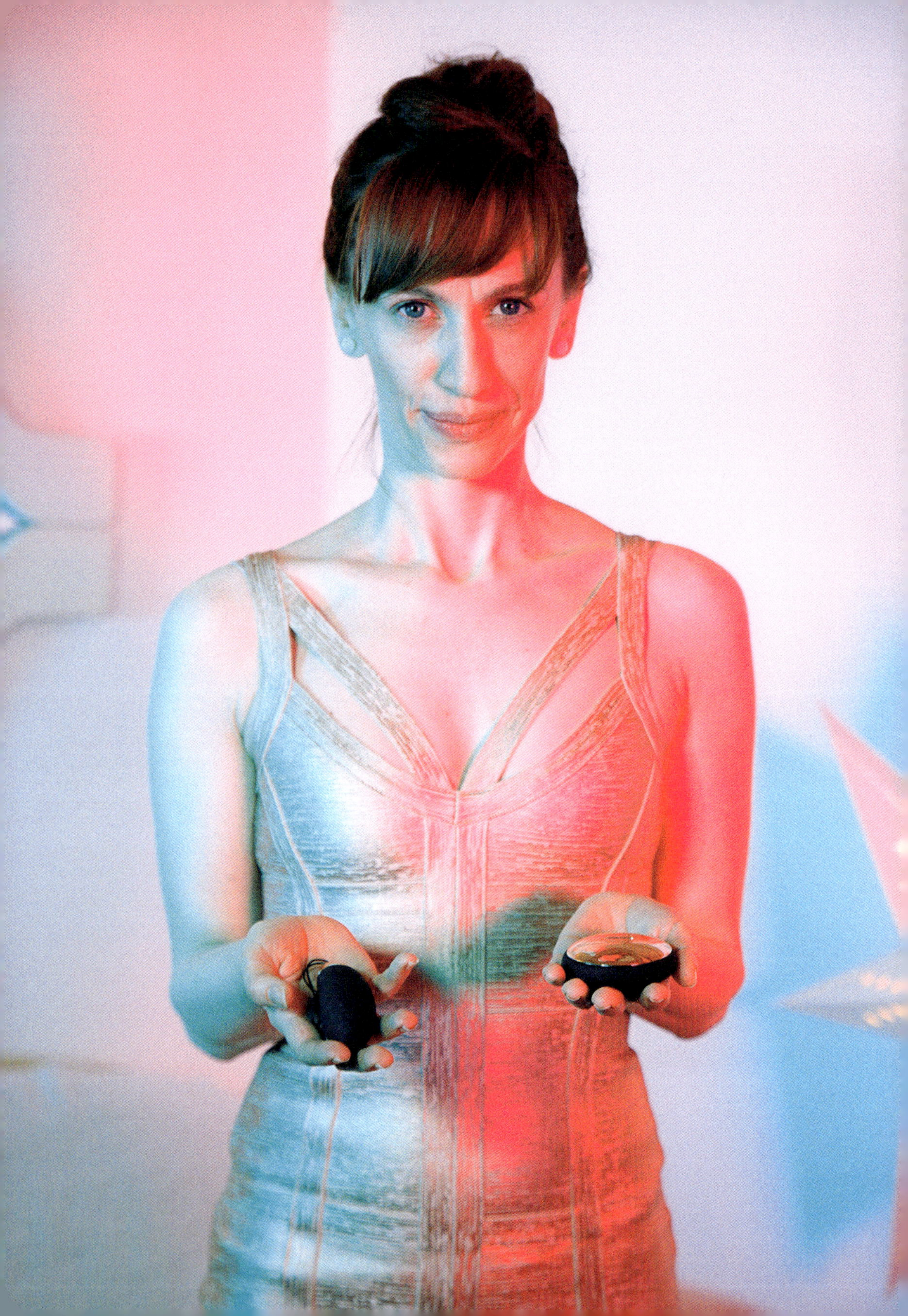

Basically, I'm a teacher who has never taught at a school. But educating has been very important for me. Let's say, you haven't learned about basic sexual health. How would you know anything about it in your adulthood? This is a lifelong process.

It's like eating or drinking. Get to know yourself sexually too. I was 31 when I bought my first vibrator. When I was younger, I used to think that things like lubricant or a dildo were for old people. But it's not, you just have to finesse this skill too.

*I know that gang-
bang scenes are usually
violent and degrading
for women, but my attrac-
tion to it comes from
the idea of having a type of
audience, a group of men
feeling pleasure at the
same time. It is not about
assault, triple or double
penetration, or even being
a slave to the group.*

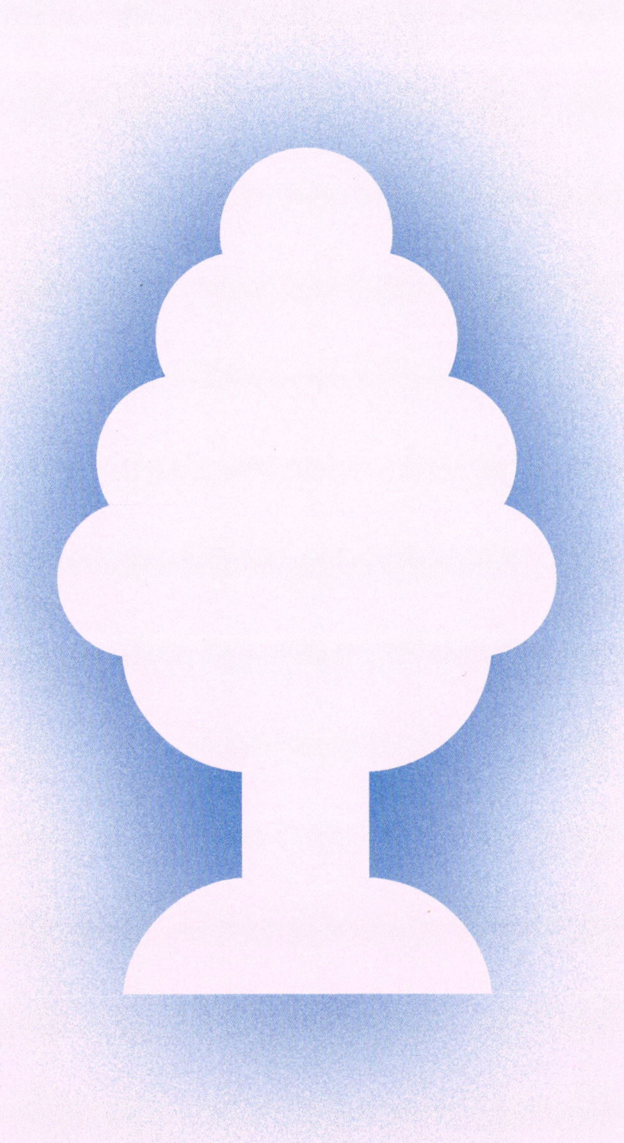

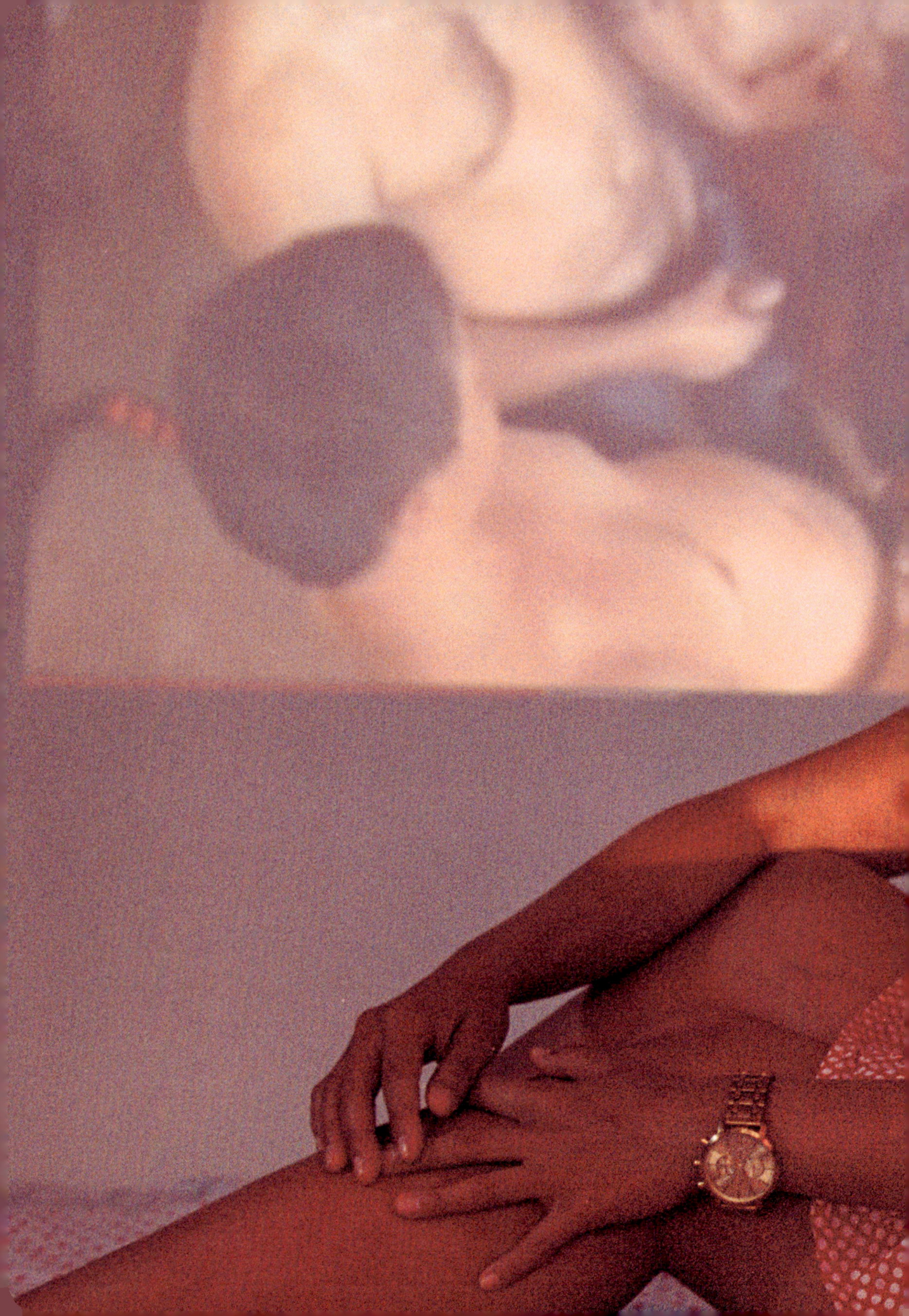

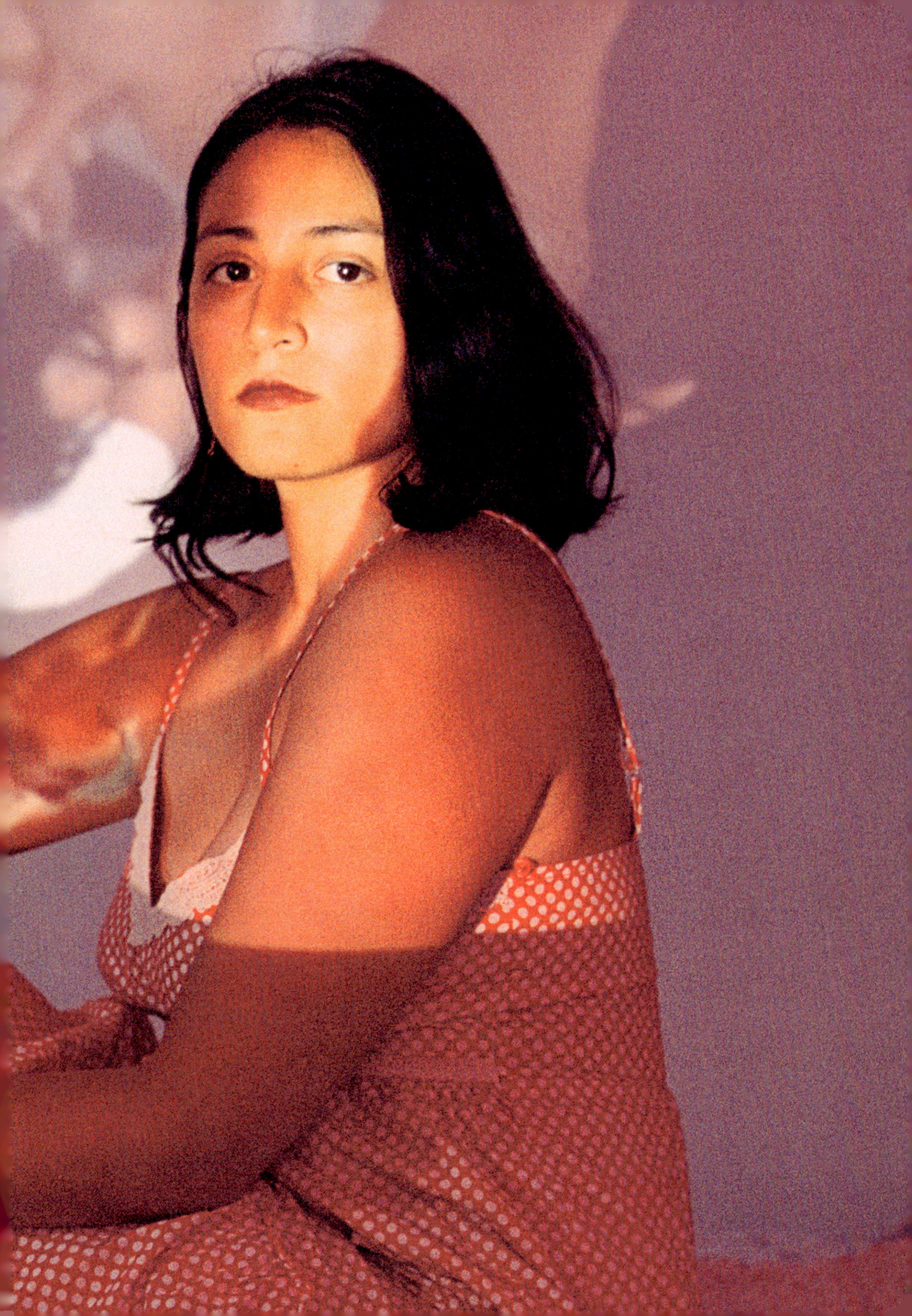

BDSM is a part of my identity and sexuality. Entering the scene was a real confidence boost.

Loads of sub men want to bow down before me and it's so fucking great.

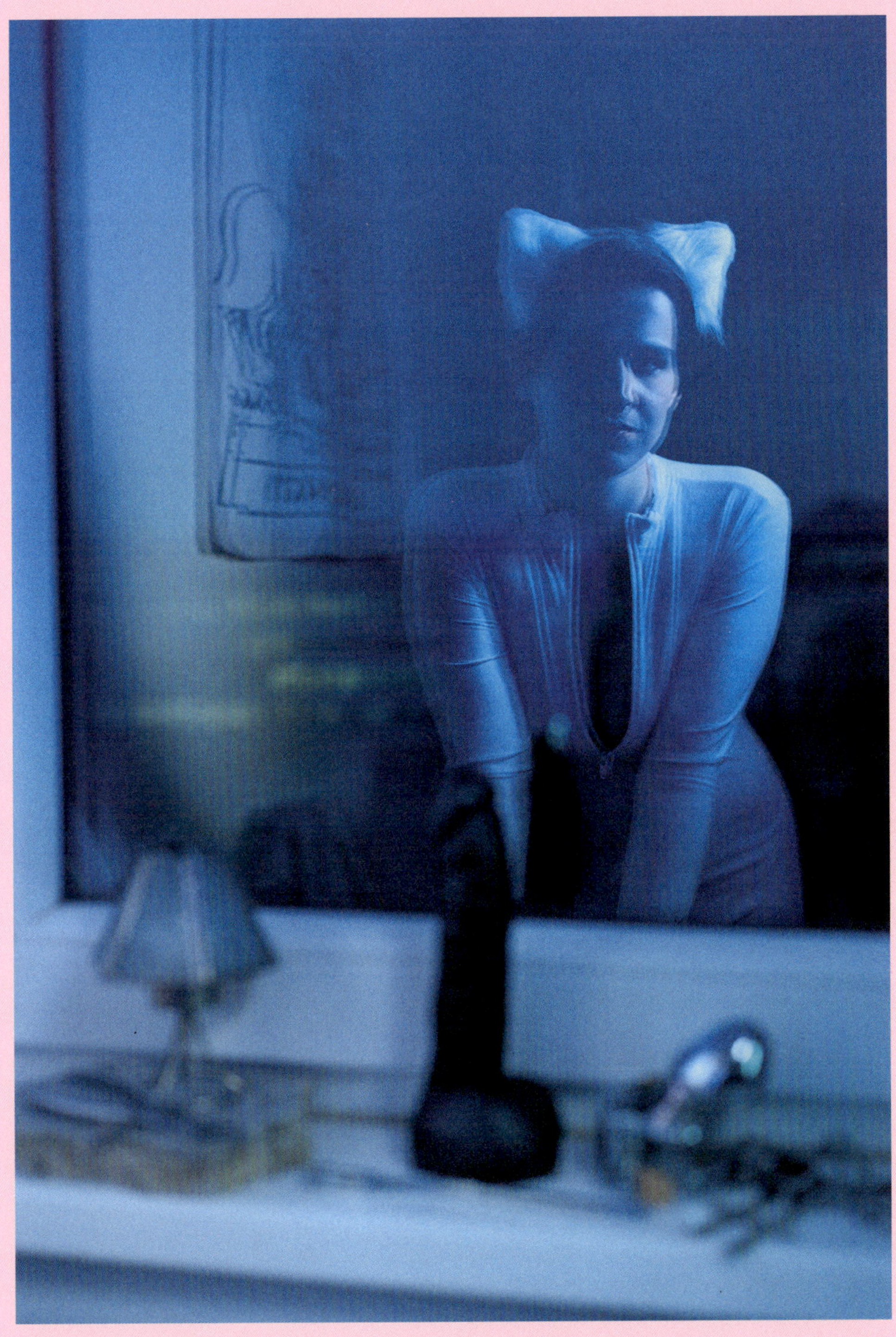

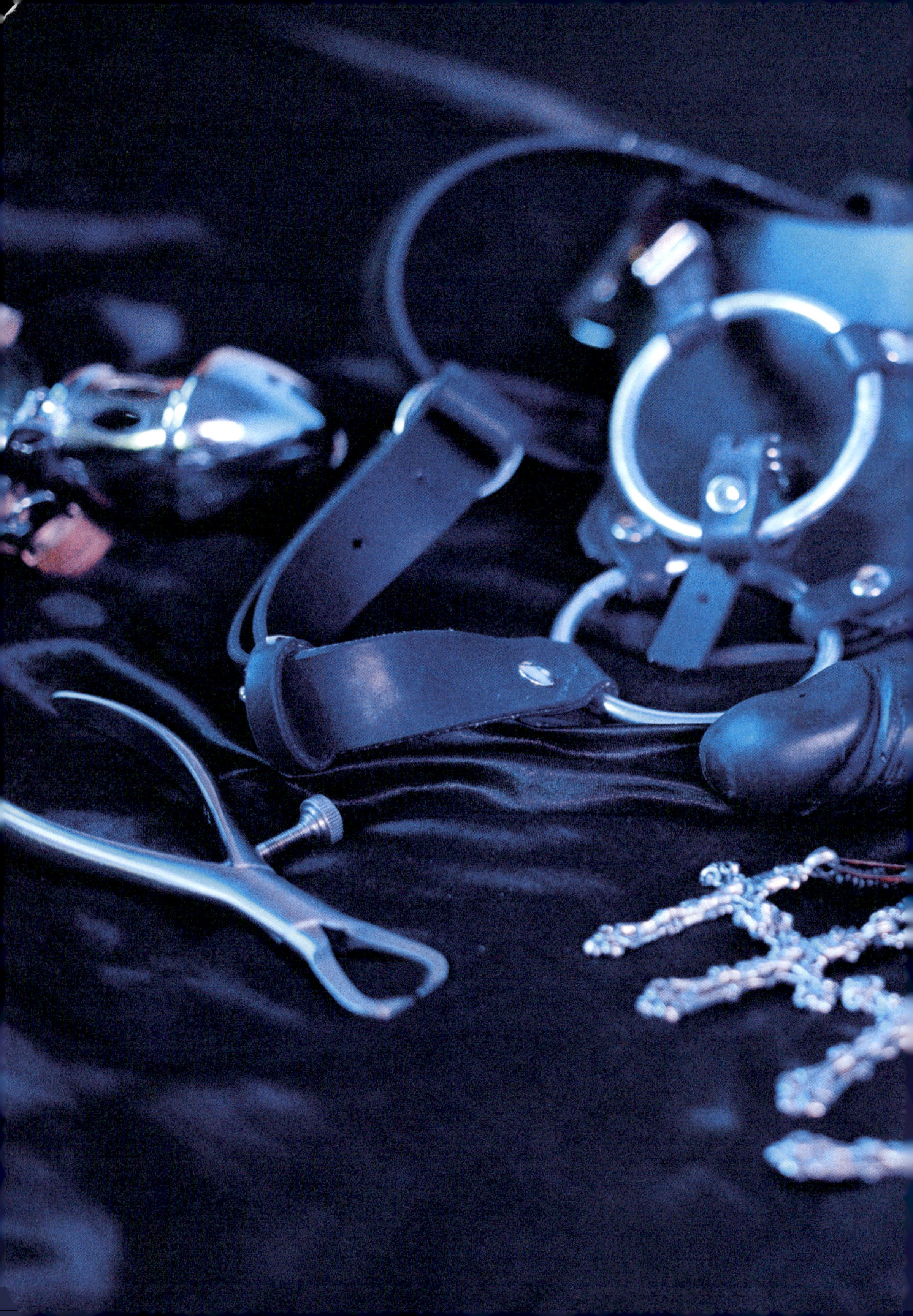

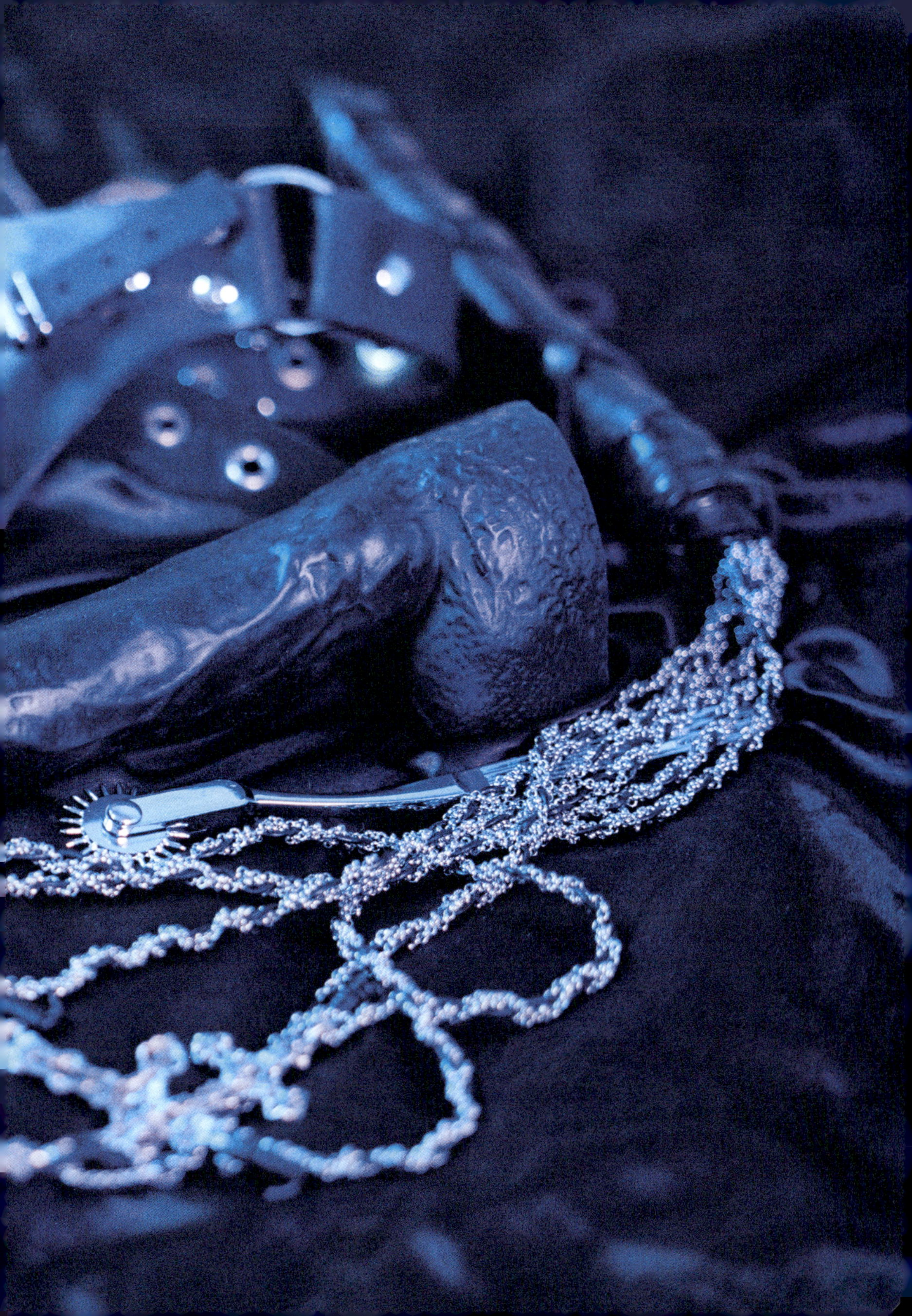

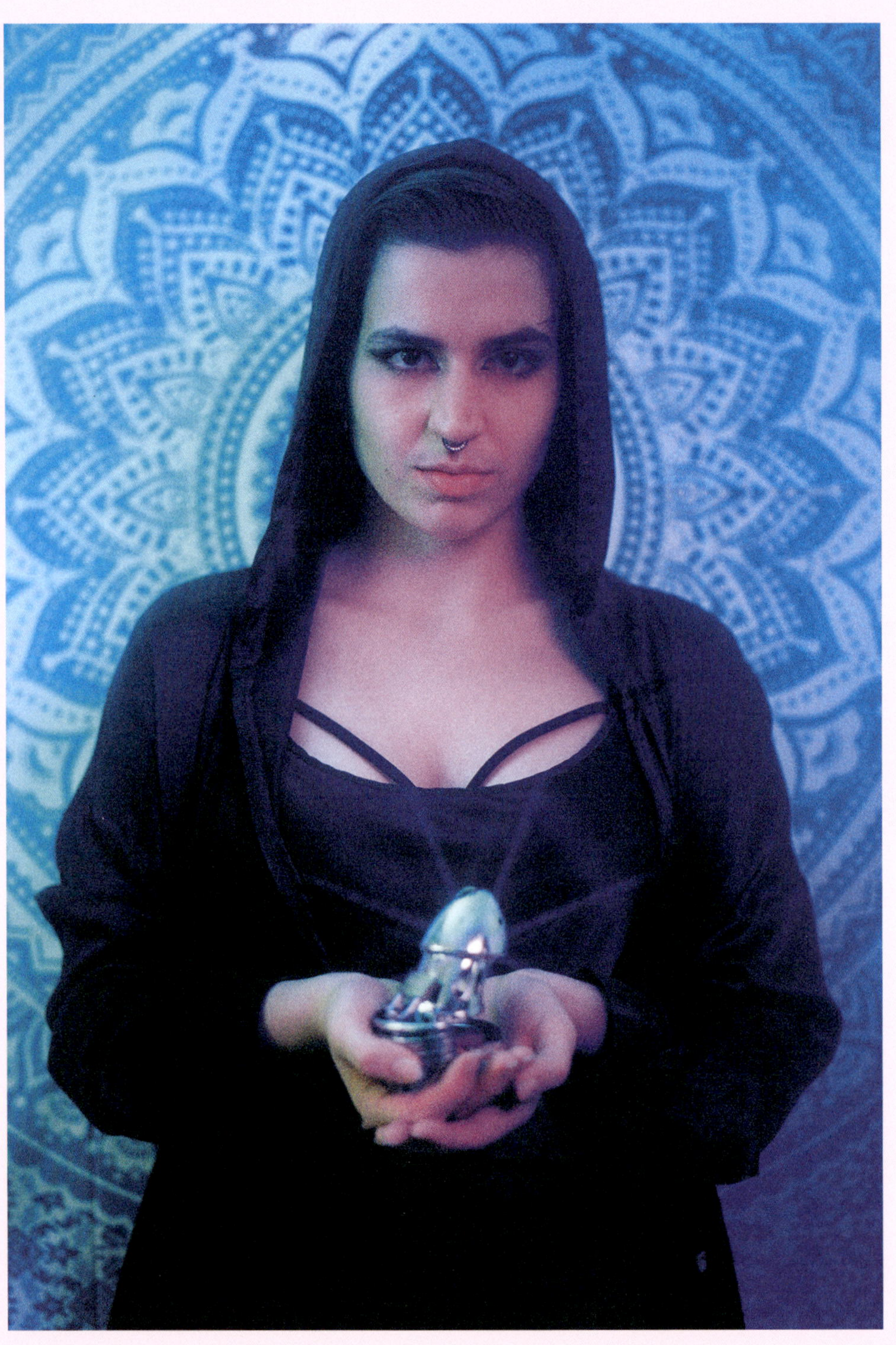

I think of BDSM as a coping mechanism, or recreation time. Sure, it's a stress release for me and for my partner too; the relationship deepens. There is a reason why I do this, there's one for everything. There aren't more trauma survivors in the BDSM community than anywhere else. I have some sadistic desires I like to realize. These experiences are very cathartic for me and for the partner I play with as well. It's deeply satisfying, it makes me really wet, but there's no need to sleep together.

Unconventional sexuality for men is not really accepted. Even less so than for women. There's a set structure for being a man. In my experience, even supposedly submissive men get their ideas from porn, since they don't have a realistic perception of dominant women. In porn, women are depicted as fetish enablers. They think dominant women live for satisfying the men's desires.

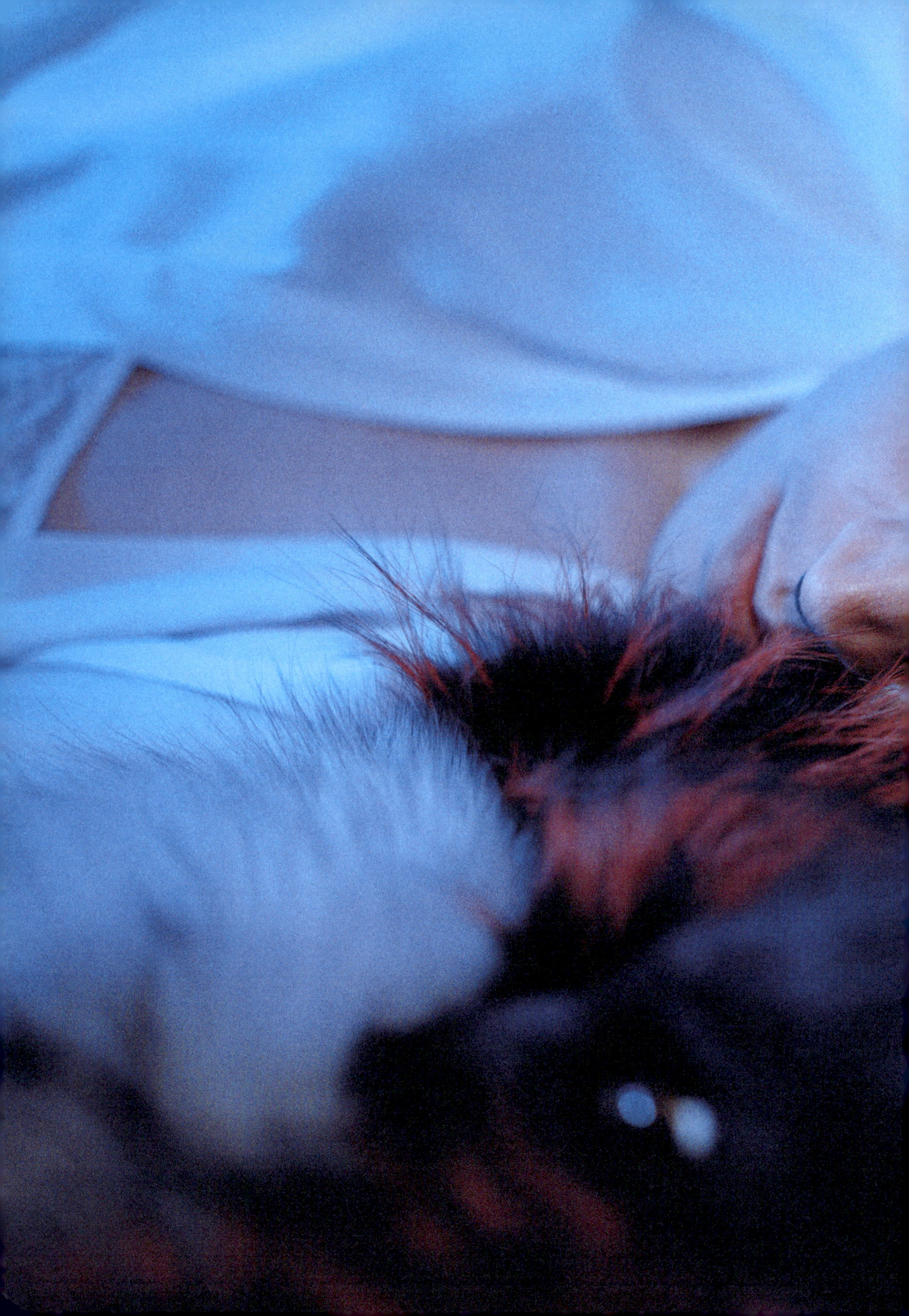

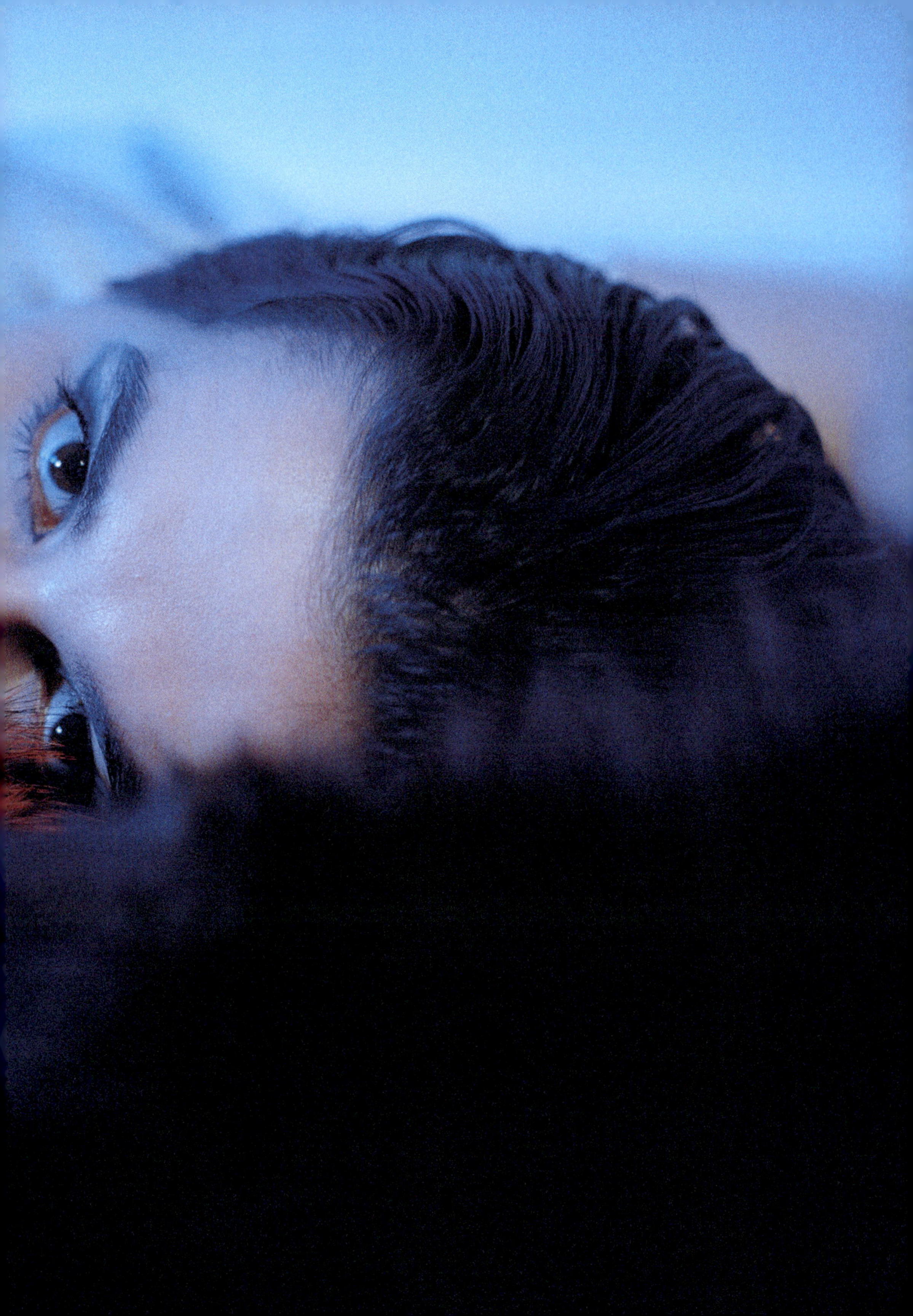

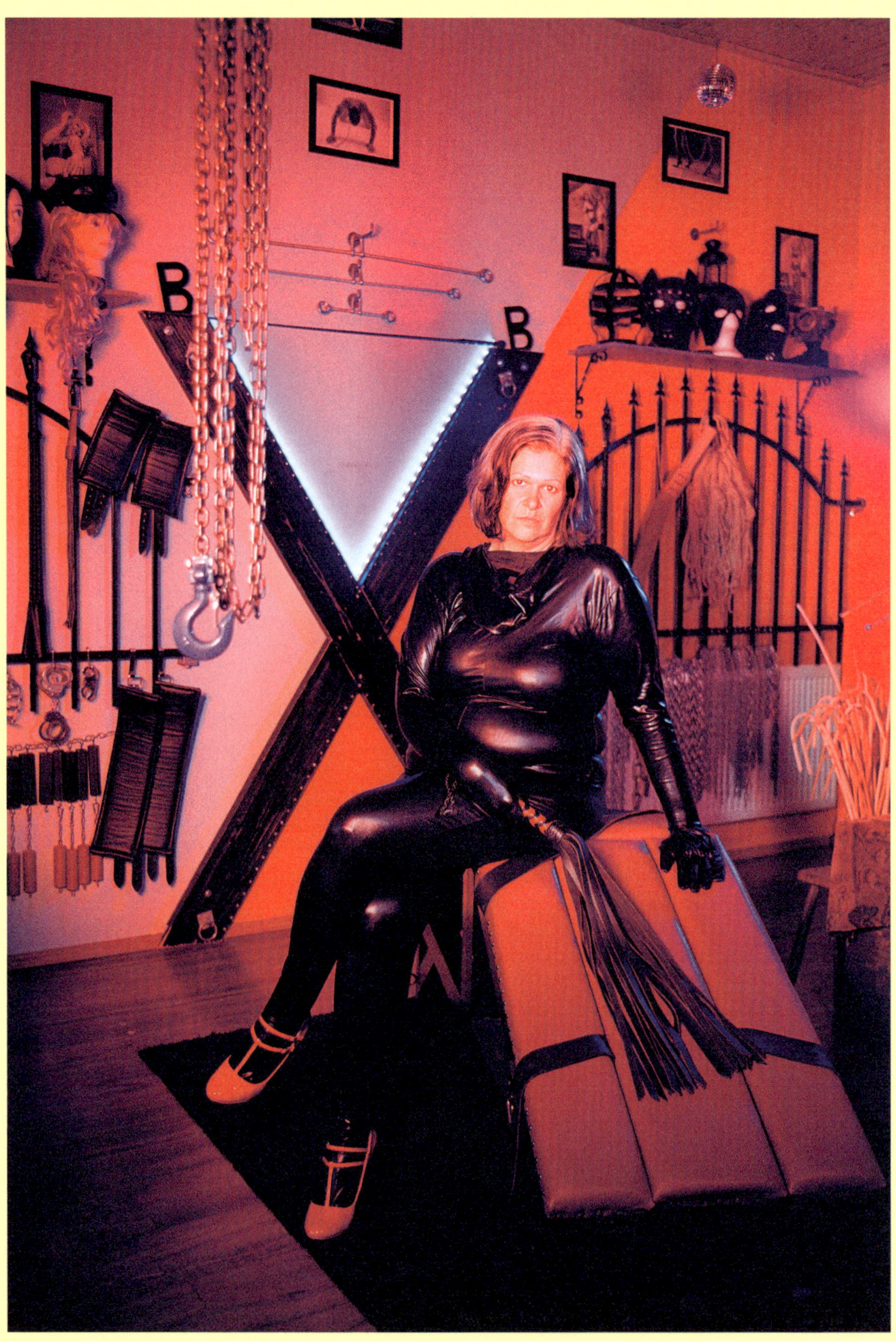

BEÁTA

People completely repress their desires because of shame. However, repressed desires cripple you. For example, I wished to be dominant over men but I repressed it.

When I realized I could change this, I got rid of the shame and tried to act on these desires. I reversed the roles, I dominated men who wished for it.

*I realized that men like
to act out social norms
that I also saw at home:
the woman serves
the man, mom cooks for
dad and maintains the
household.*

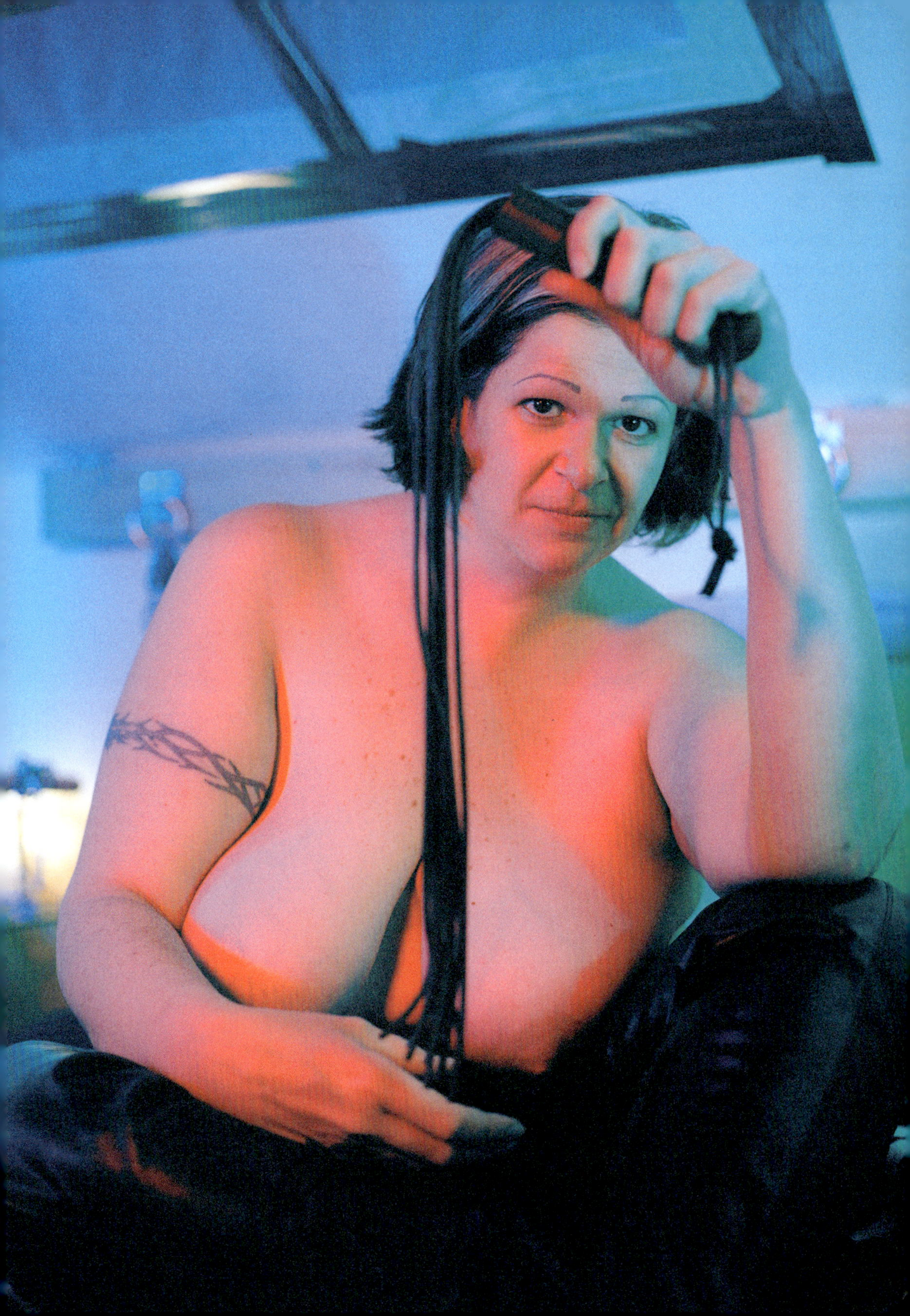

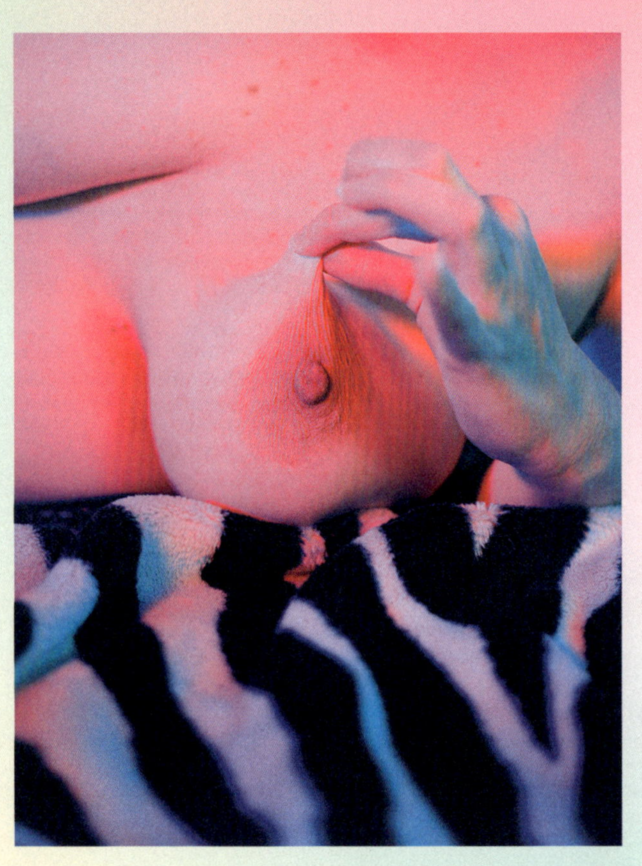

Little boys come
to me with real desires.
They process their
traumas through
BDSM.

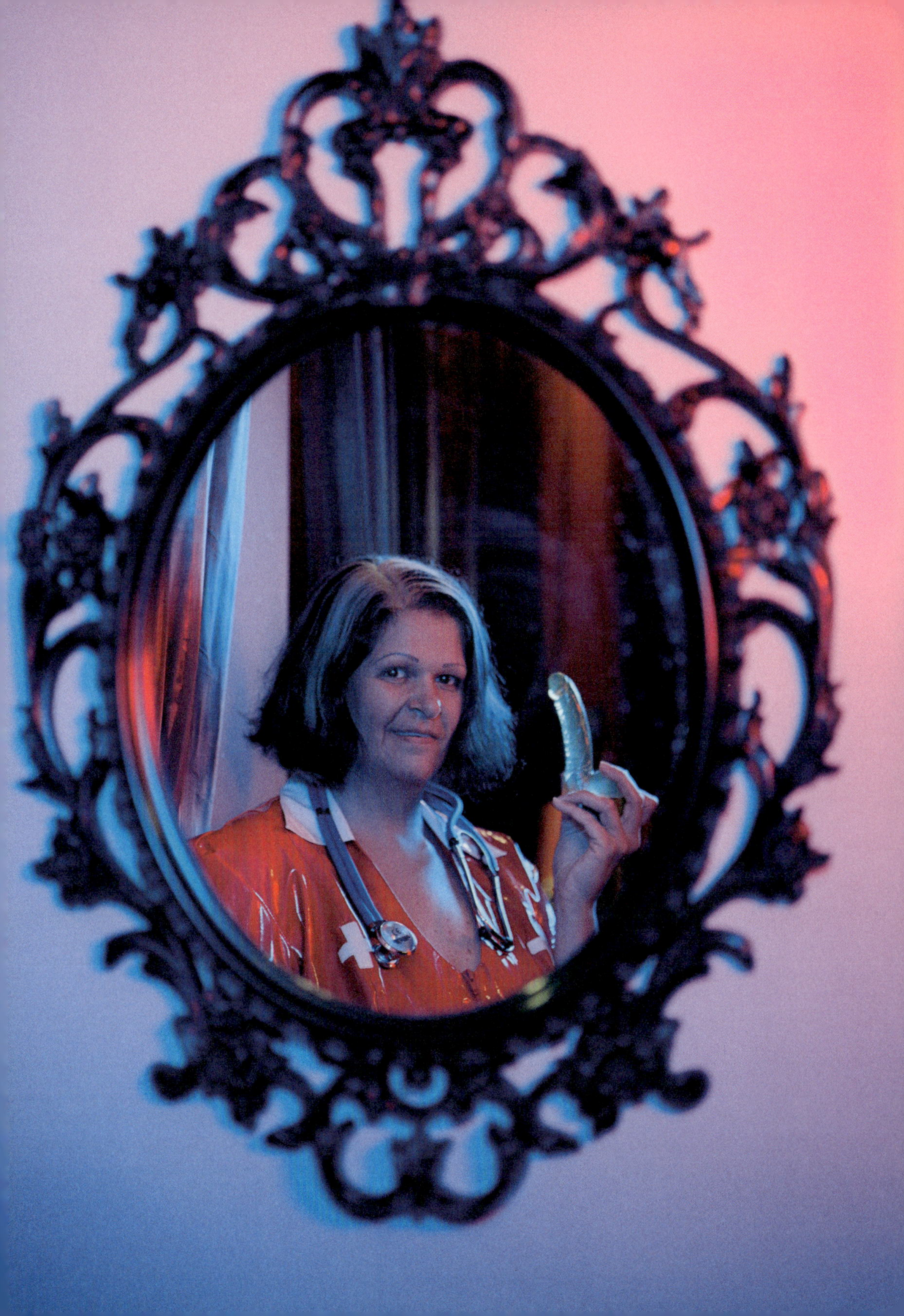

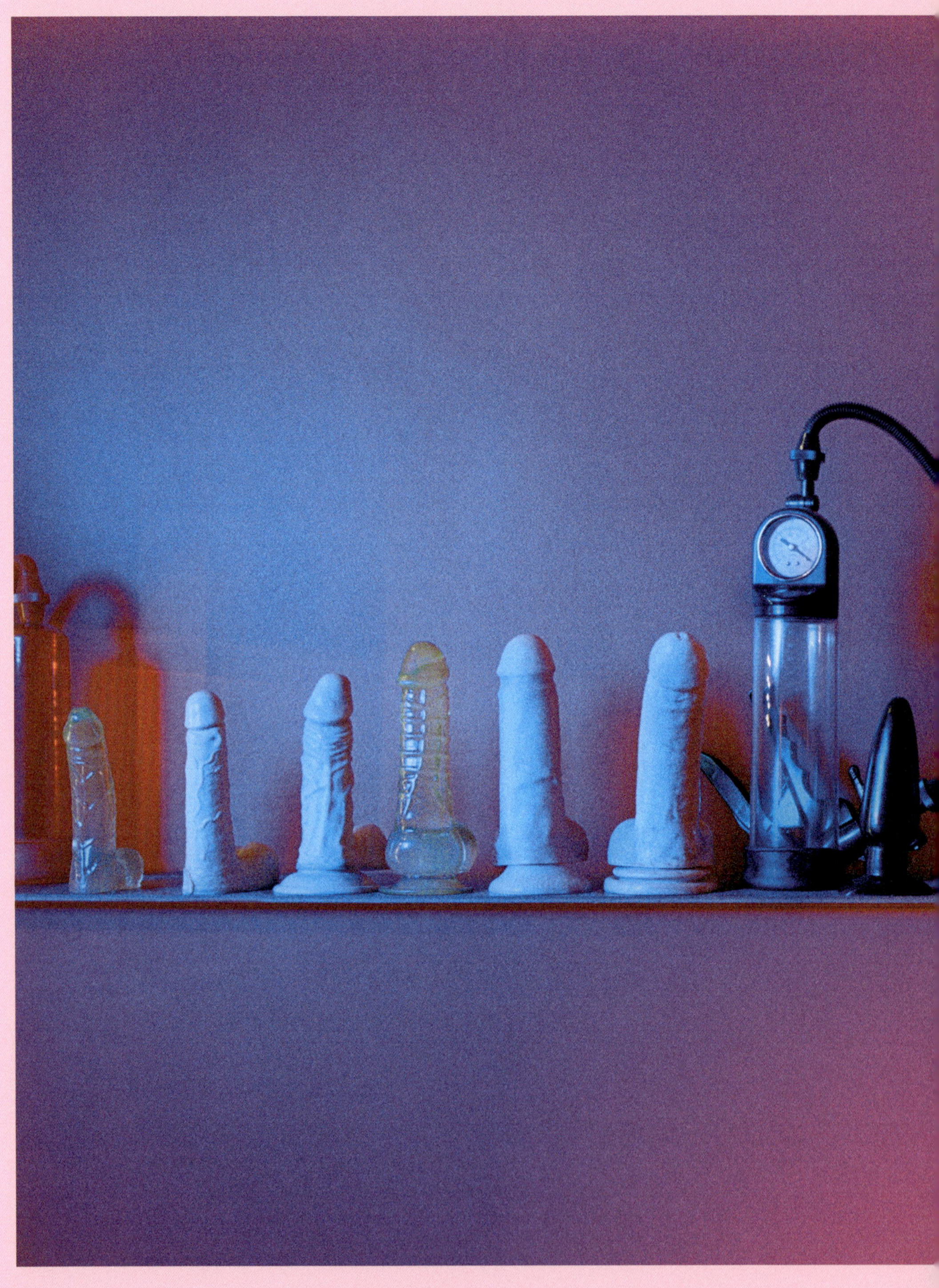

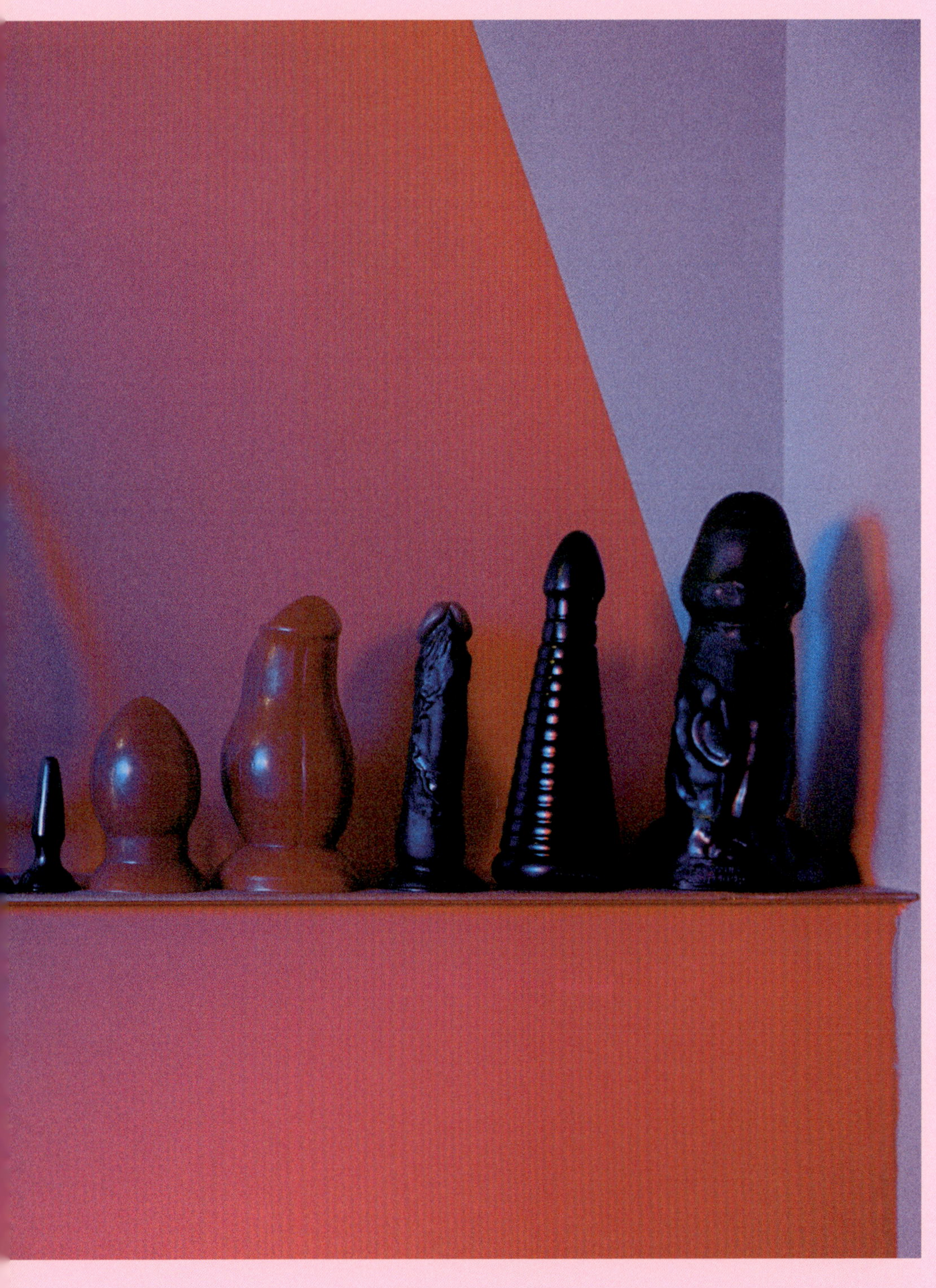

*Every secret
gets out.*

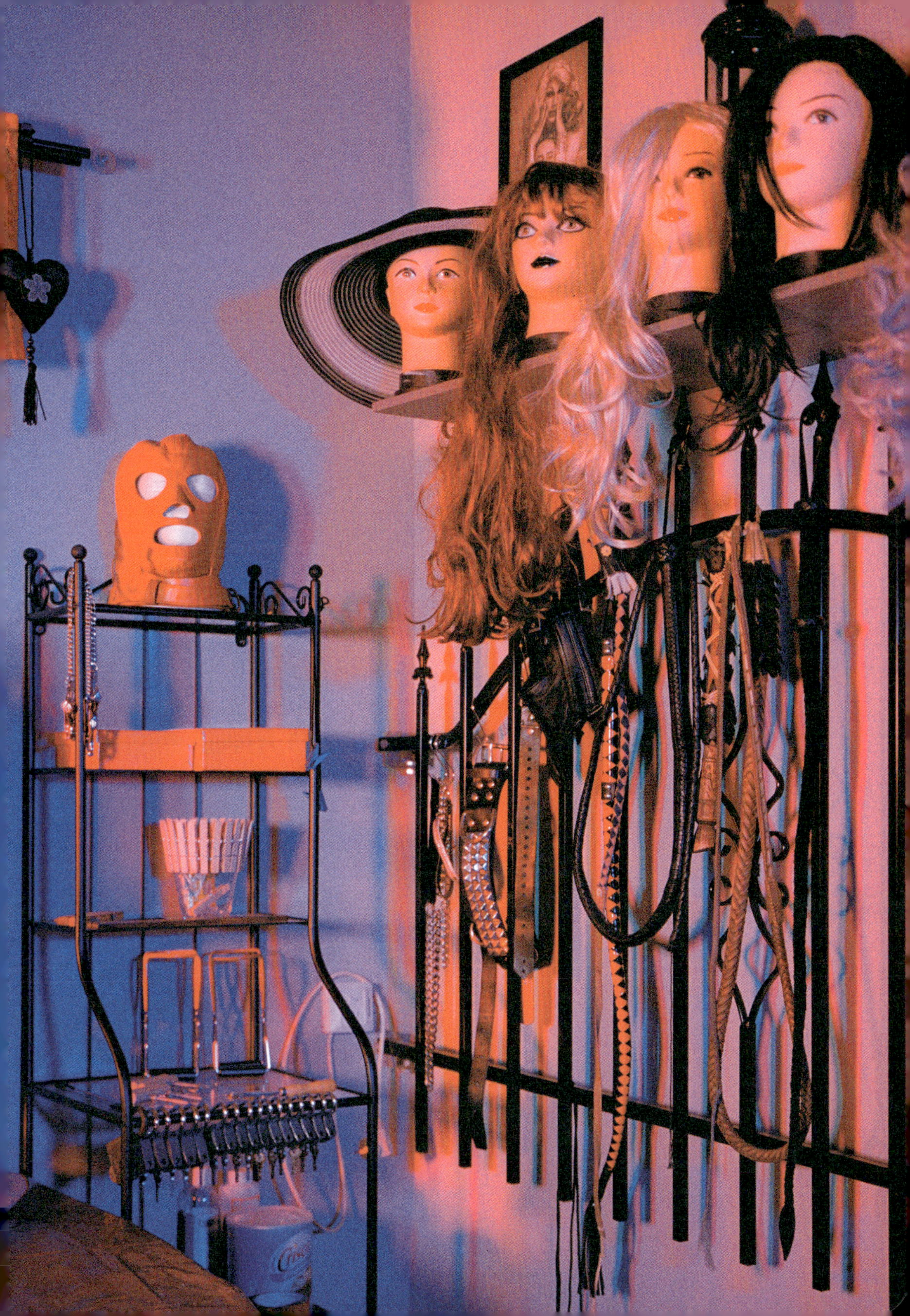

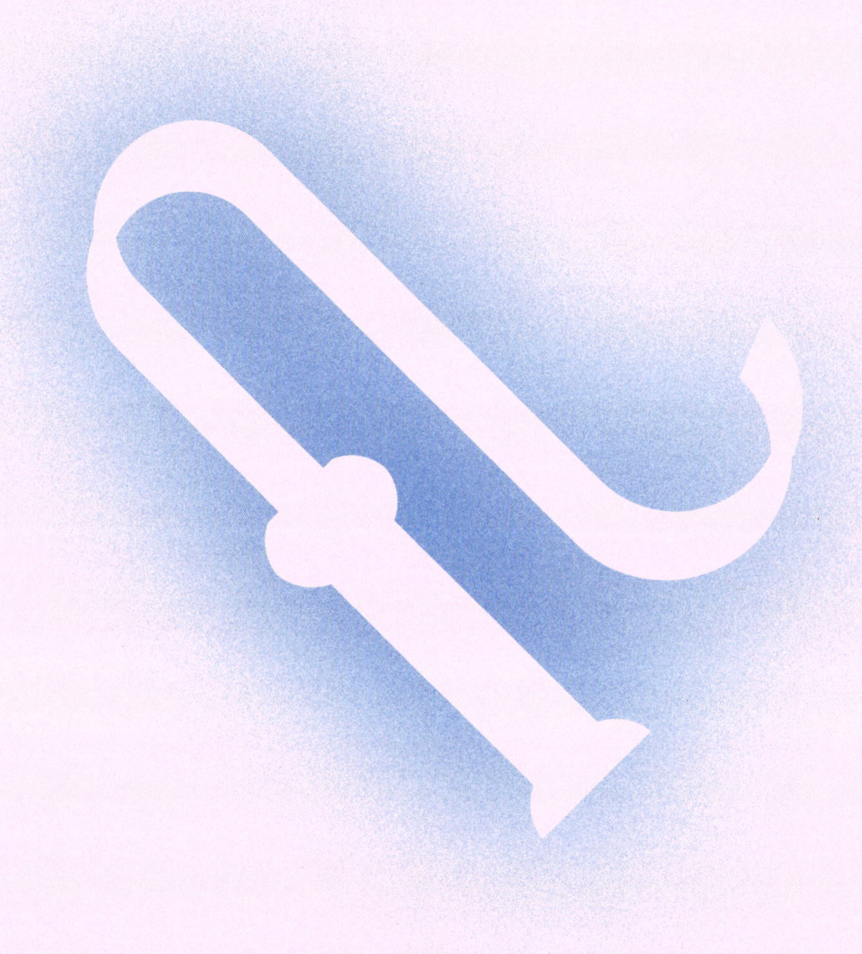

Better fucks
to every bedroom!

The Hungarian nation could be
so much happier.

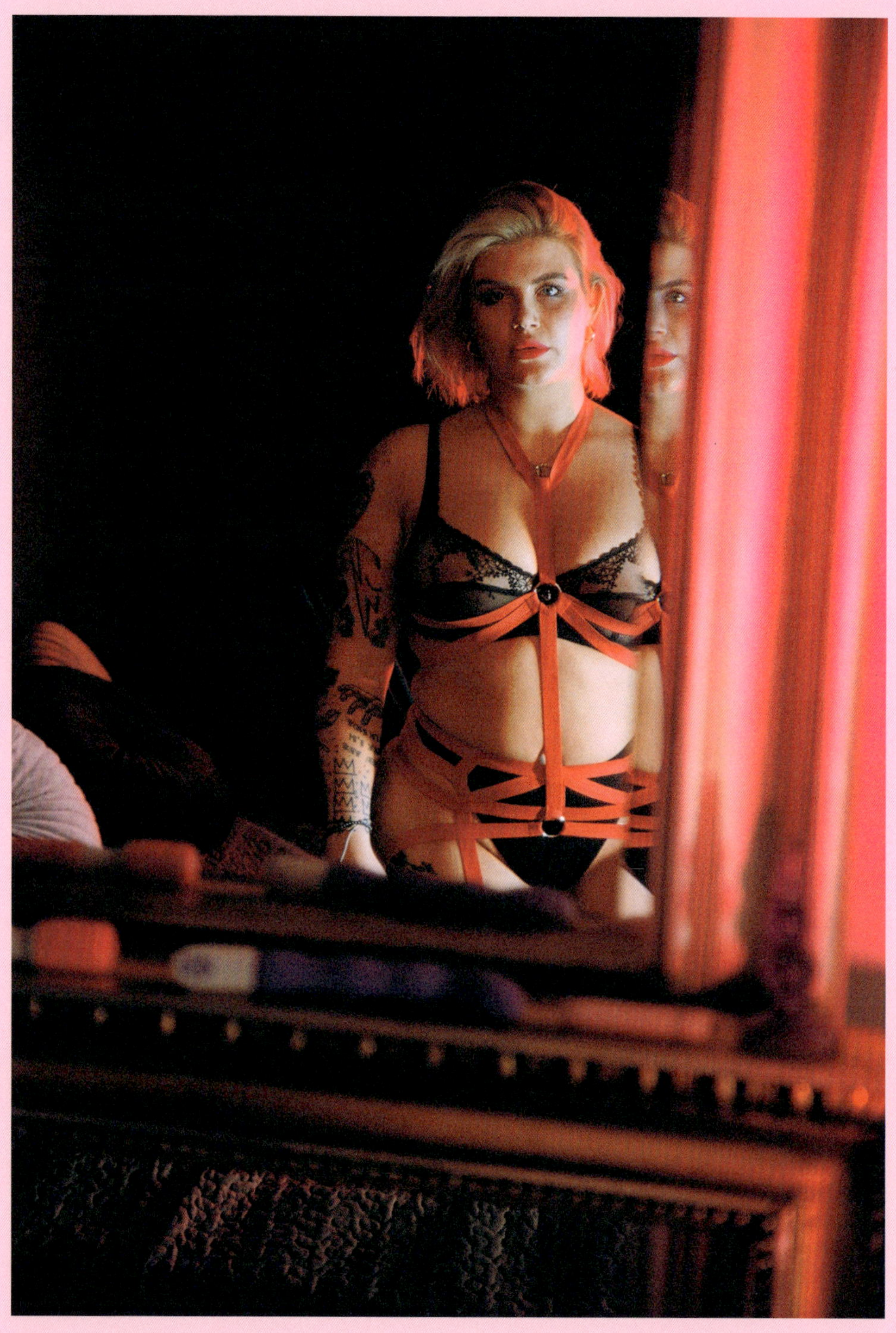

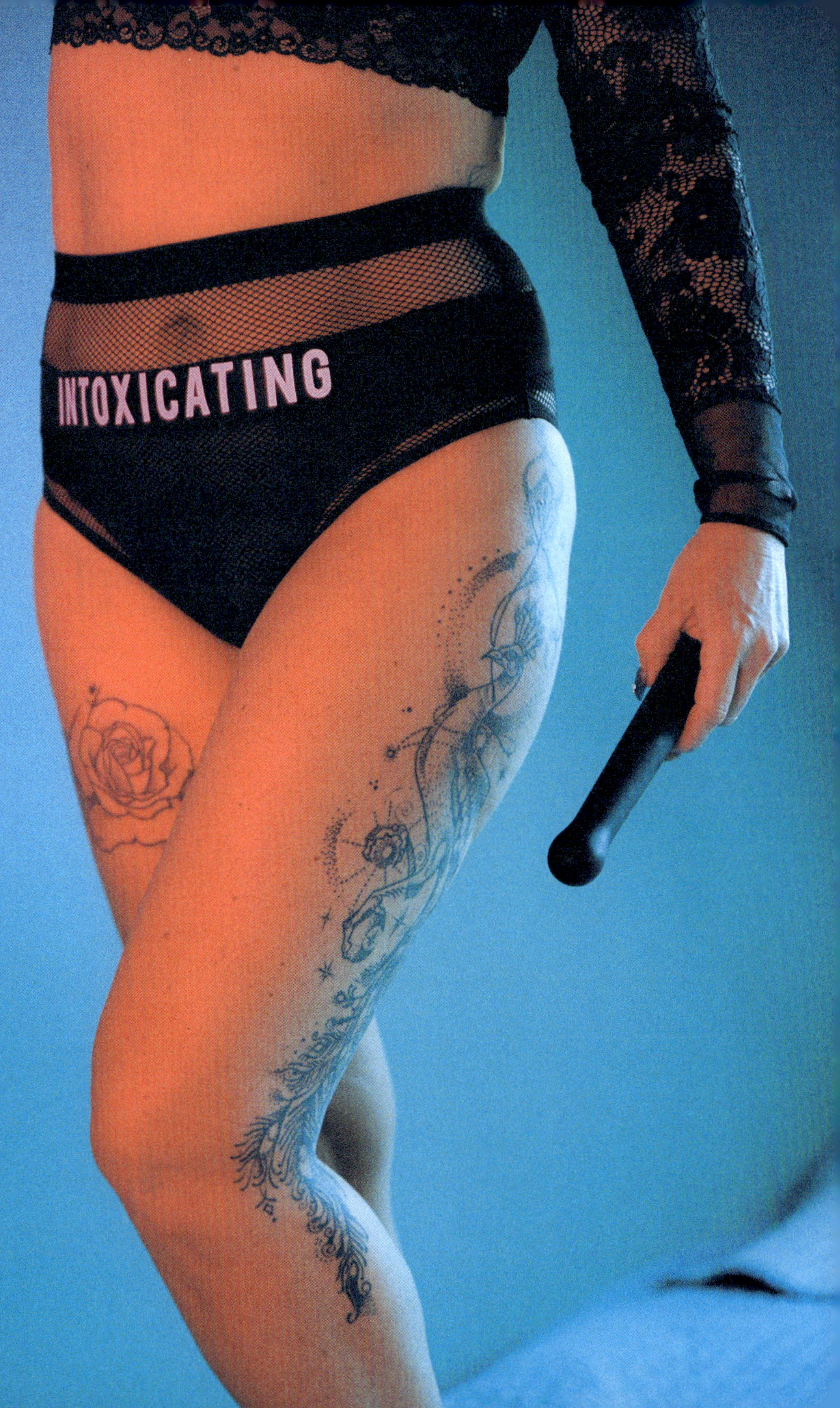
INTOXICATING

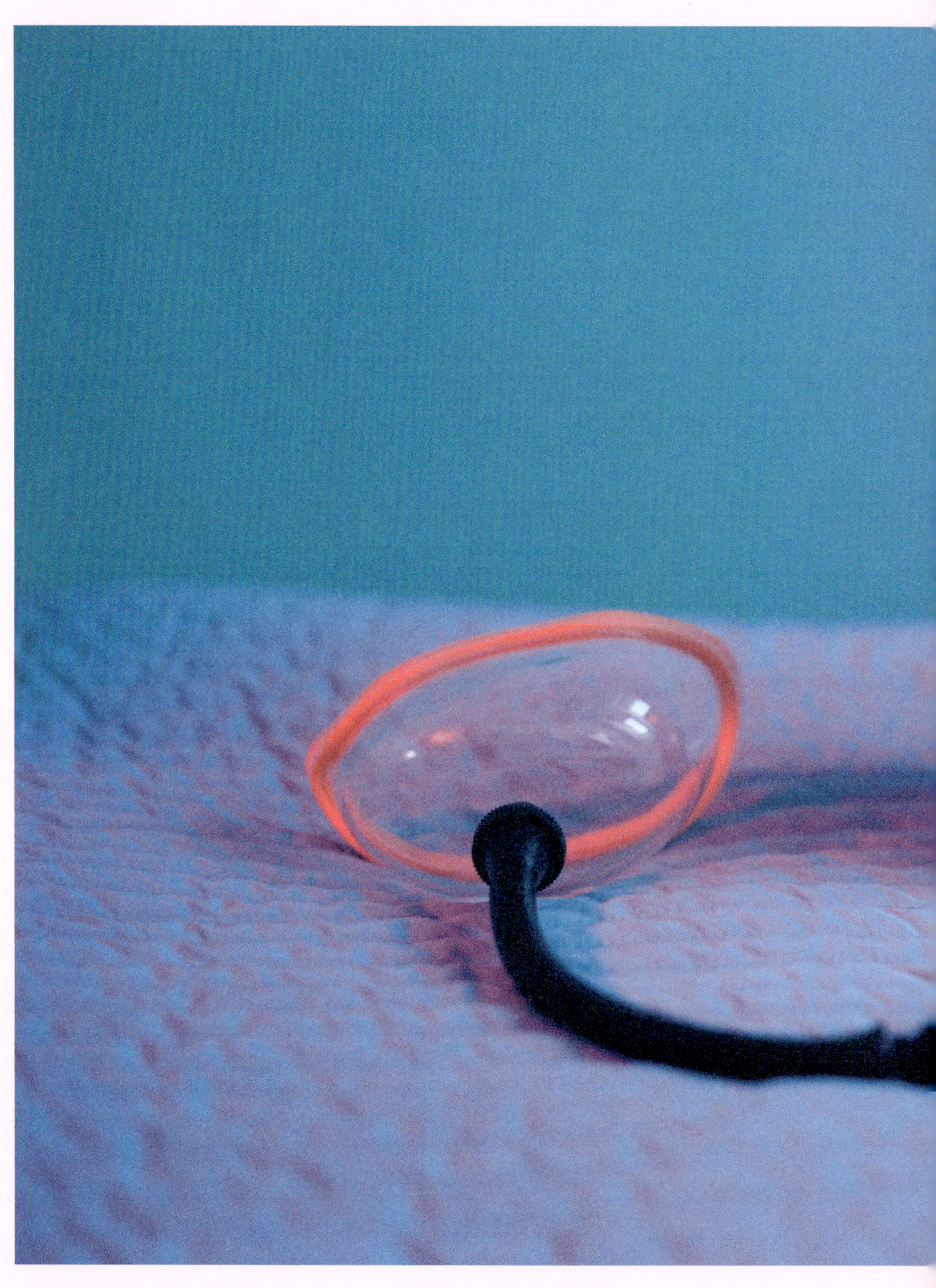

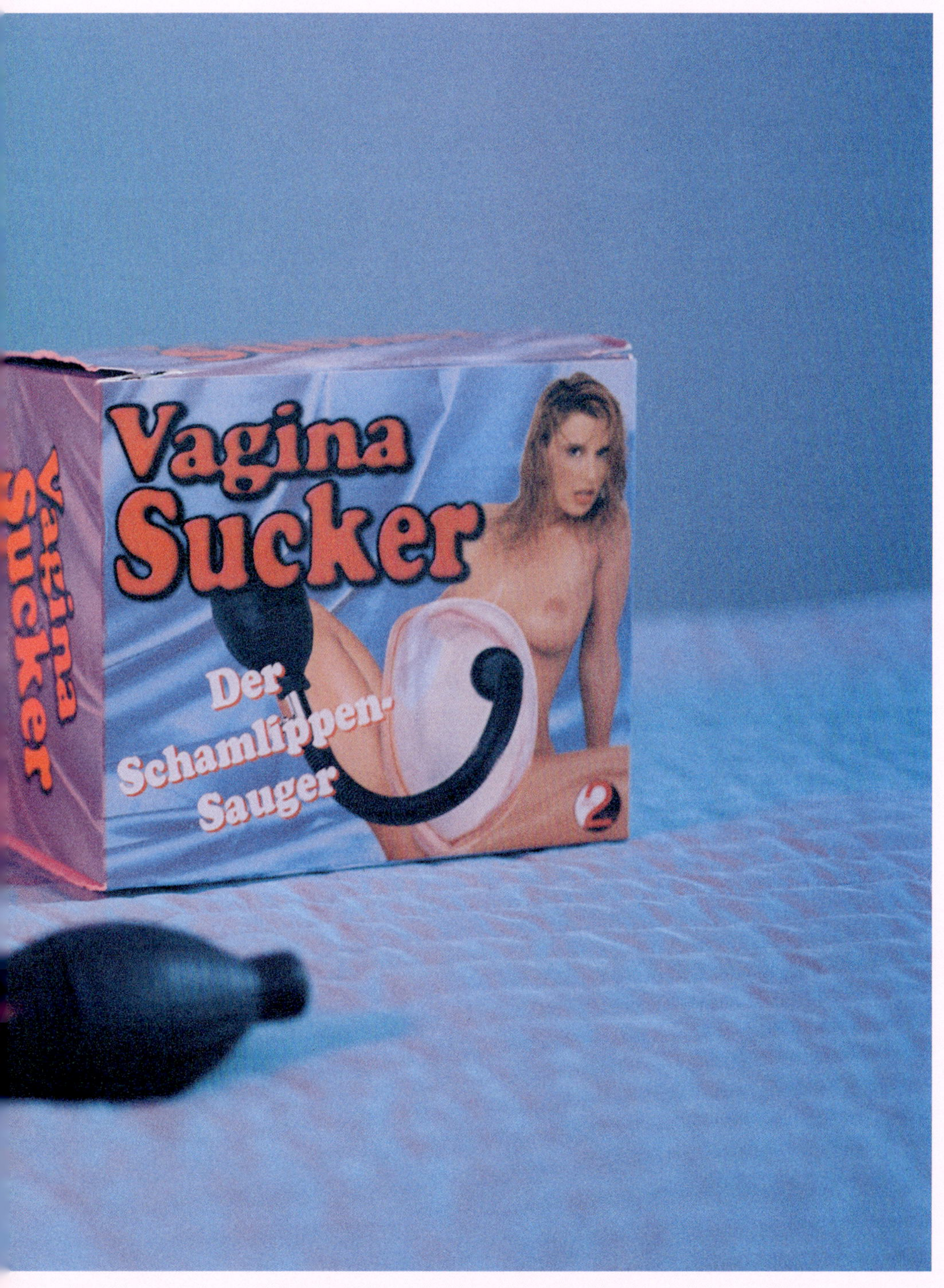

Vagina
Sucker
Der
Schamlippen-
Sauger
Vagina
Sucker

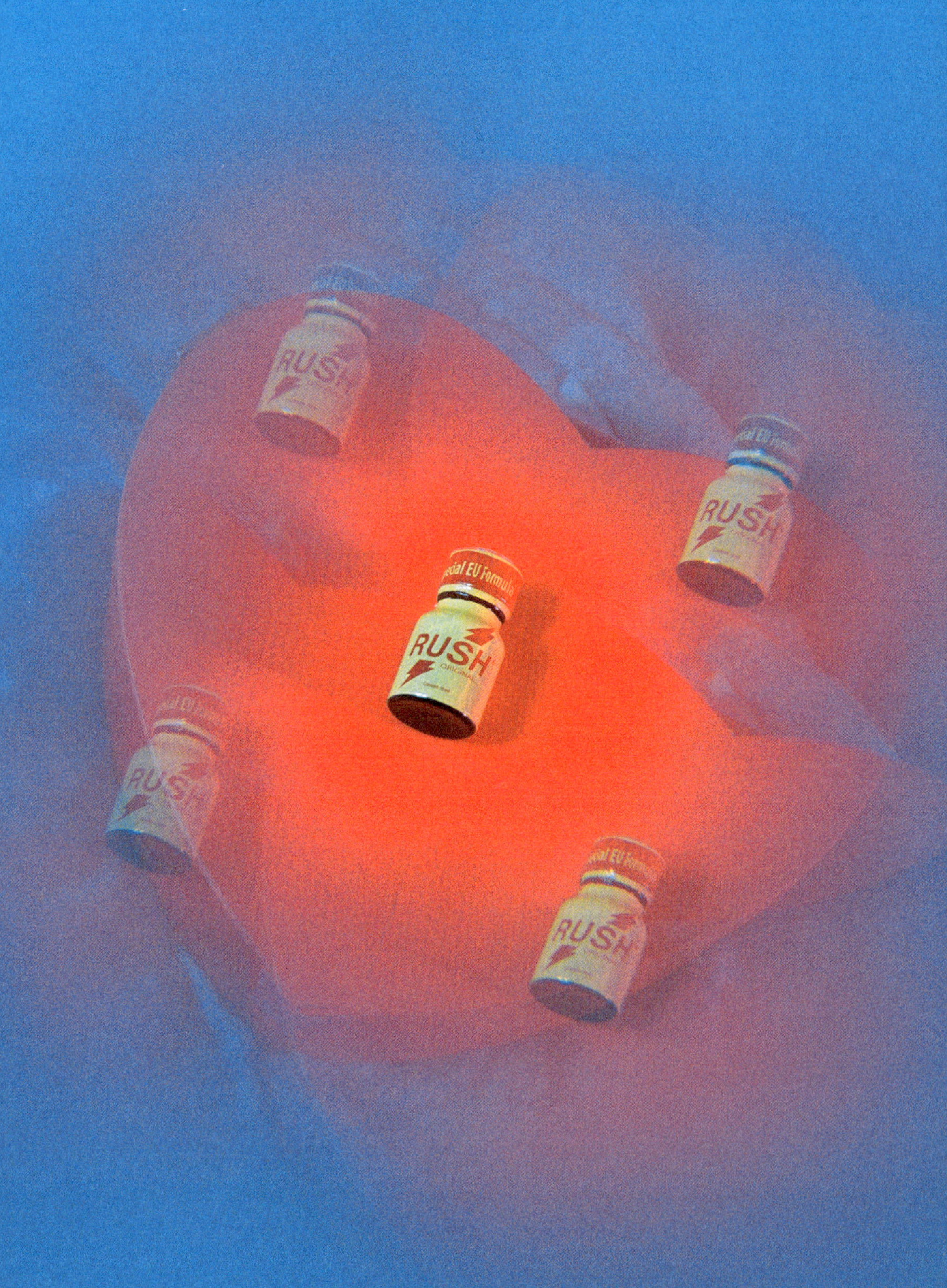

RUSH
Special EU Formula
RUSH
ORIGINAL
RUSH
RUSH
RUSH

BARBARA M.

*I'm just an
average girl
who likes to
play.*

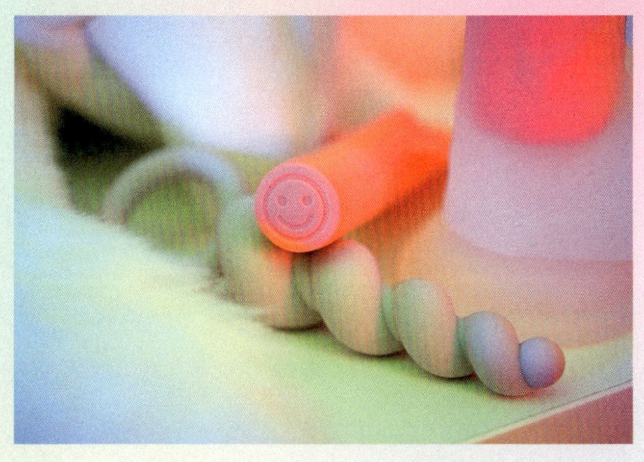

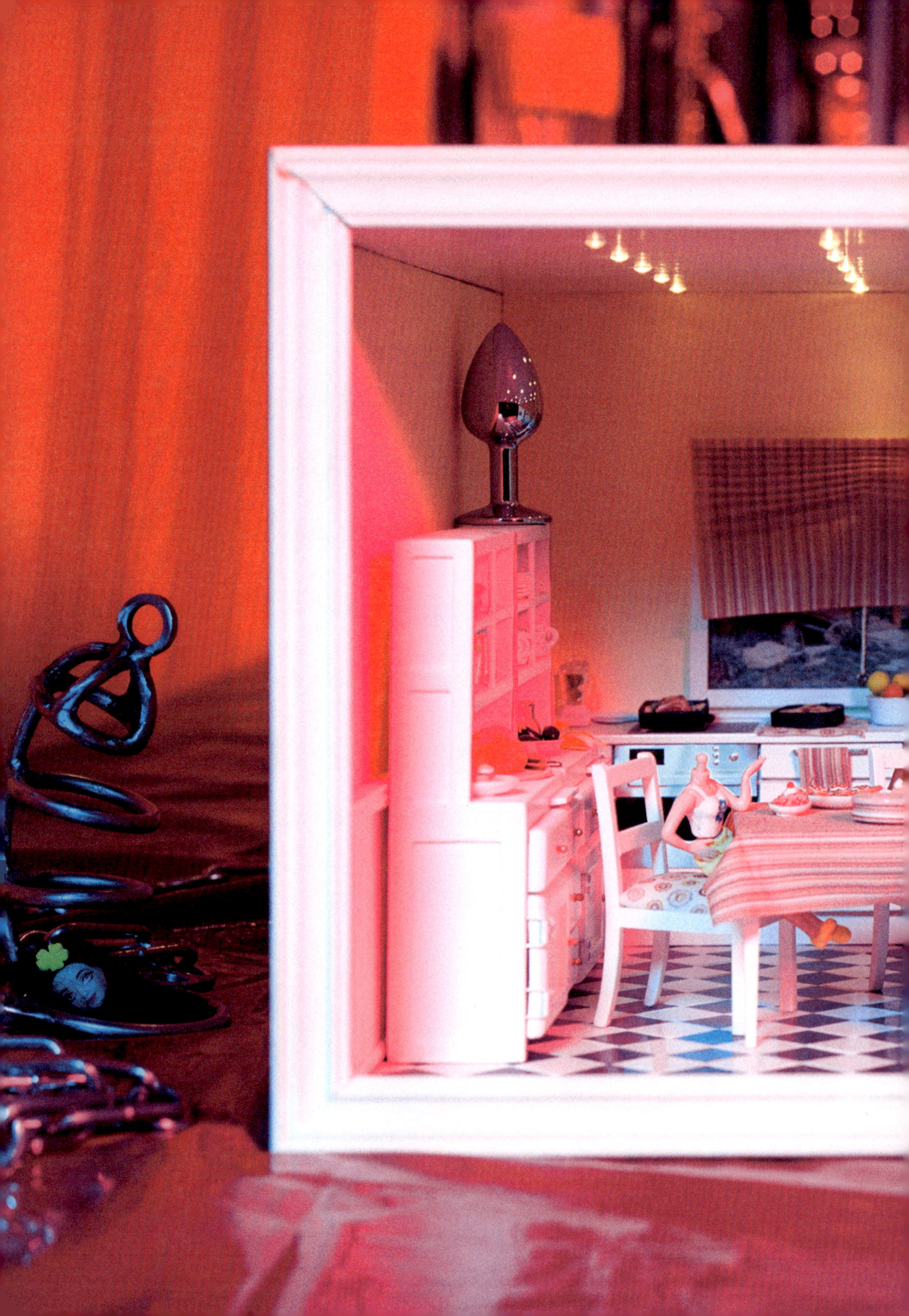

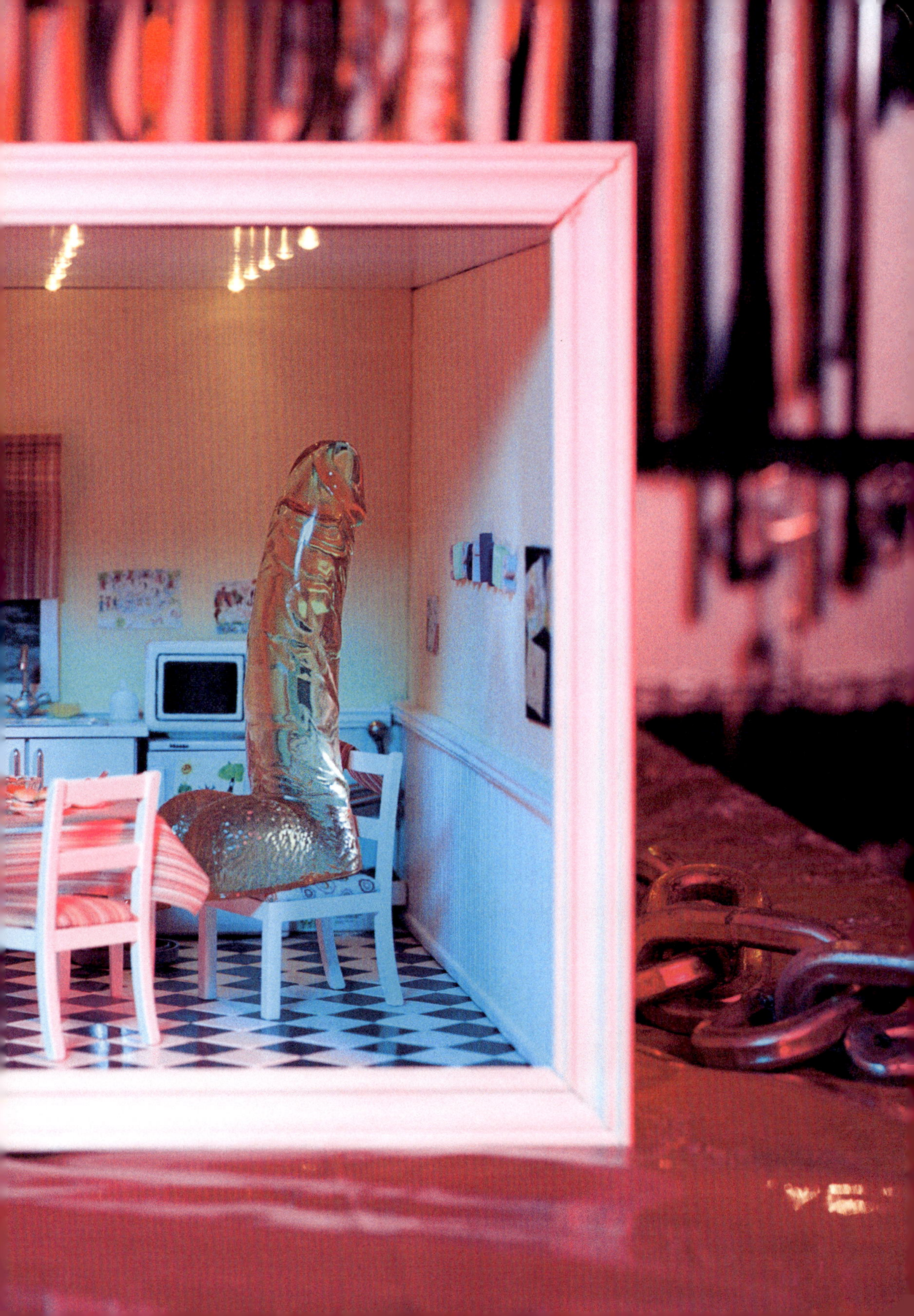

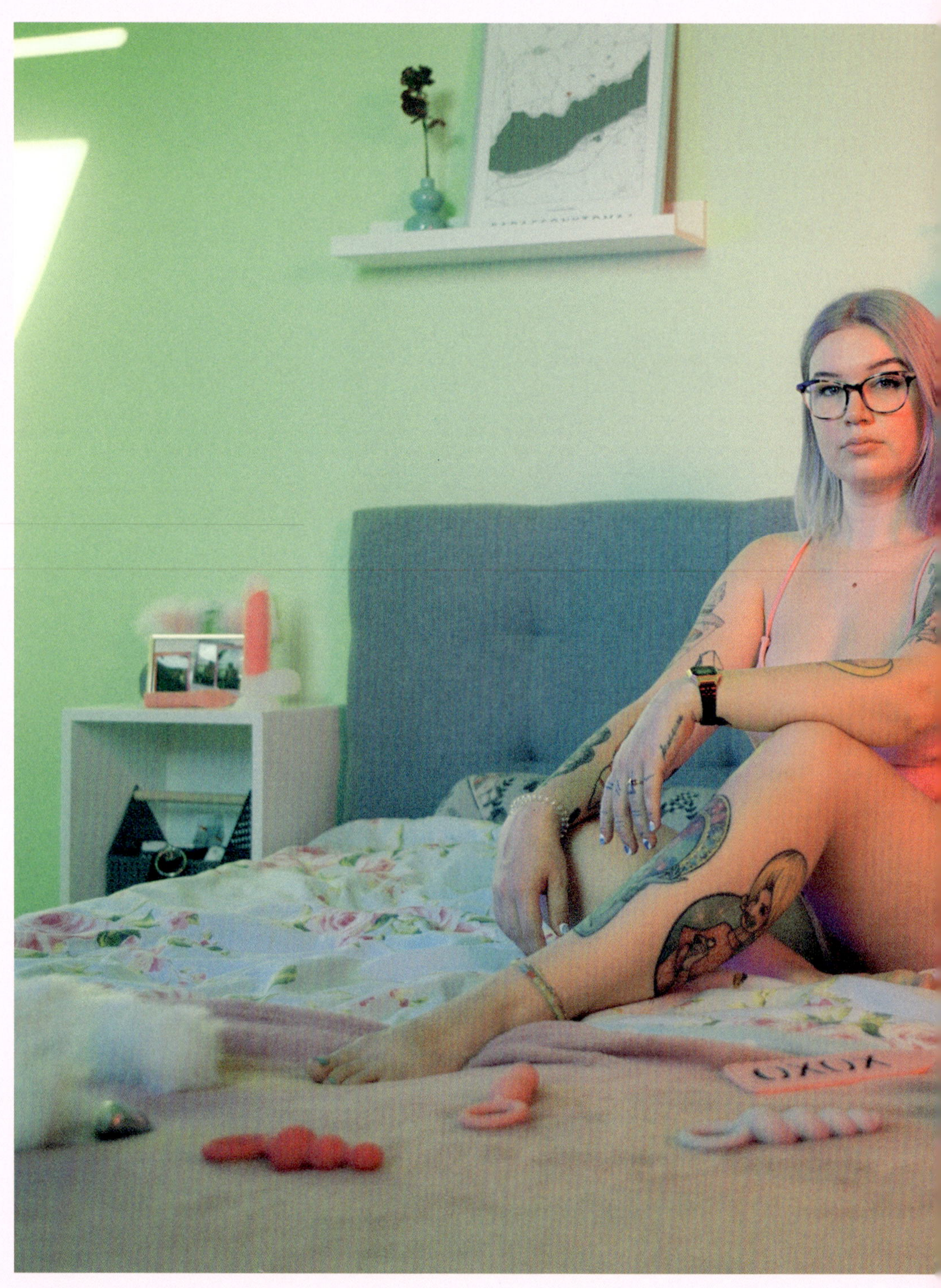

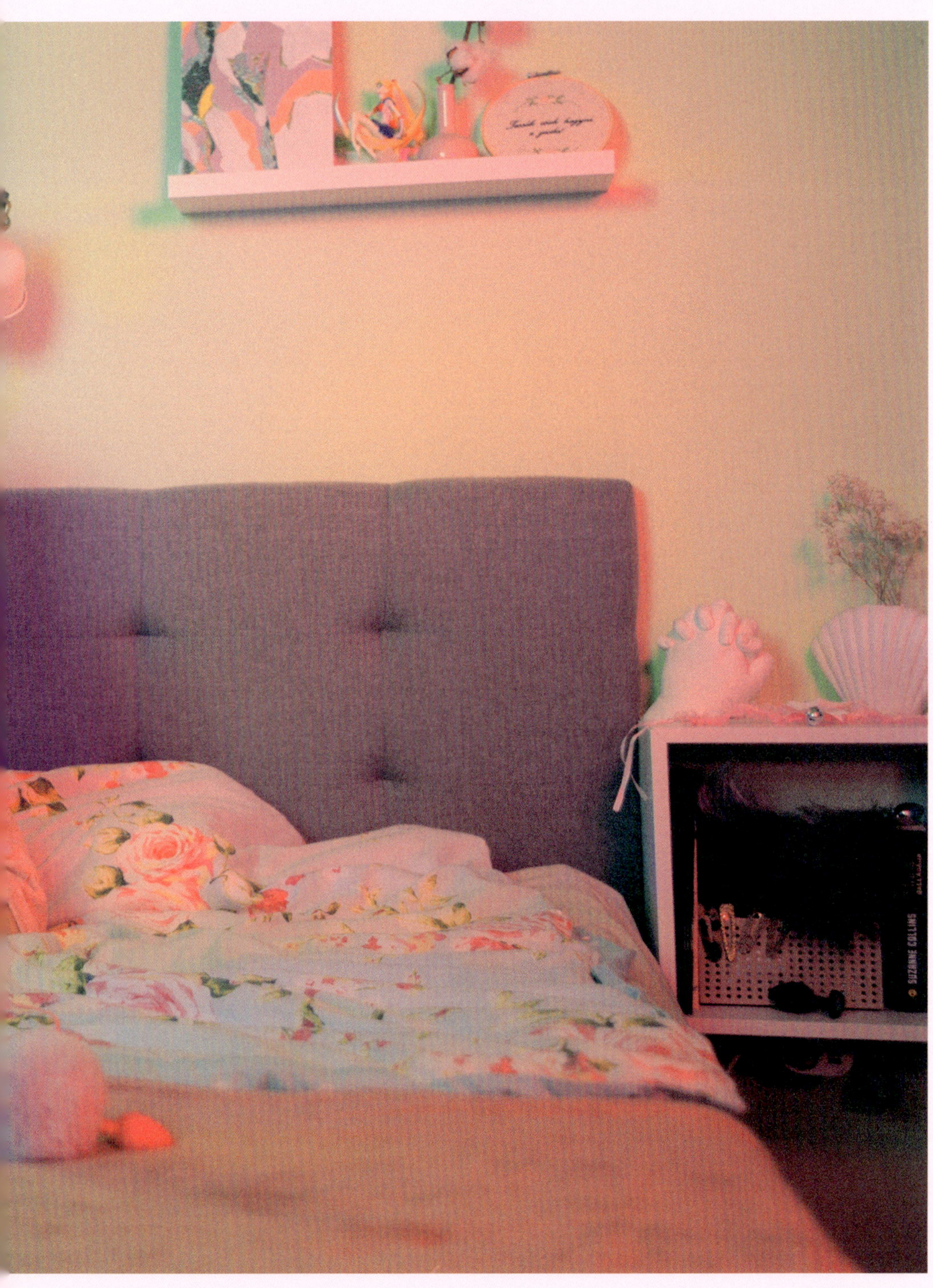

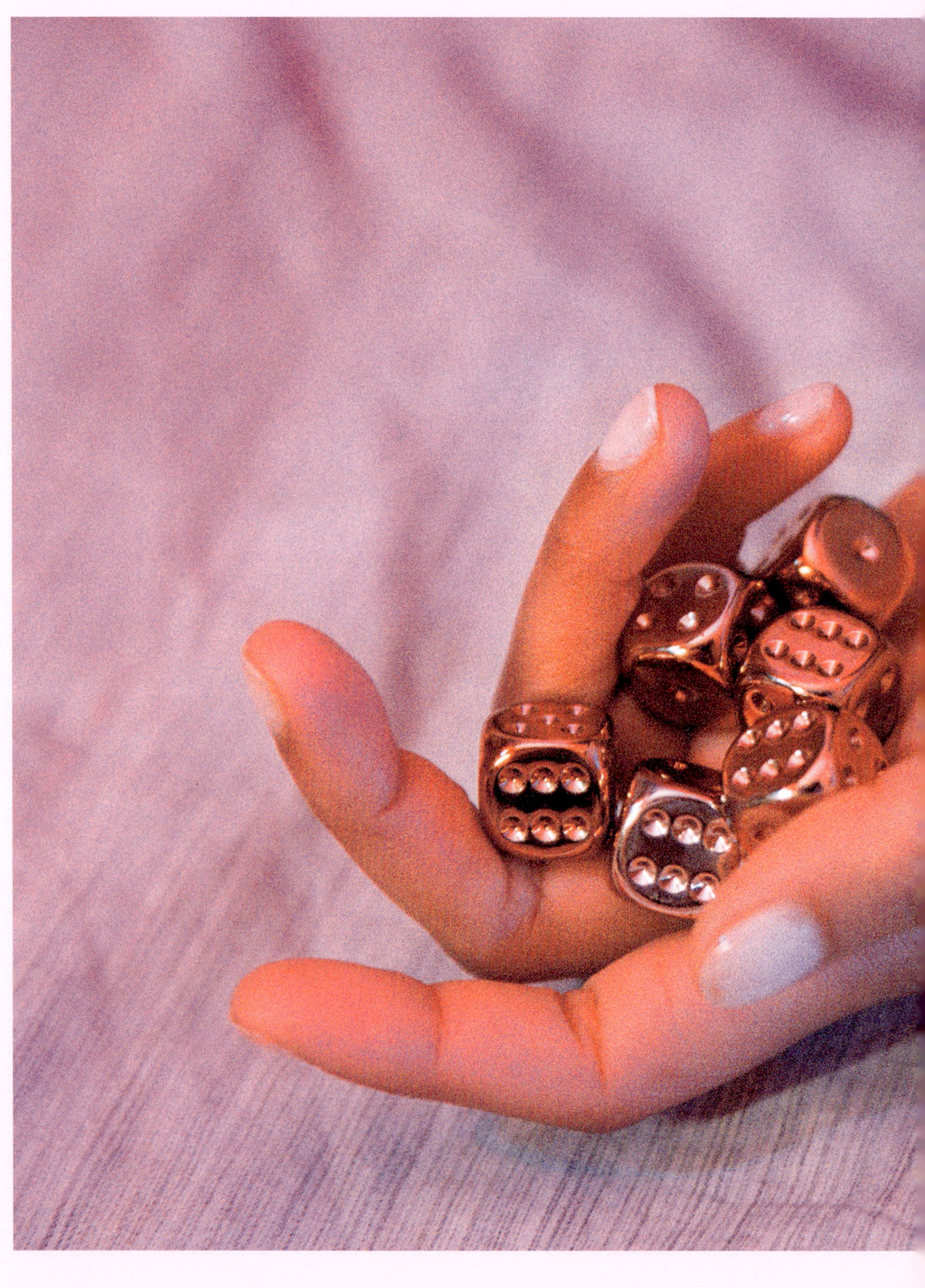

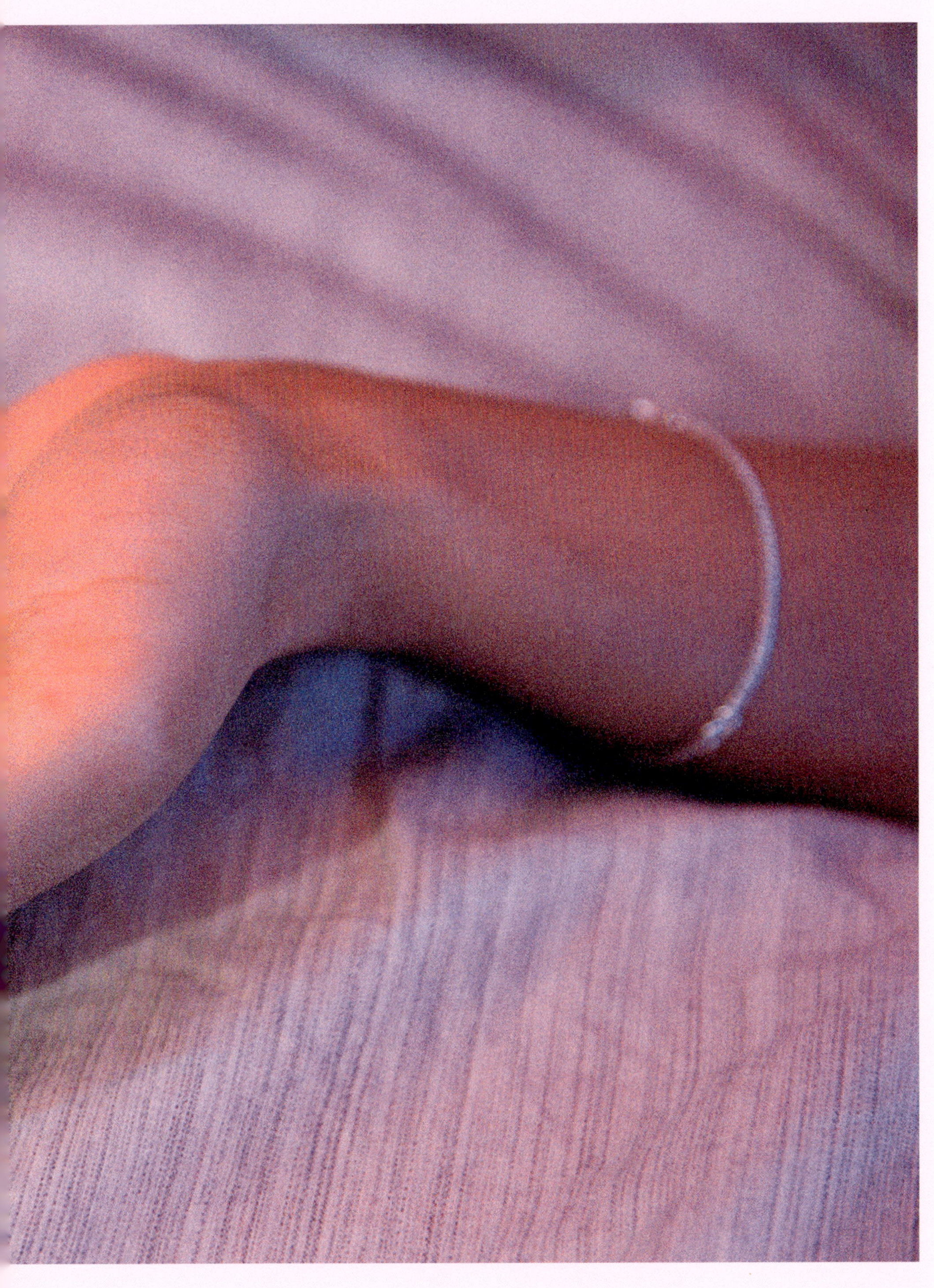

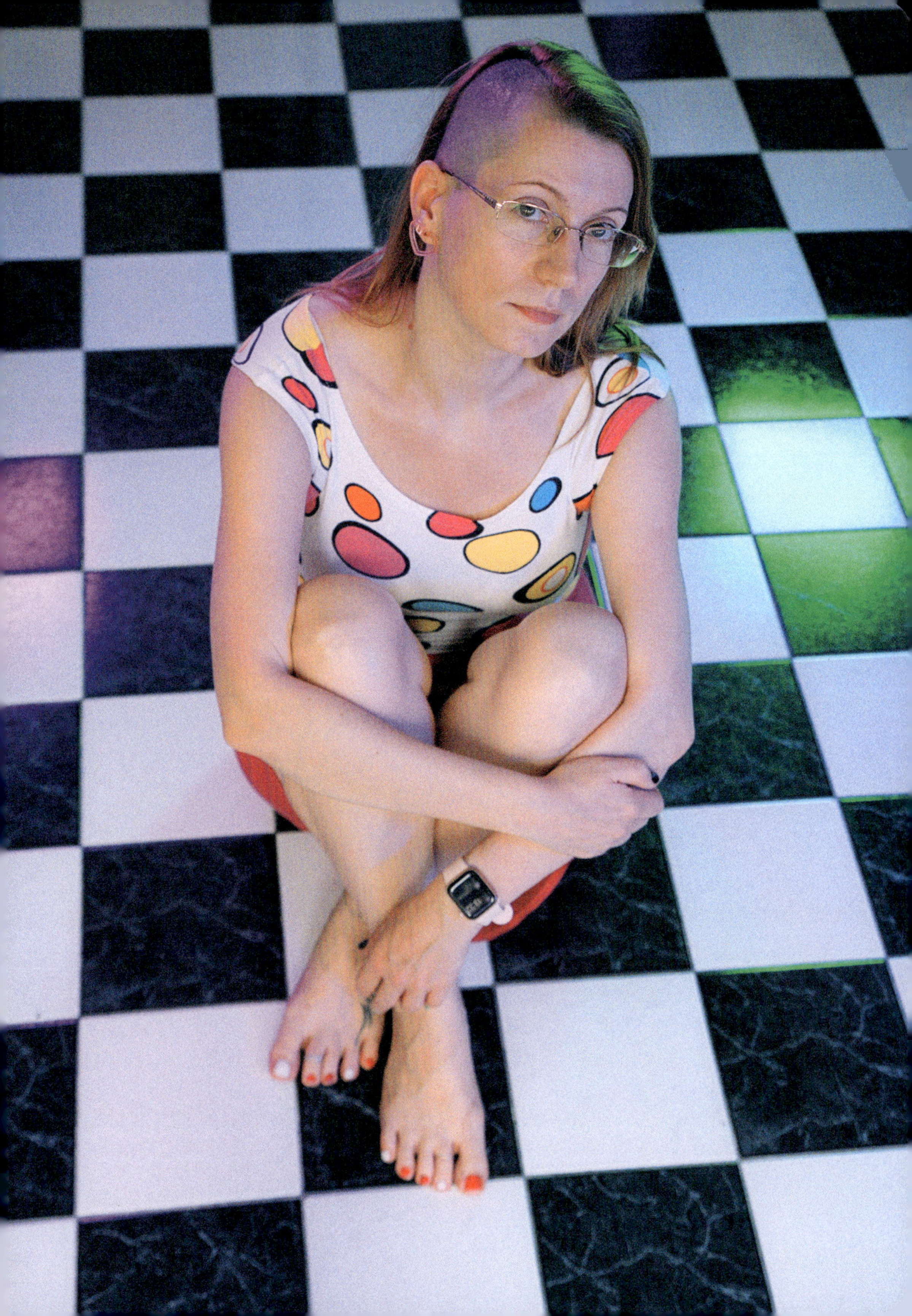

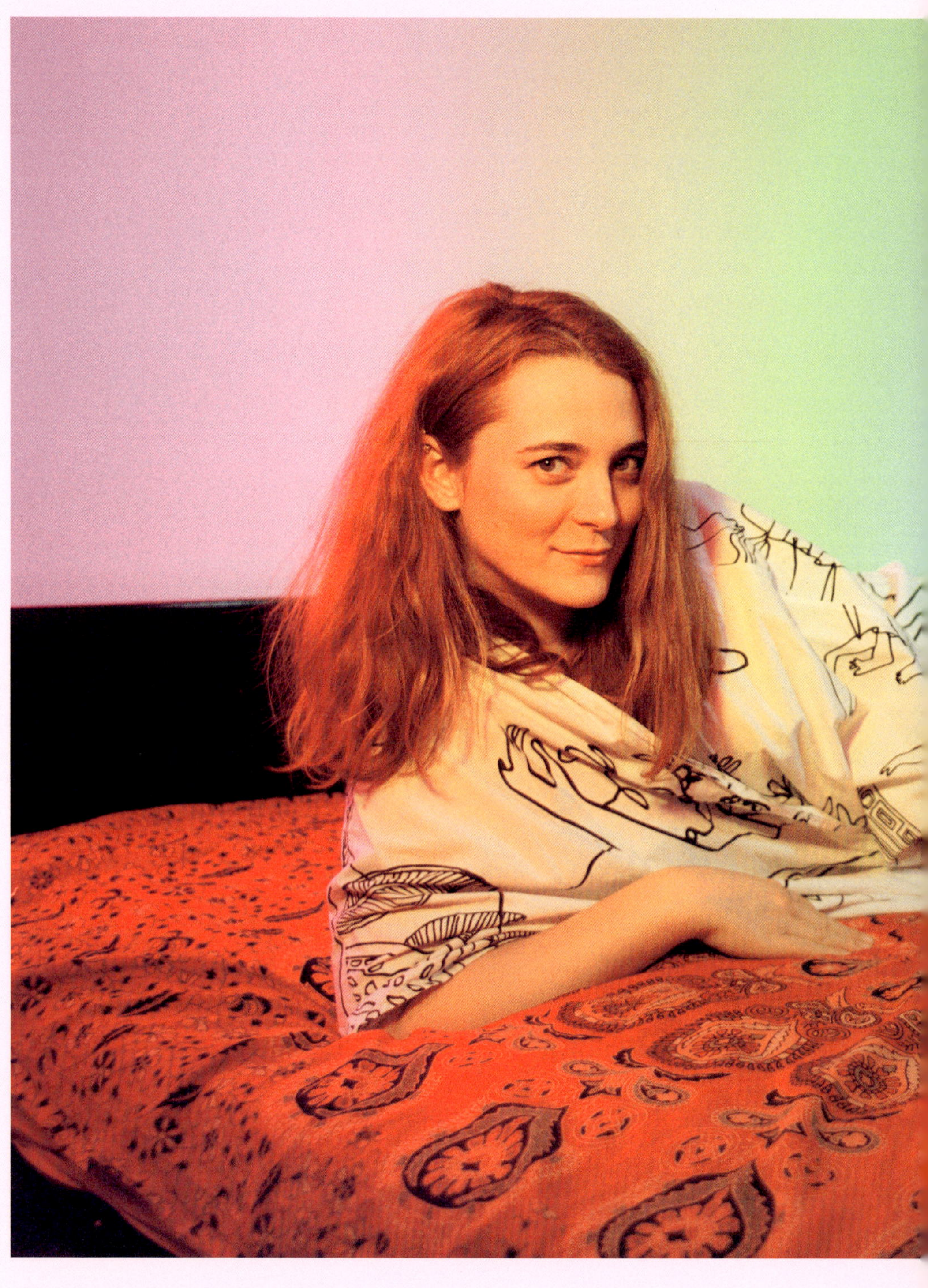

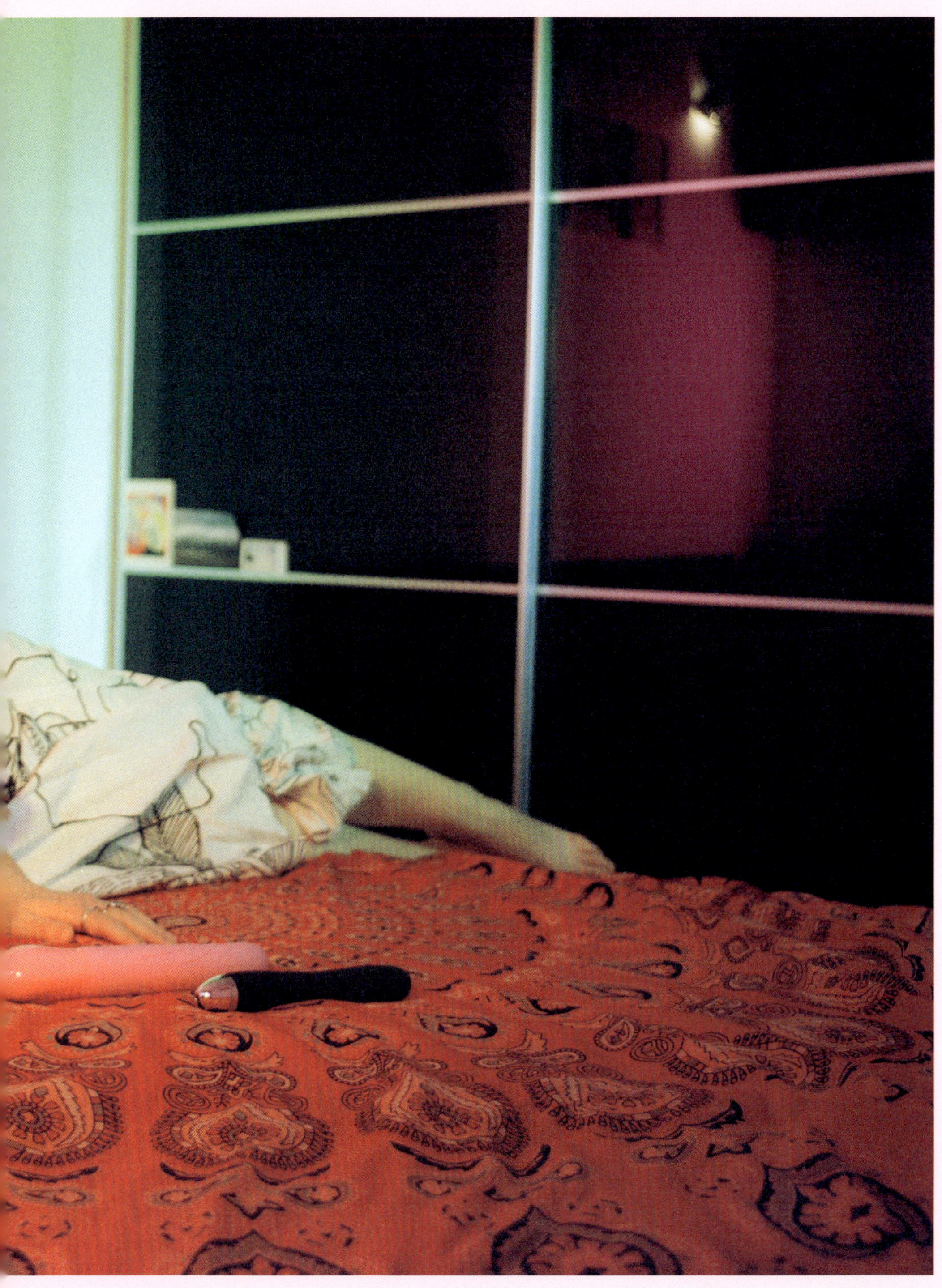

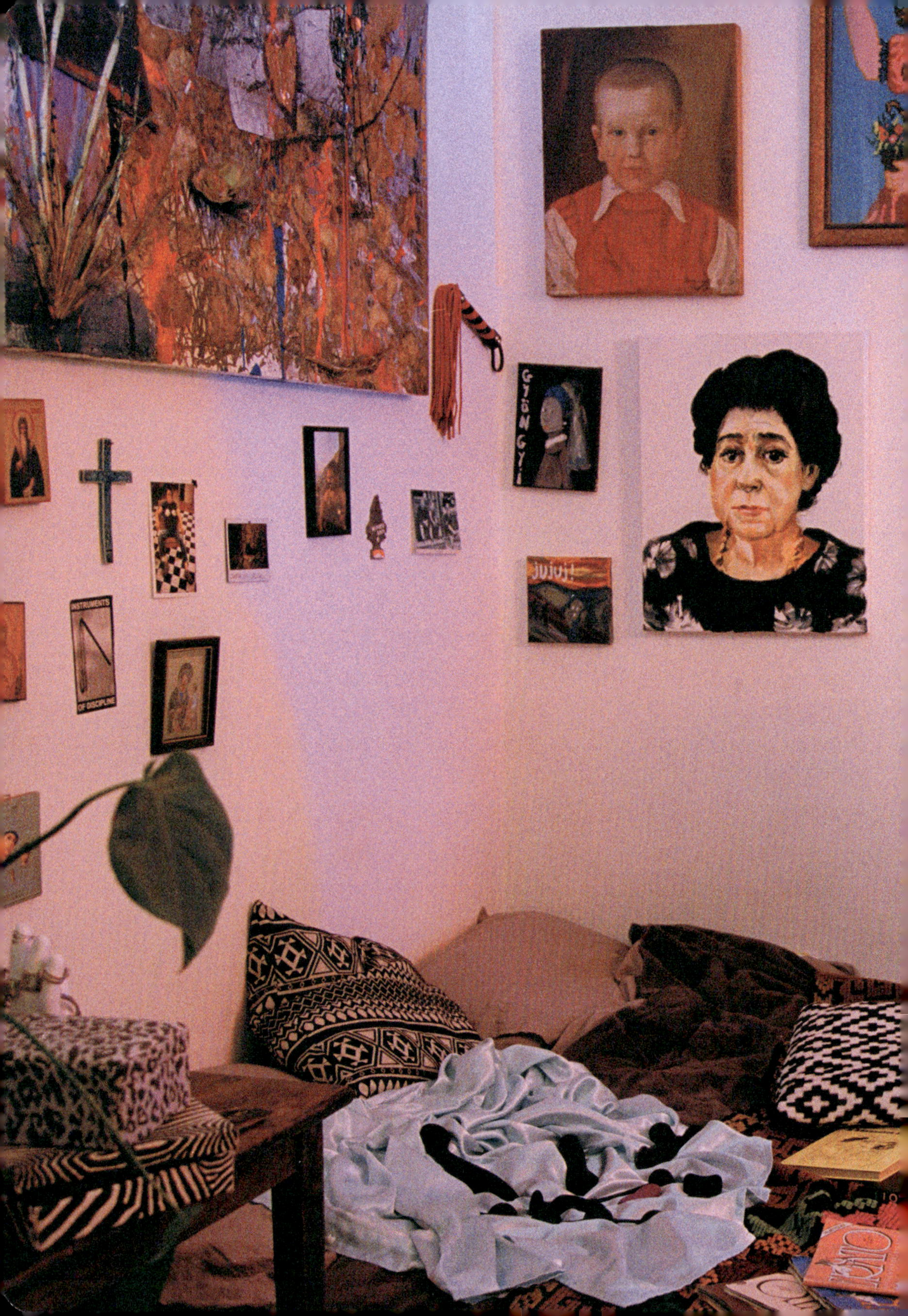
GYÖNGYI
INSTRUMENTS OF DISCIPLINE

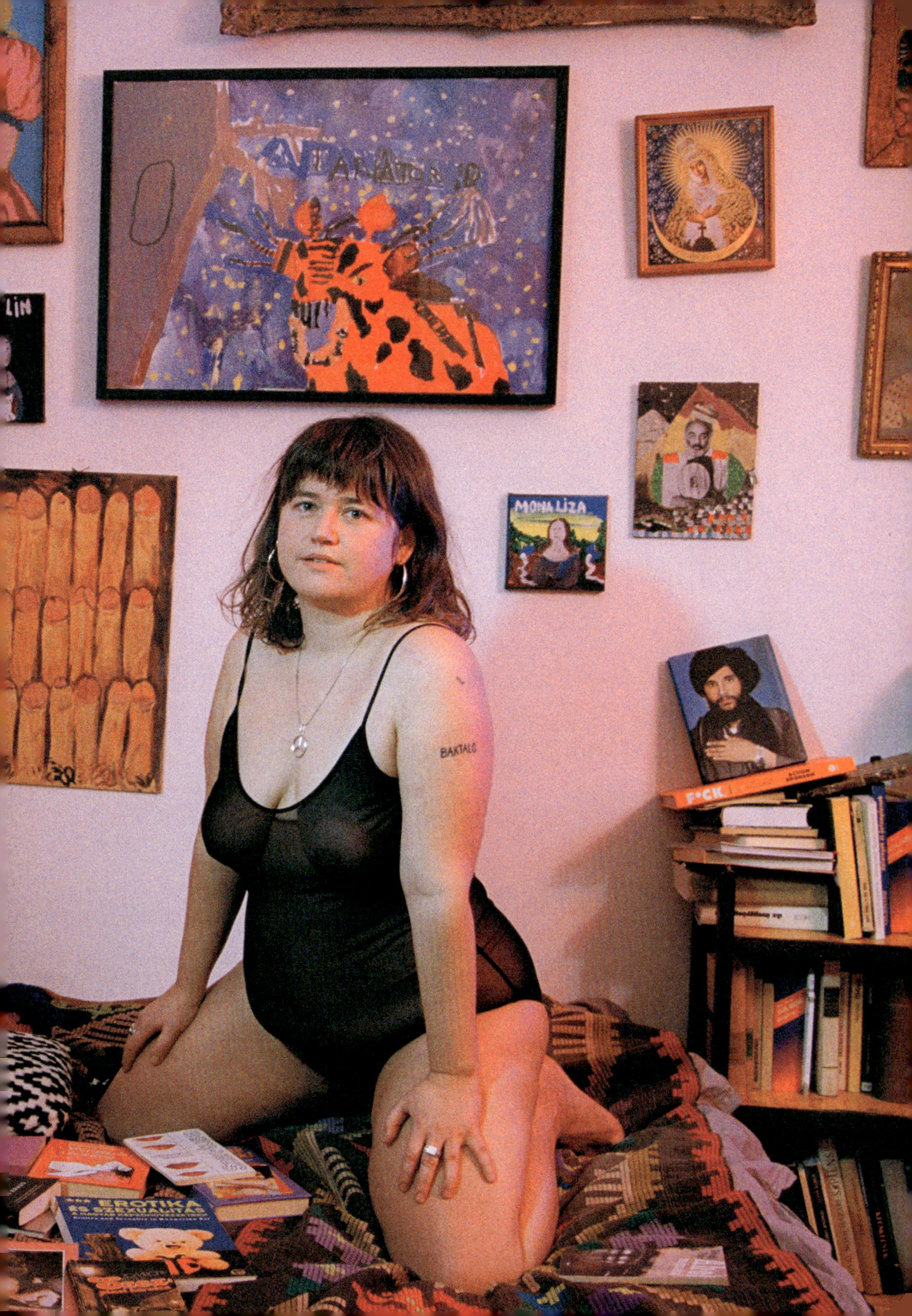

MONA LIZA
BAKTALO
F*CK
EROTIKA ÉS SZEXUALITÁS

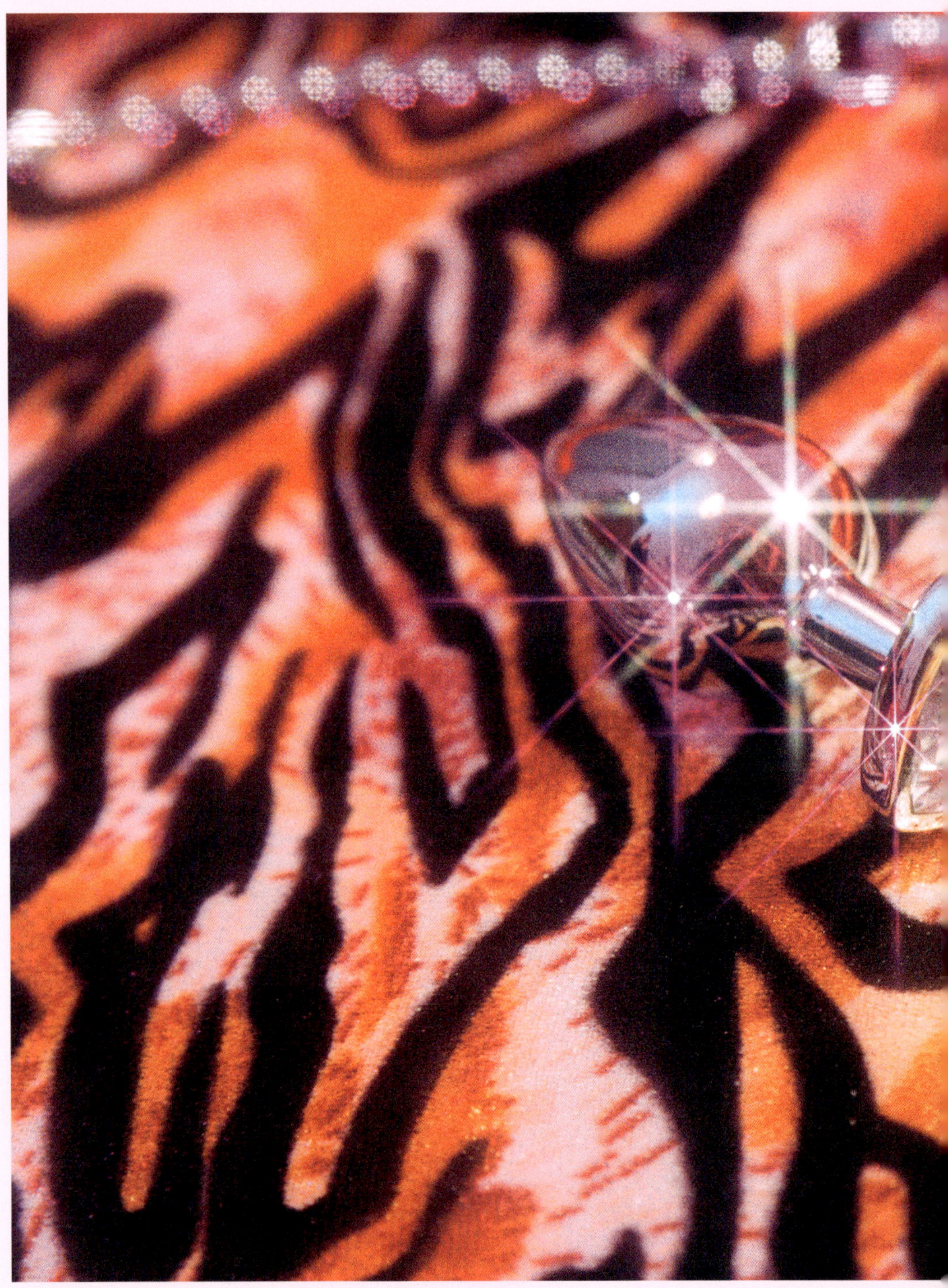

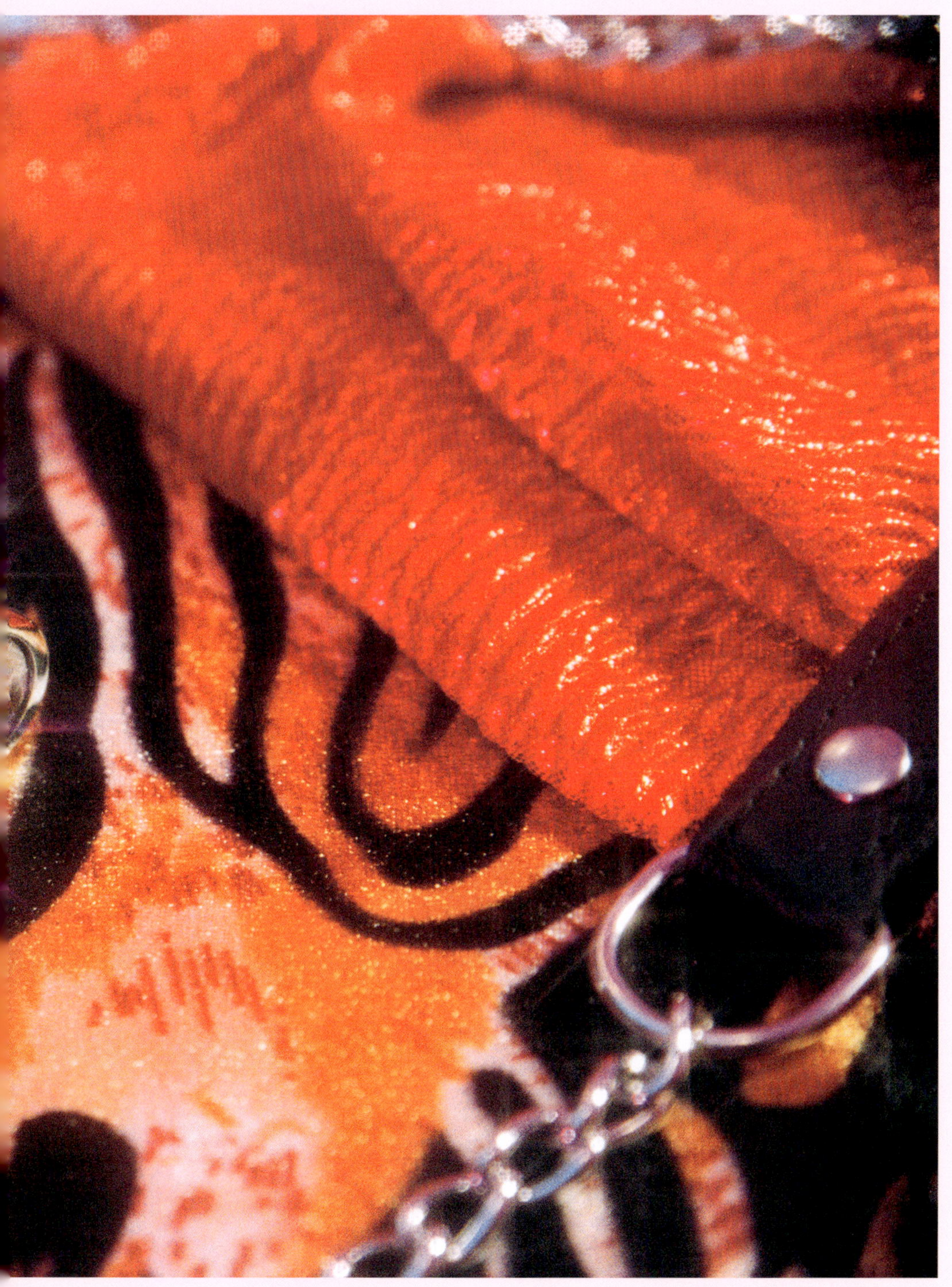

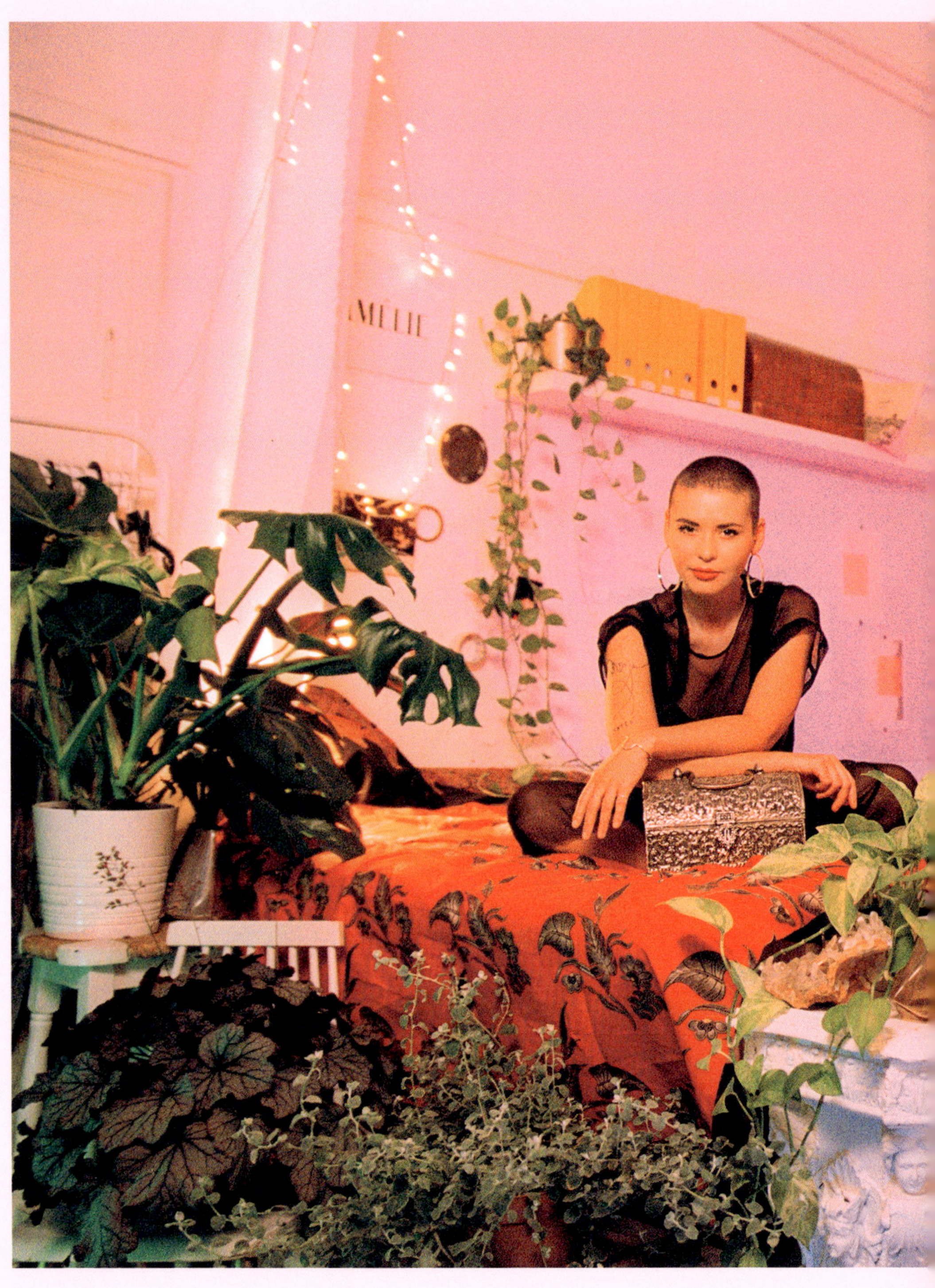
AMÉLIE

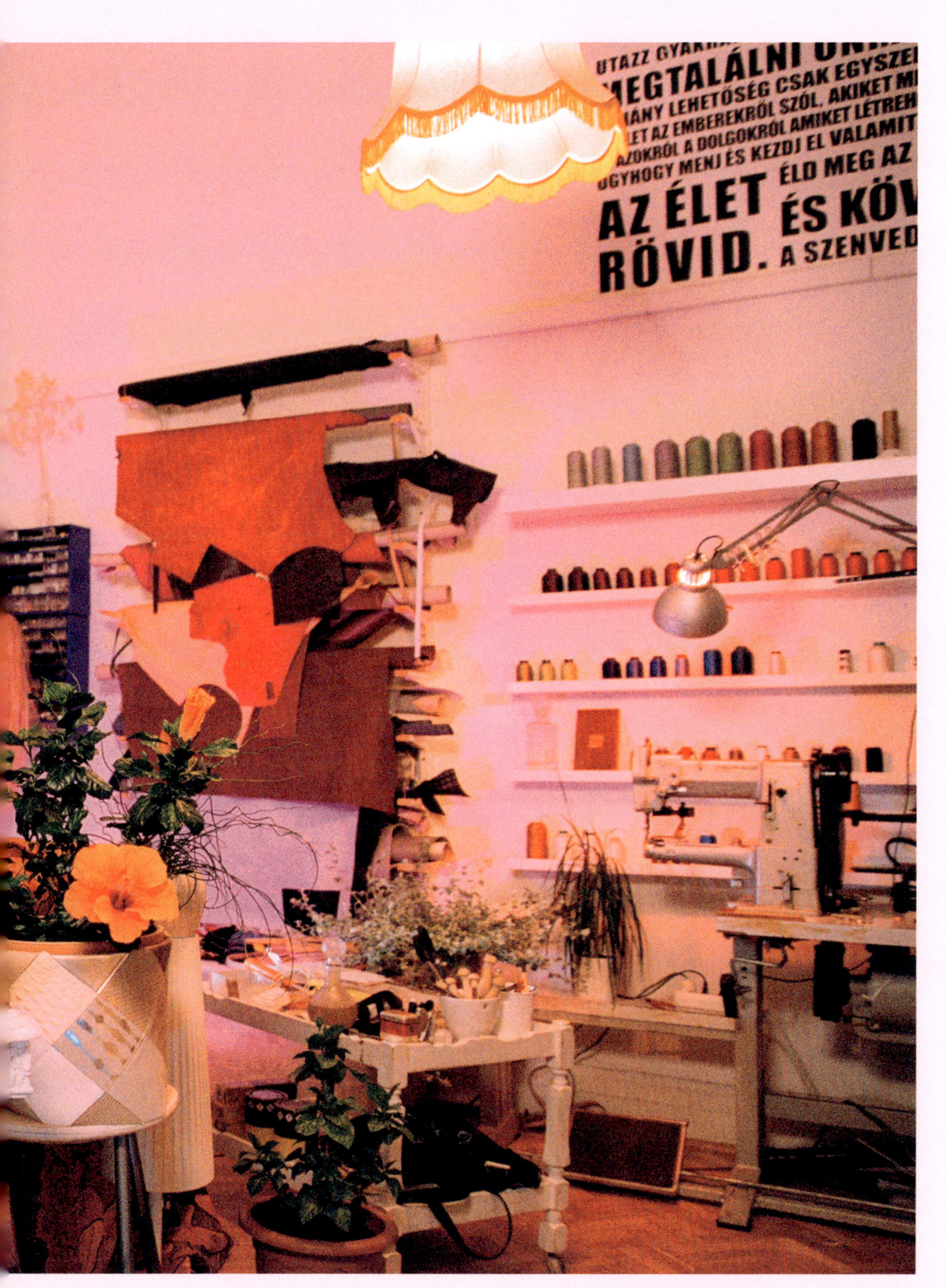
UTAZZ GYAKRA
MEGTALÁLNI ÖNM
IÁNY LEHETŐSÉG CSAK EGYSZER
ÉLET AZ EMBEREKRŐL SZÓL, AKIKET MI
AZOKRÓL A DOLGOKRÓL AMIKET LÉTREH
ÚGYHOGY MENJ ÉS KEZDJ EL VALAMIT
AZ ÉLET   ÉLD MEG AZ
RÖVID.   ÉS KÖV
A SZENVED

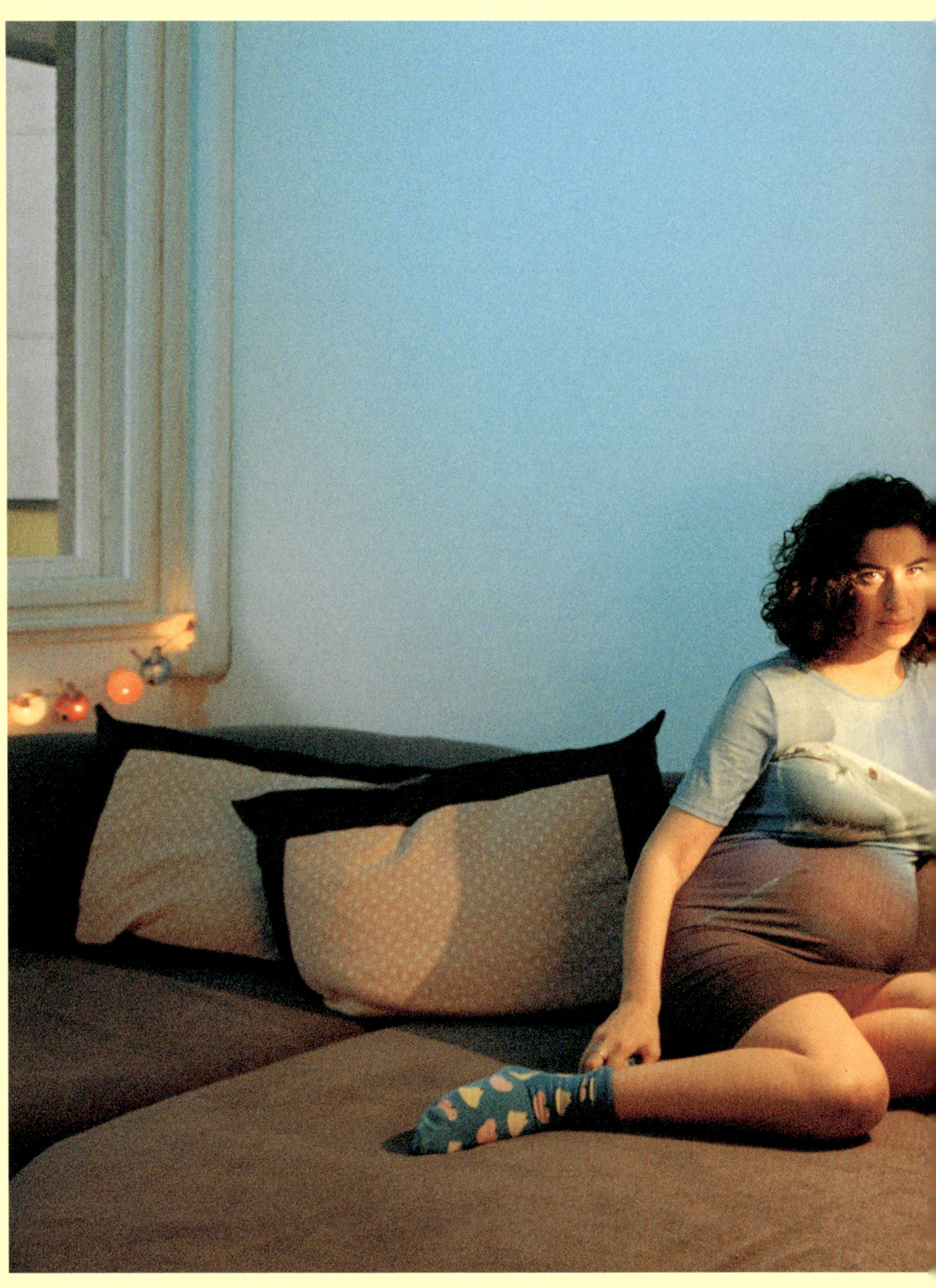

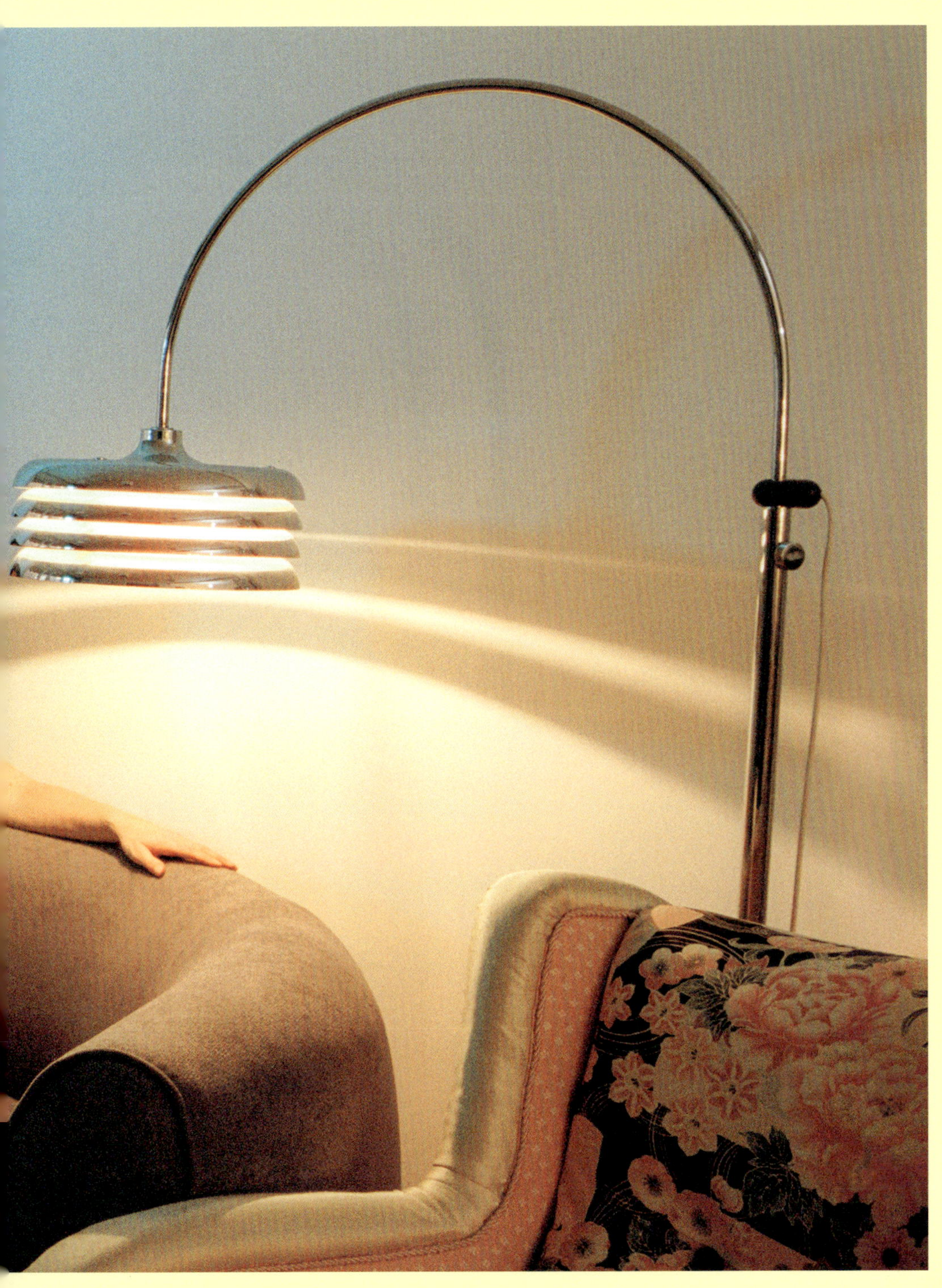

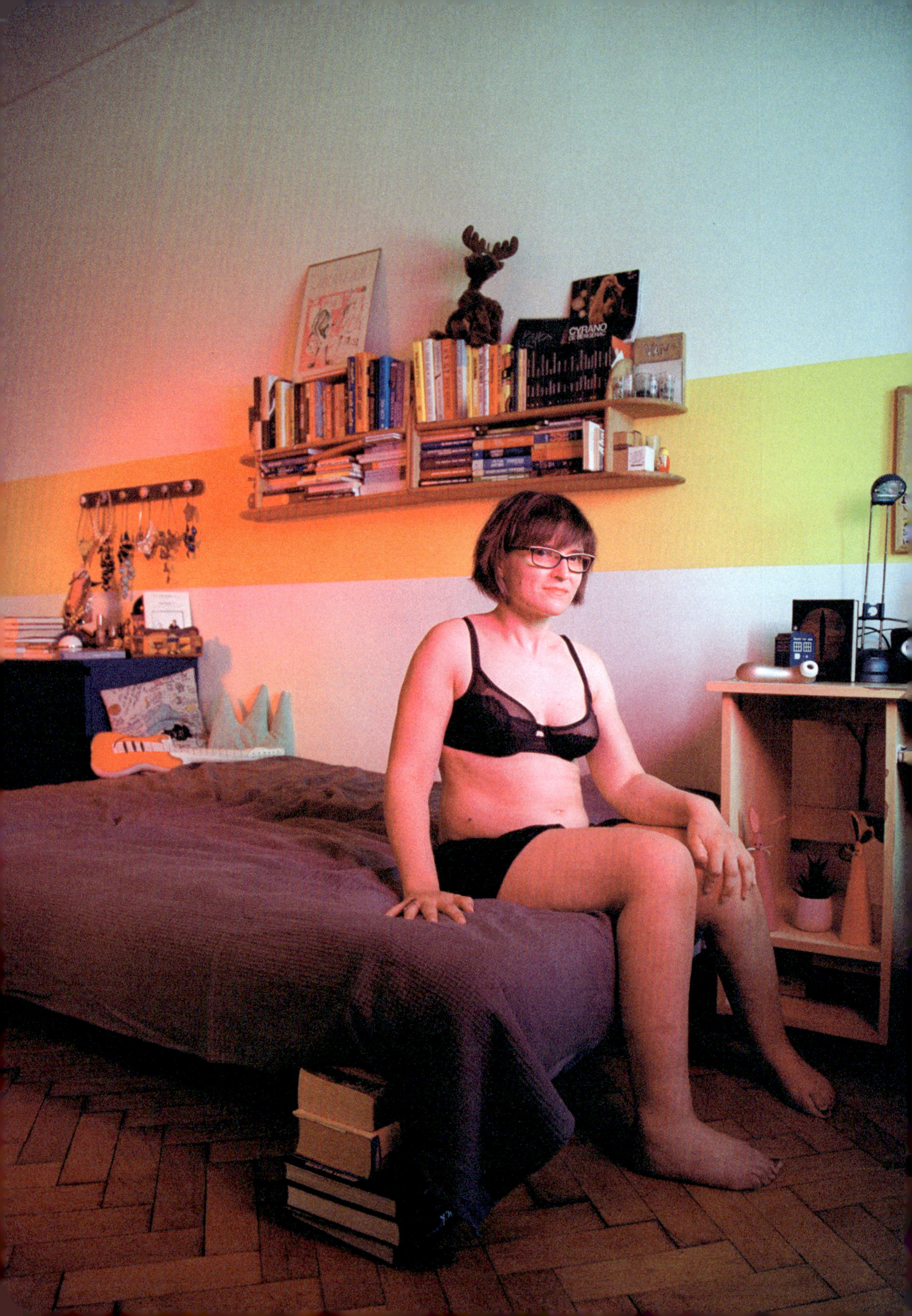

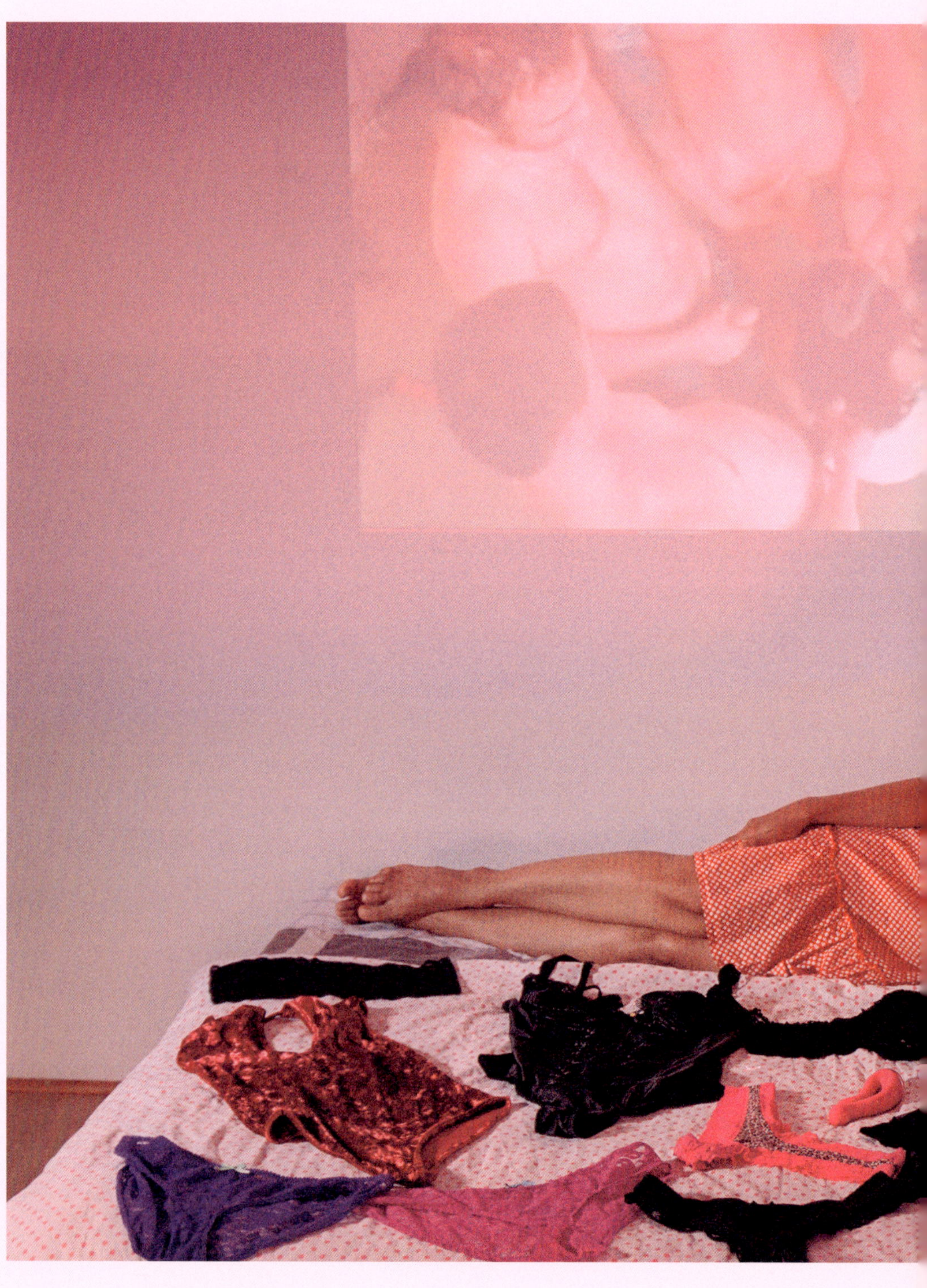

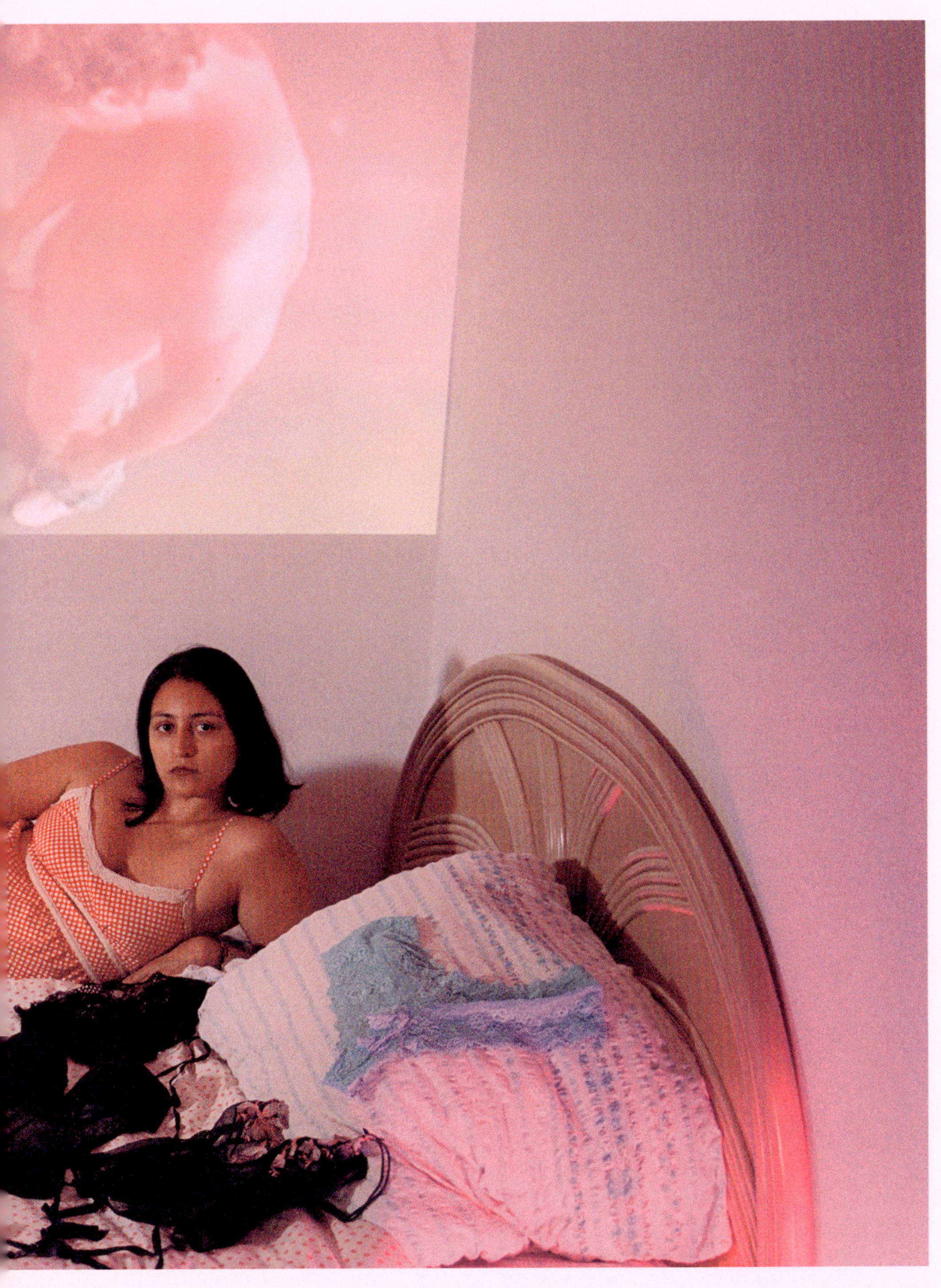

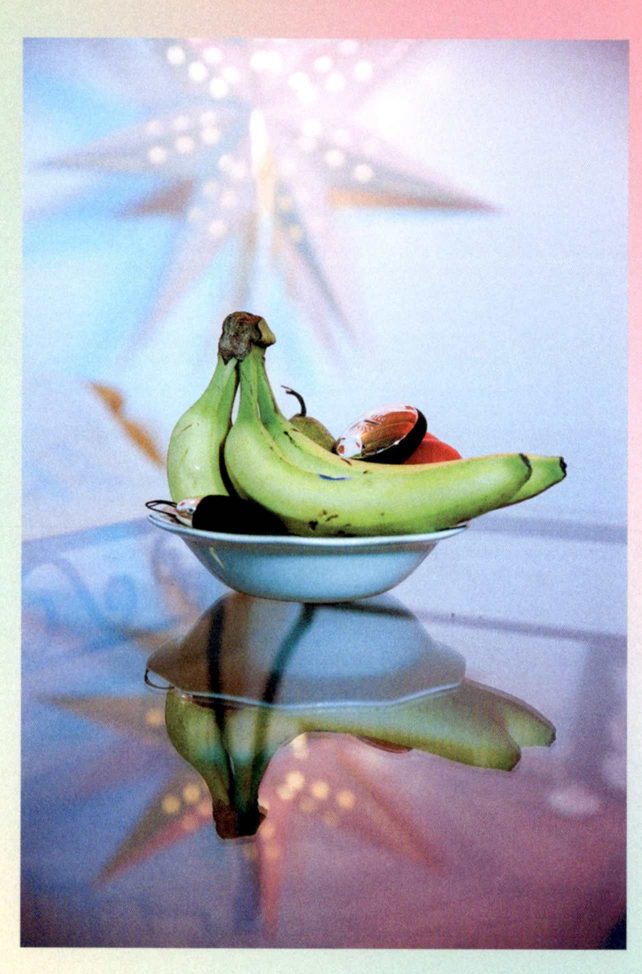

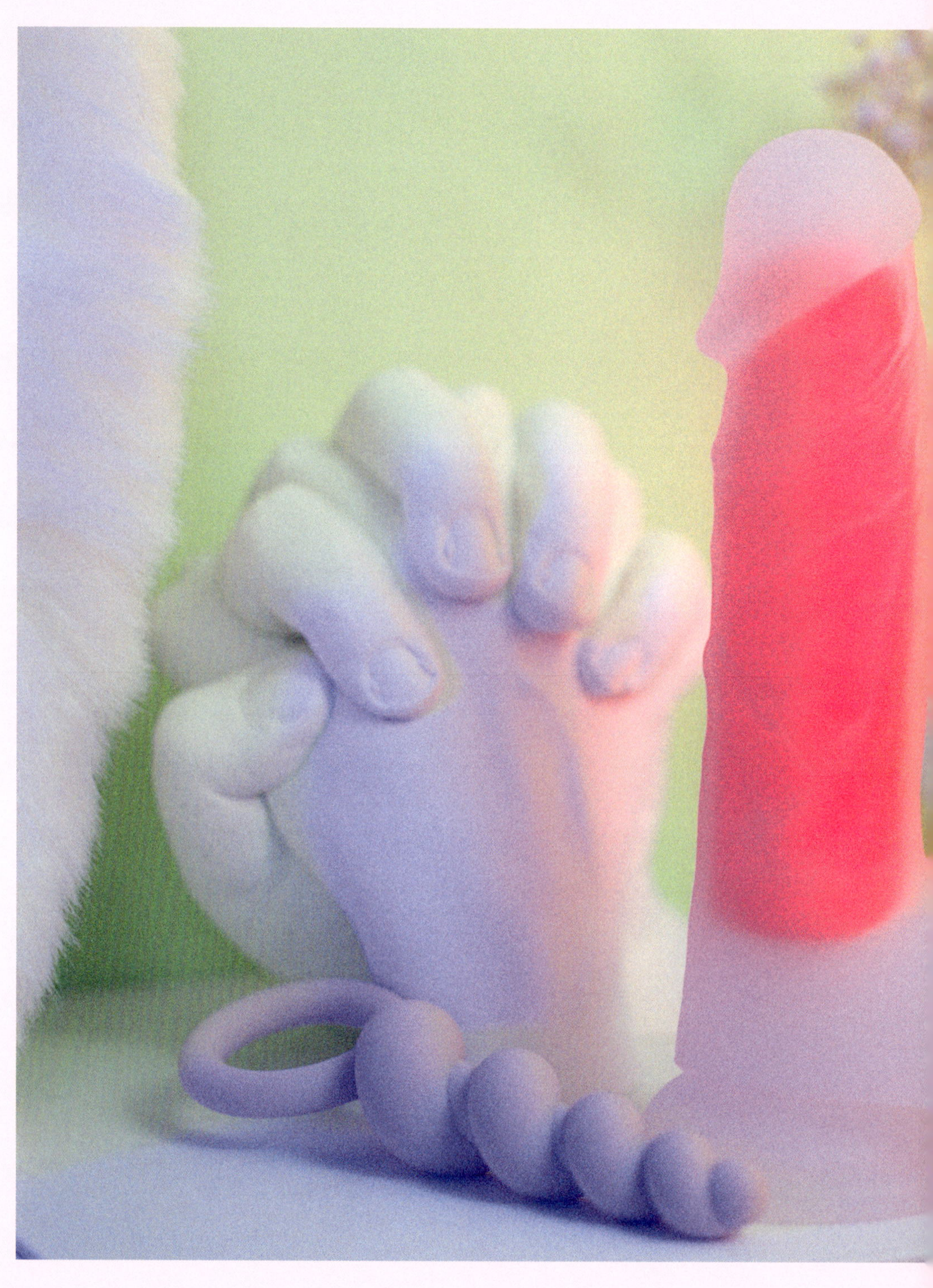

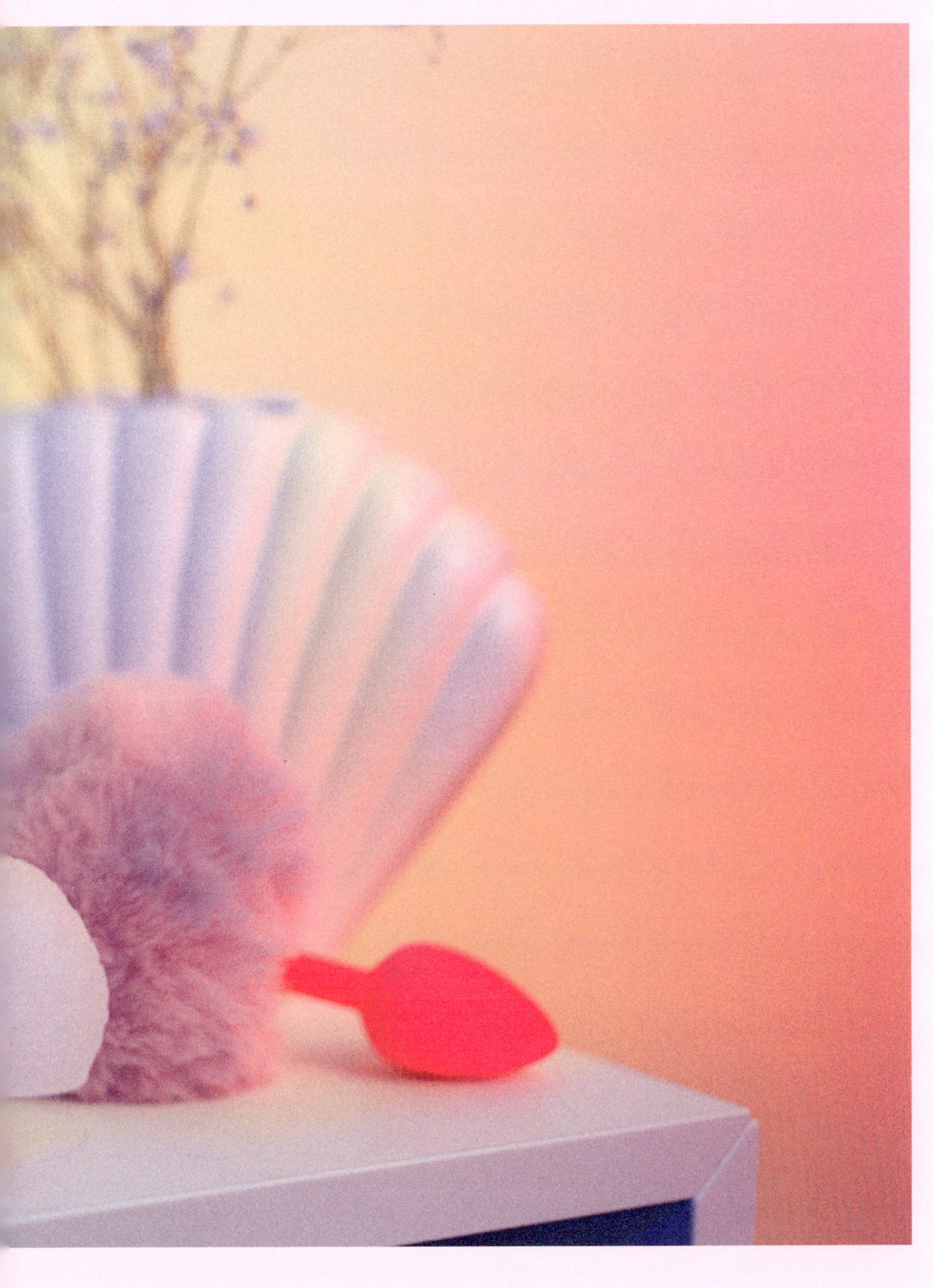

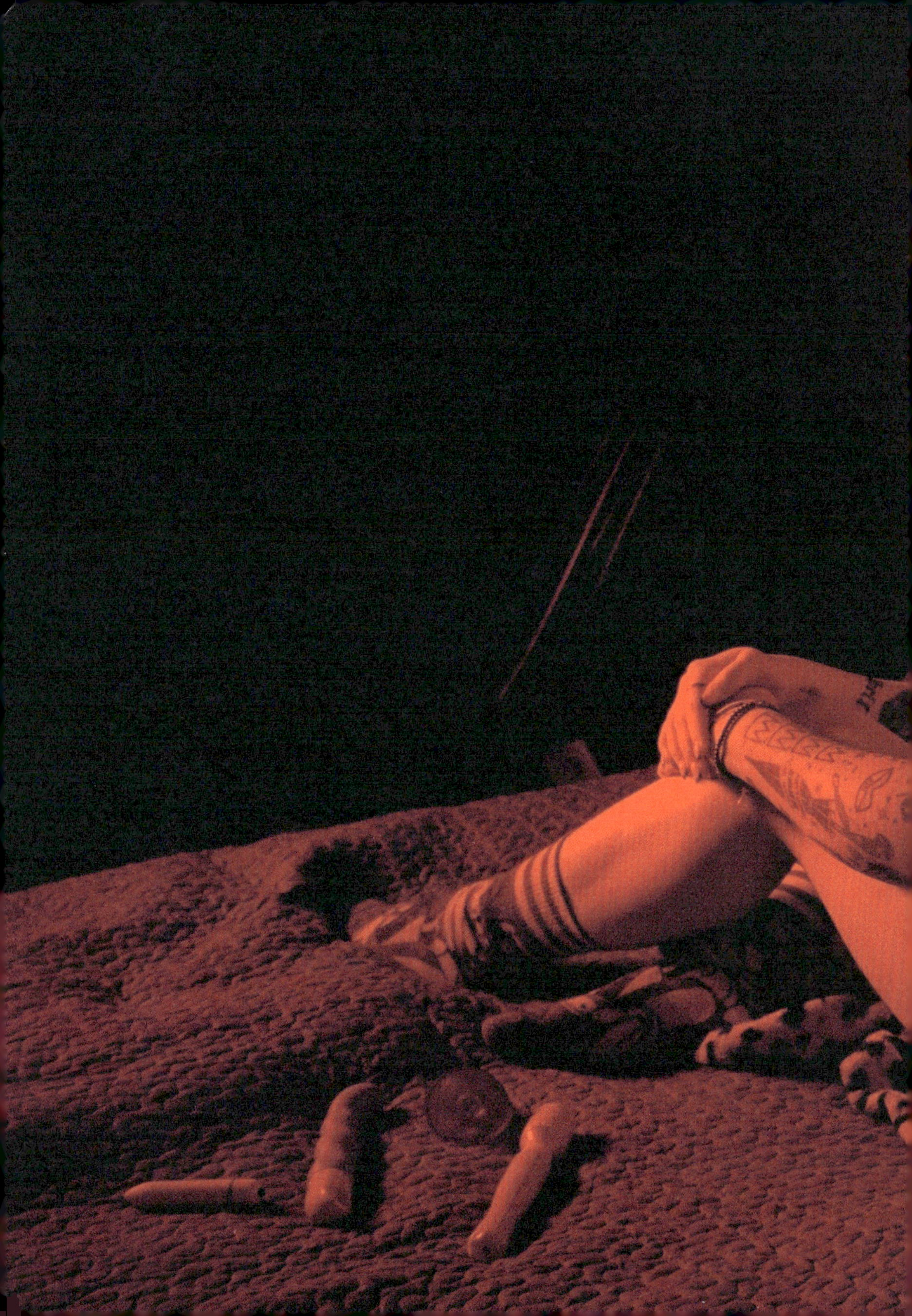

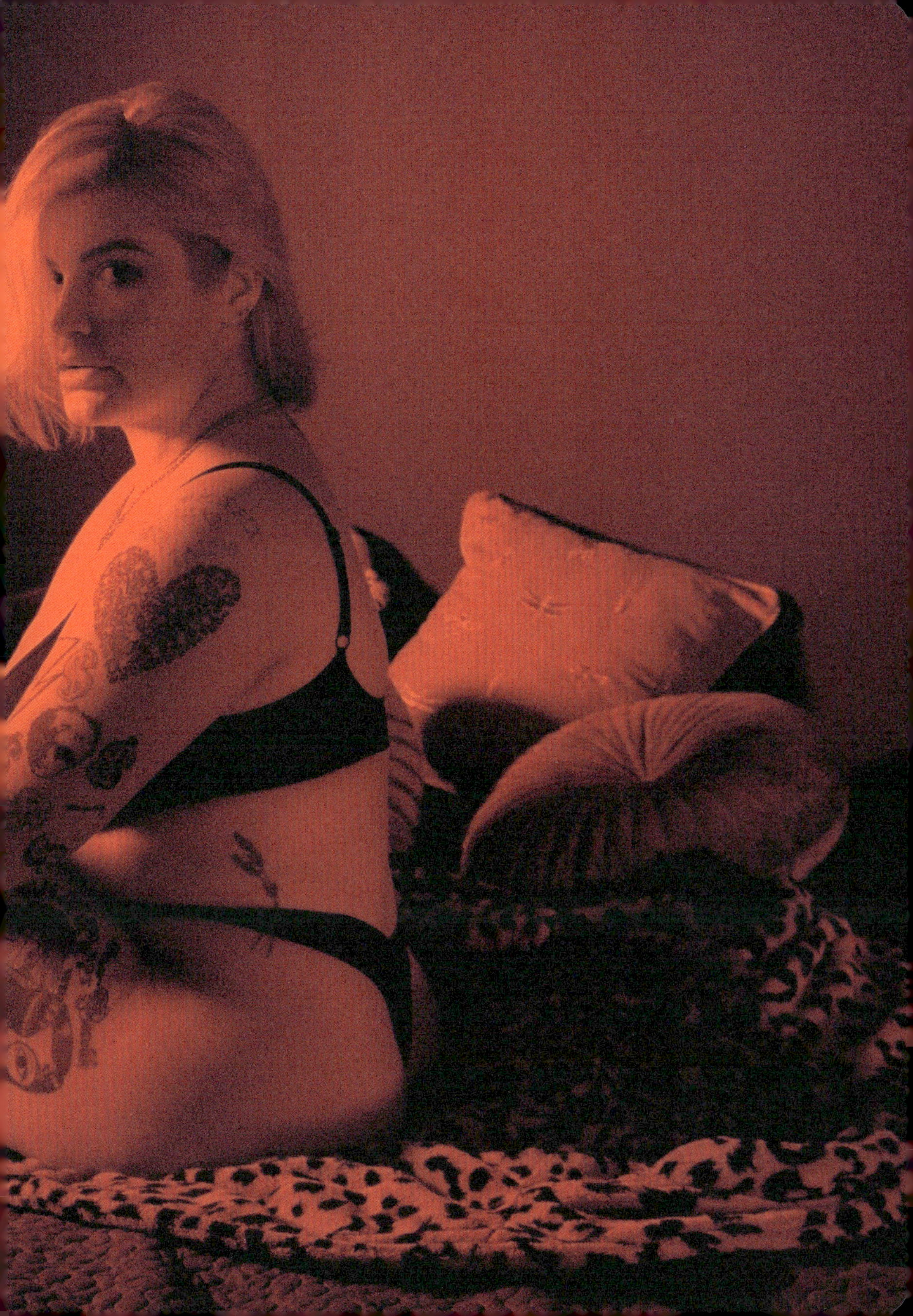

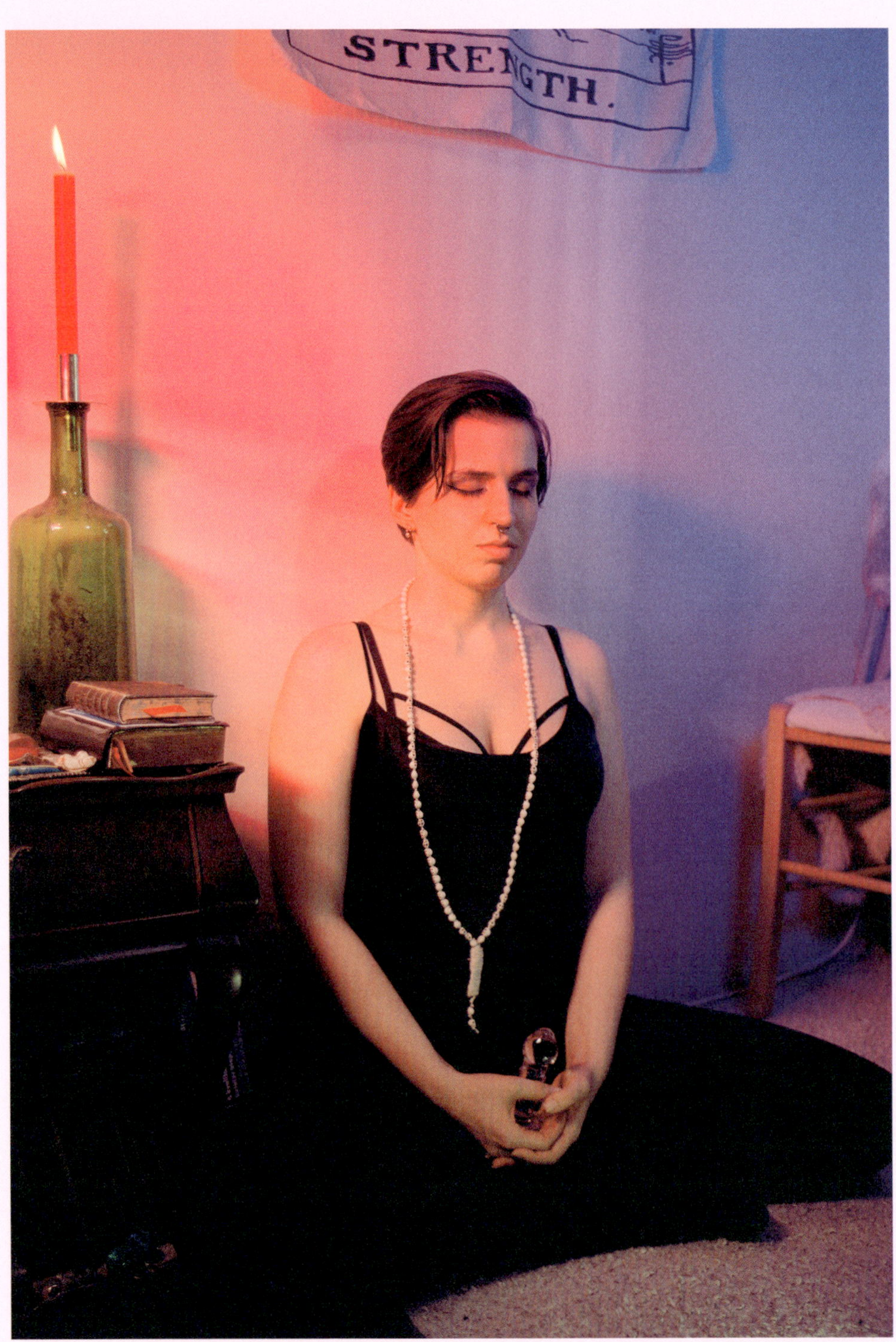

STRENGTH.
NGTH.

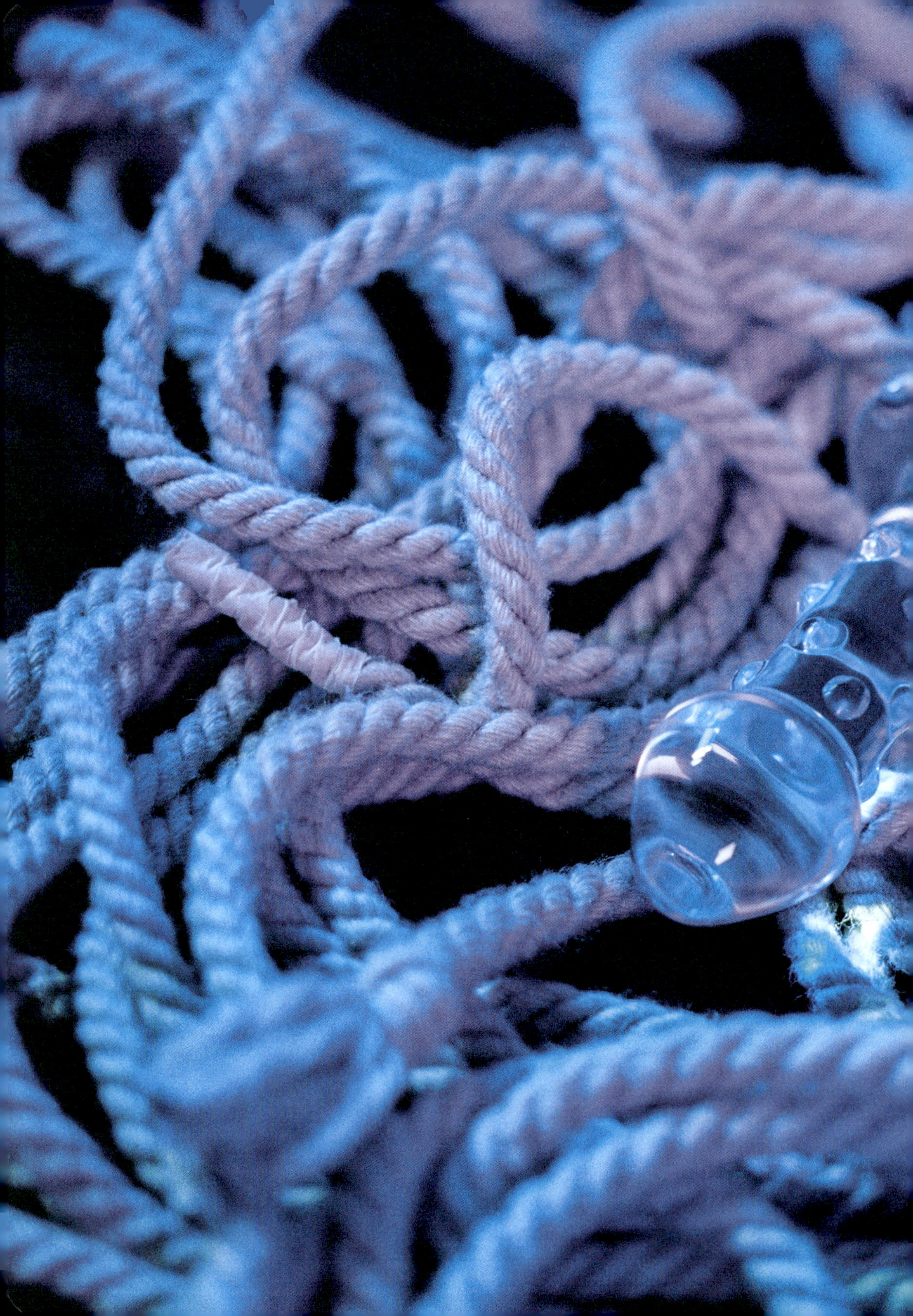

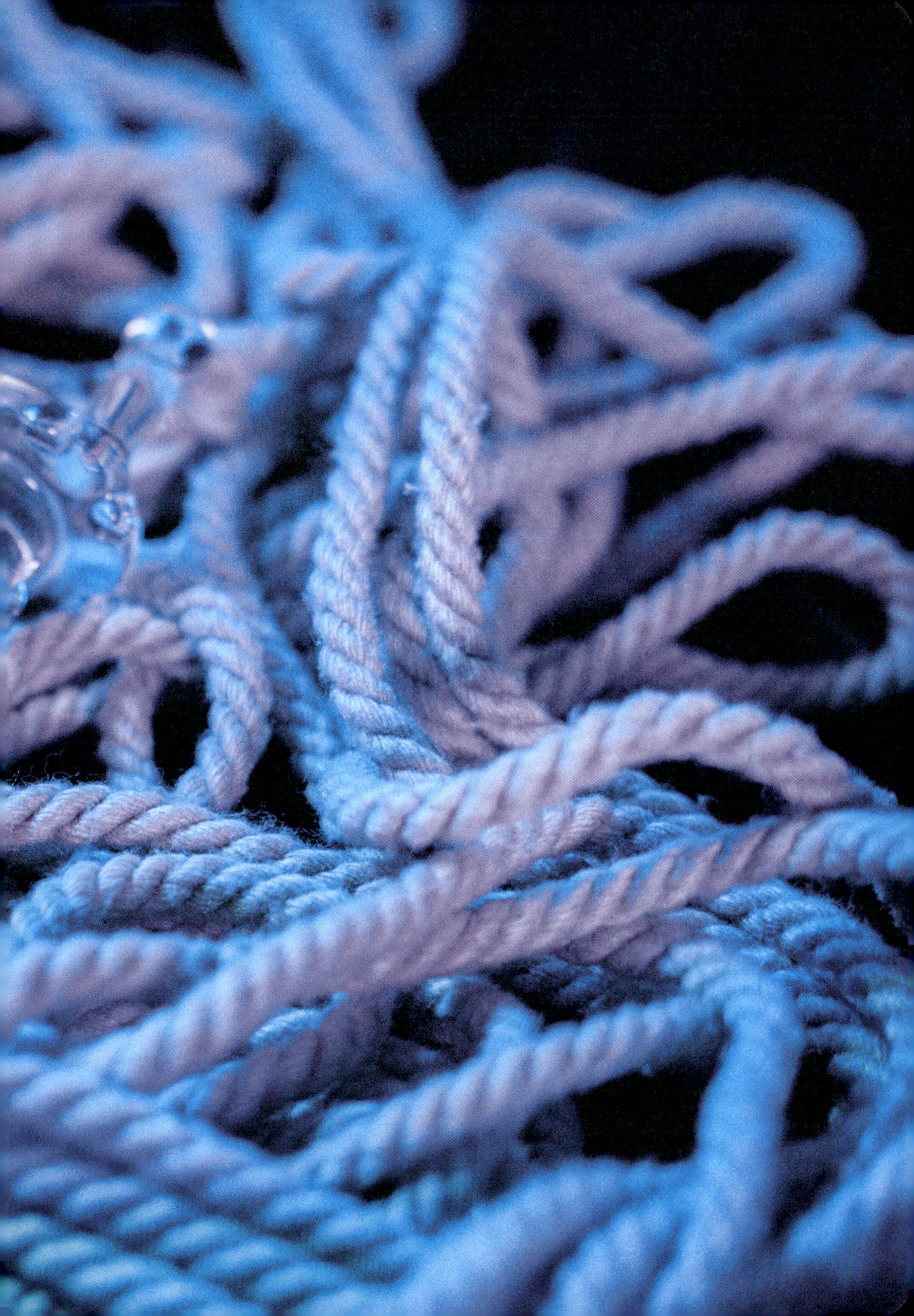

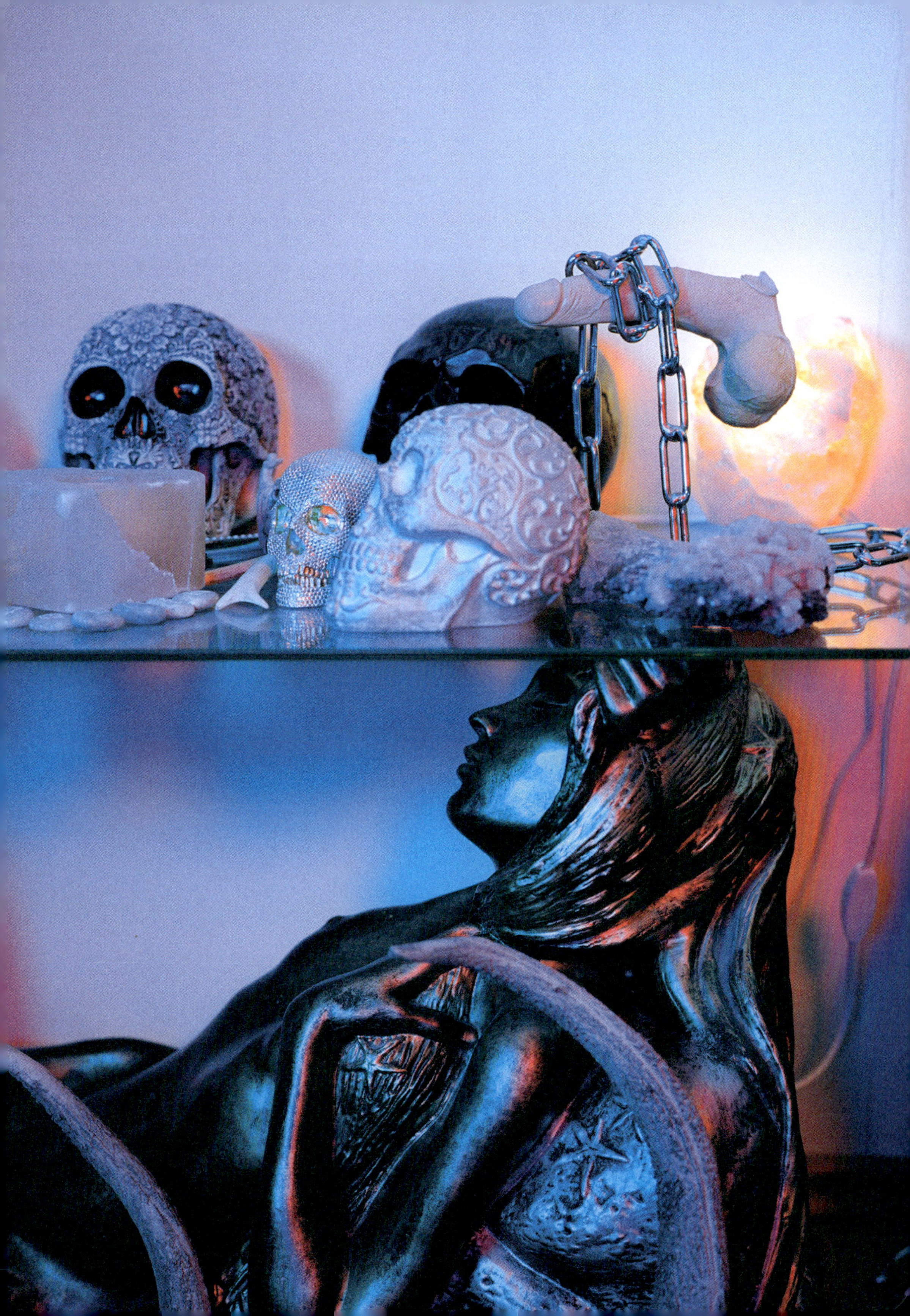

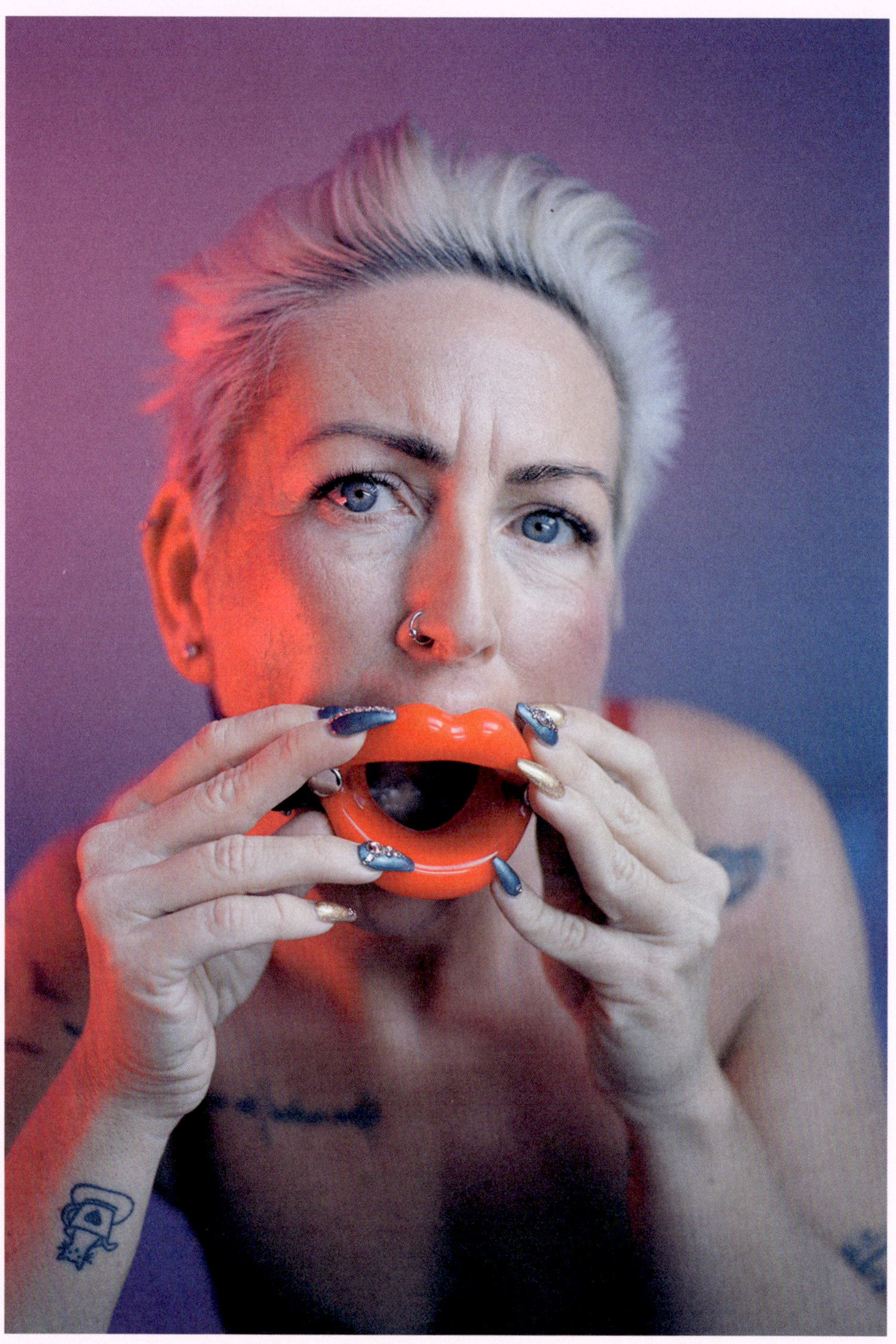

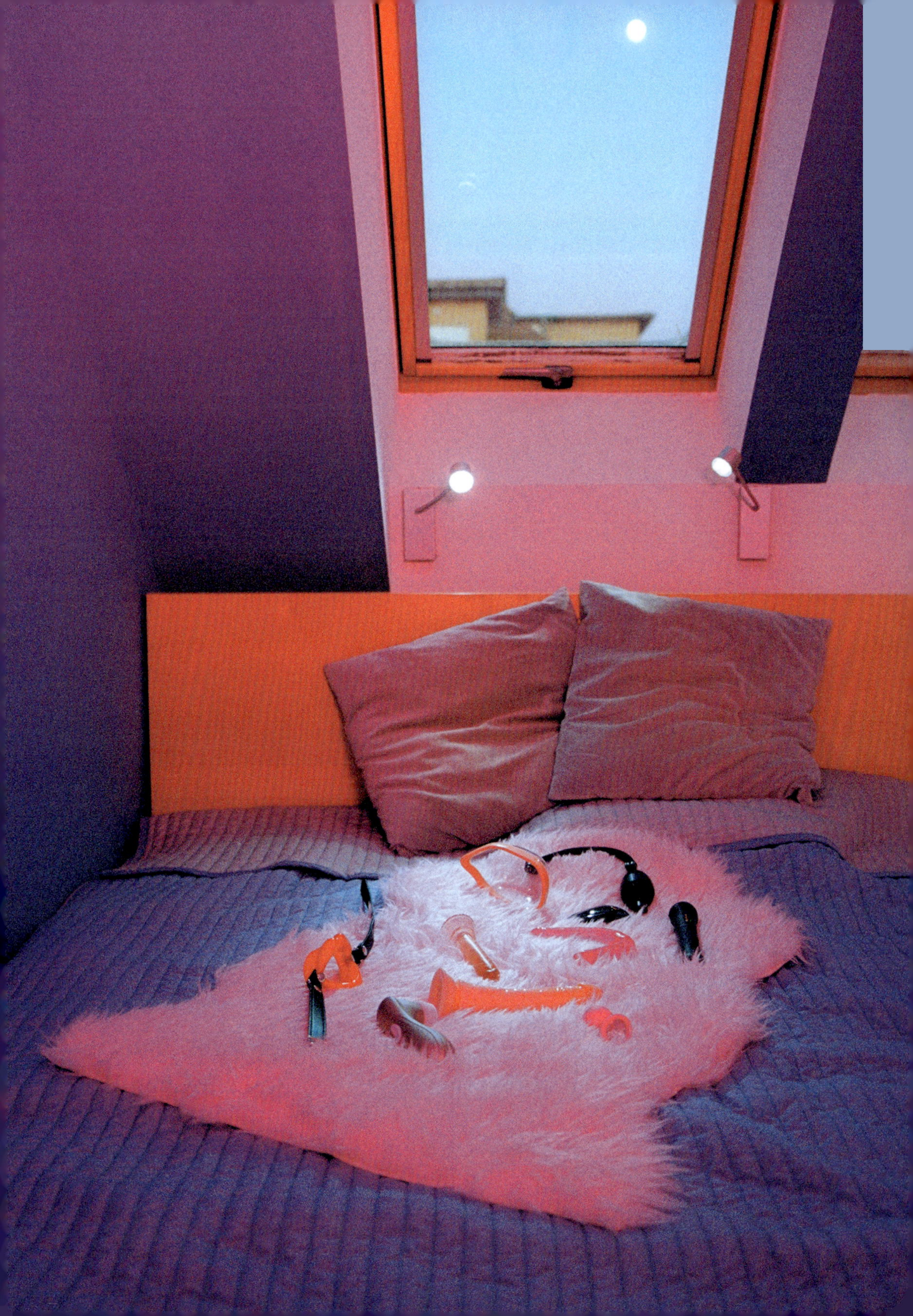

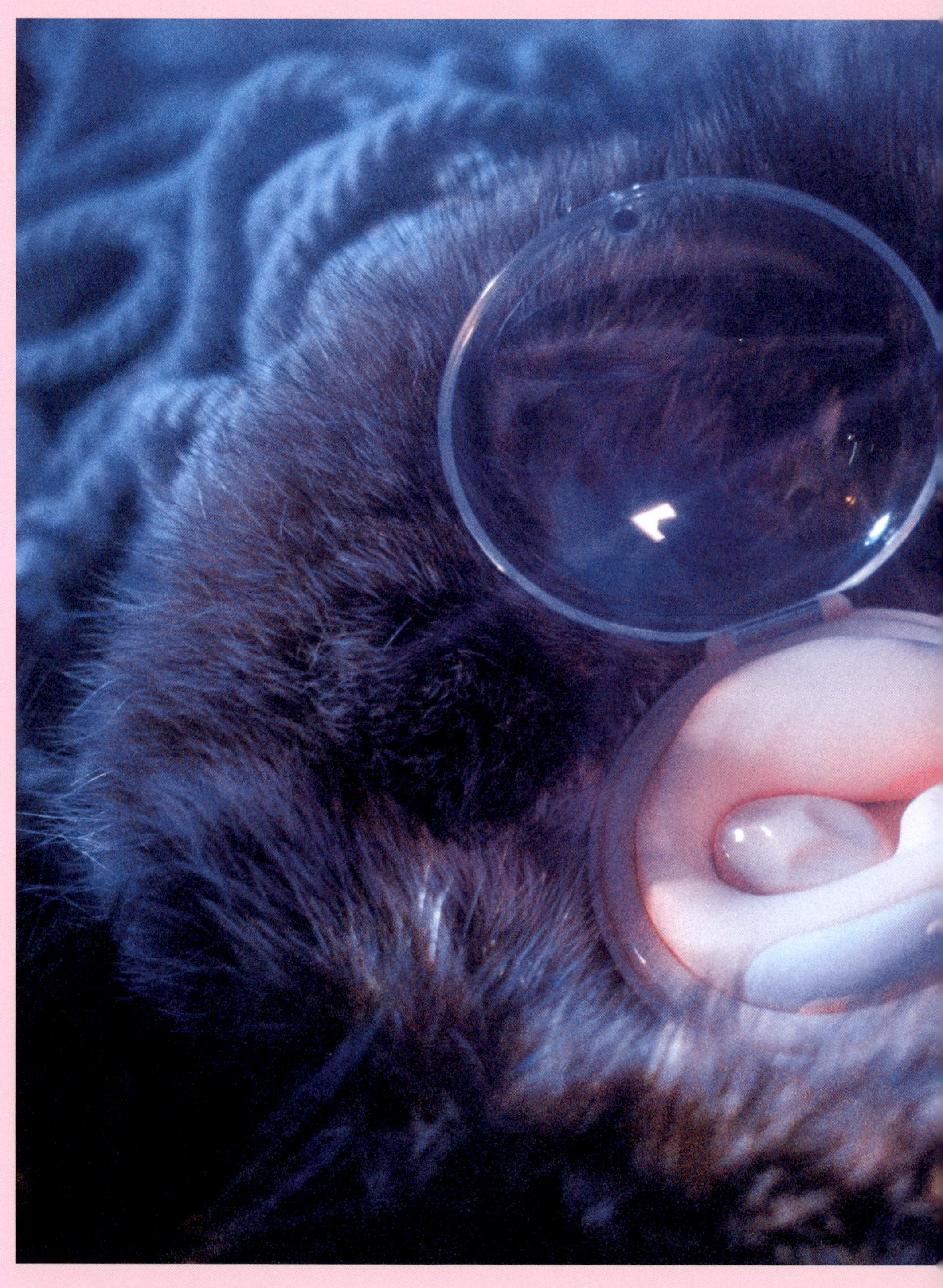

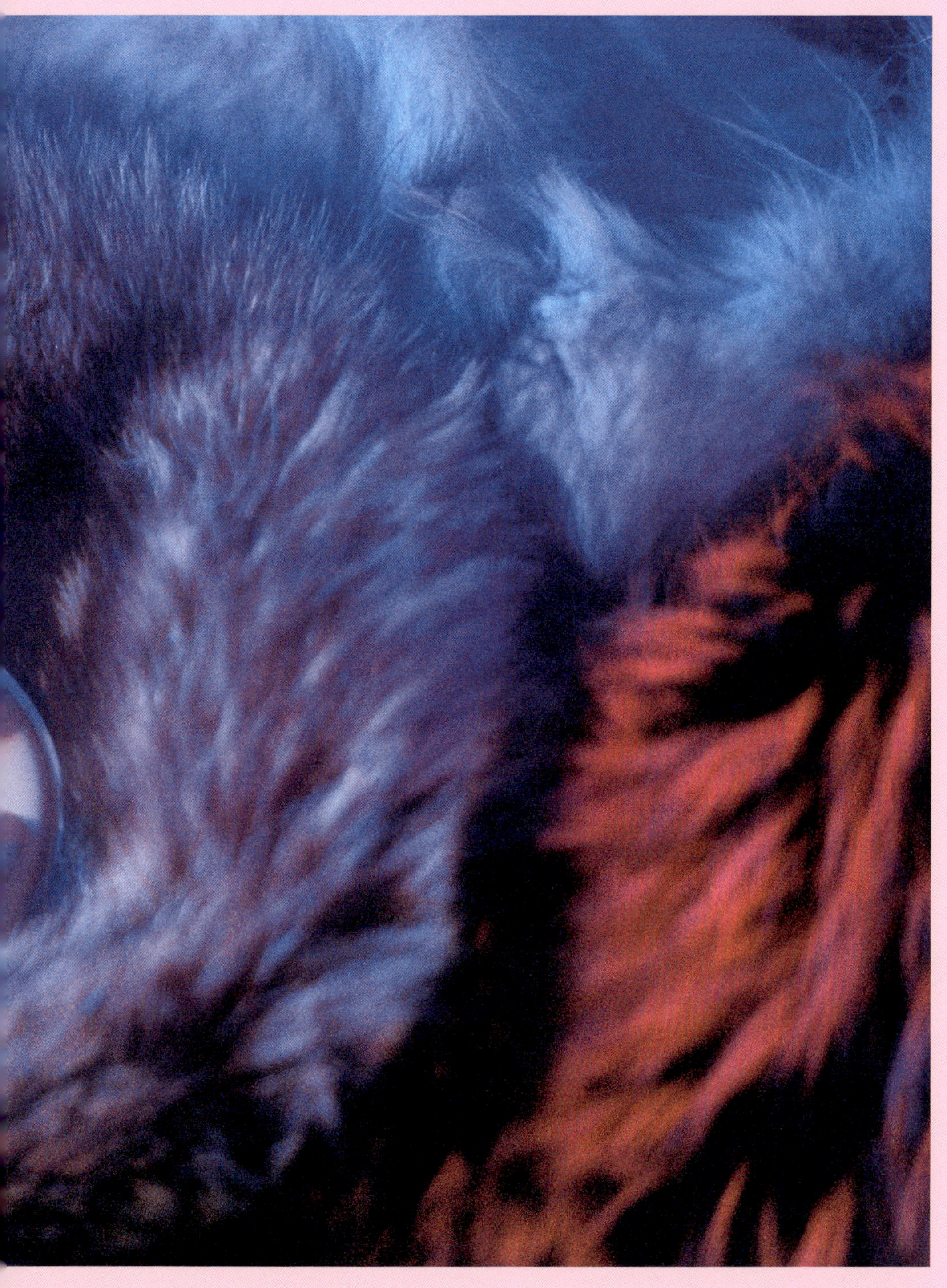

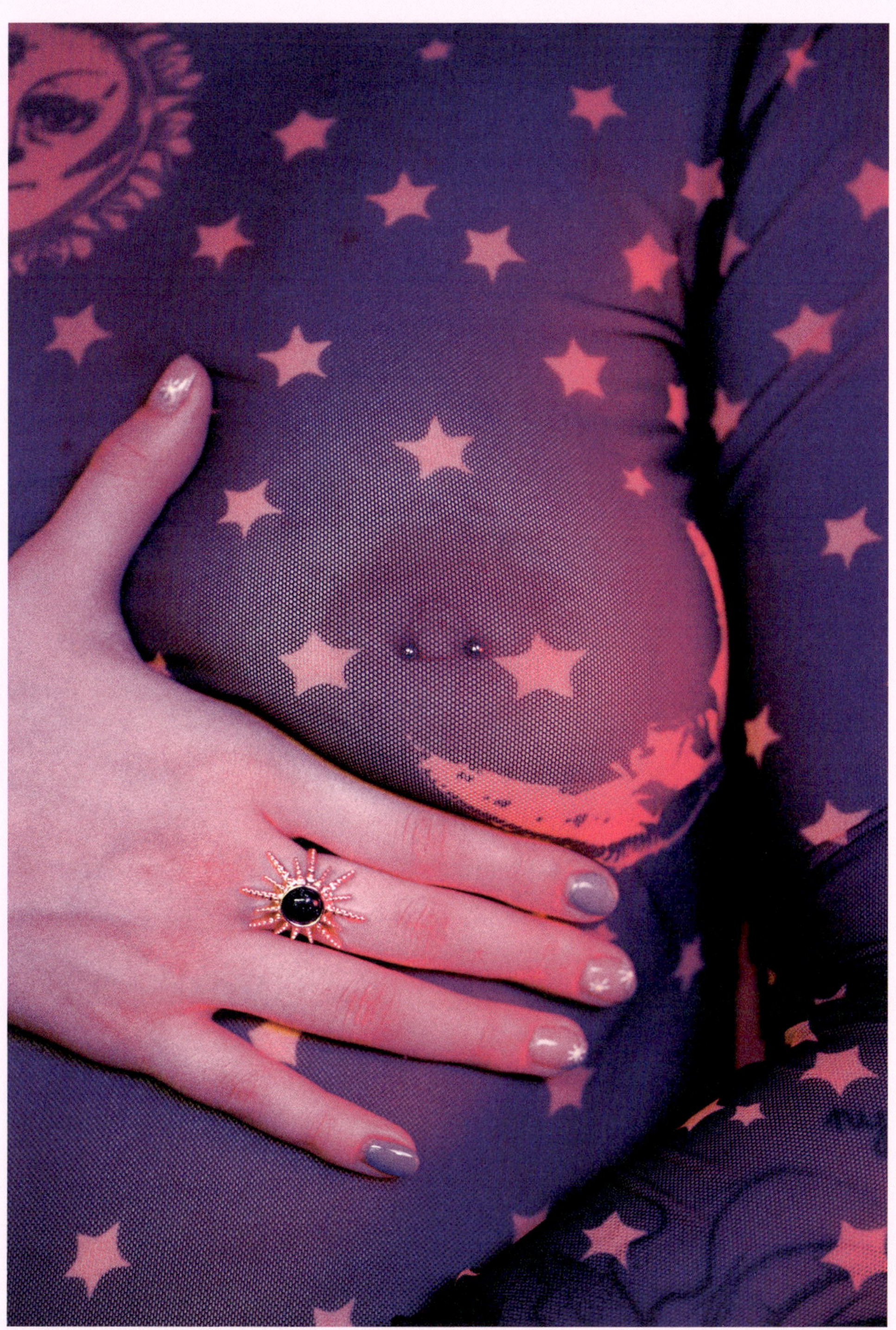

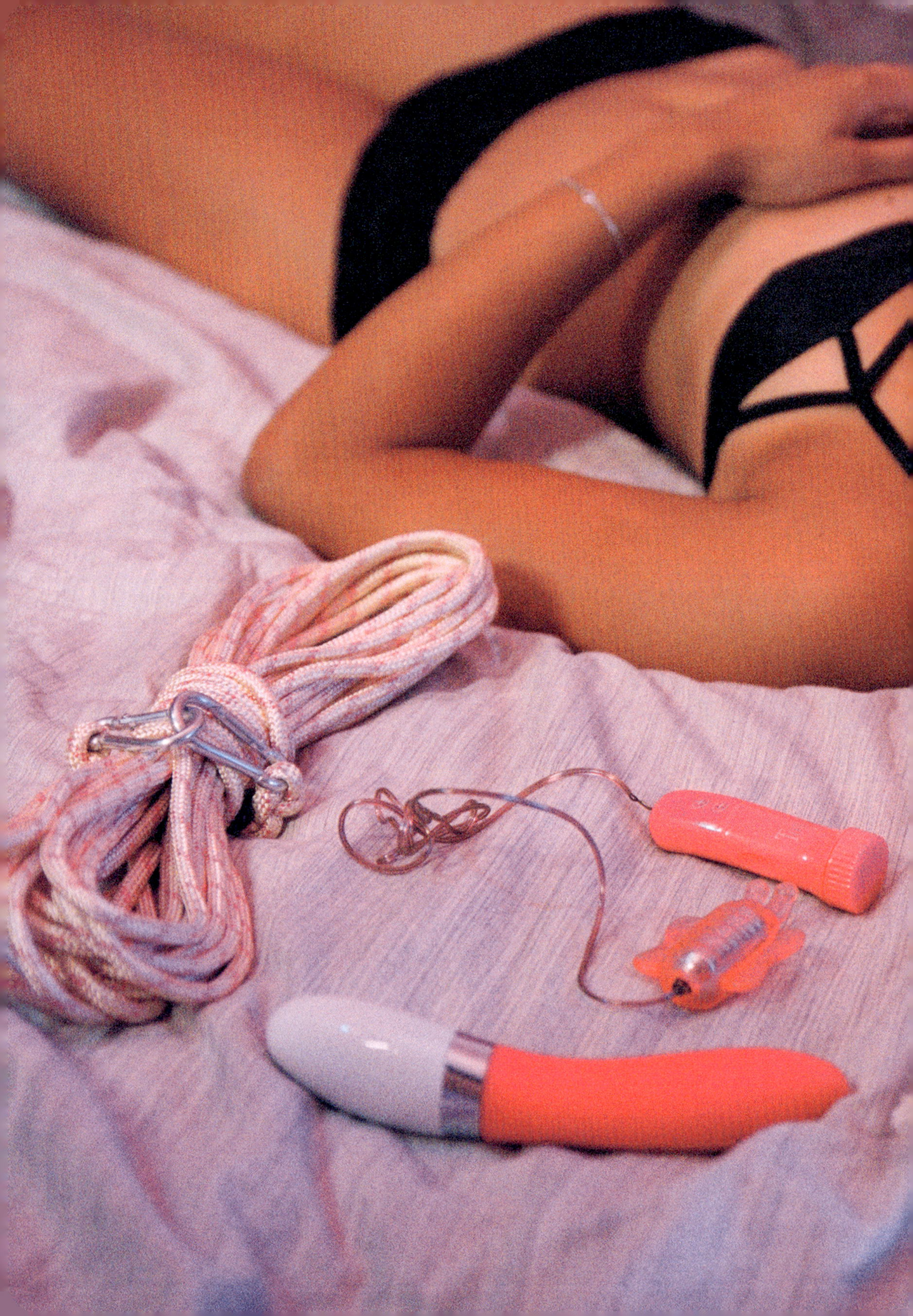

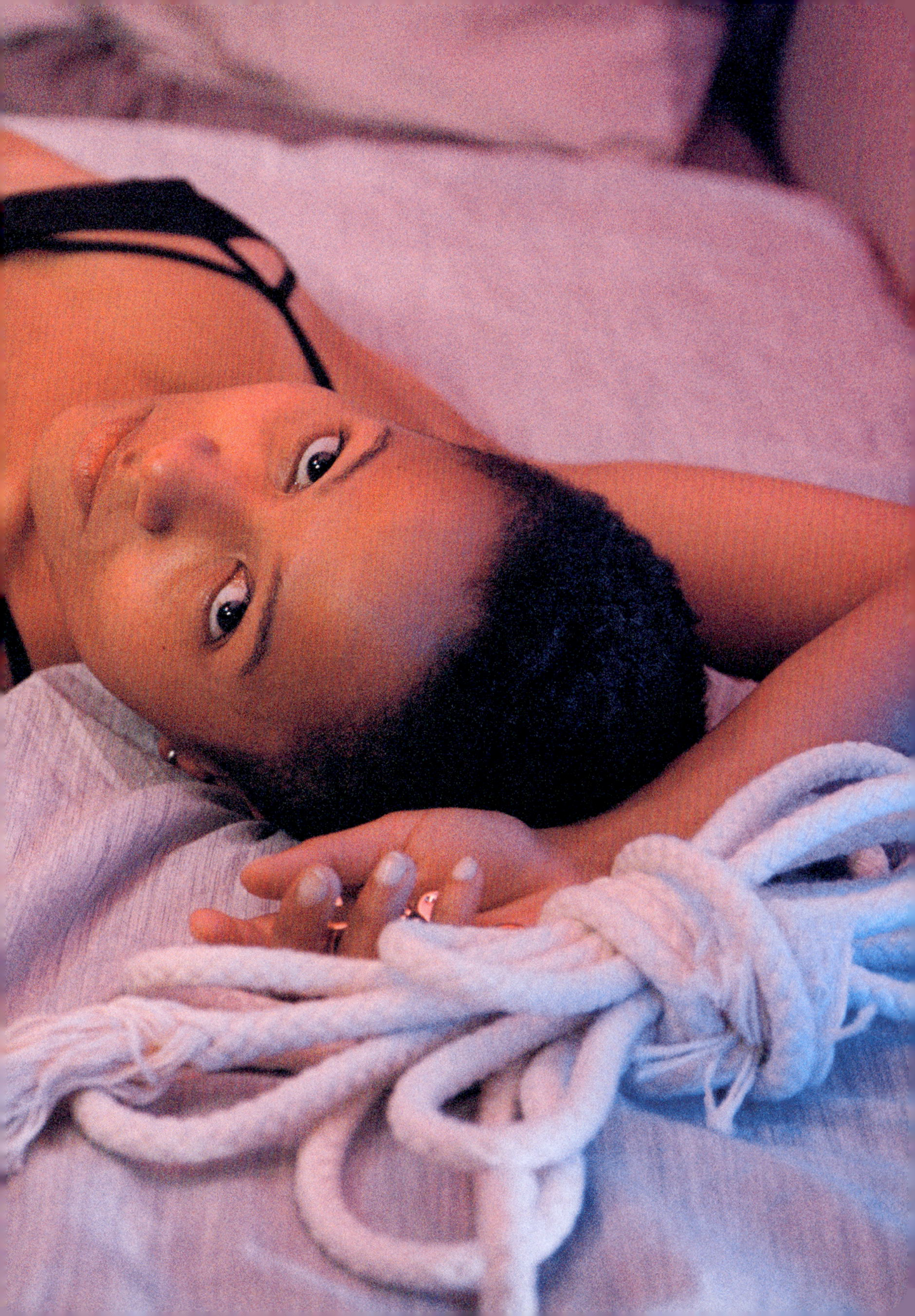

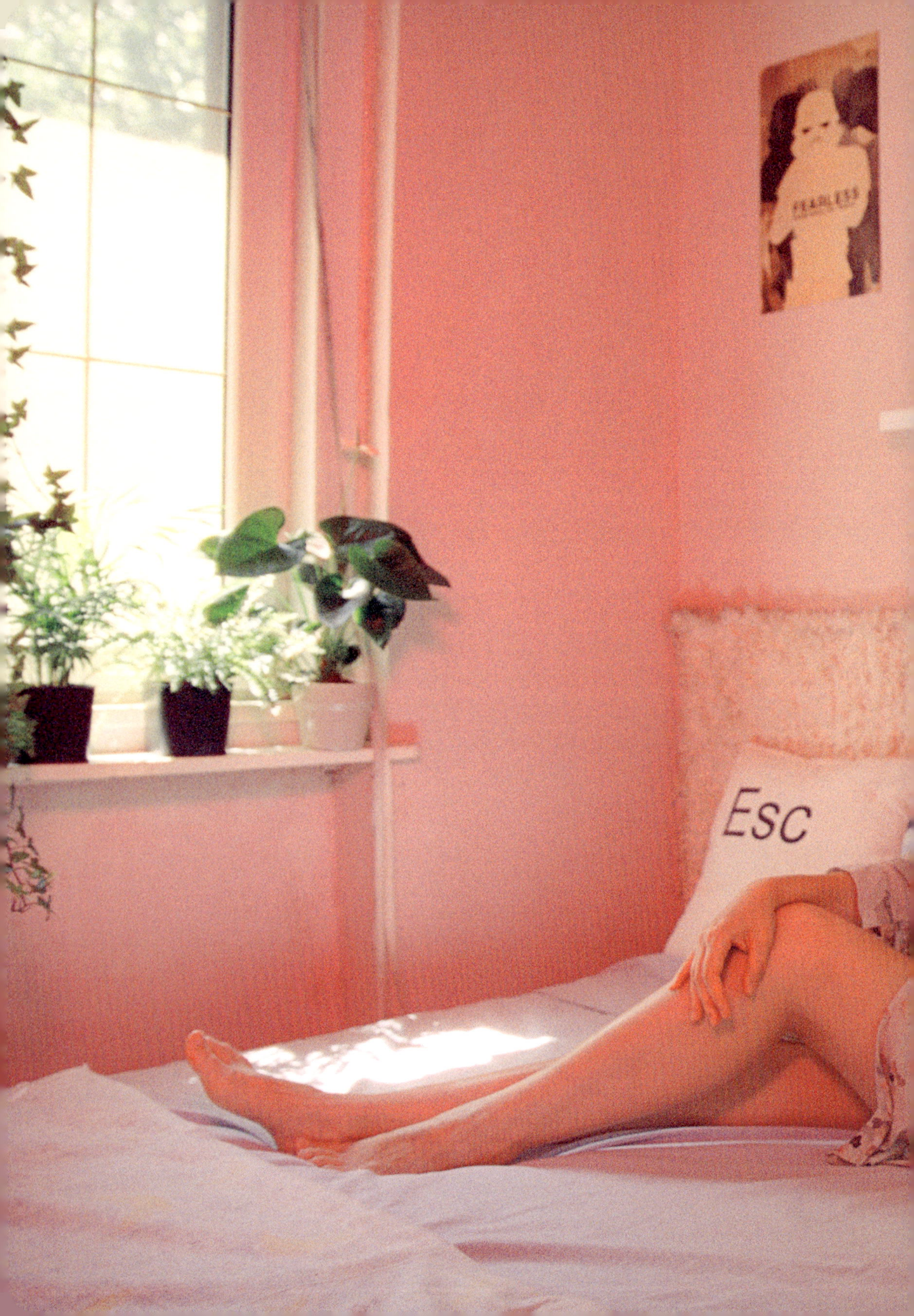

FEARLESS
Esc

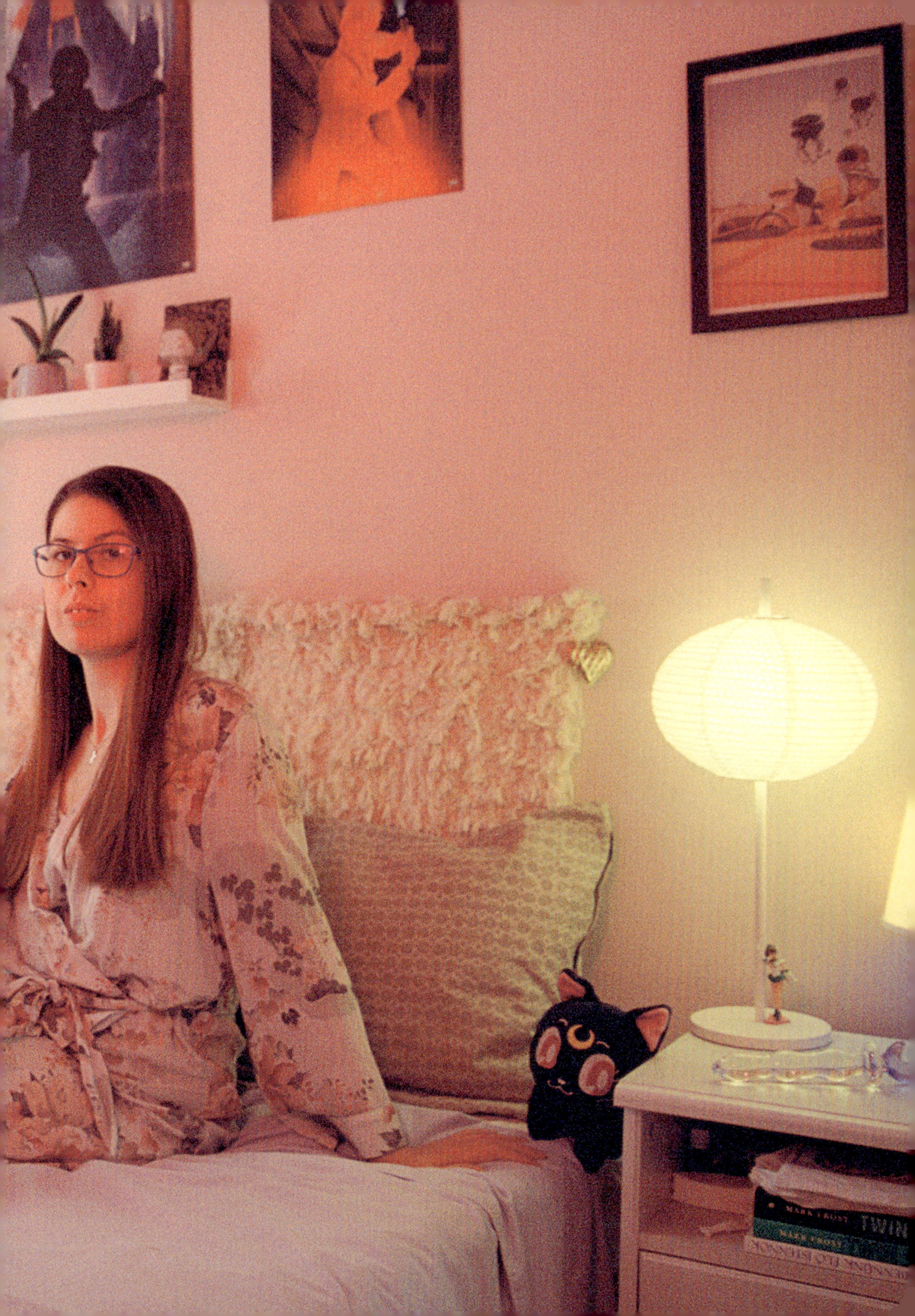

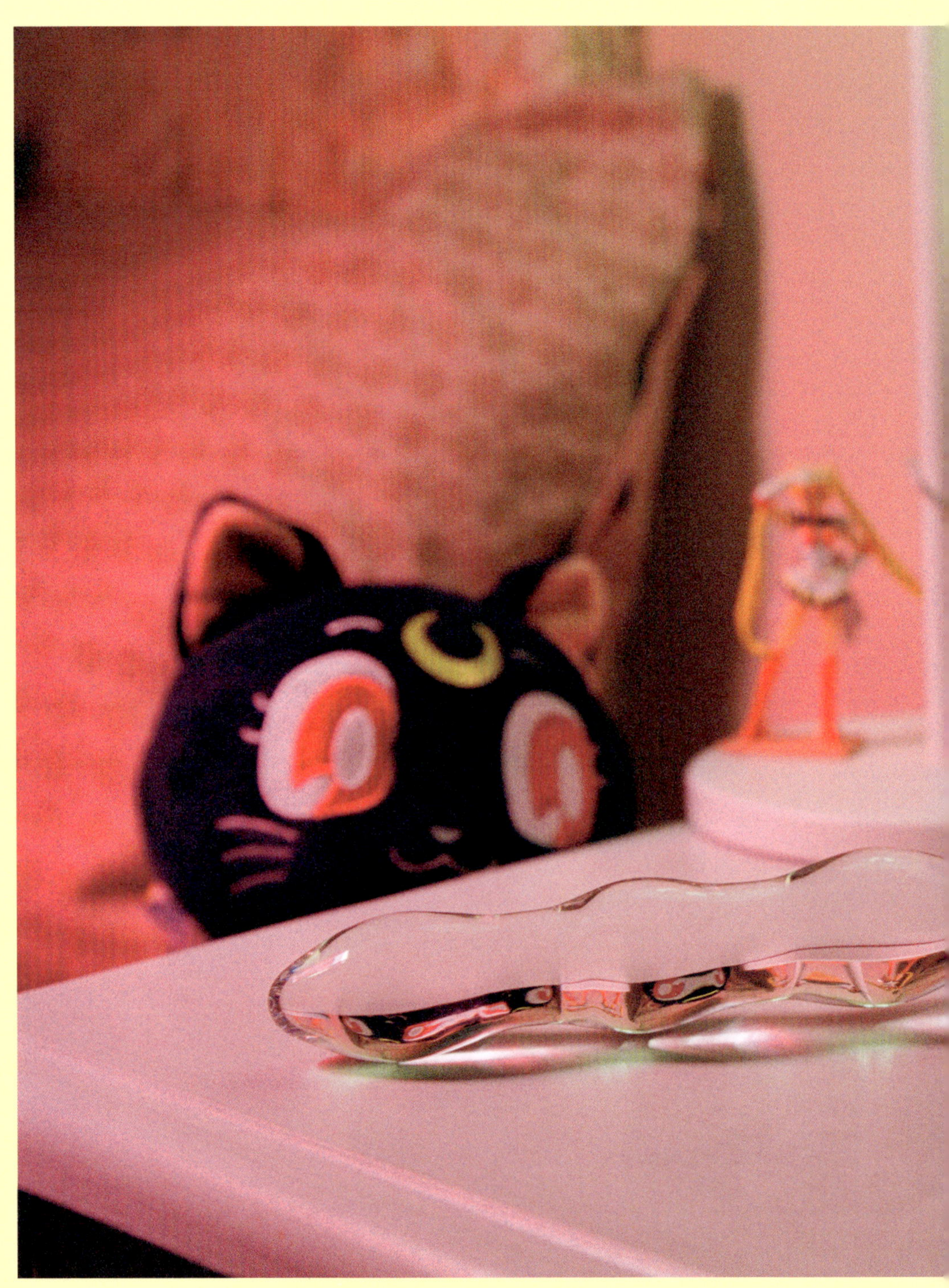

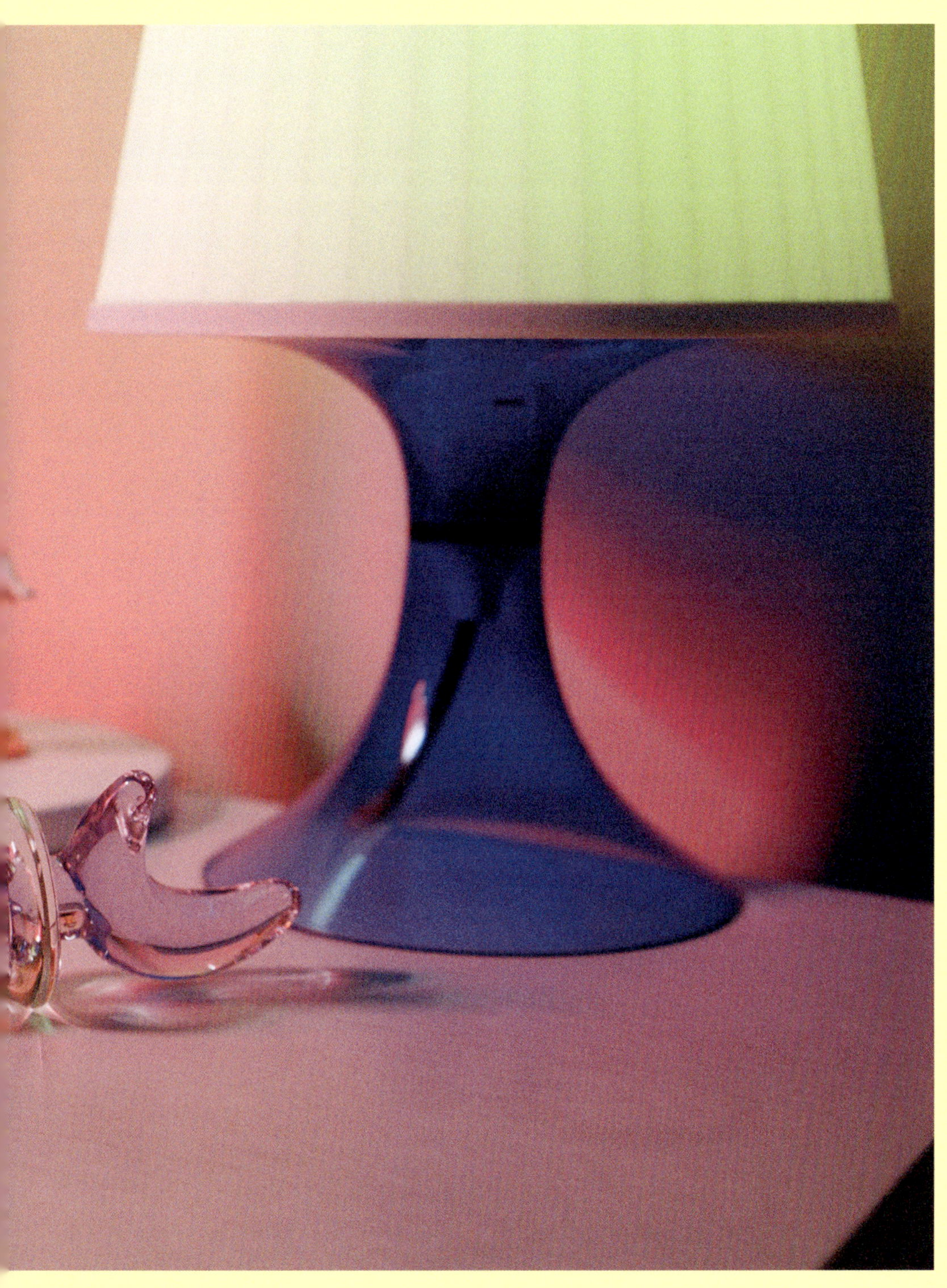

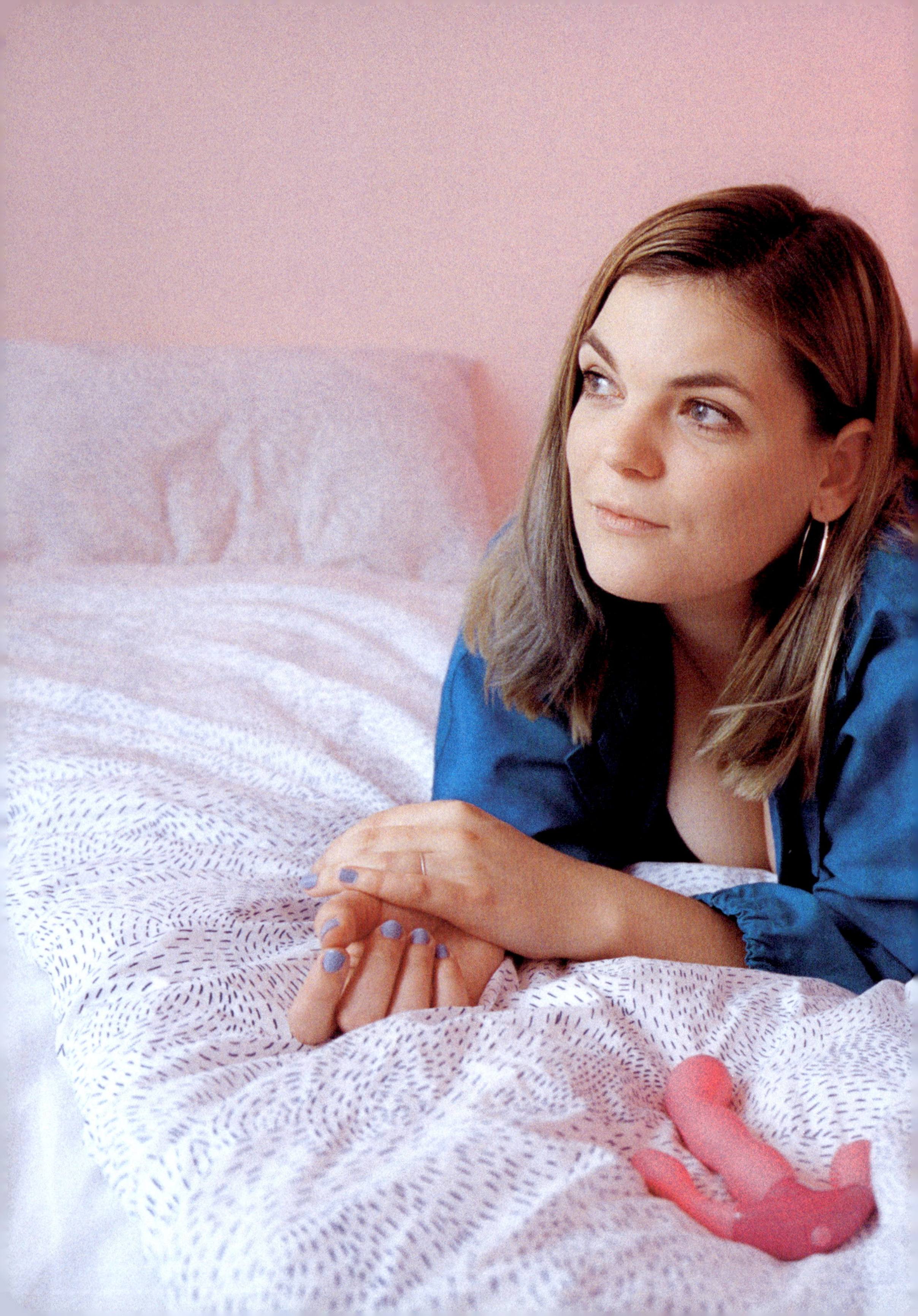

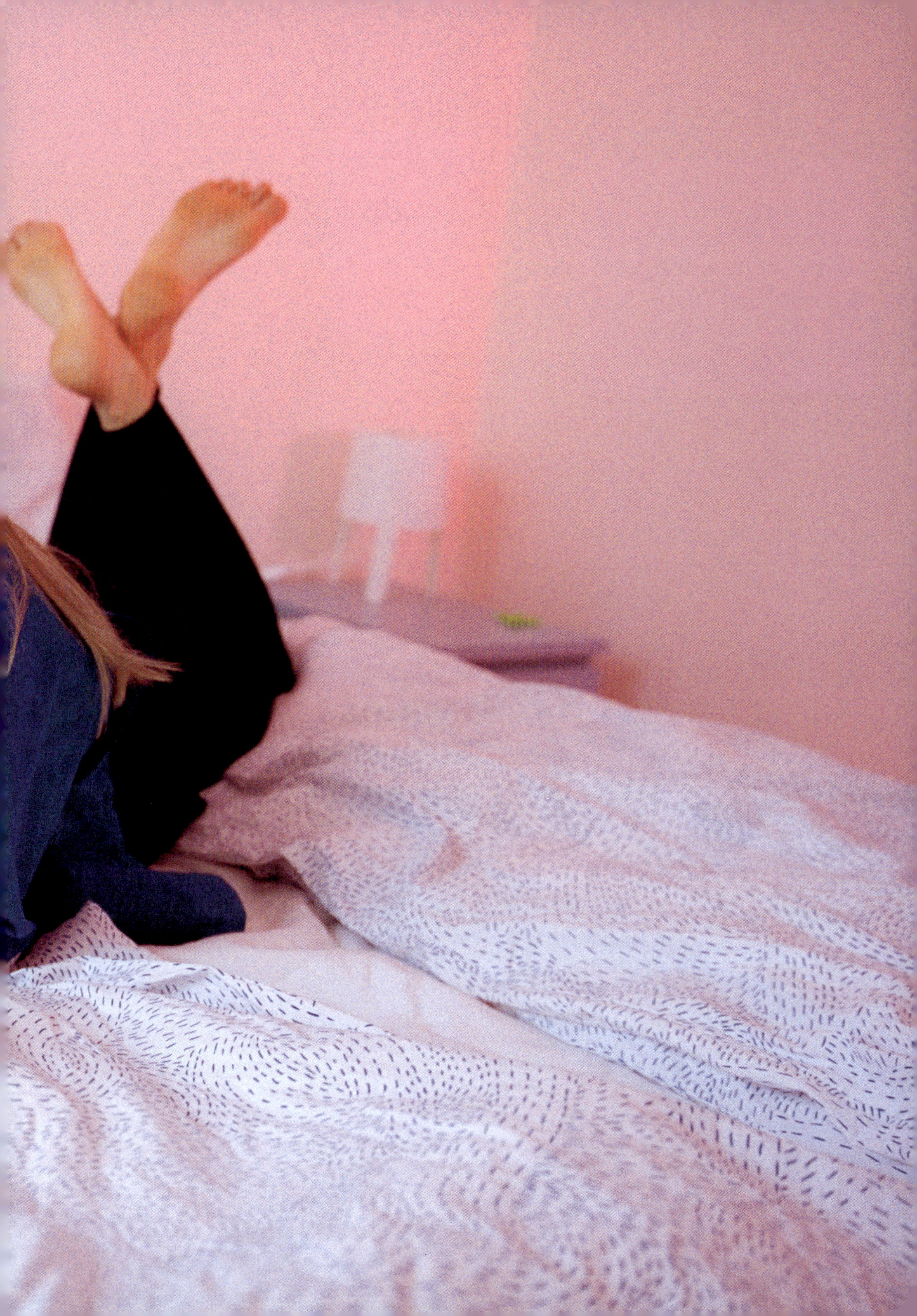

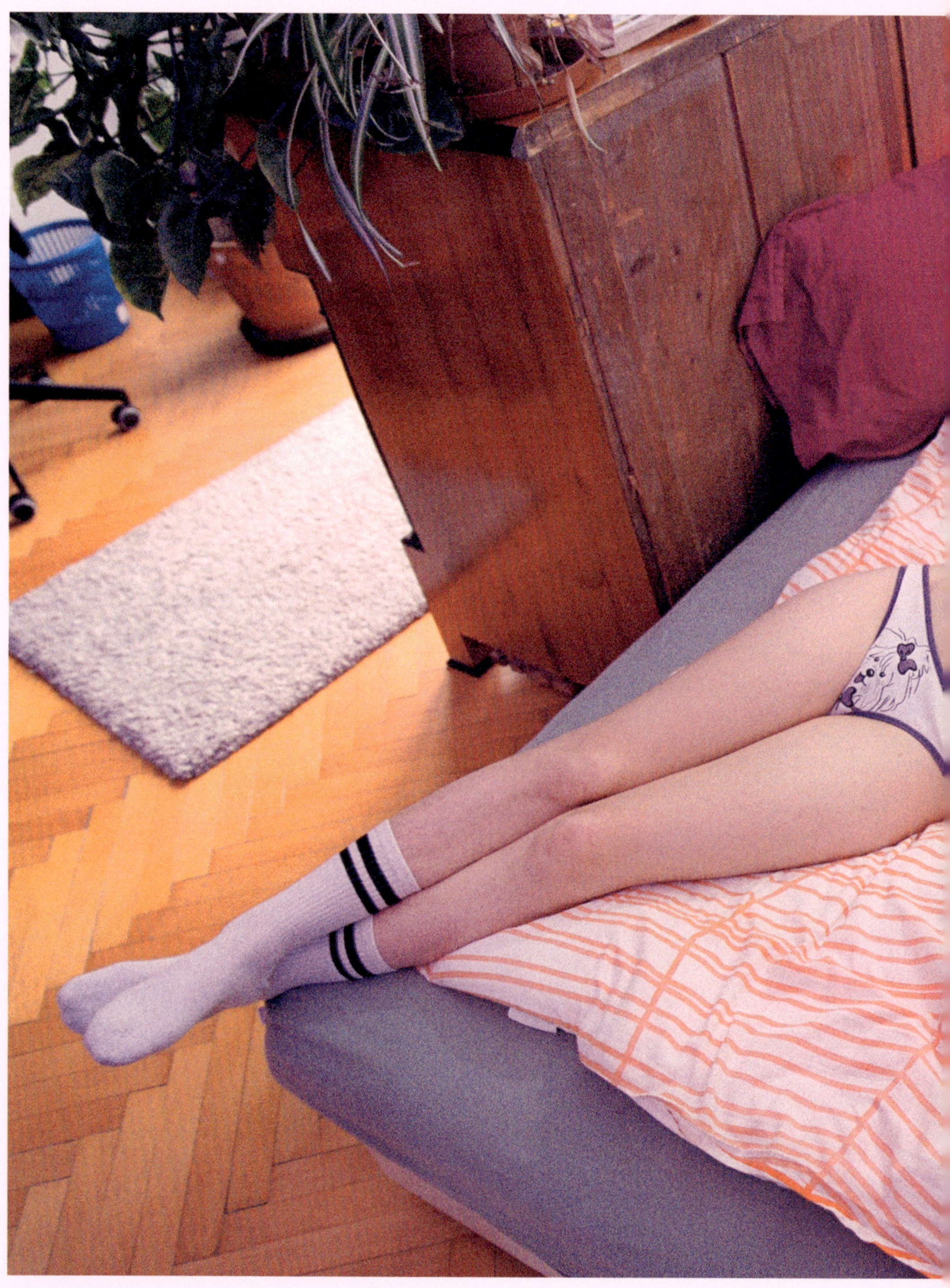

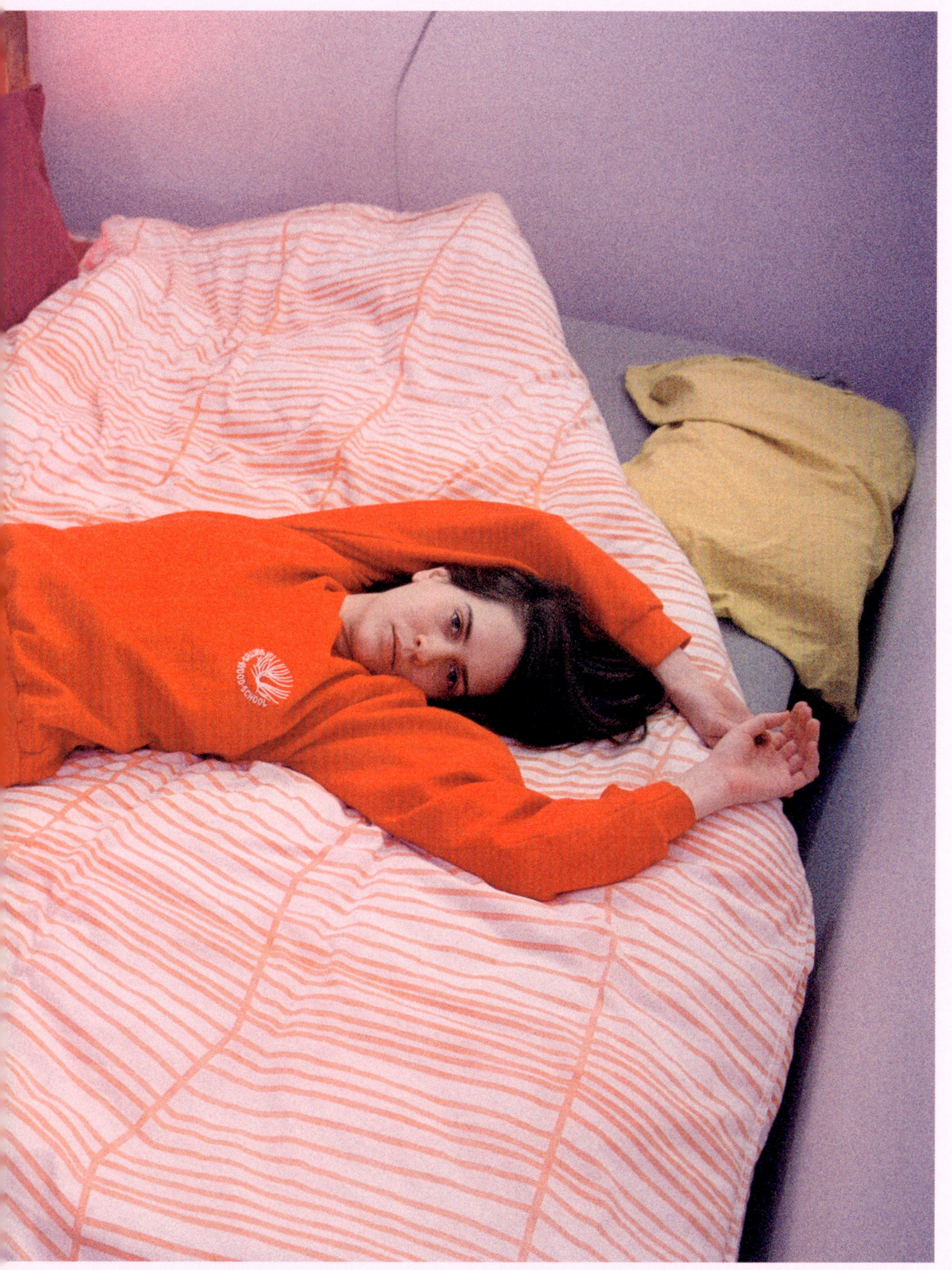

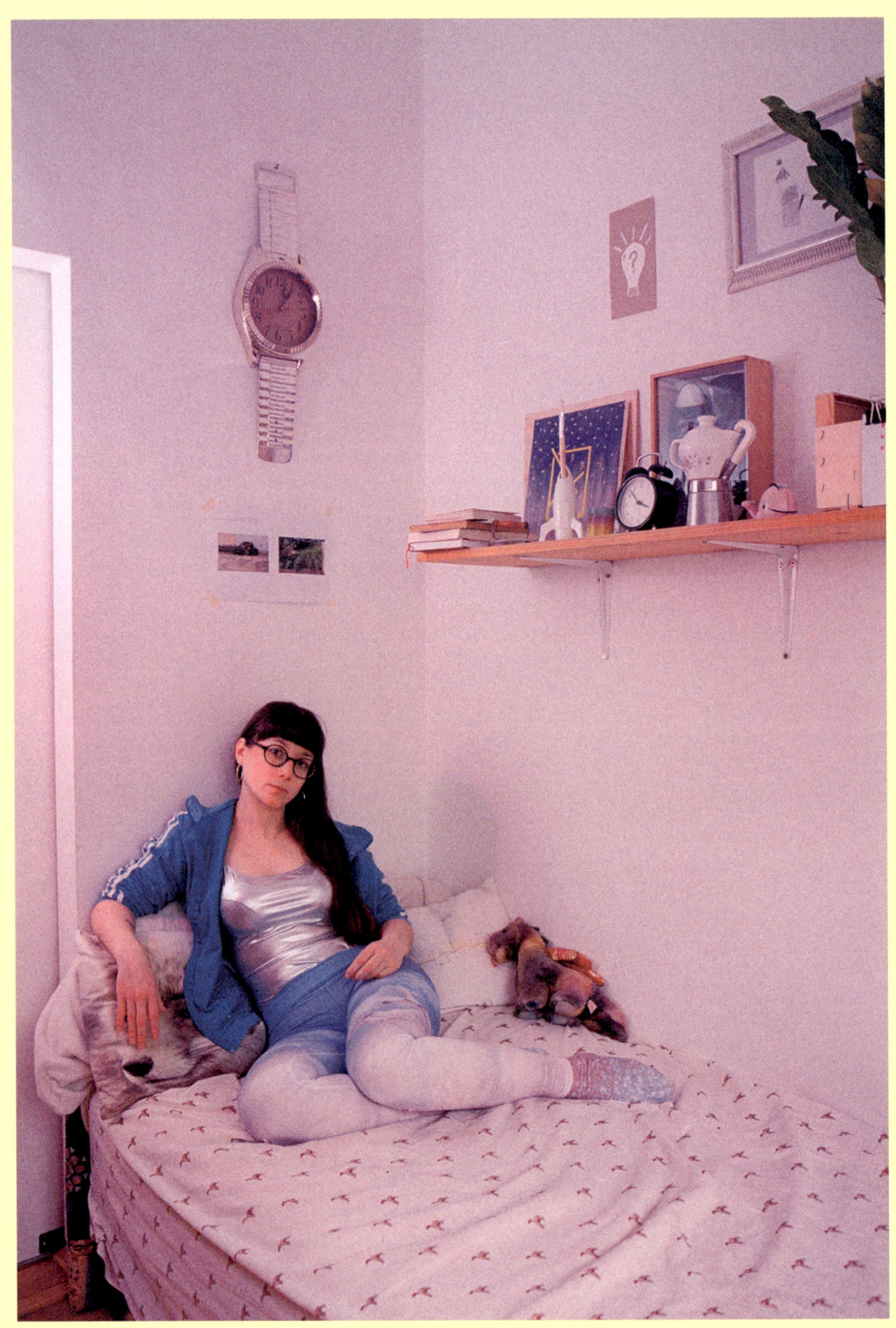

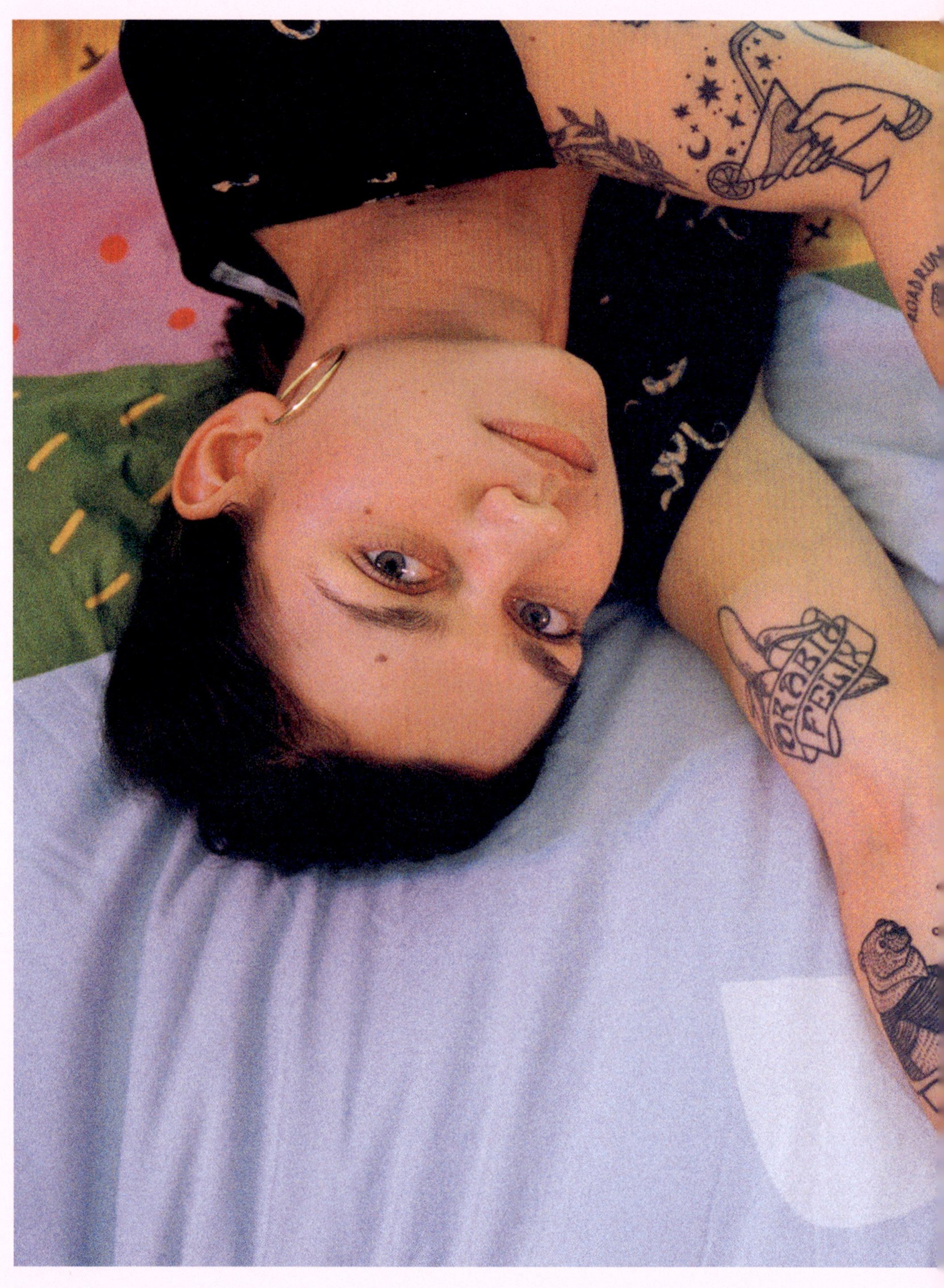

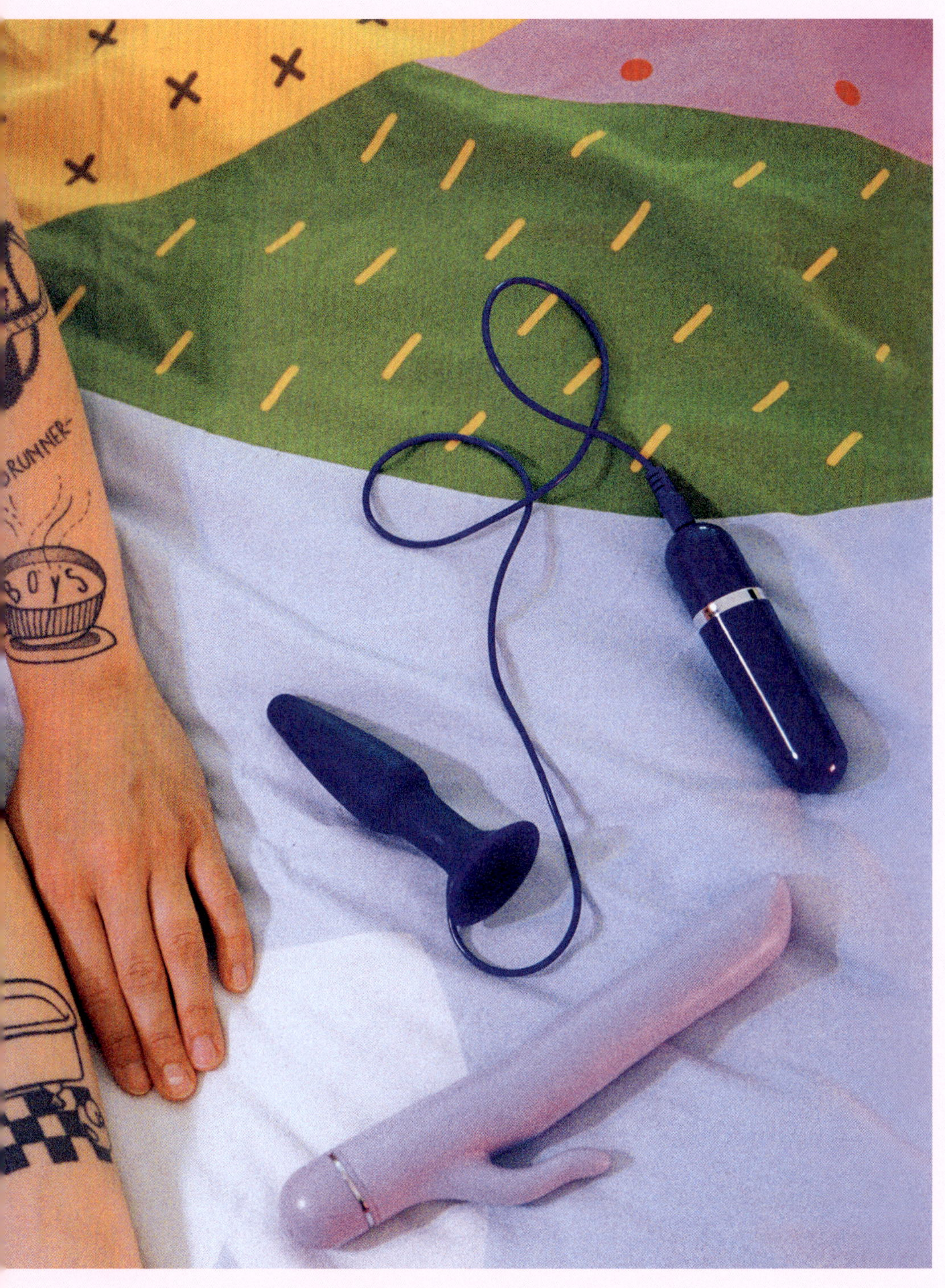

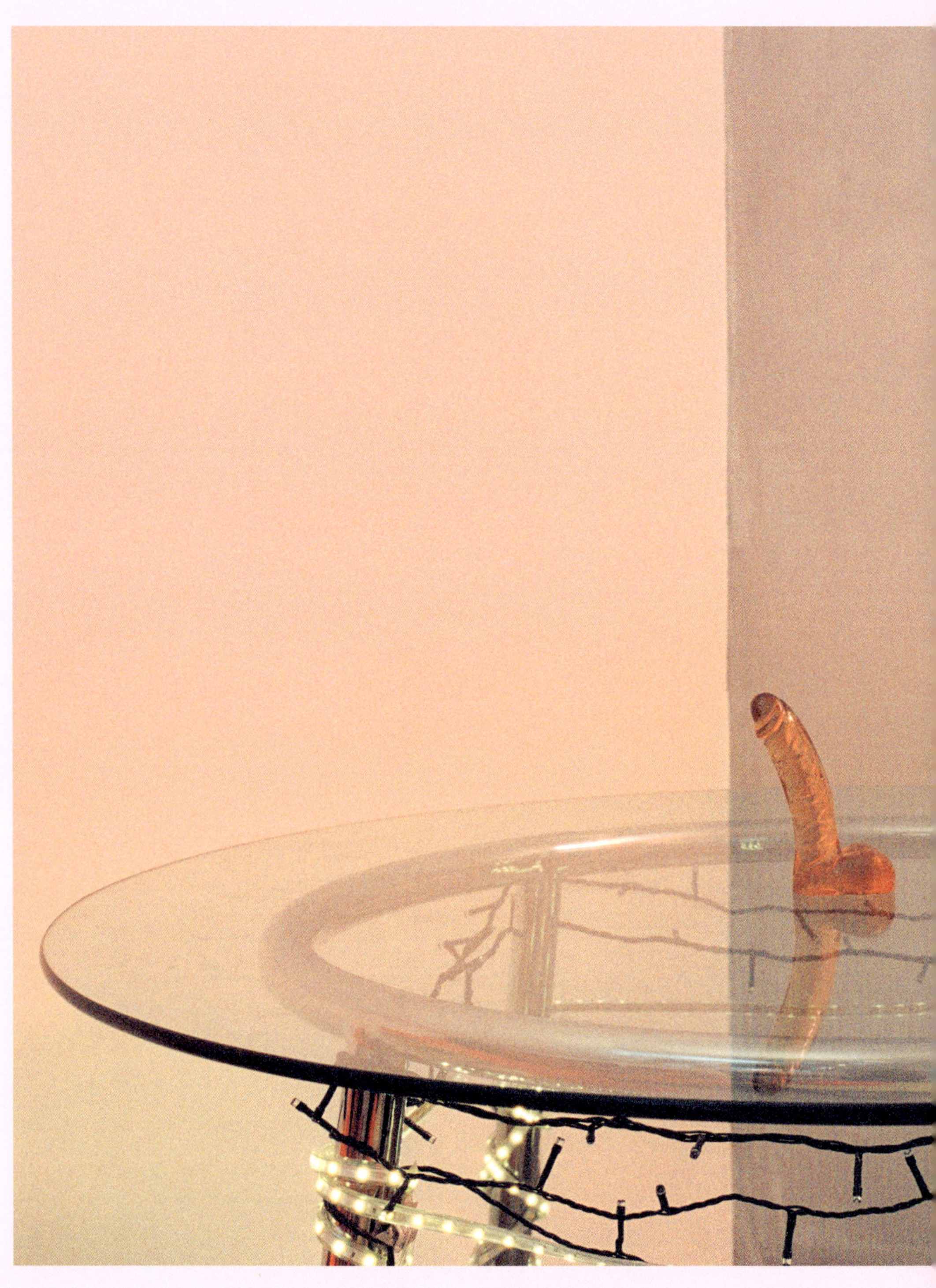

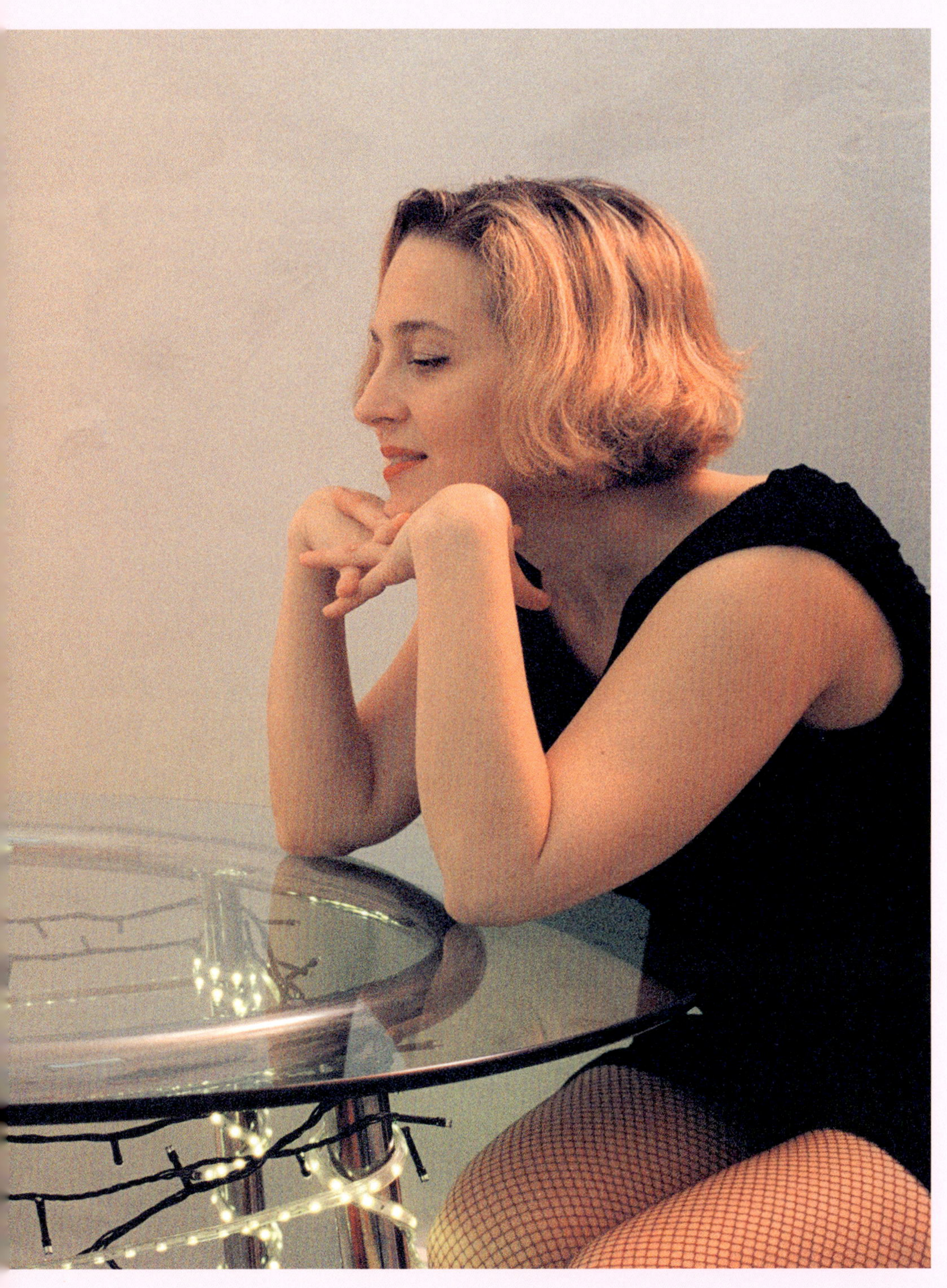

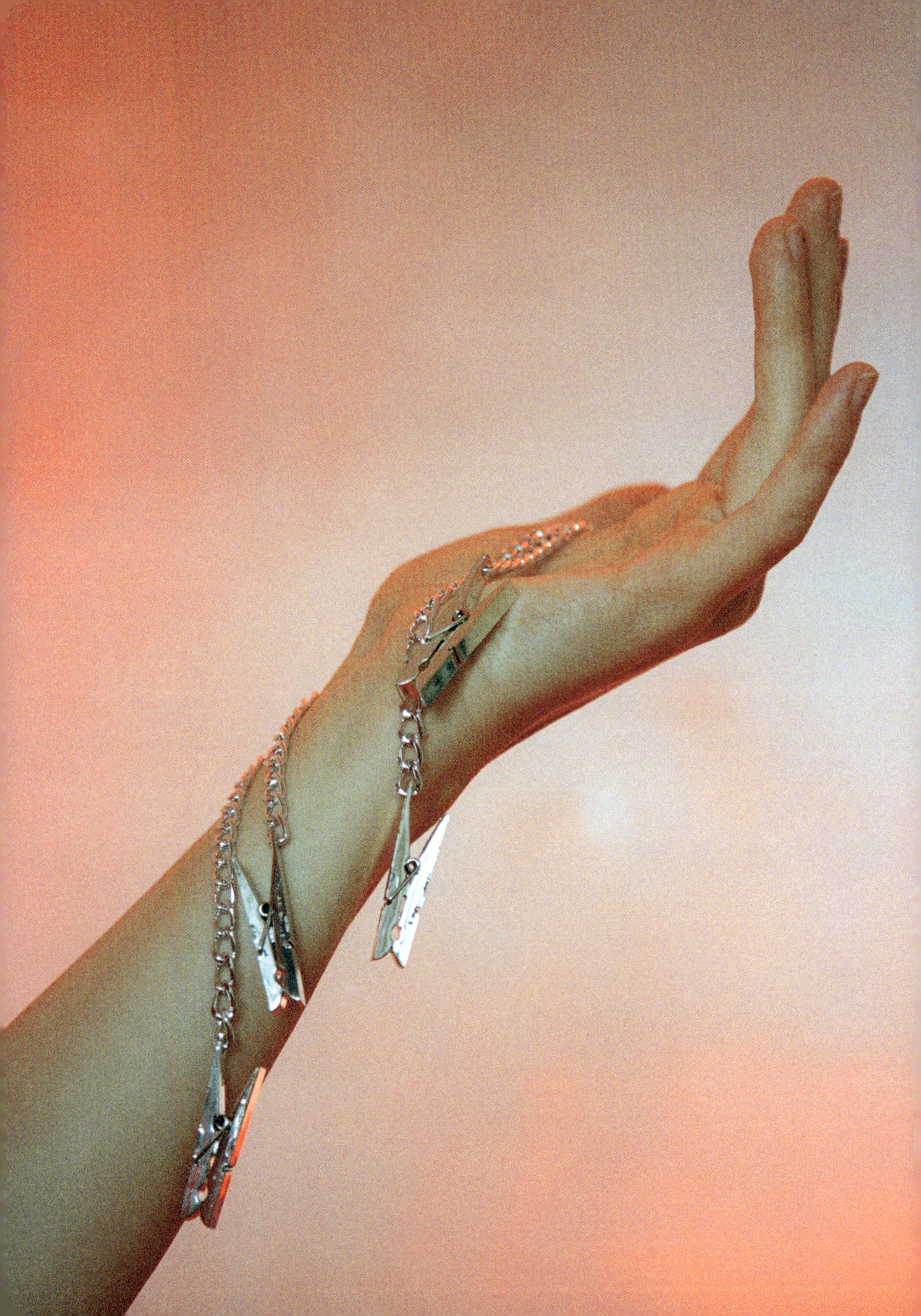

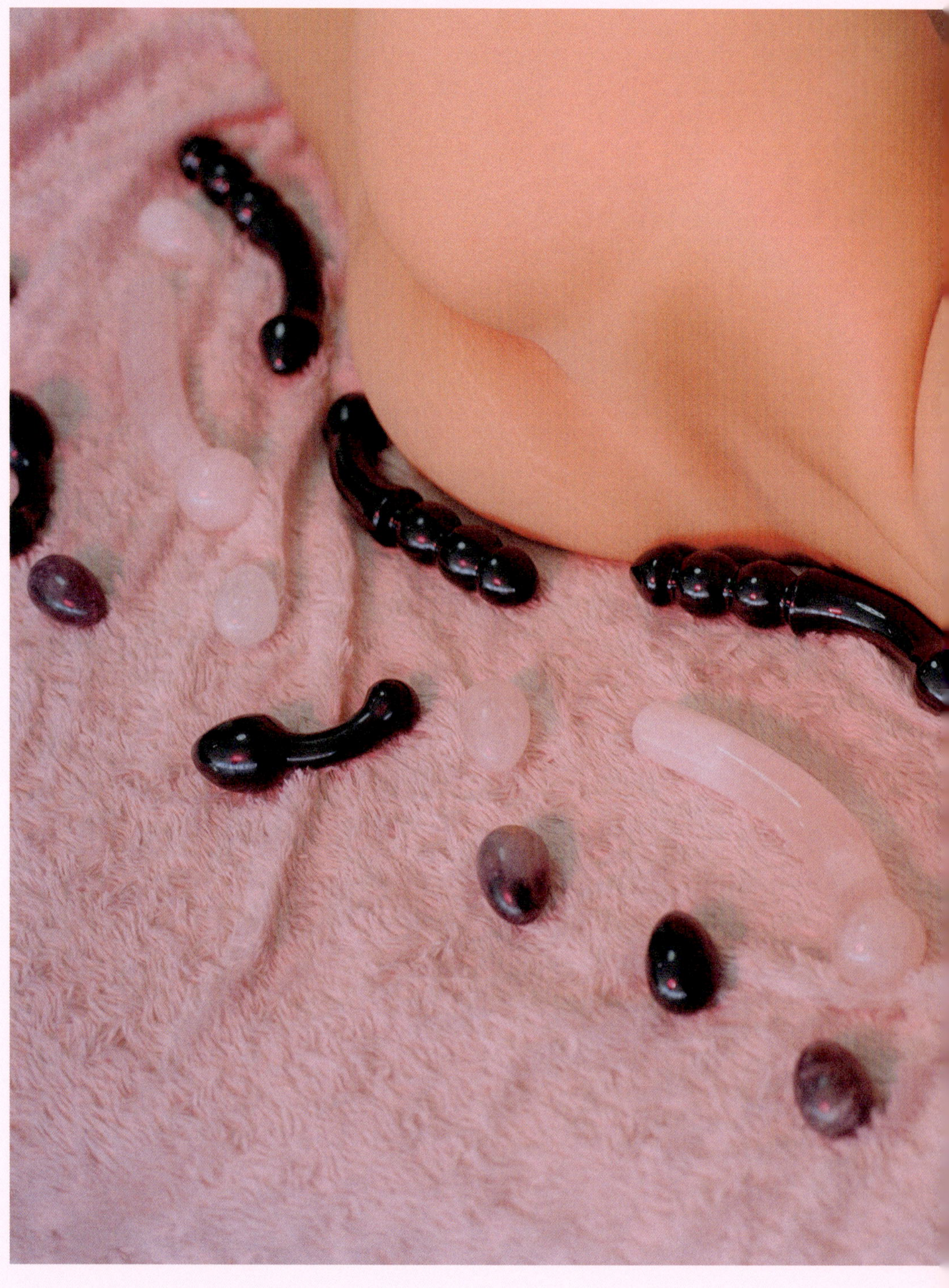

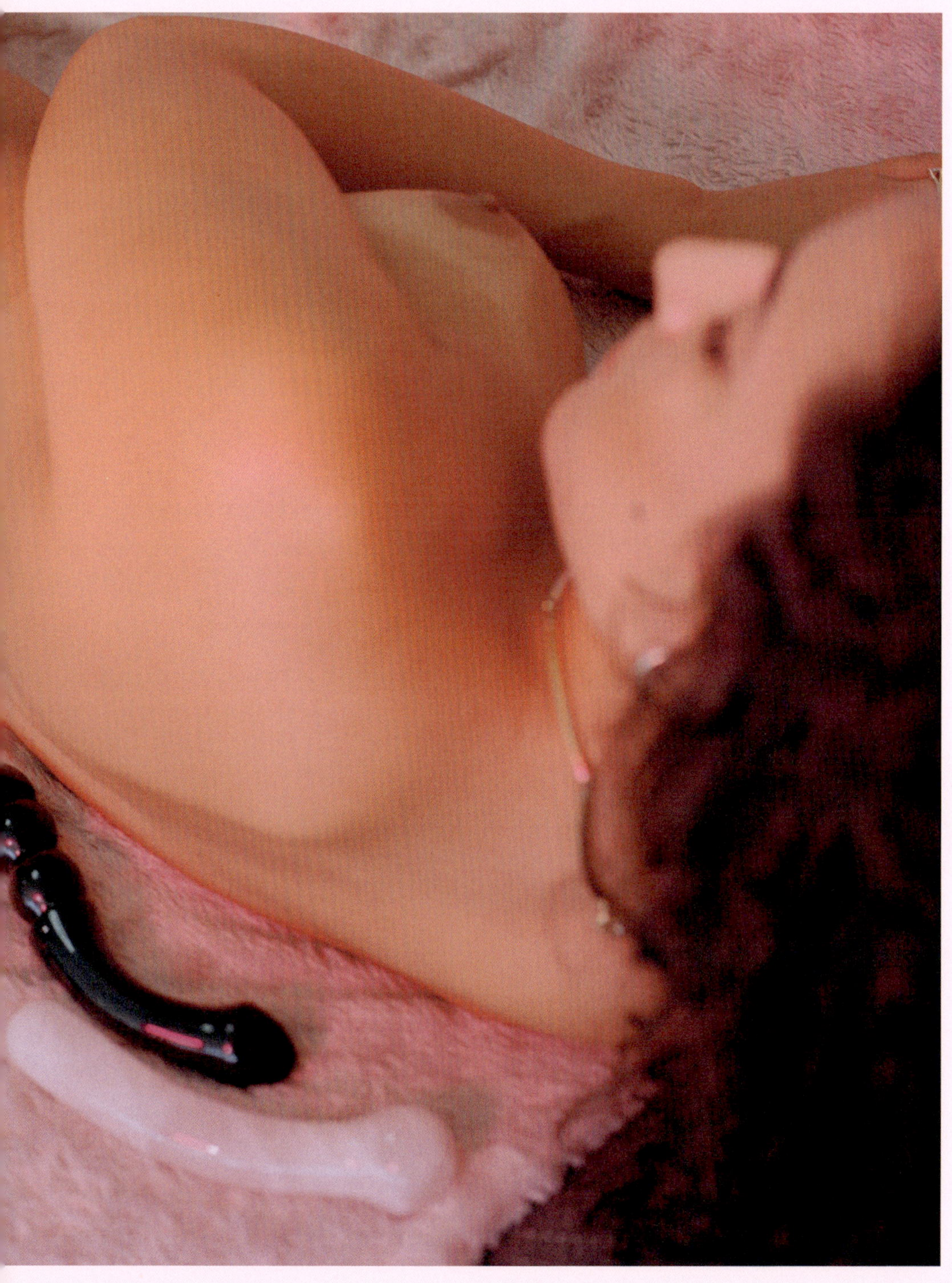

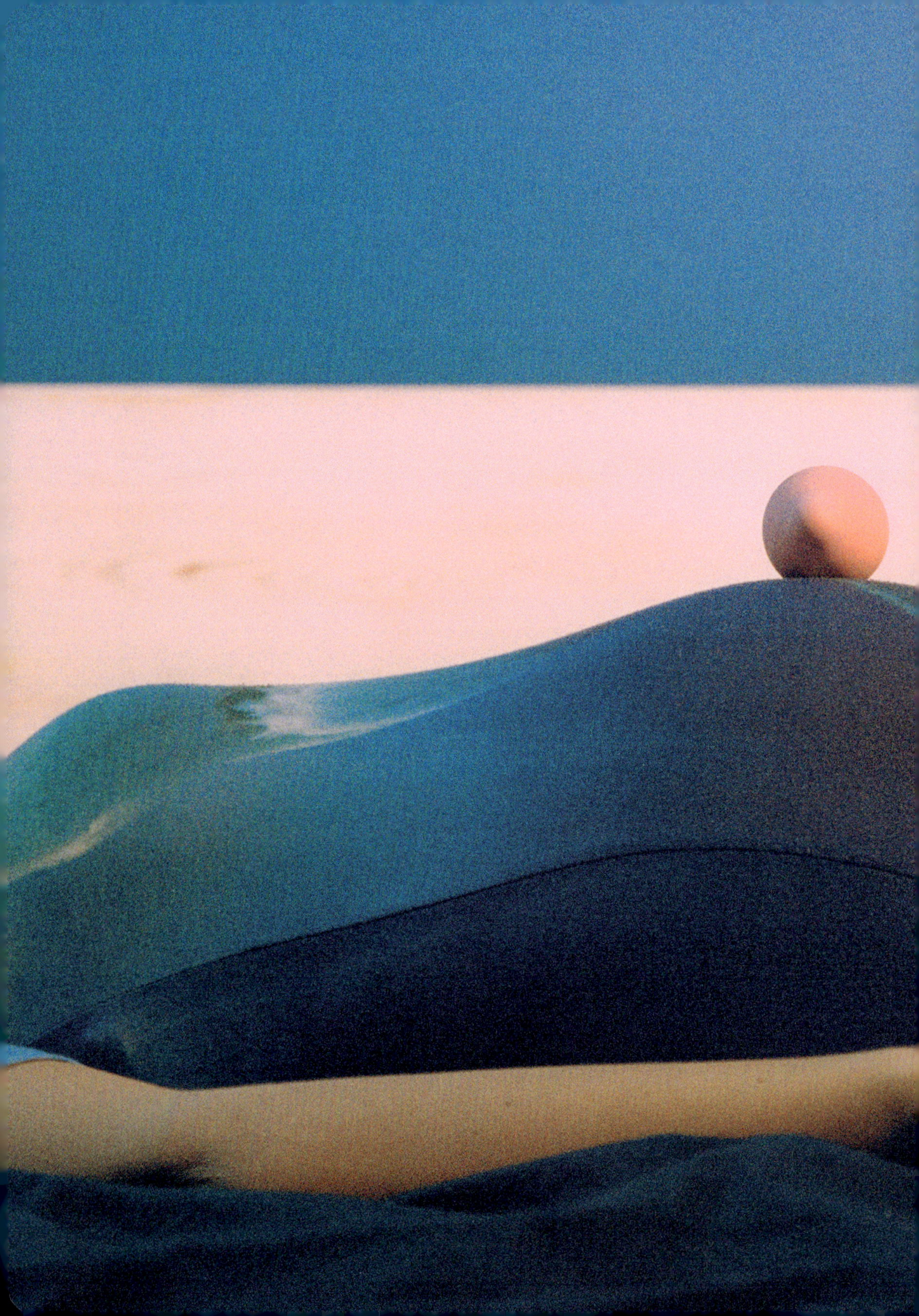

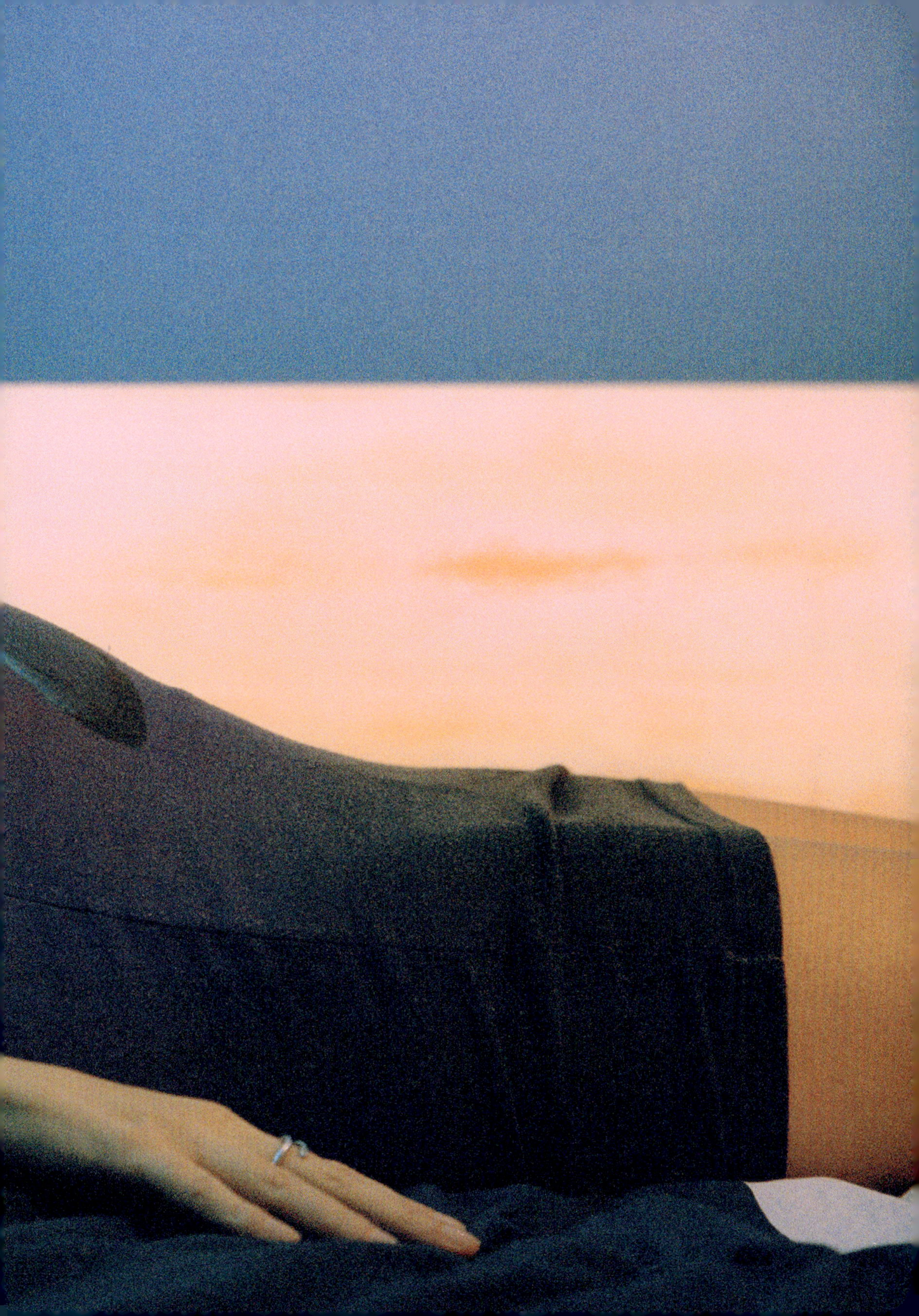

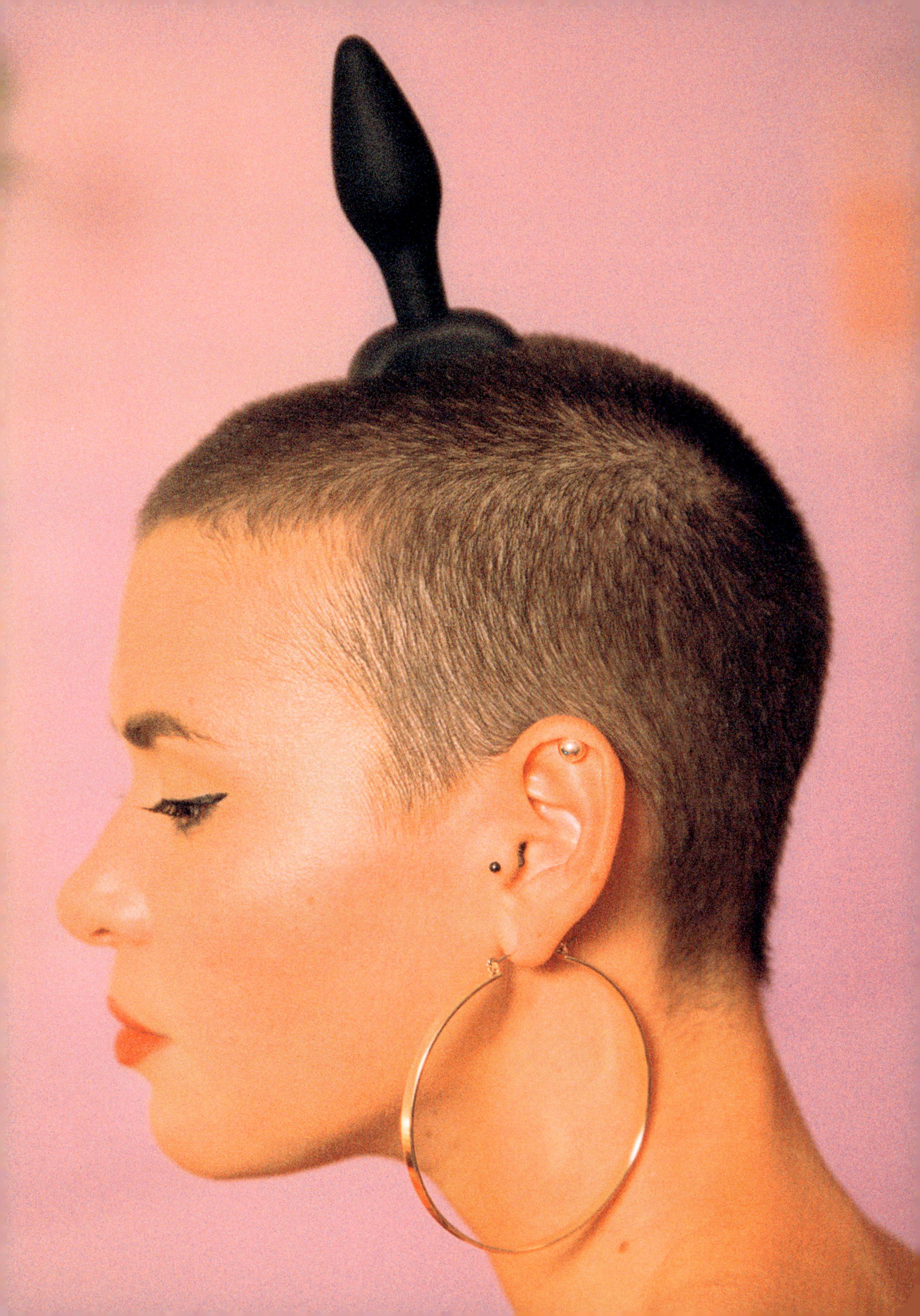

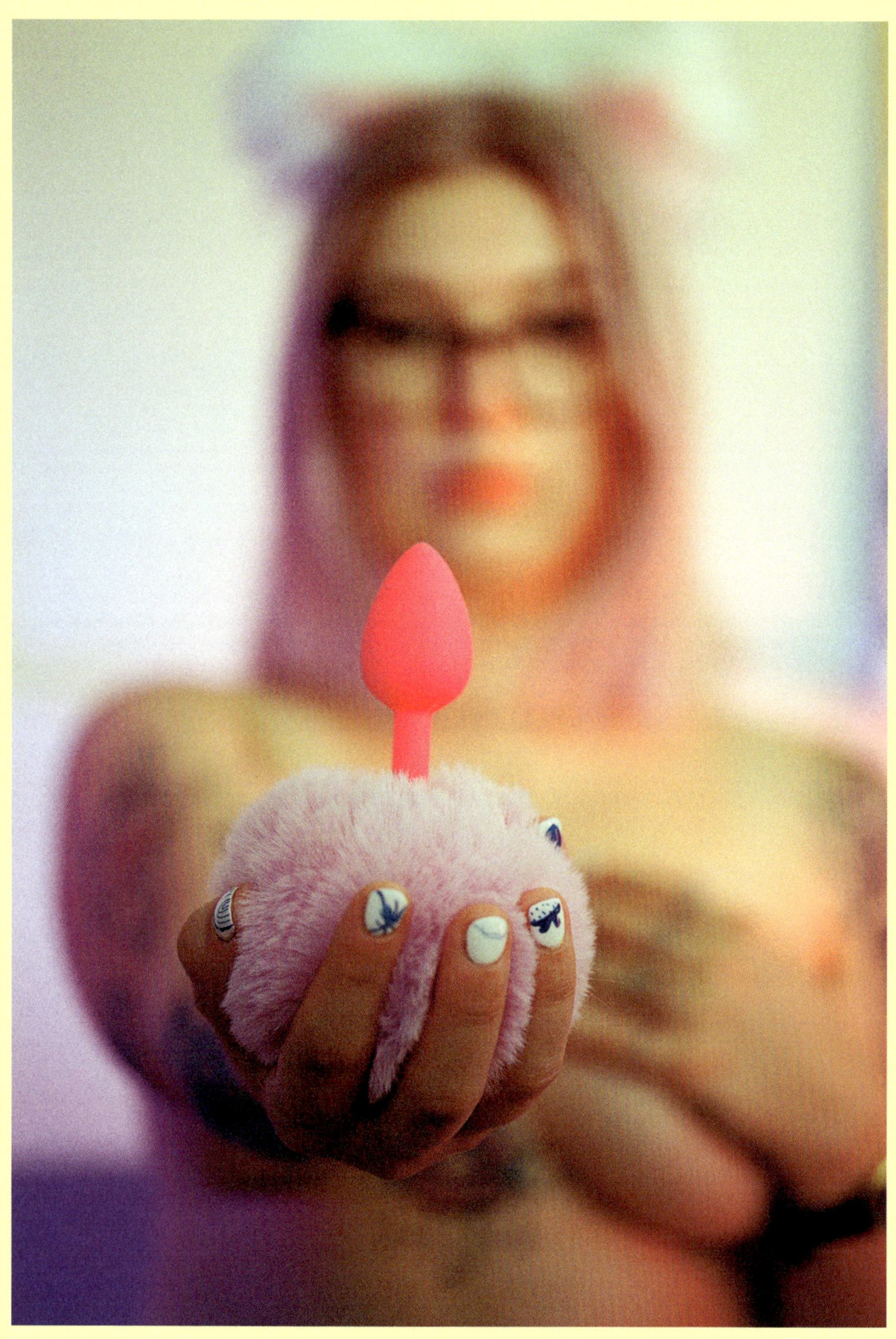

*Think what
you want.*

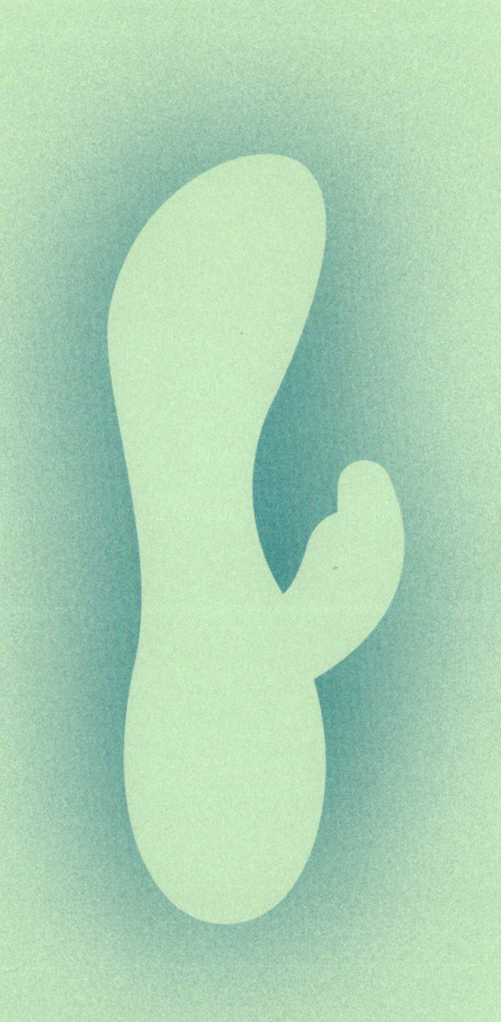

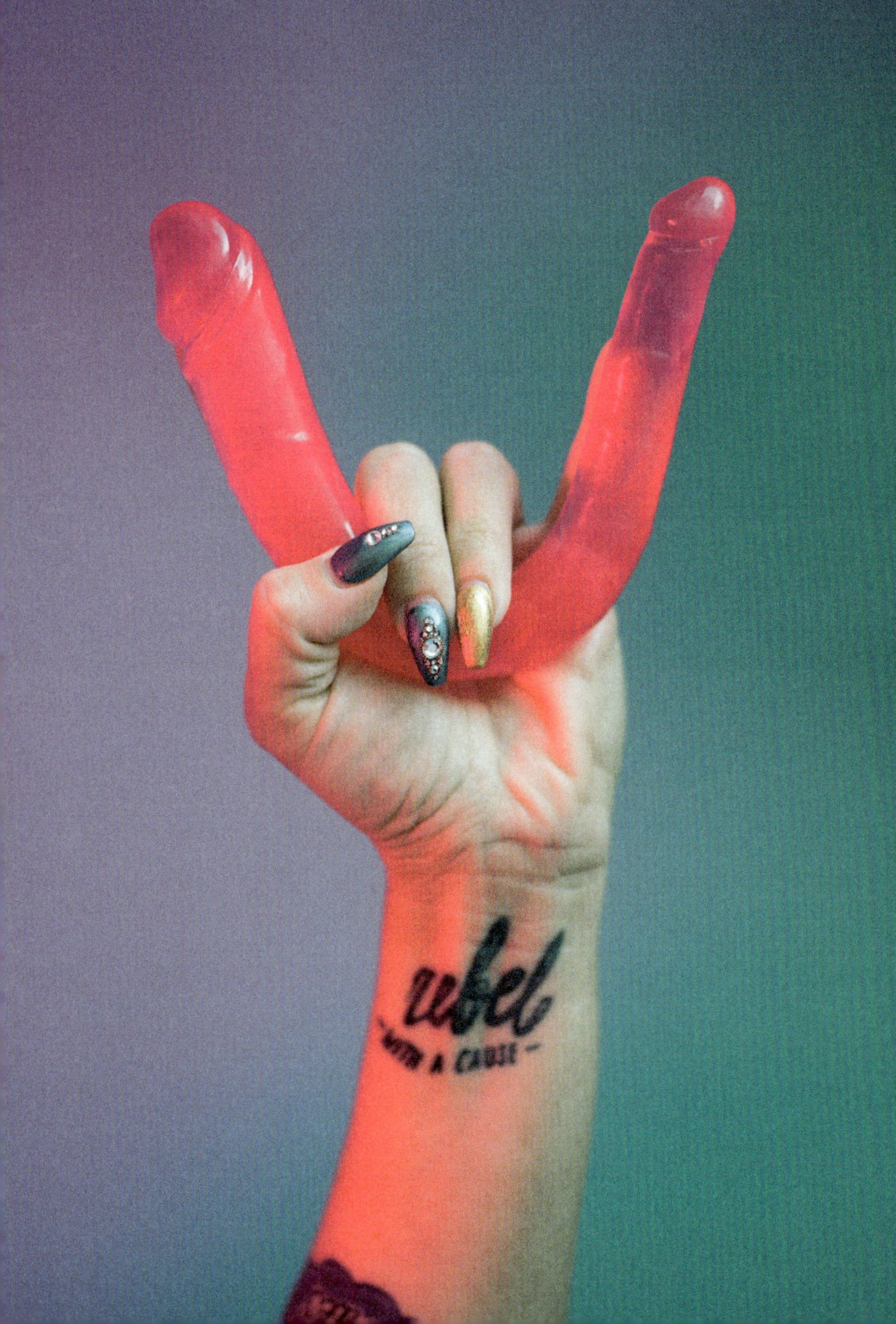
rebel
— WITH A CAUSE —

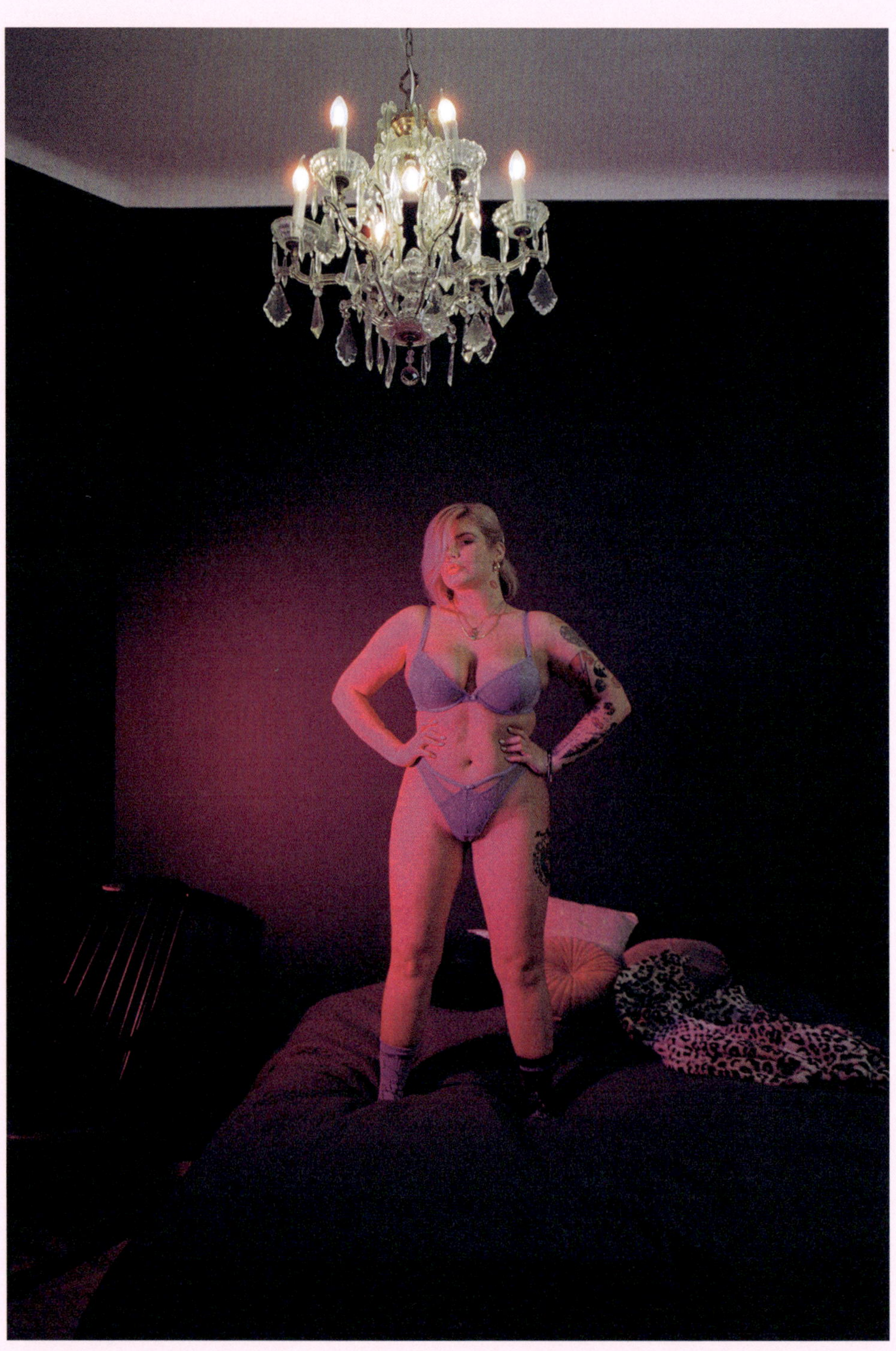

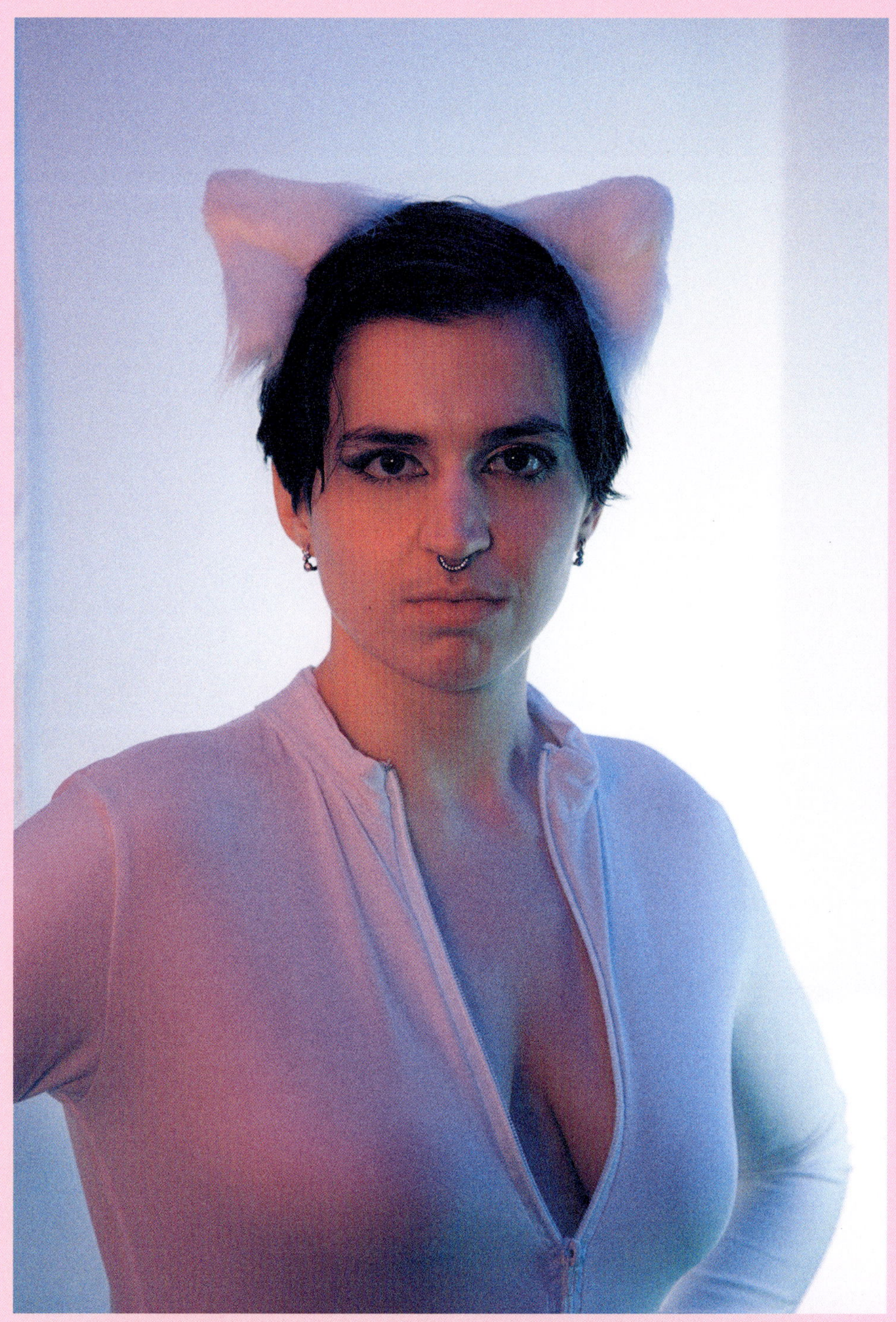

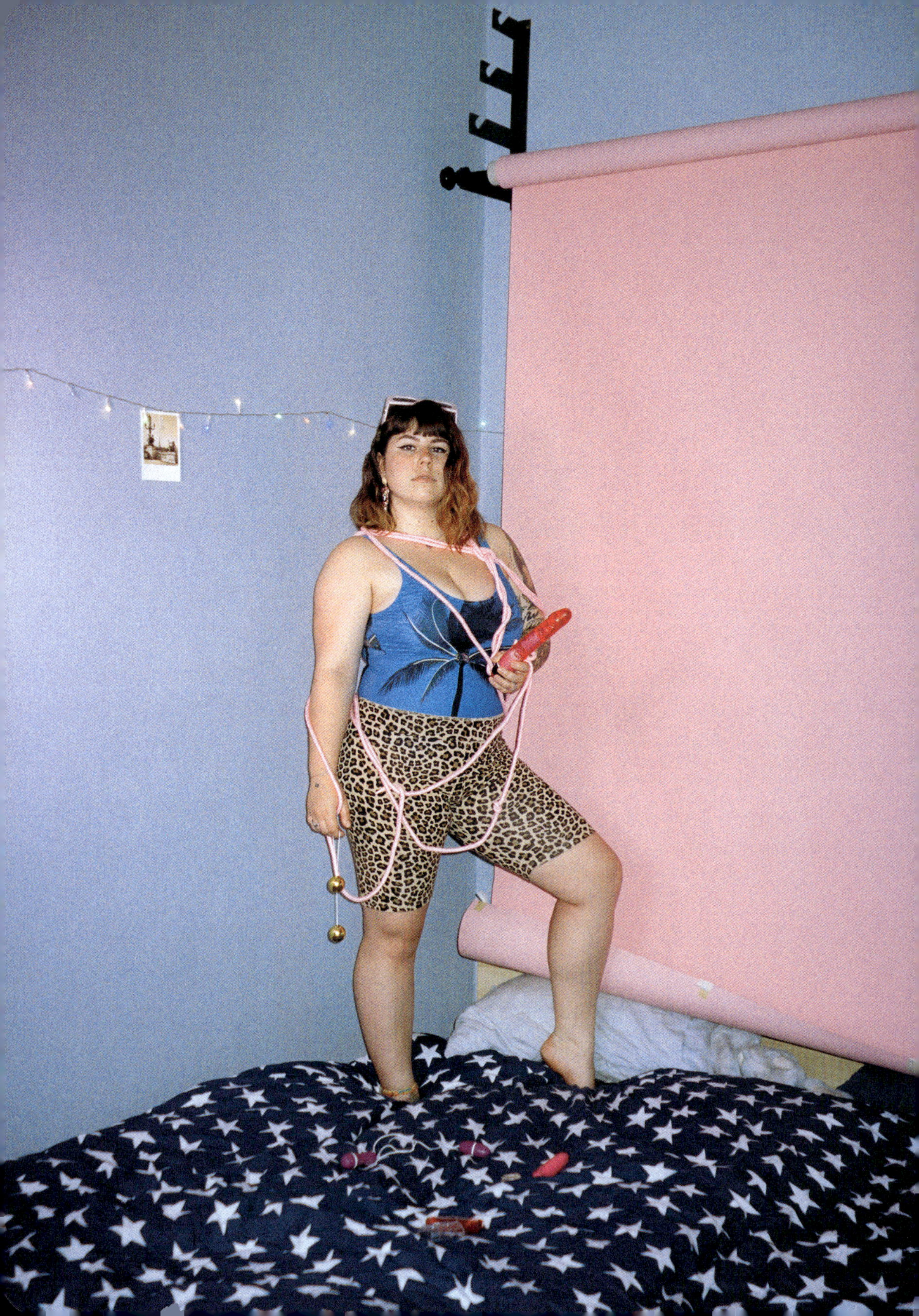

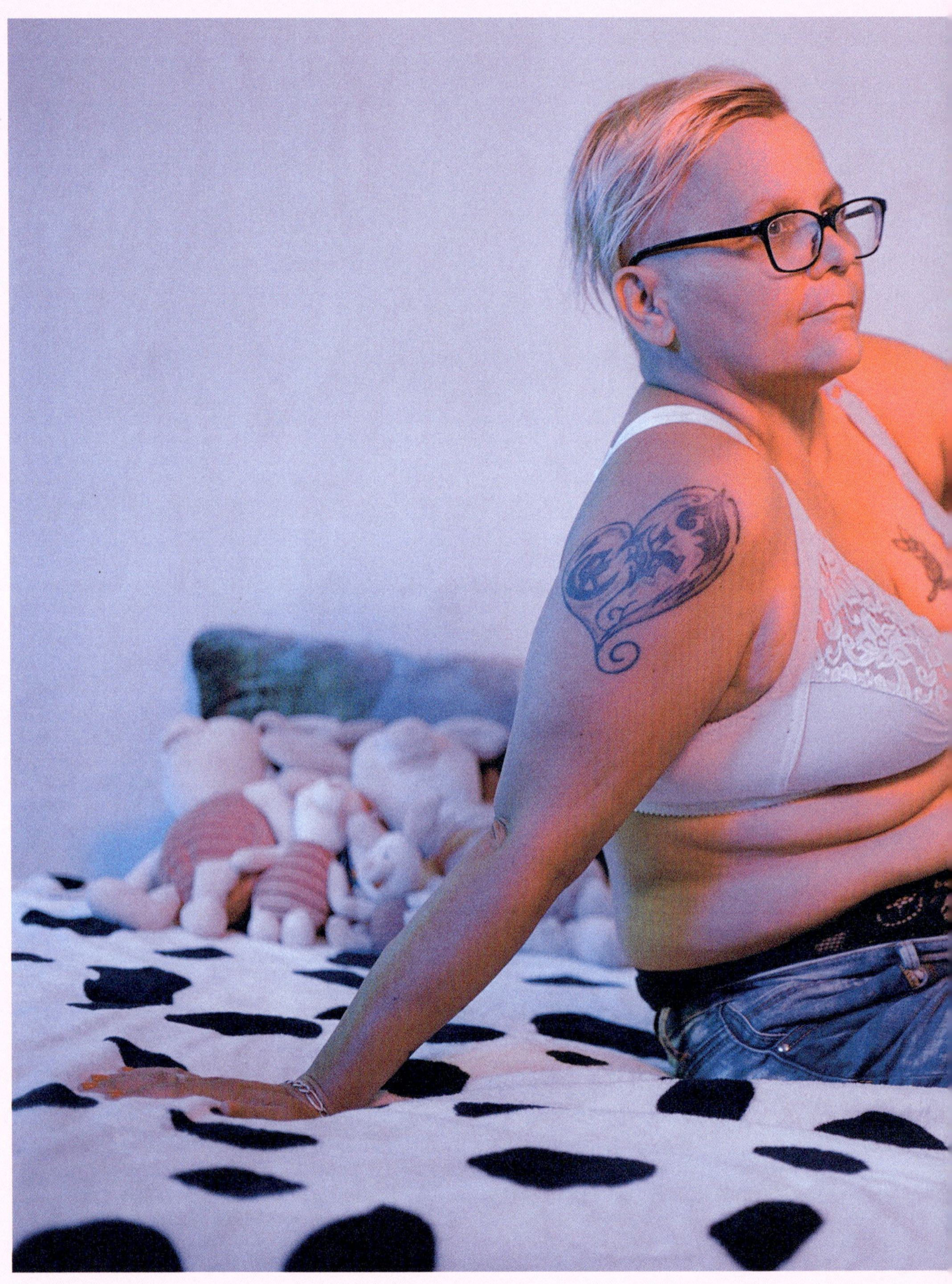

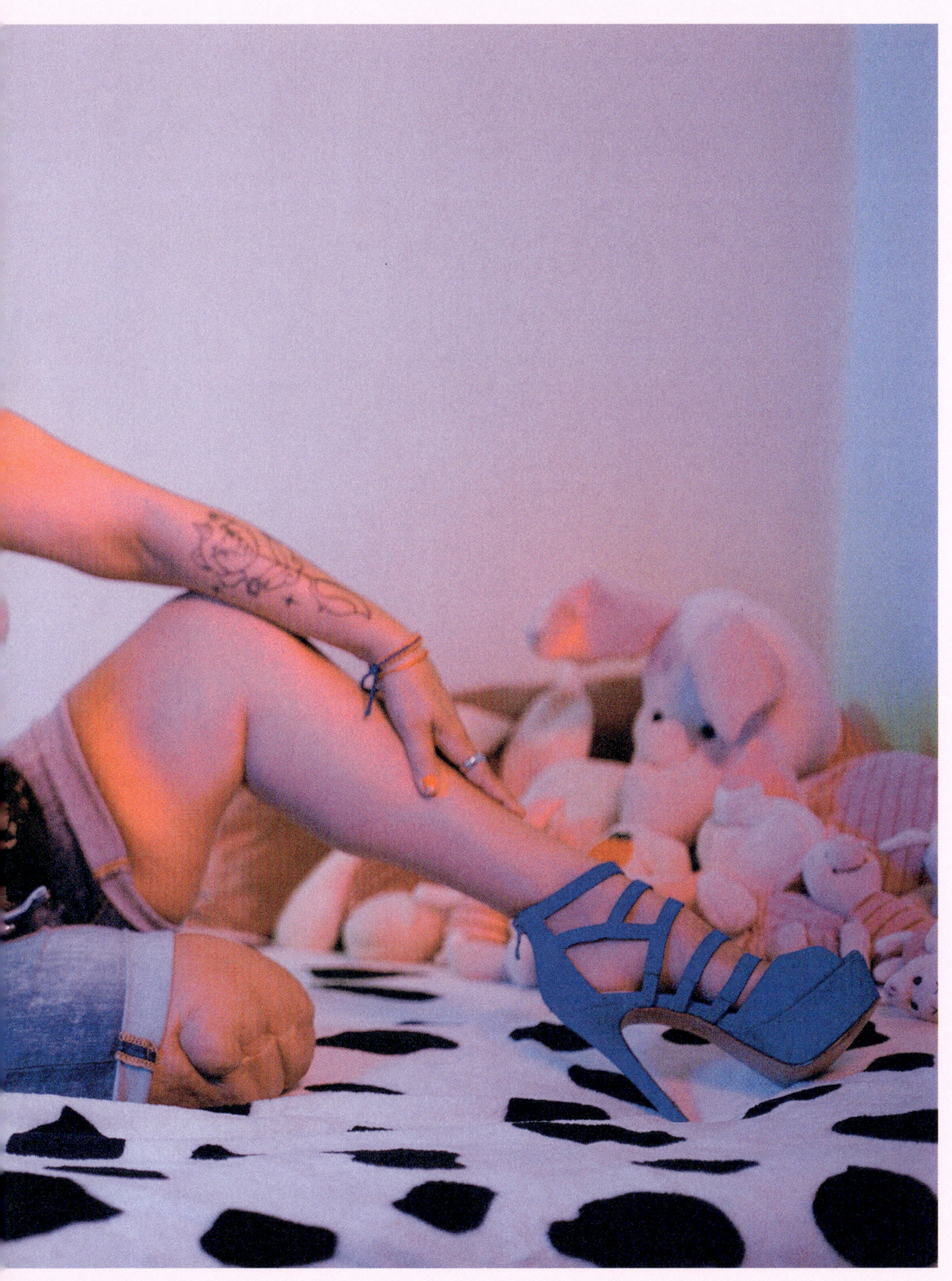

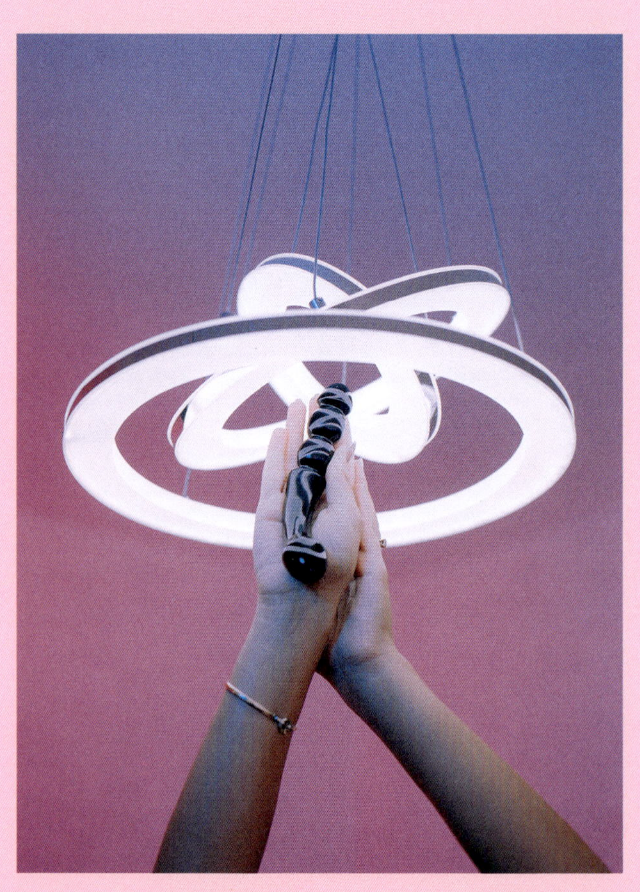

BARBARA O.

In my overly prudish family I'm proud of my public nudity and I can see that they are proud of me and they loosen up just like I do. I'm so much into what I do that I feel like I'm unbreakable. Since I'm not insecure, they can't cut me to the quick.

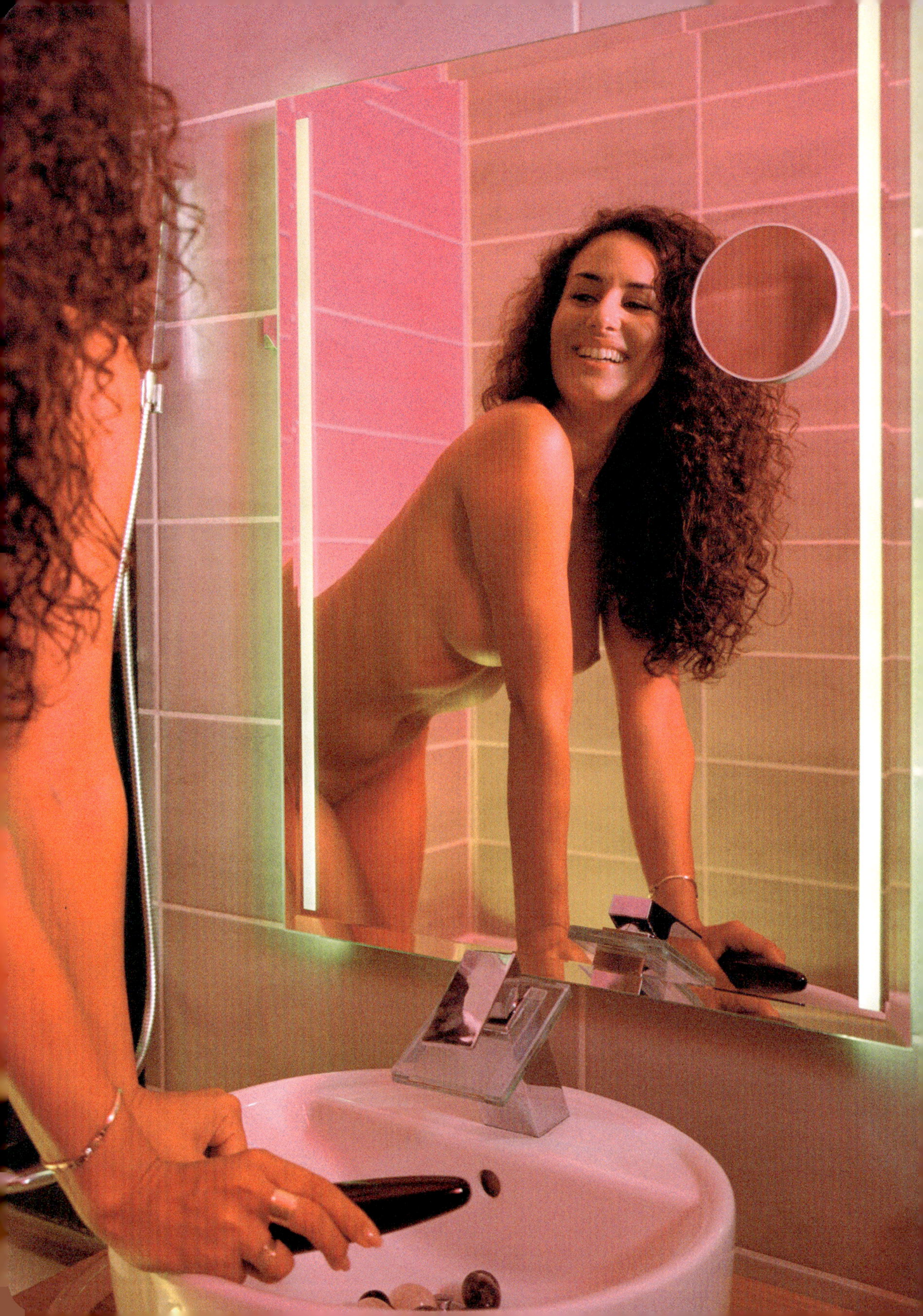

The woman who has literally come to her senses, loves herself, sexy but not sexualized. Of course anyone can say that "The stupid bitch is asking for it." But it's never on the person who's being judged. If that's what makes them complete, let them be. It's important how they feel. I can declare that I'm a sexually awakened, free woman. If someone can exist without restraint, it's a real power move. You can't manipulate them easily.

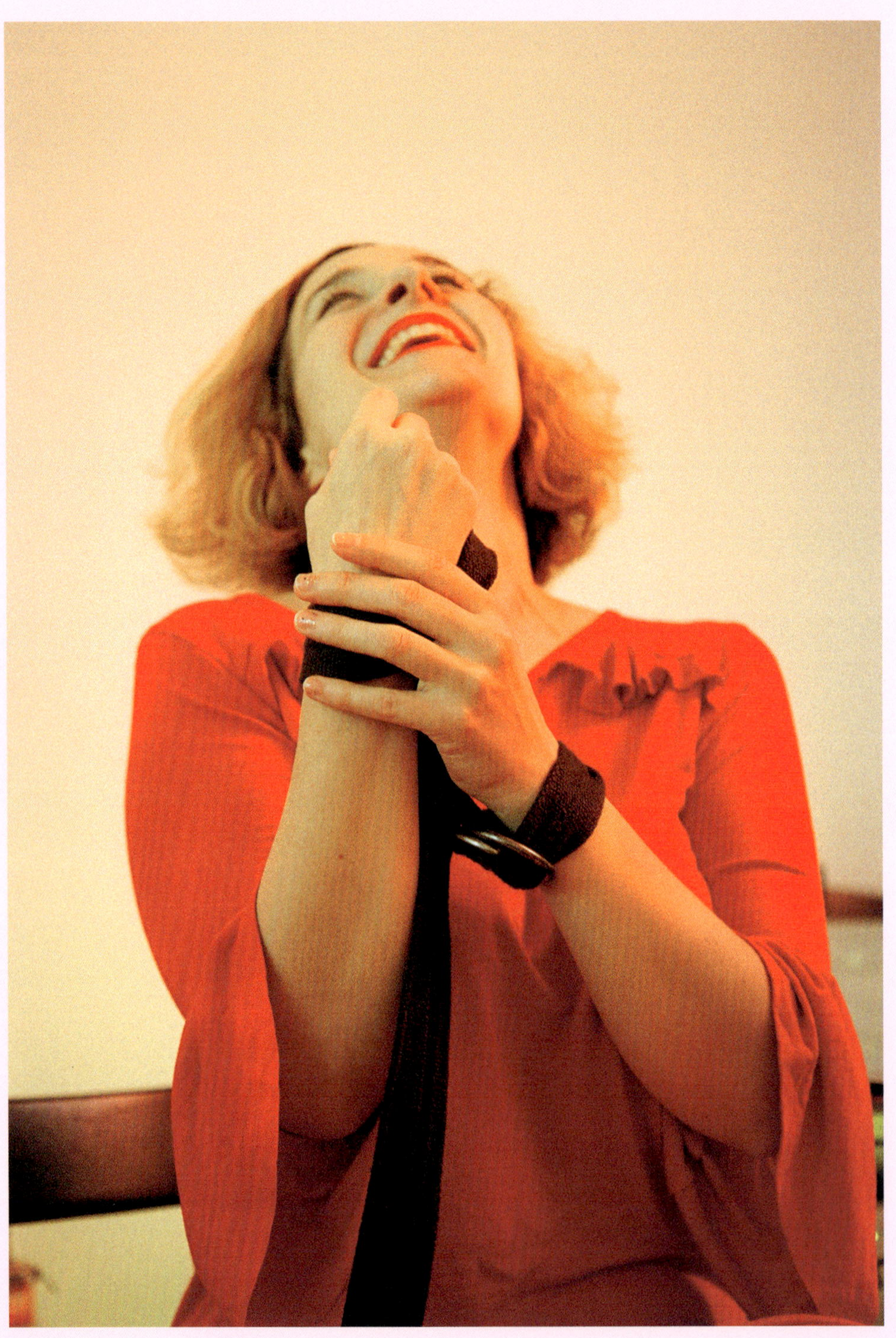

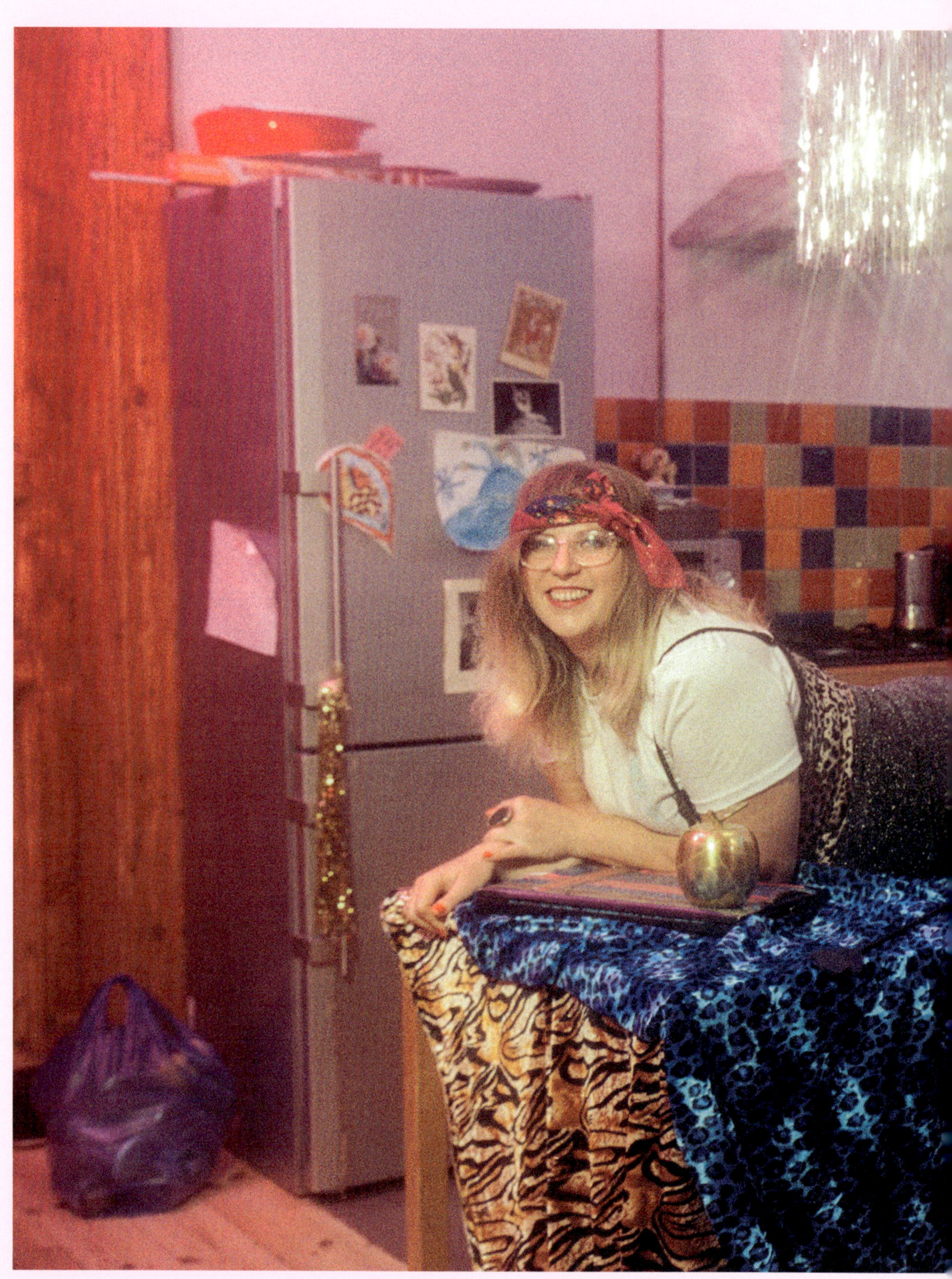

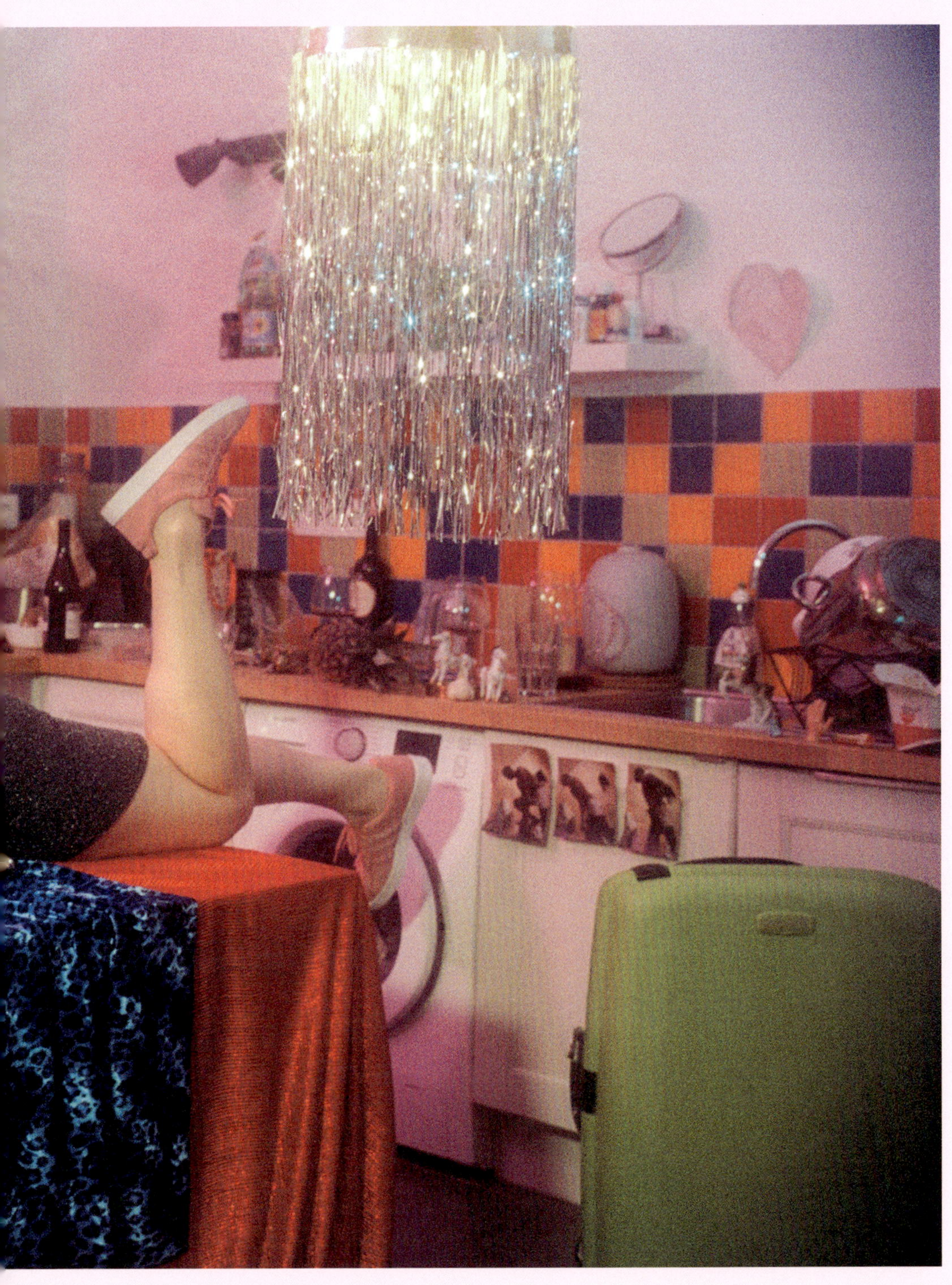

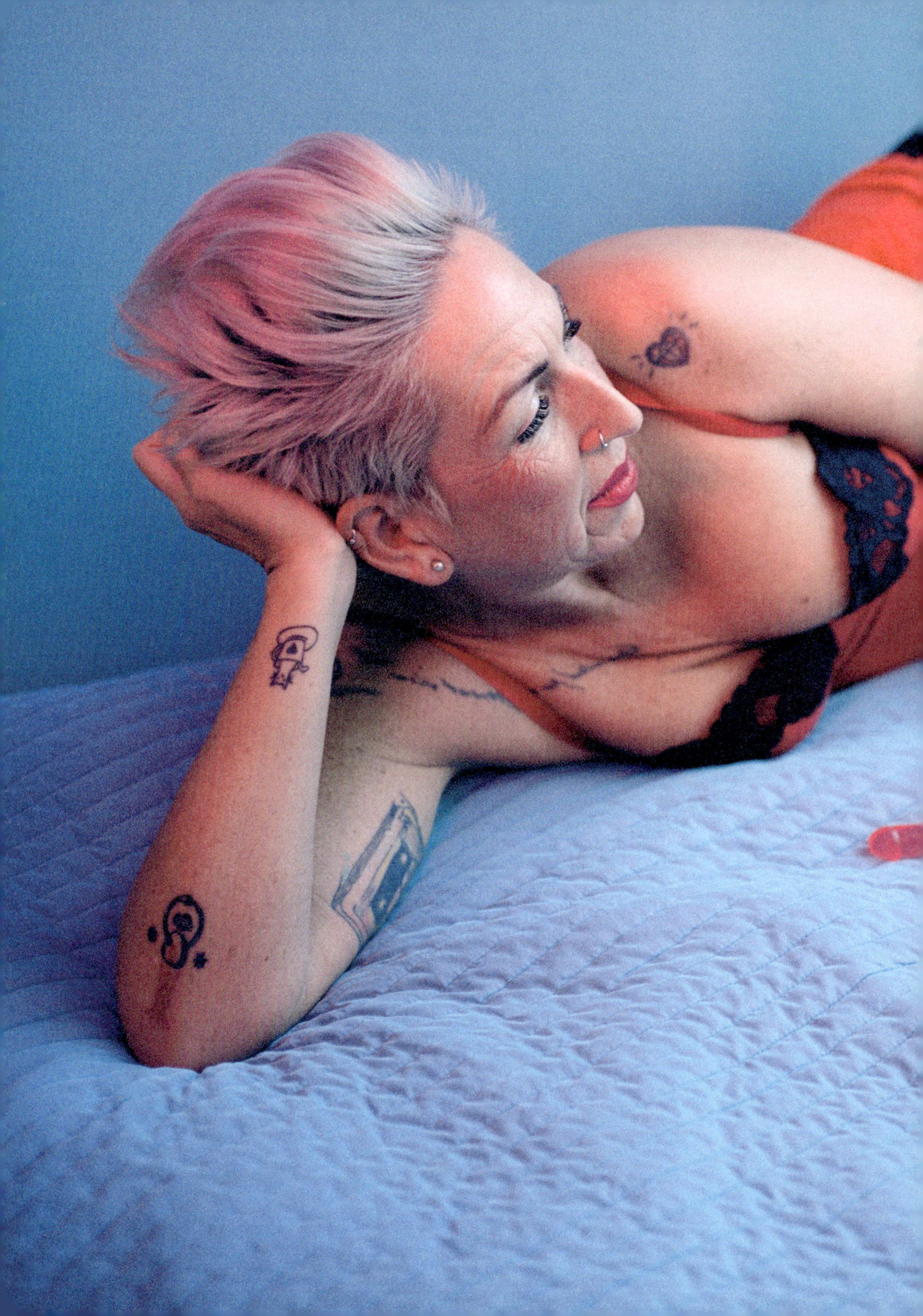

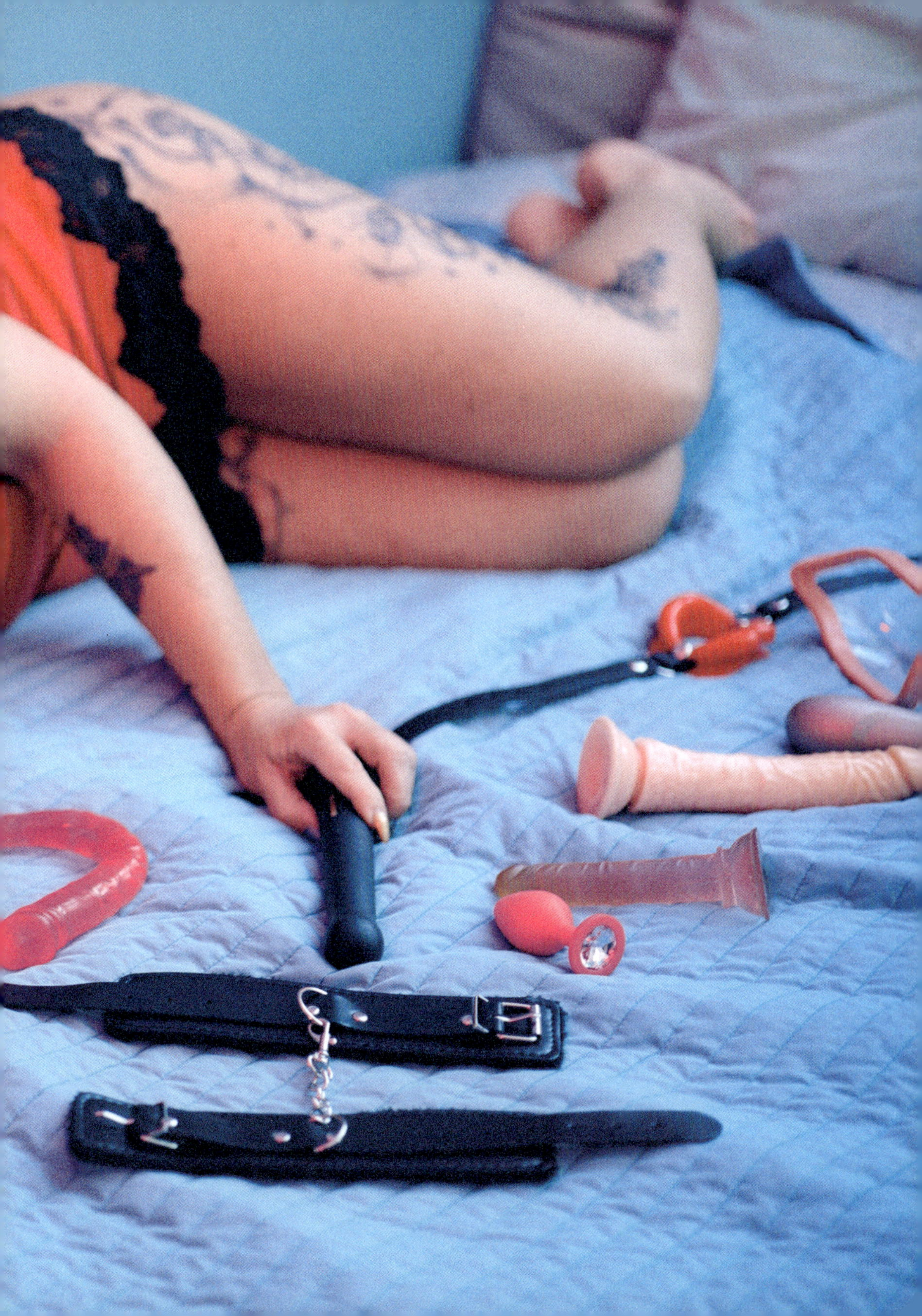

In the last three years, I feel that I've grown an awful lot. I built my self-confidence, I found a job. I'm proud of how much I've changed.

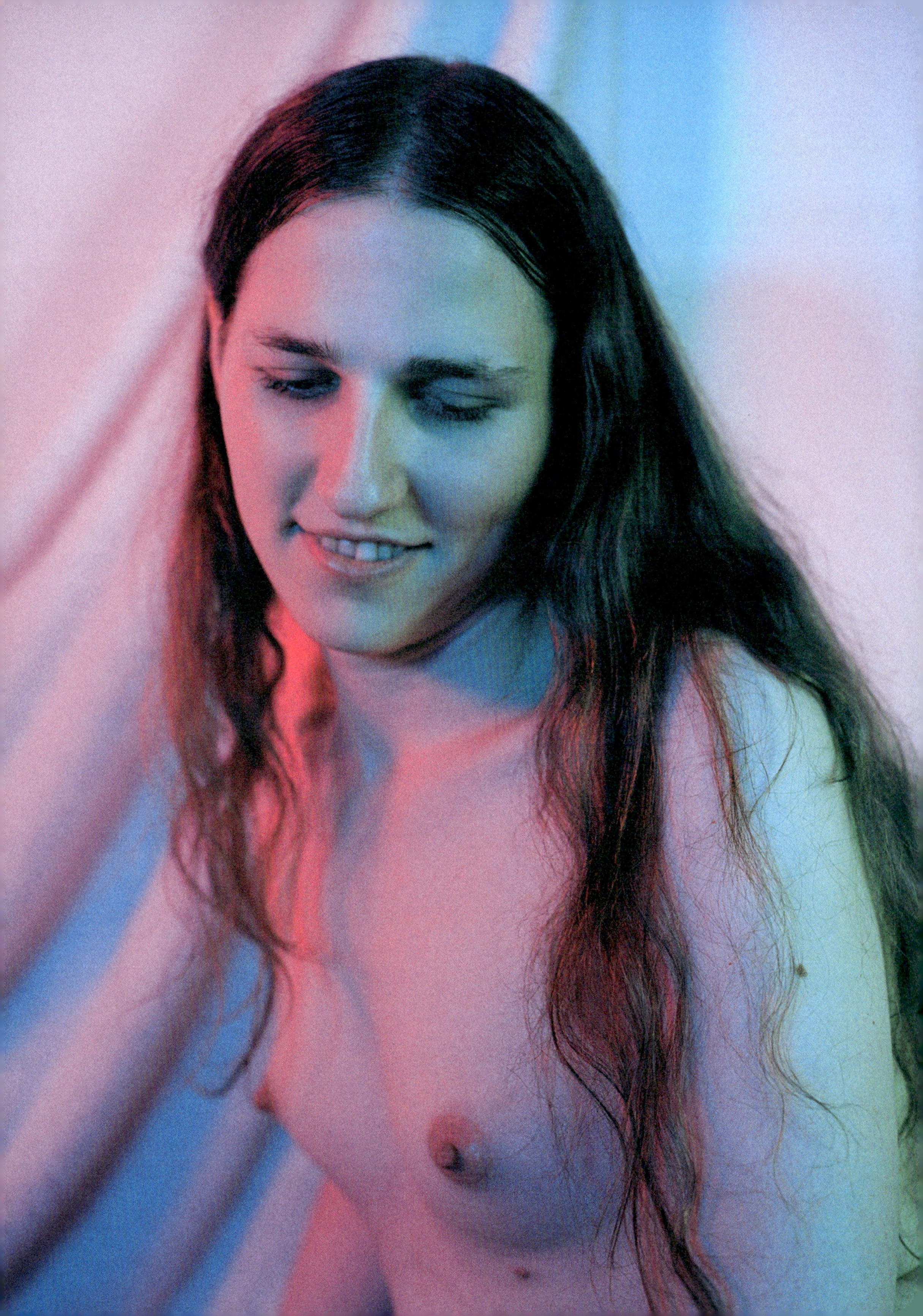

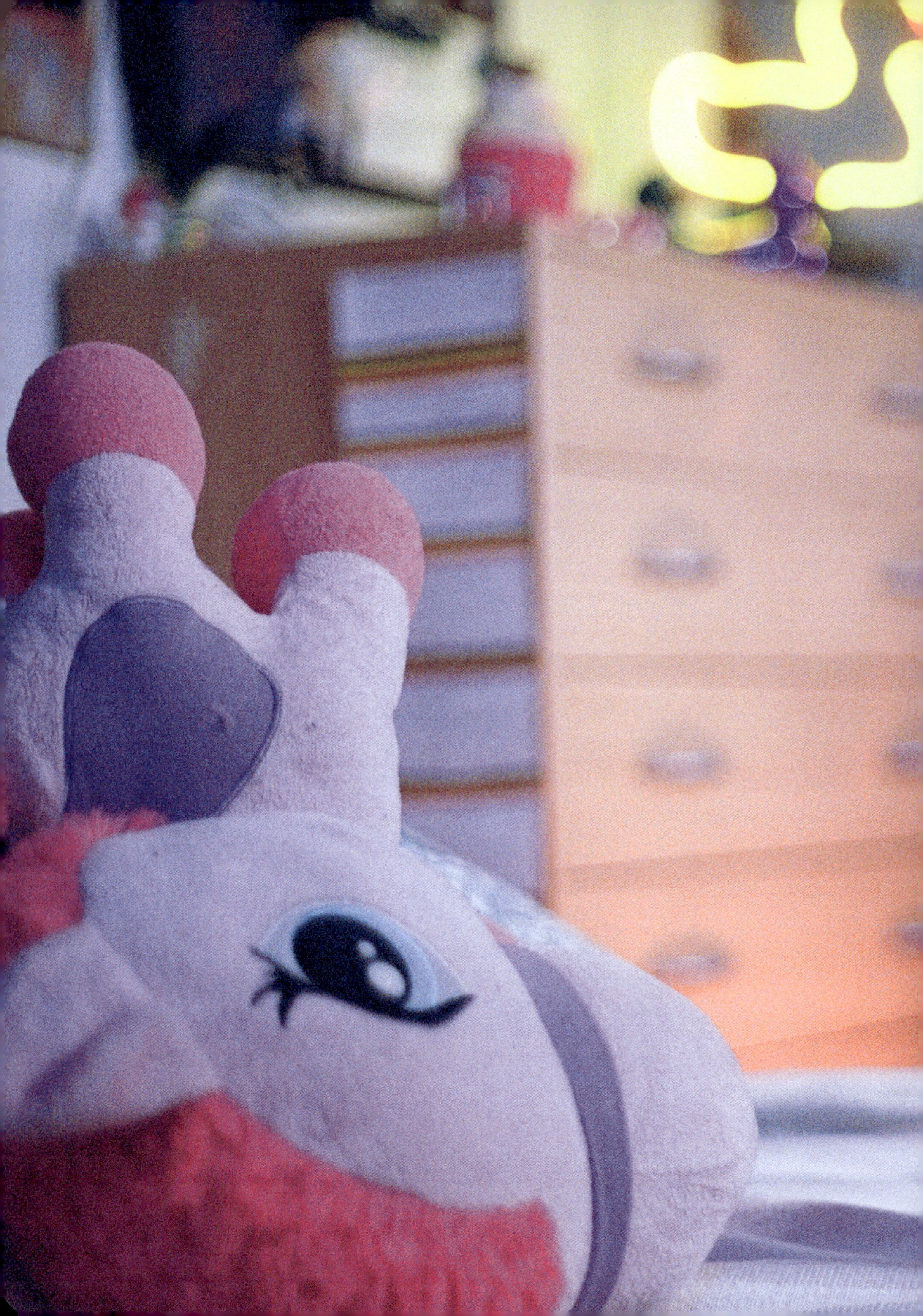

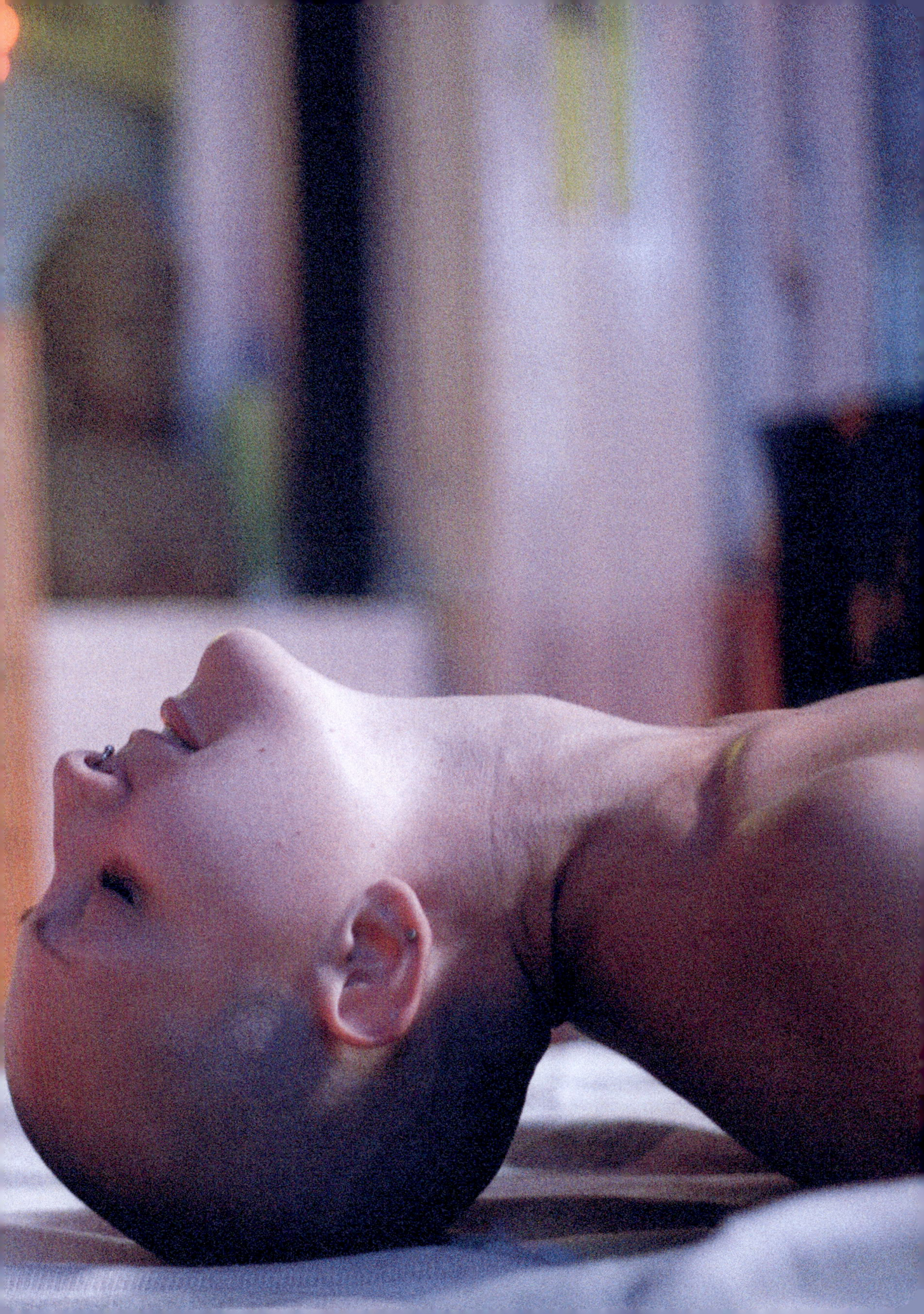

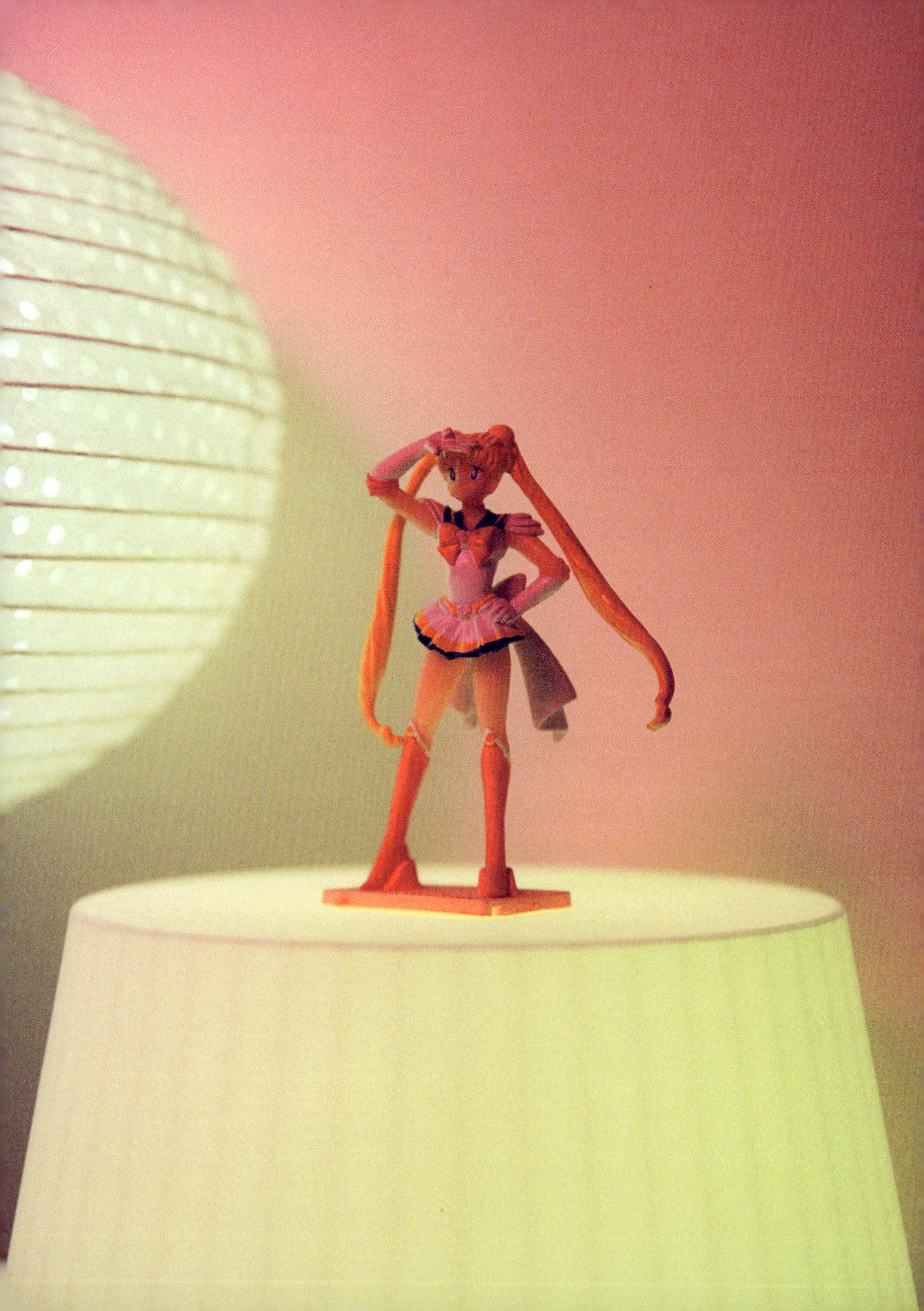

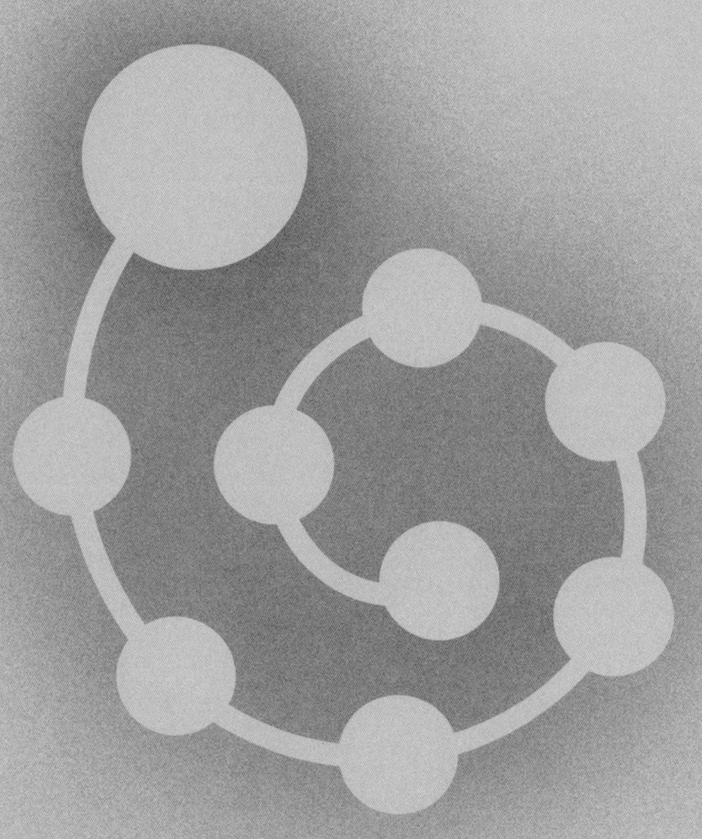

*Eventually,
I've accepted myself
and that I fucking
love sex.*

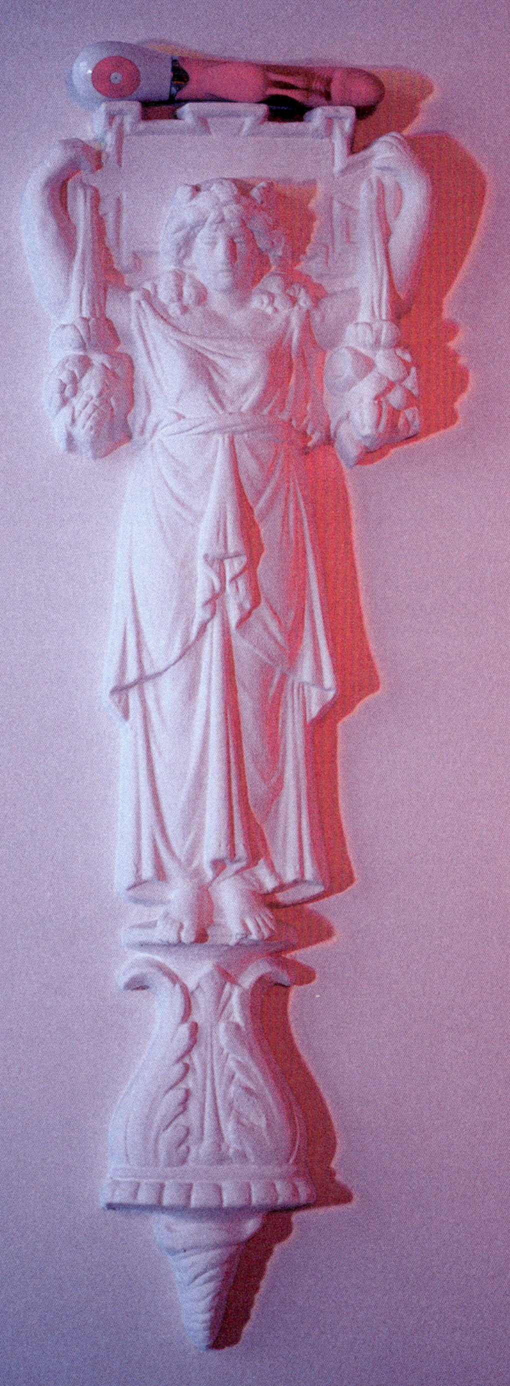

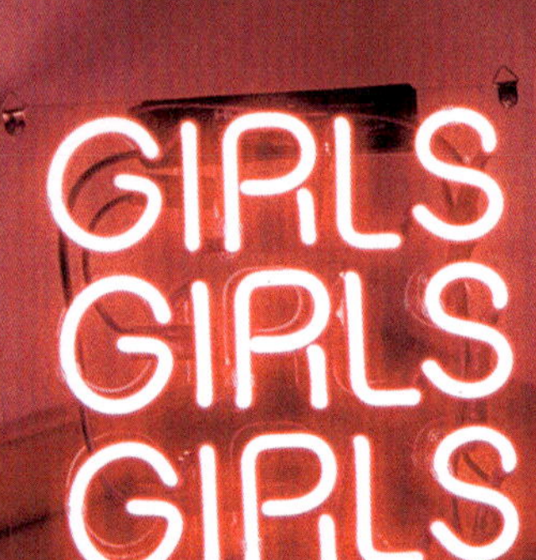
GIRLS
GIRLS
GIRLS

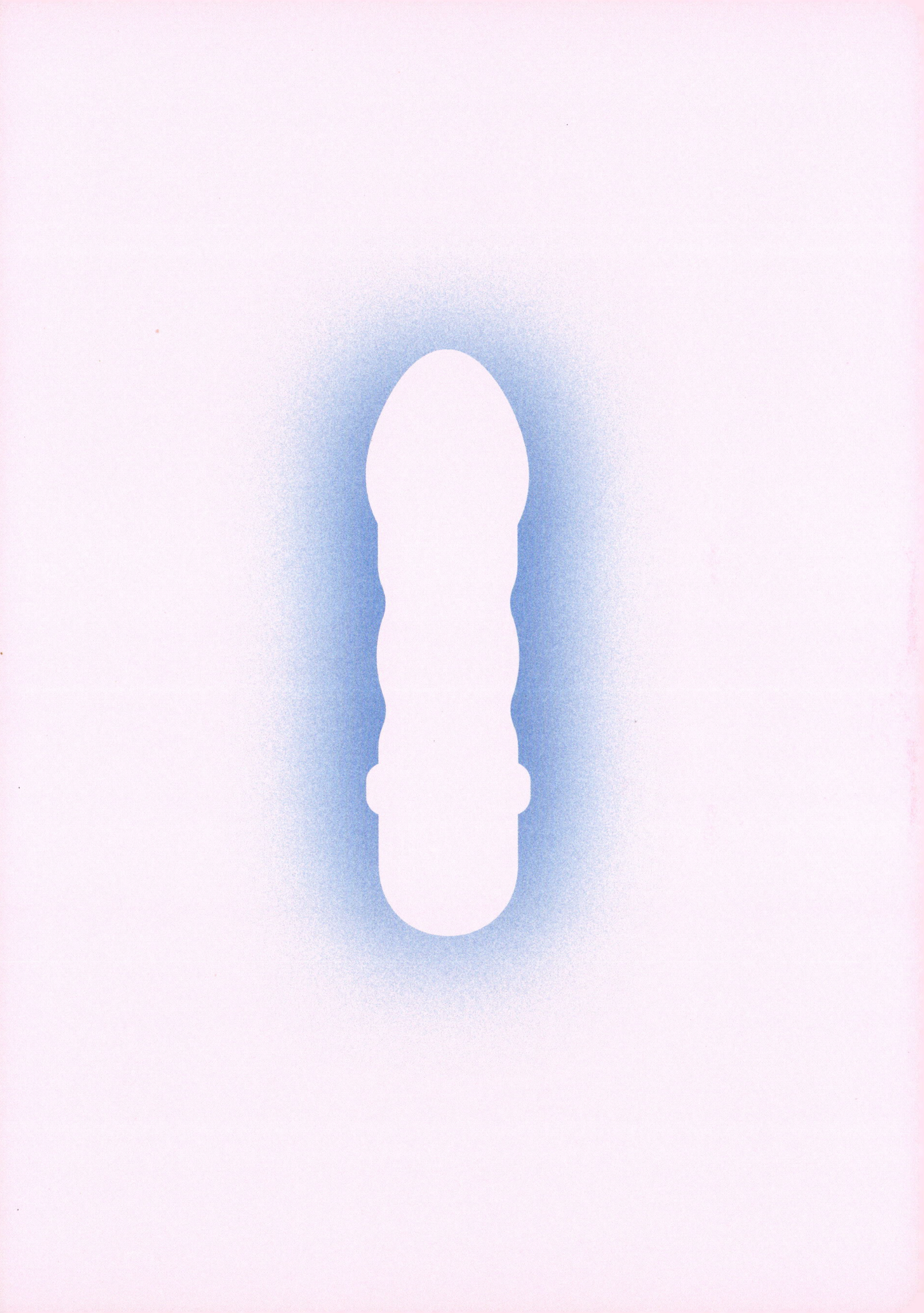

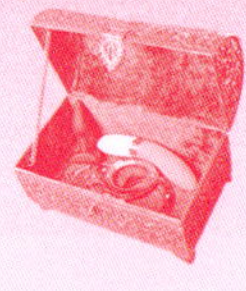

ANETT

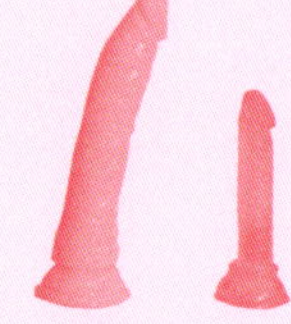

ANNA

BARBARA F.

ANNAMÁRIA

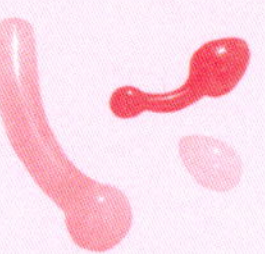

BARBARA O.

BARBARA M.

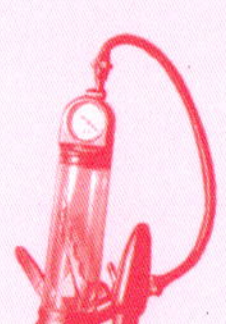

BEÁTA

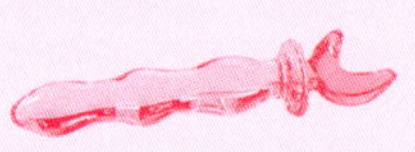

BEATRIX

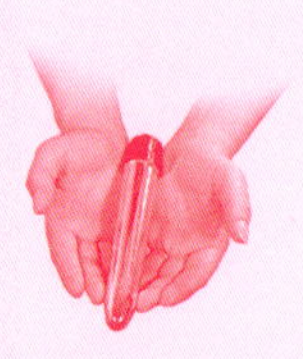

DANIELA

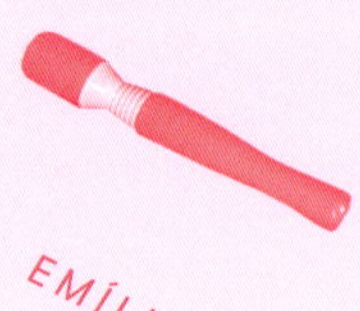

EMÍLIA

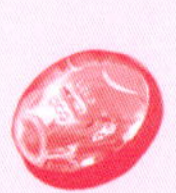

ESZTER

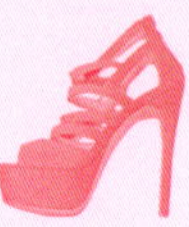

ÉVA B.

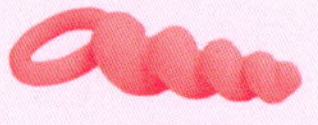

FRUZSINA

JUDIT

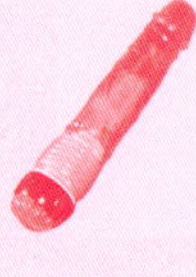

FÉDRA

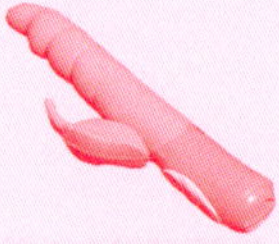

ILDIKÓ

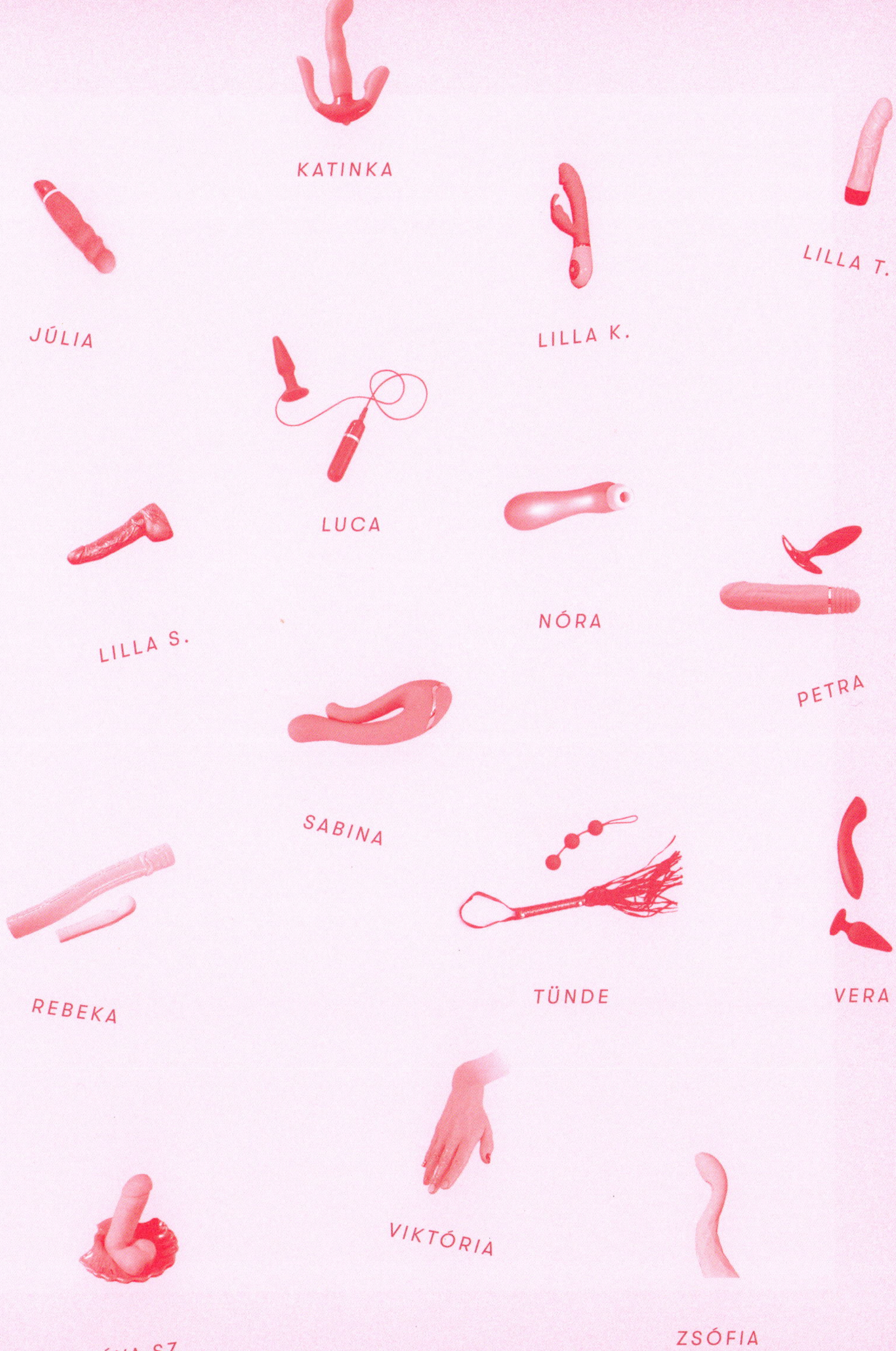

KATINKA
JÚLIA
LILLA K.
LILLA T.
LUCA
NÓRA
PETRA
LILLA S.
SABINA
REBEKA
TÜNDE
VERA
VIKTÓRIA
ÉVA SZ.
ZSÓFIA

Thanks to all featured

Rebeka Balla (36–37, 274–275), Éva Bányai (67, 90–97, 260–261), Judit Zorka Bohorquez Babinszki (10–13, 32–33, 122–123, 136–137), Beatrix Dányi (226–229, 276), Ildikó Dudás (44–45, 194–195, 268–269), Barbara Fränk (134–135, 198–199, 244–245), Anett Gálvölgyi (138–141, 186–187, 224–225), Eszter Jámbor (24–25, 112–113, 144–145, 204), Katinka Juhász (230–231), Lilla Vivien Király (28–29, 48–49, 106–109, 223, 281), Fruzsina Krasznár (46–47, 74–75, 130–131, 181, 184–185, 206–207), Júlia Lerch (234), Emília Major (126–127, 172, 208–209, 248, 254), Petra Lilla Marjai (232–233), Barbara Markó (26–27, 52–53, 128–129, 180, 190–191), Fédra Matolcsi (124–125, 258), Zsófia Németh (19–21, 115–121), Anna Oláh (196–197, 247), Barbara Oláh (22–23, 54–55, 104–105, 262–265), Tünde Ombódi (56–59, 238–240, 266), Annamária Papp, PharmD (60–63, 175–177, 216, 219, 253, 270–271), Daniela Pataki (30–31, 80–88, 272–273), Lilla Saáry (16–17, 34–35, 150–157, 210–213, 220–221, 257), Luca Séllei (132–133, 236–237, 282), Viktória Sulyok (68–73, 76–77, 110–111, 188–189), Beáta Tari (14–15, 64–65, 158–169, 182–183, 215), Lilla Török (50–51, 142–143), Sabina Triana (148–149, 202–203), Nóra Vaski (40–43, 98–101, 200), Vera Vida (192–193).

Special thanks to

Anonymous Supporters, Orsi Bakos, László Vágó, Judit Reszegi, Walter Tambke, Hetényi-Gonda Collection, Anonym = True, Péter Bencze

About the author

Éva Szombat is a photographer based in Budapest, Hungary. She got her MA in photography from Moholy-Nagy University of Art and Design (MOME), and studied visual communication at ESAG Penninghen in Paris. Her works examine the phenomenon of happiness and mental well-being, and how they can manifest in people. She previously released two books on the subject: *Happiness*, and *Practitioners*. Her works were displayed in New York, Jerusalem, Milan, Lisbon, Vienna, Berlin, Bogotá among other places. The series *I Want Orgasms, Not Roses* won the Robert Capa Photography Grand Prize in 2021. She is currently attending doctoral school and teaching photography at MOME.
www.evaszombat.com

© 2022 Kehrer Verlag Heidelberg
and Éva Szombat

Project Management

Kehrer Verlag (Aydria Stadter)

Texts

Éva Szombat
The texts are edited from interviews
conducted with the participants.

Translations

Nóra Vaski

Copy Editing

Elisabeth Buchet-Deák

Design

Anna Bárdy

Image Processing

Kehrer Design (Erik Clewe)

Production Management

Kehrer Design (Tom Streicher)

Bibliographic information published by
the Deutsche Nationalbibliothek
The Deutsche Nationalbibliothek lists this
publication in the Deutsche National-
bibliografie; detailed bibliographic
data is available on the Internet at
http://dnb.dnb.de.

Printed and bound in Germany
ISBN 978-3-96900-097-7

EVERYBODY NEEDS ART

Everybody Needs Art
www.everybodyneedsart.com
www.longtermhandstand.art

Kehrer Verlag Heidelberg
www.kehrerverlag.com

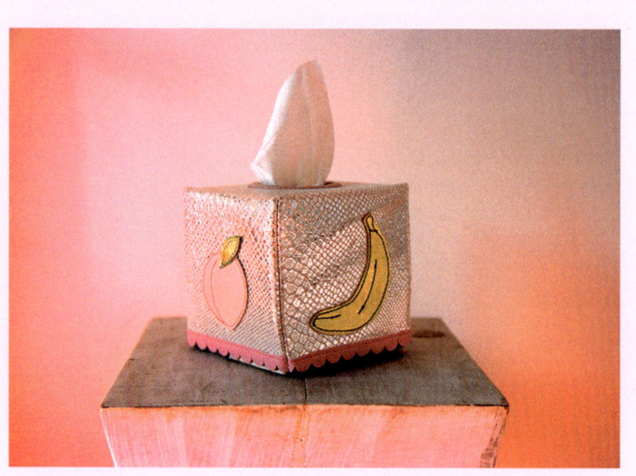